Microsoft ADO.NET Entity Framework Step by Step

John Paul Mueller

Published with the authorization of Microsoft Corporation by:
O'Reilly Media, Inc.
1005 Gravenstein Highway North
Sebastopol, California 95472

ISBN: 978-0-735-66416-6

1 2 3 4 5 6 7 8 9 LSI 8 7 6 5 4 3

Printed and bound in the United States of America.

Microsoft Press books are available through booksellers and distributors worldwide. If you need support related to this book, email Microsoft Press Book Support at *mspinput@microsoft.com*. Please tell us what you think of this book at *http://www.microsoft.com/learning/booksurvey*.

Acquisitions and Developmental Editor: Russell Jones

Production Editor: Christopher Hearse

Editorial Production: Zyg Group, LLC

Technical Reviewer: Russ Mullen

Indexer: Zyg Group, LLC

Cover Design: Twist Creative • Seattle

Cover Composition: Ellie Volckhausen

Illustrator: Rebecca Demarest

This book is dedicated to Kevin Smith, a good friend who's helped us realize some of our most special dreams. He's always helped us help ourselves—an outstanding gift that's exceptionally rare in this world.

—John Paul Mueller

Contents at a glance

Contents

Introduction

Gaining access to data in a managed way without a lot of coding—that's a tall order! The Entity Framework fulfills this promise and far more. Each version of the Entity Framework is more capable than the last. The latest version, Entity Framework version 5, provides you with access to far more database features with less work than ever before, and *Microsoft ADO.NET Entity Framework Step by Step* is your gateway to finding just how to use these phenomenal new features. In this book, you get hands-on practice with all the latest functionality that the Entity Framework provides. By the time you finish, you'll be ready to tackle some of the most difficult database management tasks without the heavy-duty coding that past efforts required.

Fortunately, this book doesn't get so immersed in high-end features that it forgets to tell you how to get started. Unlike a lot of tomes on the topic, this book starts simply and helps you gain a good foothold in understanding just why the Entity Framework is such an amazing addition to the your developer toolbox. You'll see examples where the automation does just about everything for you with little coding required, and yet you obtain professional-looking results. In fact, that's what you're buying with the Entity Framework—a reliable means of creating code quickly and successfully without the problems that would ensue if you tried to create the same code completely by hand. The book's 44 examples help you gain experience using the Entity Framework in a hands-on environment where you actually create code, rather than just reading about what might work.

Of course, you do eventually delve into higher-end topics. You'll find an entire chapter on one of the most requested features, Table-Valued Functions (TVFs). Access to this feature alone makes the upgrade to Entity Framework 5 a significant one. You'll also discover how to handle performance problems and perform low-end tasks such as using inheritance when creating a model. In short, by the time you finish this book, you will have the experience required to handle every common task that developers need to know how to perform.

Who should read this book

Anyone who creates database applications using ADO.NET and is tired of writing reams of code will definitely benefit from reading this book. What you should ask yourself is whether you want to become more productive while writing code that is both more reliable and better able to interact with the database. Although the coding examples are written in C#, several Microsoft Visual Basic developers tested this book during the writing process and found that they could follow the examples quite well. All you really need is a desire to write database applications more quickly and with less fuss.

Assumptions

To use this book successfully, you need a good knowledge of database programming concepts using a technology such as ADO.NET. Although every attempt is made to explain basic (and essential) topics, a knowledge of working with databases using the .NET Framework will make working through the examples significantly easier.

You also need to know how to write applications using the C# programming language. All of the examples are written using C#, and there isn't any attempt to explain how the language elements work. If you don't have the required C# knowledge, you should consider getting John Sharp's *Microsoft Visual C# 2010 Step by Step* (Microsoft Press, 2010).

Some of the examples also require some knowledge of Transact-Structured Query Language (T-SQL). Again, there are plenty of comments provided with the various scripts, but there isn't a lot of additional information provided about language elements. The book assumes that you know how basic SQL queries work.

Who should not read this book

This book is most definitely not aimed at the complete novice. You must know a little about both SQL and ADO.NET to work with the book successfully. In addition, you must know the C# programming language fairly well. The examples in the book focus a little more on enterprise developers, but hobbyists should be able to follow the examples without problem. If you're looking for a high-end book with lots of low-end programming examples and no hands-on techniques, this is most definitely not the book for you. This book is all about getting people started using the Entity Framework in a meaningful way to perform most common tasks, which means it uses several different techniques to convey information so that a majority of readers can understand and use the material presented.

Organization of this book

This book is organized into five parts. Each part is designed to demonstrate a particular facet of the Entity Framework, with an emphasis on the functionality provided by version 5. Here is a brief overview of the book parts (each part introduction has more detailed information about the content of the chapters in that part):

- **Part I: Introducing the Entity Framework** This part of the book introduces you to the Entity Framework version 5. You'll discover what is new in this version of the Entity Framework and also basic concepts such as the parts of a model. Unlike many other texts, this part also tells you about the three workflows available when working with the Entity Framework: model first, database first, and code first. Every chapter includes coding examples that emphasize the basics so that you can see precisely how the Entity Framework works at a basic level.
- **Part II: Completing basic tasks** Once you have a basic understanding of what the Entity Framework does and why you'd want to use it, it's time to see how to perform basic Create, Review, Update, and Delete (CRUD) operations. This part of the book provides an essential discussion of how to perform essential tasks with full automation in place. It's the part of the book you want to read to emphasize speed of development over flexibility in accessing database functionality.
- **Part III: Manipulating data using the Entity Framework** Most applications require more than a display of raw database data and simple CRUD operations. This part of the book takes the next step in your journey of actually controlling how the data appears and precisely what data is retrieved from the database. You discover two client-side techniques for manipulating data (Language Integrated Query [LINQ] and Entity Structured Query Language [Entity SQL]). In addition, you see how to use server-based techniques that include stored procedures, views, and TVFs.
- **Part IV: Overcoming entity errors** It's nearly impossible to create an application that is free from error. In fact, smart developers know that it is impossible because you really never have full control over absolutely all of the code that goes into your application. This part of the book discusses three realms of error: exceptions, concurrency issues, and performance problems.

- **Part V: Advanced management techniques** This is the low-level-coding part of the book. This is where you learn how to create custom entities and use inheritance as a tool to create more robust models. You also discover techniques for mapping various kinds of data to the Entity Framework, even when the Entity Framework normally doesn't support the data type. The key thing to remember about this part is that you discover manual methods for modifying how the automation works.

Finding your best starting point in this book

The different sections of *Microsoft® ADO.NET Entity Framework Step by Step* cover a wide range of technologies associated with the Entity Framework. Depending on your needs and your existing understanding of Microsoft data tools, you may wish to focus on specific areas of the book. Use the following table to determine how best to proceed through the book.

If you are	Follow these steps
New to the Entity Framework	Begin with Chapter 1, "Getting to know the Entity Framework," and move through Chapter 13, "Handling performance problems." Skip the last part of the book until you have gained some experience using the automation that the Entity Framework provides.
Familiar with earlier releases of the Entity Framework	Read through Chapter 1 and Chapter 3, "Choosing a workflow," carefully. Chapter 3 is especially important because it helps you understand the new workflows. Work through Parts III, IV, and V as needed to update your knowledge.
Interested in learning advanced Entity Framework techniques	Move directly to Part V of the book. The first four parts of this book are designed to help you learn about the Entity Framework and interact successfully with the automation it provides.
Interested in using the existing database infrastructure of your organization	Read Parts I and II to ensure you understand the basics of how the Entity Framework works, and then skip to Chapter 8, "Interaction with stored procedures," Chapter 9, "Interaction with views," and Chapter 10, "Interaction with table-valued functions."

Every chapter in this book contains at least one hands-on example (and usually more). The only way you'll actually gain a full understanding of the Entity Framework is to download the sample code and then work through the hands-on examples. Each of these procedures demonstrates an important element of the Entity Framework.

Conventions and features in this book

This book presents information using conventions designed to make the information readable and easy to follow.

Note Note boxed elements tell you about additional information that will prove useful in working with the Entity Framework. Notes normally include text about techniques used to create examples or the sources of information used in creating the chapter's content.

Tip Tip boxed elements provide additional information that will enhance your productivity, make it easier to perform tasks, or help you locate additional sources of information. Most tips provide helpful information that you don't need to know in order to use the book, but the information will prove helpful later as you work with real-world code.

Warning Warning boxed elements describe potentially dangerous situations where performing an act could result in damage to your application, the data it manages, or the user environment (such as the need to keep certain types of information secure). Pay special attention to warning elements because they'll save you time and effort.

- Each exercise consists of a series of tasks, presented as numbered steps (1, 2, and so on) listing each action you must take to complete the exercise.
- Sidebars contain useful information that isn't part of the main flow of discussion in a chapter. These elements always have a title that tells you about the topic of discussion. You can safely skip sidebars if desired or simply read them later. Sidebars always provide you with helpful real-world resource information that will help you as you create or manage applications.
- Text that you type (apart from code blocks) appears in bold.
- A plus sign (+) between two key names means that you must press those keys at the same time. For example, "Press Alt+Tab" means that you hold down the Alt key while you press the Tab key.

- A vertical bar between two or more menu items (for example, File | Close) means that you should select the first menu or menu item, then the next, and so on.

System requirements

You will need the following hardware and software to complete the practice exercises in this book:

- A copy of Microsoft Windows that will work with Microsoft Visual Studio 2012, which can include Windows 7 SP1 (x86 and x64), Windows 8 (x86 and x64), Windows Server 2008 R2 SP1 (x64), or Windows Server 2012 (x64).
- A copy of Visual Studio 2012 Professional or better. This book won't work well with Visual Studio 2012 Express Edition. In fact, many of the examples won't work at all, even if you use the downloaded source code.
- A copy of Microsoft SQL Server 2012 Express Edition with SQL Server Management Studio 2012 Express or higher (included with Visual Studio). You can also use the full-fledged version of SQL Server 2012.

Your computer must also meet these minimum requirements (although higher ratings are always recommended):

- 1.6 GHz or faster processor
- 1 GB of RAM (1.5 GB if running on a virtual machine)
- 10 GB of available hard disk space
- 600 MB of available hard disk space
- 5400 RPM hard drive
- DirectX 9–capable video card running at 1024×768 or higher display resolution
- DVD drive

Your computer must also have access to an Internet connection to download software or chapter examples.

Note Many of the tasks in this book require that you have local administrator rights. Newer versions of Windows include stricter security that requires you to have additional rights to perform tasks such as creating copies of database files.

Code samples

Most of the chapters in this book include exercises that let you interactively try out new material learned in the main text. All sample projects can be downloaded from the following page:

http://aka.ms/ADONETEFSbS/files

Follow the instructions to download the zip file.

Note In addition to the code samples, your system should have Visual Studio 2012 Professional (or better) and SQL Server 2012 Express Edition (or better) installed. The exercises will include instructions for working with SQL Server 2012. In most cases, the exercises rely on Server Explorer to make it easy to perform all tasks from the Visual Studio Integrated Development Environment (IDE).

Installing the code samples

All you need to do to install the code samples is download them and unzip the archive to a folder on your hard drive. The complete source code file will include all of the databases used in the book. Simply attach these databases to your copy of SQL Server or open them in Visual Studio by right-clicking Data Connections in Server Explorer and choosing Add Connection. Use the Microsoft SQL Server Database Connection option when creating the connection. If you encounter problems installing the code samples, please contact me at *John@JohnMuellerBooks.com*. You can also find answers to common questions for this book on my blog, at *http://blog.johnmuellerbooks.com/categories/263/entity-framework-development-step-by-step.aspx*.

Using the code samples

The downloaded source code includes one folder for each chapter in the book. Simply open the chapter folder and then the example folder for the example you want to work with in the book. The downloaded source contains the completed source code so that you can see precisely how your example should look. If you want to work through the examples from scratch, the book contains complete instructions for developing them.

The downloaded source code also contains a Databases folder that contains all of the databases for the book. Simply create a connection to the database you need to use. The example will tell you which database is required. If you desire, the exercises also tell you how to create the databases from scratch so that you can use whatever setup you like.

Acknowledgments

Thanks to my wife, Rebecca, for working with me to get this book completed. I really don't know what I would have done without her help in researching and compiling some of the information that appears in this book. She also did a fine job of proofreading my rough draft. Rebecca keeps the house running while I'm buried in work.

Russ Mullen deserves thanks for his technical edit of this book. He greatly added to the accuracy and depth of the material you see here. Russ is always providing me with great URLs for new products and ideas. However, it's the testing Russ does that helps most. He's the sanity check for my work. Russ also has different computer equipment from mine, so he's able to point out flaws that I might not otherwise notice.

Matt Wagner, my agent, deserves credit for helping me get the contract in the first place and taking care of all the details that most authors don't really consider. I always appreciate his assistance. It's good to know that someone wants to help.

A number of people read all or part of this book to help me refine the approach, test the coding examples, and generally provide input that all readers wish they could have. These unpaid volunteers helped in ways too numerous to mention here. I especially appreciate the efforts of Eva Beattie and Glenn Russell, who provided general input, read the entire book, and selflessly devoted themselves to this project.

Finally, I would like to thank my editor, Russell Jones; Christopher Hearse; Damon Larson; and the rest of the editorial and production staff at O'Reilly for their assistance in bringing this book to print. It's always nice to work with such a great group of professionals.

Errata & book support

We've made every effort to ensure the accuracy of this book and its companion content. Any errors that have been reported since this book was published are listed on our Microsoft Press site at oreilly.com:

http://aka.ms/ADONETEFSbS/errata

If you find an error that is not already listed, you can report it to us through the same page.

If you need additional support, email Microsoft Press Book Support at *mspinput@microsoft.com*.

Please note that product support for Microsoft software is not offered through the addresses above.

We want to hear from you

At Microsoft Press, your satisfaction is our top priority, and your feedback our most valuable asset. Please tell us what you think of this book at

http://www.microsoft.com/learning/booksurvey

The survey is short, and we read every one of your comments and ideas. Thanks in advance for your input!

Stay in touch

Let's keep the conversation going! We're on Twitter: *http://twitter.com/MicrosoftPress*.

PART I

Introducing the Entity Framework

Creating a database can be difficult. A database models information in the real world using a collection of tables, indexes, views, and other items. In other words, a database is an abstraction of the real-world information that it's supposed to represent. When a developer is tasked with creating an application that relies on the data within a database, the developer must create a second level of abstraction because the application won't see the data in precisely the same way that the database does. Defining this second level of abstraction is even harder than creating the original database, because it requires interpreting the real world through an abstraction. In order to define a realistic presentation of the data in the database—one that precisely represents the real world—a developer needs help. That's what the Entity Framework does. It provides help to a developer in the form of a modeling methodology that eases the amount of work the developer must perform to create a realistic presentation. To make things even easier, the Entity Framework relies on a graphical presentation of the data so that the developer can literally see the relationships between the various tables and other database items.

Even though the concept of the Entity Framework is straightforward, you need to know more about it before you can simply use it to create a connection between the database and your application. Working with models is definitely easier than working with hand-coded connections. However, you still need to have a good understanding of how those models work and the various ways you can interact with them. The purpose of the three chapters in this part is to introduce you to the Entity Framework concepts. You'll use this information to build a picture of how the Entity Framework performs its task so that you can perform more complex operations with the Entity Framework later in the book.

CHAPTER 1

Getting to know the Entity Framework

After completing the chapter, you'll be able to

- Define what an entity is and why it's important.
- Specify the major elements of the Entity Framework.
- List and describe the files used to store Entity Framework information.
- Create a simple Entity Framework example.

When an architect wants to design a real-world building by creating a blueprint, one of the tools used to ensure the blueprint is accurate is a *model*. Often you see a model of the building as part of the presentation for that building. Models are helpful because they help others visualize the ideas that reside in the architect's head. In addition, the models help the architect decide whether the plan is realistic. Likewise, software developers can rely on models as a means of understanding a software design, determining whether that design is realistic, and conveying that design to others. The Entity Framework provides the means to create various kinds of models that a developer can interact with in a number of ways. As with the architect's model, the Entity Framework uses a graphical interface to make information about the underlying database structure easier to understand and modify.

The Entity Framework is actually a Microsoft ActiveX Data Object .NET (ADO.NET) technology extension. When you create the model of the database, you also make it possible for the Integrated Development Environment (IDE) to automatically create some of the code required to make the connection between an application and the database real. Because of the way ADO.NET and the Entity Framework interact, it's possible to create extremely complex designs and then use those designs directly from your code in a way that the developer will understand. There isn't any need to translate between the levels of abstraction—the Entity Framework performs that task for you.

Before you can begin using the Entity Framework to perform useful work, however, you need to know a little more about it. For one thing, you need to know why it's called an Entity Framework. It's also important to know how the various models work and how they're stored on your system, should you ever need to access them directly. The following sections provide this information and more about the Entity Framework. You'll then use the knowledge you've gained to create a very simple example. This example will help you better understand what the Entity Framework can do because you'll actually use it to interact with a simple database.

Defining an entity

An *entity* is the data associated with a particular object when considered from the perspective of a particular application. For example, a customer object will include a customer's name, address, telephone number, company name, and so on. The actual customer object may have more data than this associated with it, but from the perspective of this particular application, the customer object is complete by knowing these facts. If you want to understand this from the traditional perspective of a database administrator, the entity would be a single row in a view that contains all of the related information for the customer. It includes everything that the database physically stores in separate tables about that particular client. When thinking about entities, you need to consider these views of the data:

- **Physical** The tables, keys, indexes, views, and other constructions that hold and describe the data associated with a real-world object such as a customer. All of these elements are optimized to make it easier for the Database Management System (DBMS) to store and manipulate the data efficiently and reliably, without error. As such, a single customer data entry can appear in multiple tables and require the use of multiple keys to create a cohesive view of that customer. The physical storage of the data is efficient for the DBMS, but difficult for the developer to understand.

- **Logical** The combined elements required to define the data used with a single object, such as a client. From a database perspective, the logical view of the data is often encapsulated in a *view.* The view combines the data found within tables using keys and other database elements that describe the relationships and order required to re-create the customer successfully. Even so, the logical view of a database is still somewhat abstract and could cause problems for the developer, not to mention require a lot of code to manage successfully. ADO.NET does reduce the amount of coding the developer performs through the use of built-in objects, but the developer must still understand the underlying physical construction of that data.

- **Conceptual** The real-world view of the data as it applies to the object. When you view a customer, you see attributes that define the customer and remember items that describe the customer, such as the customer's name. A conceptual view of the data presents information in this understandable manner—as objects where the focus is on the data, not on the structure of the underlying database.

When you want to think about customers as a group, you work with entities. Each entity is a single customer, and the customers as a group are entities as well. In order to visualize the data that comprises a customer, the Entity Framework relies on models. These models help the developer conceptualize the entities. In addition, the Entity Framework stores these models in XML format for use in automatically generating code to create objects based on the models. Working with objects makes life easier for the developer.

Note You may be tempted to think of the Entity Framework as a technology that only applies to Microsoft SQL Server and other relational databases. The Entity Framework is a full solution that works with any data source, even flat-file and hierarchical databases. For the sake of making the discussion clear, this book will rely upon SQL Server for the examples, but you should know that using SQL Server is only a convenience, and you can use the Entity Framework for any data source your application needs to work with. In addition, you can mix and match data sources as needed within a single application.

In times past, developers needed to consider the physical (tables), logical (views), and conceptual (data model) perspectives of data stored in a database. A developer had to know precisely which table stored a particular piece of data, how that table was related to other tables in the database, and how to relate the data in such a way as to create a complete picture of a particular entity. The developer then wrote code to make the connectivity between the application and the database work. The Entity Framework reduces the need to perform such tasks. A developer focuses on the entity, not the underlying physical or logical structure of the database that contains the data. As a result, the developer is more productive. Working with entities also makes the data easier to explain to others.

An entity contains *properties*. Just as objects are described by the properties they contain, entities contain individual properties that describe each data element. A customer's last name would be a property of a customer entity. Just as classes have configurable getters and setters, so do properties in the Entity Framework. Every entity has a special property called the key property. The *key property* uniquely defines the entity in some way. An entity can have more than one key property, but it always has at least one. An entity can also group multiple properties together to create a complex type that mimics the use of user-defined types with standard classes.

Note It's important to remember that properties can contain either simple or complex data. Simple data is of a type defined by the .NET Framework, such as *Int32*. Complex data is more akin to a user-defined type and consists of multiple base types within a structure-like context.

It's possible to create a relationship between two entities through an association. For example, you might create an association between a customer entity and the order entities associated with the customer. The association type defines the specifics of the association. In some respects, an association is similar to a database-level join. One or more properties in each entity, called *association endpoints*, define the relationship between the two entities. The properties can define both single and multicolumn connections between the two entities. The multiplicity of the association endpoints determines whether the association is one-to-one, one-to-many, or some other combination. The association is bidirectional, so entities have full access to each other. In addition, an entity association can exist even when the target data lacks any form of database-level join specification. All of the association instances used to define an association type make up what is called the *association set*.

In order to allow one entity to view the data provided by an associated entity, the entities have a navigation property. For example, a customer entity that's associated with multiple order entities will have a navigation property that allows each order to know that it's associated with that customer. Likewise, each order will have a navigation property that allows each customer entity to see all of the orders associated with it. The use of navigation properties allows your code to create a view of the entities from the perspective of a particular entity. When working with a customer entity, the application can gain access to all of the orders submitted by that customer. In some respects, this feature works much like a foreign key does in a database, but it's easier to work with and faster to implement.

Some entities derive from other entities. For example, a customer can create an order. However, the order will eventually have a state that creates other entities, such as a past-due order entity or a delivered-order entity. These derived entities exist in the same container as the order entity as part of an entity set. You can view the relationship between entities and derived entities as being similar to a database and its views. The database contains all of the data, but a view looks at the data in a particular way. In the same way, a derived entity would help you create applications that view a particular entity type within the set of entities.

The final piece of information you need to know for now about entities concerns the *entity container*. In order to provide a convenient means to hold all of the entity information together, the Entity Framework employs the entity container. Before you can interact with an entity, your application creates an entity container instance. This instance is known as the *context*. Your application accesses the entities within a particular context.

Understanding the Entity Framework elements

The Entity Framework relies on XML files to perform its work. These files perform three tasks: defining the conceptual model, defining the storage model, and creating mappings between the models and the physical database. Even though the Entity Framework does a lot of the work for you, it's still important to understand how these elements work together to create a better environment in which to write applications.

Note This chapter discusses the idea of models generically. However, it's important to realize that the Entity Framework lets you interact with the database using one of three techniques:

- **Database first** The Entity Framework creates classes that reflect an existing database design.
- **Design first** You define a model of the database that the Entity Framework then creates on the database server.
- **Code first** You create an application, and the Entity Framework defines a model that it then uses to create the database on the database server.

In all three cases, the Entity Framework eventually creates a model that follows the standards described in this chapter. You'll learn more about the methods of working with the Entity Framework in Chapter 3, "Choosing a workflow." For now, the important consideration is the model itself.

Now that you a have a little idea of what constitutes the Entity Framework elements, it's time to discuss them in greater detail. In this case, we're looking at the logical structure of the Entity Framework. The physical structure (the XML files and their content) is discussed in the "Introducing the Entity Framework files" section of the chapter. The following sections discuss the conceptual model, storage model, and model mappings.

Considering the conceptual model

The conceptual model is the part of the Entity Framework that developers interact with most. This model defines how the database looks from the application's perspective. Of course, the application view must somehow match the physical realities of the underlying database, but there are many ways in which this happens. For example, a C# application will use an *INT32* value, rather than the Structured Query Language (SQL) *int* type. The conceptual model will refer to the data type as *INT32*, but the reality is that the database itself stores the data as an *int*.

The conceptual model is also used to create the classes used to interact with the database. The Entity Framework manages the conceptual model. As you make changes to the conceptual model, the changes are reflected in both the classes that the Entity Framework creates for your application and in the structure of the database. In addition, the Entity Framework automatically tracks changes to the database design and incorporates them into your implementation classes. As a result, your application can always access the data and functionality included with the target database.

Note It's important to realize that changes to the database design can occur at several levels. The two most common levels are from the developer, when making changes to the database model to accommodate application requirements; and from the Database Administrator (DBA), to accommodate enterprise-wide changes to the database as needed to efficiently and reliably store information. No matter how a change occurs, the database structure is ultimately affected, at which point the Entity Framework detects the change and updates the application using the data.

A conceptual model also incorporates the concept of a namespace, just as your applications do. An Entity Framework namespace performs the same functions as the namespace in your application. For example, it helps define entities with the same name as unique features. Using namespaces also helps group like entities together. For example, everything related to a customer can appear in the same namespace, making it easier to interact with the customer in every way needed.

At the heart of the conceptual model are the entity and association definitions used to create the view of the database. Each entity definition includes the information described in the "Defining an entity" section earlier in this chapter. When you use the designer to interact with the database model, what you're really doing is modifying the XML entries that create and define each of these entity definitions. The XML entries are stored on disk and used to re-create the graphic appearance of the model when you reopen the project.

Considering the storage model

The storage model is the part of the Entity Framework that defines how the database looks from the database manager's perspective. However, this model provides this view within Microsoft Visual Studio, and it provides support for the conceptual model. This model is often called the logical model because it provides a logical view of the database that ultimately translates into the physical database (see the "Defining an entity" section earlier in this chapter for a description of the various database views).

As with the conceptual model, the storage model consists of entity and association definitions. However, these definitions reflect the logical appearance of the actual database, rather than the presentation of the conceptual model within the application. In addition to the entity and association definitions, the storage model includes actual database data such as commands used to query the information within the database. You'll also find stored procedures in this model. All of this additional information is used by ADO.NET to create connection and command objects automatically, so that you don't have to hand-code the information as part of your application.

Considering the model mappings

At this point, you know that there are two models used with the Entity Framework—the conceptual model presents the application view of the database and the storage model presents the logical database manager view of the database. These two models are necessarily different. If they were the same, you wouldn't need two models. The need for two models is also easy to understand once you consider that the application's use of the database is always going to differ from the database manager's goals of storing the data efficiency and reliably. In order to make the two models work together, the Entity Framework requires model mapping—a third element that describes how something in the conceptual model translates to the storage model, and vice versa.

The overall goal of the model-mapping part of the Entity Framework is to create a definition of how the entities, properties, and associations in the conceptual model translate to elements within the storage model. This mapping makes it possible for the application to create a connection to the database, modify its structure, manage data, and perform other tasks with a minimum of manually written code. Most of the code used to interact with the database is automatically generated for the developer using the combination of the conceptual model, storage model, and this mapping layer.

Introducing the Entity Framework files

As previously mentioned, all of the files used with the Entity Framework rely on XML. The use of XML makes the files portable and easy to use with other applications. You can also view the content of these files and reasonably expect to understand much of what they contain. However, each of the Entity Framework elements uses a different XML file with a different file extension and a different language inside.

After you create a new application that relies on the Entity Framework and define the required database models, you can find the resulting files in the main folder of the project. When working with Visual Studio 2012, you'll find a single Entity Data Model XML (.EDMX) file. However, when working with older versions of Visual Studio, you may find individual files for each of the Entity Framework elements.

Providing a complete tutorial on each of these files is outside the scope of this book. The following sections provide a useful overview of the files, which you can use for further study.

Viewing the Conceptual Schema Definition Language file

The Conceptual Schema Definition Language (.CSDL) file contains the XML required to build the conceptual model of the database content as viewed by the application. You see this content in graphical format when working with Visual Studio. To see it in plain-text form, locate the .CSDL or .EDMX file for your application in the project folder. Right-click this file in Microsoft Windows Explorer and choose Open With from the context menu. Locate Notepad or some other suitable text editor in the Open With dialog box, clear any option that says that this program will become the default program for opening this file, and click OK. You'll see the XML for the conceptual model for the application. Following is the XML for the sample application that appears later in the chapter (some *<Schema>* attributes are removed to make the listing easier to read).

Note When using Visual Studio design tools to create the .CSDL, Store Schema Definition Language (.SSDL), and Mapping Specification Language (.MSL) files, all three are stored in a single .EDMX file, rather than in separate files. Whether the data appears in a single file or within multiple files, it's always stored as XML. An .EDMX file also contains some designer information not found in the separate files. You can safely ignore the designer information when viewing the .EDMX file in order to understand how the conceptual model, storage model, and model mapping interact.

```
<!-- CSDL content -->
<edmx:ConceptualModels>
  <Schema xmlns="http://schemas.microsoft.com/ado/2009/11/edm"...>
    <EntityContainer Name="Model1Container" annotation:LazyLoadingEnabled="true">
      <EntitySet Name="Customers" EntityType="Model1.Customer" />
    </EntityContainer>
    <EntityType Name="Customer">
      <Key>
        <PropertyRef Name="CustomerID" />
      </Key>
      <Property Type="Int32" Name="CustomerID" Nullable="false"
                annotation:StoreGeneratedPattern="Identity" />
      <Property Type="String" Name="FirstName" Nullable="false" />
      <Property Type="String" Name="LastName" Nullable="false" />
      <Property Type="String" Name="AddressLine1" Nullable="false" />
      <Property Type="String" Name="AddressLine2" Nullable="false" />
      <Property Type="String" Name="City" Nullable="false" />
      <Property Type="String" Name="State_Province" Nullable="false" />
      <Property Type="String" Name="ZIP_Postal_Code" Nullable="false" />
      <Property Type="String" Name="Region_Country" Nullable="false" />
    </EntityType>
  </Schema>
</edmx:ConceptualModels>
```

The XML makes it easier to understand the preceding discussion of how an *Entity* object works. Notice that the XML describes an entity container, used to hold all of the entities for this particular model. Within that container is a single *EntityType* named *Customer*. As with all *Entity* objects, this one has a *Key* property named *CustomerID* that gives the *Entity* a unique value. In addition, there are a number of properties associated with this *Entity*, such as *FirstName*. You'll see how the properties work later in the chapter. Of course, an *Entity* can have other elements associated with it, and you'll see them at work later in the book.

Look at the individual *<Property>* entries. Each one includes a .NET type. In this case, the types are limited to *Int32* and *String*, but you have access to a number of other types. You can see the primitive data types supported by the Entity Framework at *http://msdn.microsoft.com/library/ee382832.aspx*.

Viewing the Store Schema Definition Language file

The .SSDL file contains the XML required to define the storage model of the database content as viewed by the database manager. As with the conceptual model, you see the database described in terms of the entities required to create it. The entries rely on SQL data types, rather than .NET data types. Here's an example of the XML used to create a storage model for the example that appears later in the chapter (the *<Schema>* has been shortened to make the text easier to read):

```
  <!-- SSDL content -->
  <edmx:StorageModels>
  <Schema Namespace="Model1.Store" Alias="Self"...>
<EntityContainer Name="Model1StoreContainer">
  <EntitySet Name="Customers" EntityType="Model1.Store.Customers" store:Type="Tables"
             Schema="dbo" />
</EntityContainer>
<EntityType Name="Customers">
  <Key>
    <PropertyRef Name="CustomerID" />
  </Key>
  <Property Name="CustomerID" Type="int" StoreGeneratedPattern="Identity"
            Nullable="false" />
  <Property Name="FirstName" Type="nvarchar(max)" Nullable="false" />
  <Property Name="LastName" Type="nvarchar(max)" Nullable="false" />
  <Property Name="AddressLine1" Type="nvarchar(max)" Nullable="false" />
  <Property Name="AddressLine2" Type="nvarchar(max)" Nullable="false" />
  <Property Name="City" Type="nvarchar(max)" Nullable="false" />
  <Property Name="State_Province" Type="nvarchar(max)" Nullable="false" />
  <Property Name="ZIP_Postal_Code" Type="nvarchar(max)" Nullable="false" />
  <Property Name="Region_Country" Type="nvarchar(max)" Nullable="false" />
</EntityType>
```

Viewing the Mapping Specification Language file

The .MSL file creates a relationship between the .CSDL and .SSDL files. The mapping serves to define how the application view and the database manager view reflect the same database, but from differing perspectives. For example, the model mapping defines which conceptual model property translates into a particular storage model property. Here's the model-mapping content for the example that appears later in the chapter:

```
<!-- C-S mapping content -->
<edmx:Mappings>
<Mapping Space="C-S" xmlns="http://schemas.microsoft.com/ado/2009/11/mapping/cs">
<EntityContainerMapping StorageEntityContainer="Model1StoreContainer"
                        CdmEntityContainer="Model1Container">
  <EntitySetMapping Name="Customers">
    <EntityTypeMapping TypeName="IsTypeOf(Model1.Customer)">
```

```
        <MappingFragment StoreEntitySet="Customers">
          <ScalarProperty Name="CustomerID" ColumnName="CustomerID" />
          <ScalarProperty Name="FirstName" ColumnName="FirstName" />
          <ScalarProperty Name="LastName" ColumnName="LastName" />
          <ScalarProperty Name="AddressLine1" ColumnName="AddressLine1" />
          <ScalarProperty Name="AddressLine2" ColumnName="AddressLine2" />
          <ScalarProperty Name="City" ColumnName="City" />
          <ScalarProperty Name="State_Province" ColumnName="State_Province" />
          <ScalarProperty Name="ZIP_Postal_Code" ColumnName="ZIP_Postal_Code" />
          <ScalarProperty Name="Region_Country" ColumnName="Region_Country" />
        </MappingFragment>
      </EntityTypeMapping>
    </EntitySetMapping>
  </EntityContainerMapping>
</Mapping>
</edmx:Mappings>
```

Developing a simple Entity Framework example

The best way to begin learning about the Entity Framework is to use it. This example won't do anything too spectacular. In fact, it's downright mundane, but it does reflect a process that many developers use to experiment with the Entity Framework. In this case, you'll use the model-first technique to create an example application. Remember that in the model-first approach, you begin by creating a model that's then added to the database, rather than relying on an existing database to define the model. The model-first technique has the advantage of allowing you to create and manipulate a database that won't have any impact on anyone else, so you're free to experiment as much as you want.

The example will start with a Windows Forms application. You'll create the model needed to make the database work with SQL Server Express (installed automatically on your system), and then use the resulting model to create a functional application. You'll test the application by managing some data you create with it. The entire process will take an amazingly short time to complete, as described in the following sections.

Starting the Entity Data Model Wizard

The first step is to create the database model. You can perform this task using a number of methods, most of which developers never use. The easy method is to start the Entity Data Model Wizard and have it do the work for you. That's the approach this example takes, as described in the following steps (you can find this project in the \Microsoft Press\Entity Framework Development Step by Step\Chapter 01\SimpleEF folder of the downloadable source code):

Creating the *SimpleEF* application and adding a database model to it

1. Start Visual Studio 2012.

> **Note** This book is designed around Entity Framework 5 and Visual Studio 2012 Professional or above. You could possibly try other versions of Visual Studio, but there is no guarantee that the examples will work. You will most definitely encounter problems trying to work through the examples using any of the Microsoft Express editions of Visual Studio.

2. Choose File | New | Project to display the New Project dialog box, as shown here:

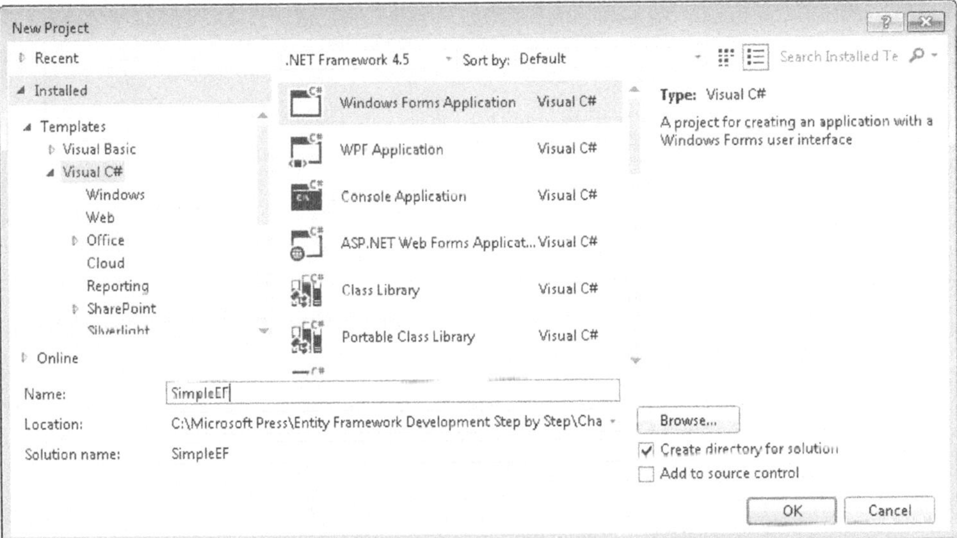

3. Type **SimpleEF** in the Name field and click OK. You'll see a new Windows Forms project.

4. Choose View | Other Windows | Data Sources. You'll see the Data Sources window, as shown here:

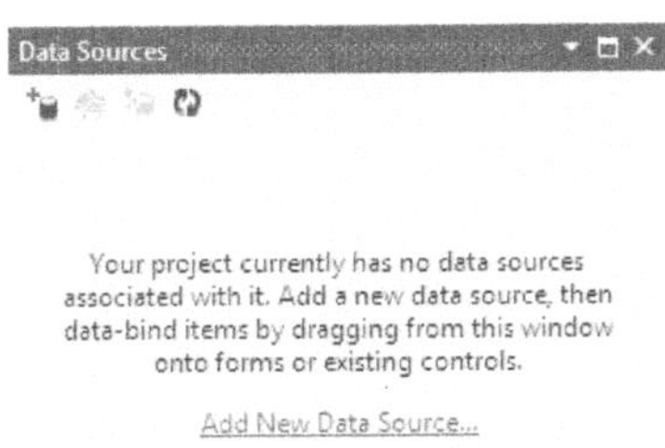

5. Click Add New Data Source. You'll see the Data Source Configuration Wizard dialog box. The wizard asks you to select a data source type, as shown here:

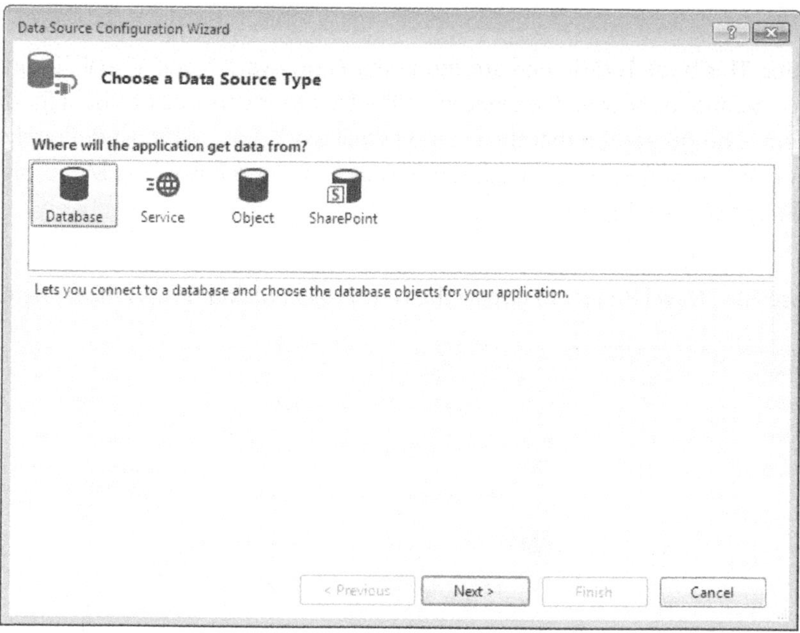

6. Select Database and click Next. The Data Source Configuration Wizard asks you to select a database model, as shown here:

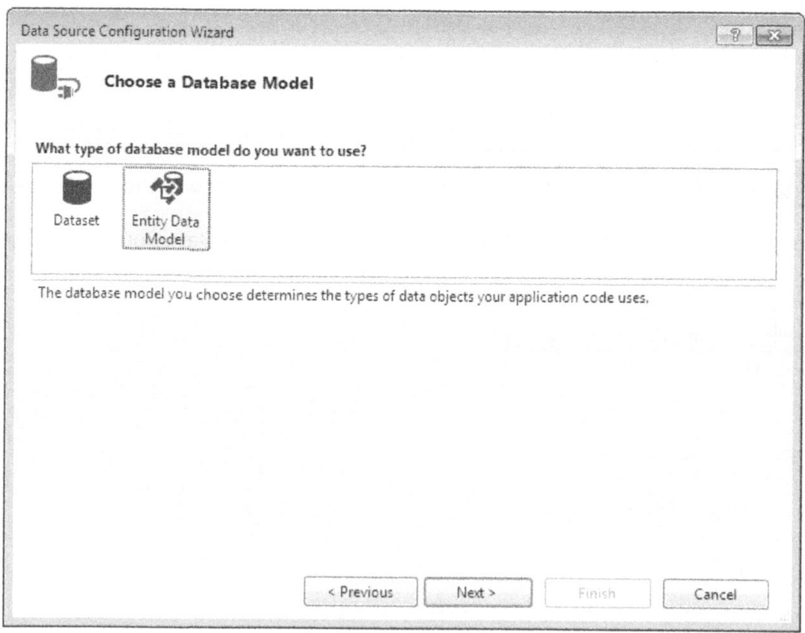

Note The Data Source Configuration Wizard provides access to a number of data source types, not just a database. For example, you could create an application that relies on access to a web service or uses a special kind of object to interact with data. There's also an option to create a data source from your Microsoft SharePoint installation. These other sources are helpful, but discussing them is outside the scope of this book. For the purposes of this book, you work with databases as a data source because the Entity Framework deals with databases, not the other data sources at your disposal.

7. Choose Entity Data Model and click Next. The Data Source Configuration Wizard asks you to choose the model content, as shown here:

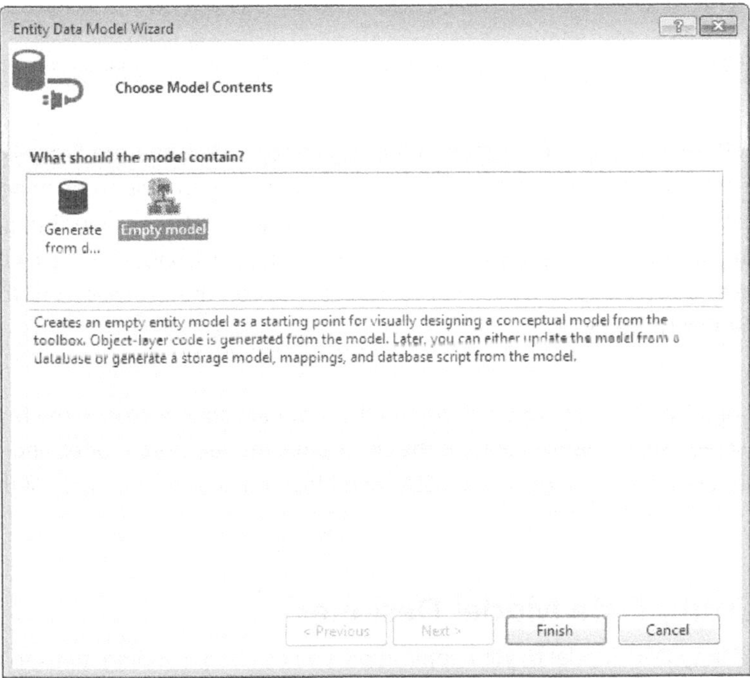

8. Choose Empty Model and click Finish. You'll see Visual Studio perform a few tasks. When you have the default User Access Control (UAC) set up, you'll see a Security Warning dialog box telling you that running the script required to generate the Entity Data Model could harm your system. If you see this message, check the Do Not Show This Message Again option and click OK to continue generating the Entity Data Model. It's during this phase of the procedure that you'll see the Entity Data Model Wizard perform the tasks required to generate an empty model for you. After a few additional moments, you'll see a blank Entity Data Model Designer window like the one shown here:

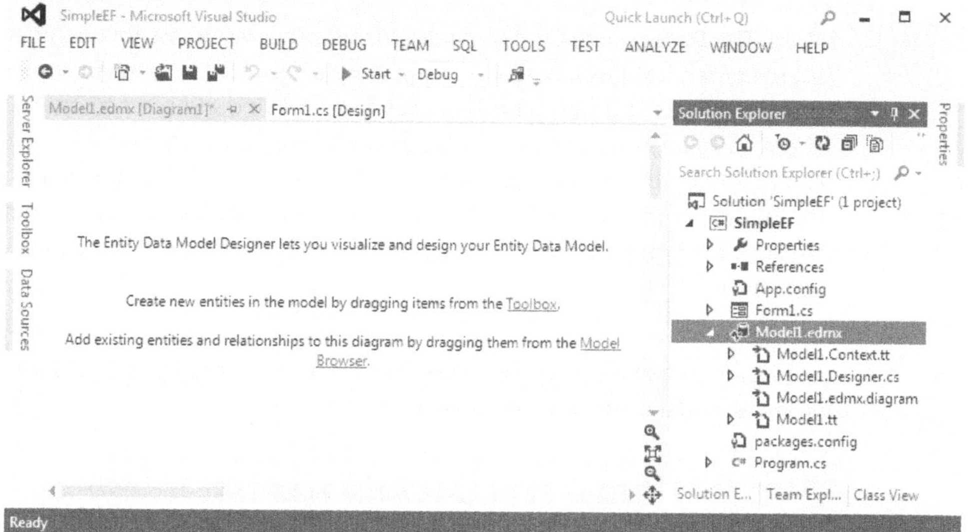

Note When working with existing data, you choose the Generate From Database option instead. The Entity Data Model Wizard will ask you a number of additional questions and create a model based on the existing database, including a full set of diagrams graphically displaying the database structure. Chapter 3 shows how the database-first technique works. For now, just focus on the process used to interact with the Entity Framework.

Solution Explorer also shows the result of adding the new data source. Notice the Model1.EDMX file shown in the screen shot. This file contains the conceptual model, store model, and model mappings. Each feature uses the language (CSDL, SSDL, and MSL) required for that part of the Entity Framework data.

Using the Entity Data Model Designer

After you add an Entity Data Model to your application, you can begin adding items to it from the toolbox—just as you do when adding controls to your application. For example, if you want to add an entity to the model, you drag and drop it onto the Entity Data Model Designer. The toolbox, shown here, contains the elements described earlier in the chapter.

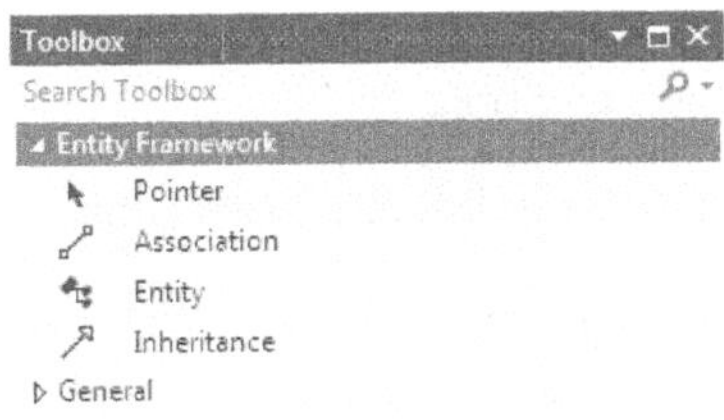

You'll begin working with a model by adding an Entity to it and then configuring the Entity as needed. The example uses a simple Entity named *Customer* with just a few properties that describe the resulting *Customer* object. In this case, you'll use the following properties:

- First Name (*FirstName*)
- Last Name (*LastName*)
- First Address Line (*AddressLine1*)
- Second Address Line (*AddressLine2*)
- City (*City*)
- State/Province (*State_Province*)
- ZIP/Postal Code (*ZIP_Postal_Code*)
- Region/Country (*Region_Country*)

Defining the *SimpleEF* Entity Data Model

1. Drag an *Entity* object from the toolbox to the Entity Data Model Designer. You'll see a new square added containing a blank entity, as shown here:

   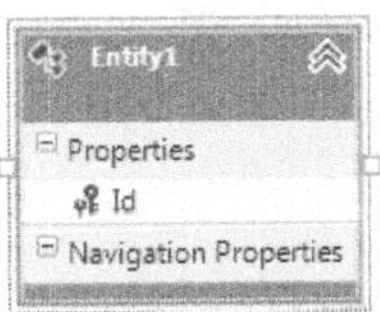

   Notice that the designer automatically adds an *Id* property for you. This property uniquely identifies a particular entry.

2. Right-click the *Entity1* object and choose Rename from the context menu. The Entity1 entry changes to a text box. Type **Customer** and press Enter.

3. Right-click the *Id* property and choose Rename from the context menu. The *Id* property changes to a text box. Type **CustomerID** and press Enter.

4. Right-click the *Customer* object and choose Add New | Scalar Property from the context menu. You'll see a new property added with the name as a text box.

5. Type **FirstName** (the value shown in parentheses in the previous list) and press Enter.

6. Perform steps 4 and 5 for all of the properties described earlier in this section. When you're finished, your entity should look like this one:

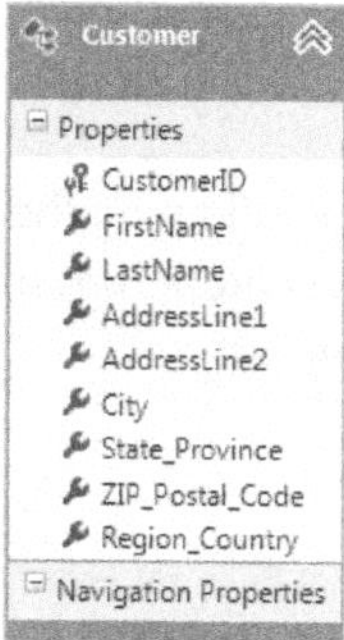

At this point, you could select any of these entity properties and change their properties using the Properties window, just as you would with any application feature. For example, you could change the *Type* property to any of the supported data types. However, for the purposes of this example, you don't actually need to change anything.

Notice that the default *Entity* object color is blue. When working with a complex design, you may want to color code the entities to make them easier to identify. For example, you may want to color customer entities blue and employee entities red. Color coding can make it easier to find the specific entity group you want. To change the color of an entity, select the entity in the designer and change the Fill Color property in the Properties window.

Working with the mapping details

At this point, you've defined a model for the example application. Right-click the *Customer* entity and choose Validate from the context menu. The IDE tells you that entity *Customer* isn't mapped, as shown here:

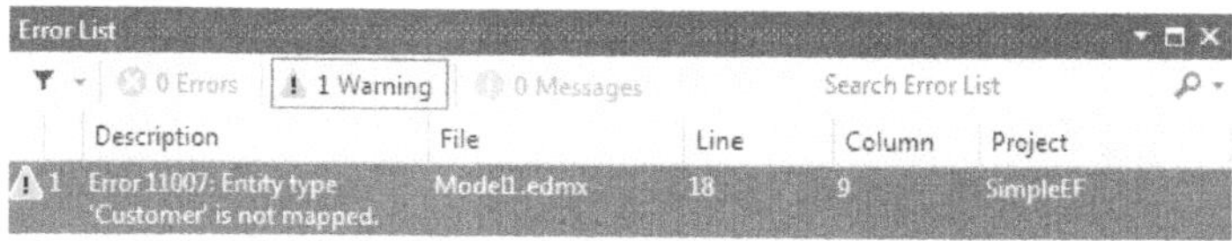

Creating a model doesn't create the required mapping. In fact, the database you just created doesn't exist at all. The model for the database exists, but you still need to tell Visual Studio to interact with the database manager (SQL Server Express in this case) to create the physical database and develop a map between your model and the logical database.

Developing the database and the required mapping

1. Right-click the *Customer* entity and choose Generate Database From Model on the context menu. You'll see the Generate Database Wizard dialog box, as shown here:

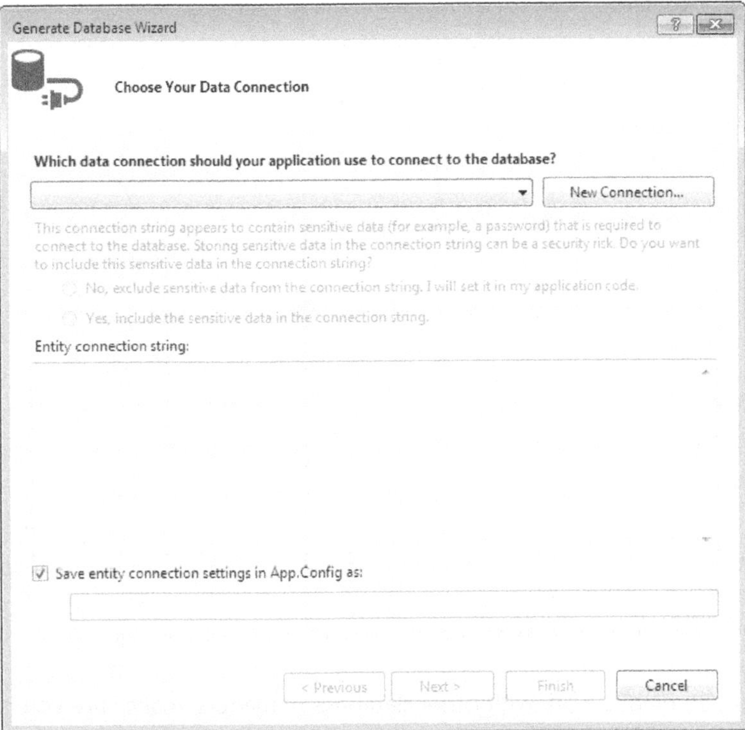

2. Click New Connection. You'll see the Choose Data Source dialog box shown here:

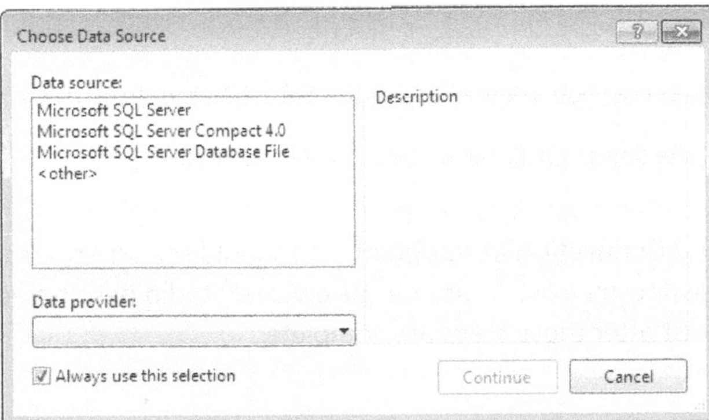

3. Select Microsoft SQL Server and then click Continue. You'll see a Connection Properties dialog box like the one shown here:

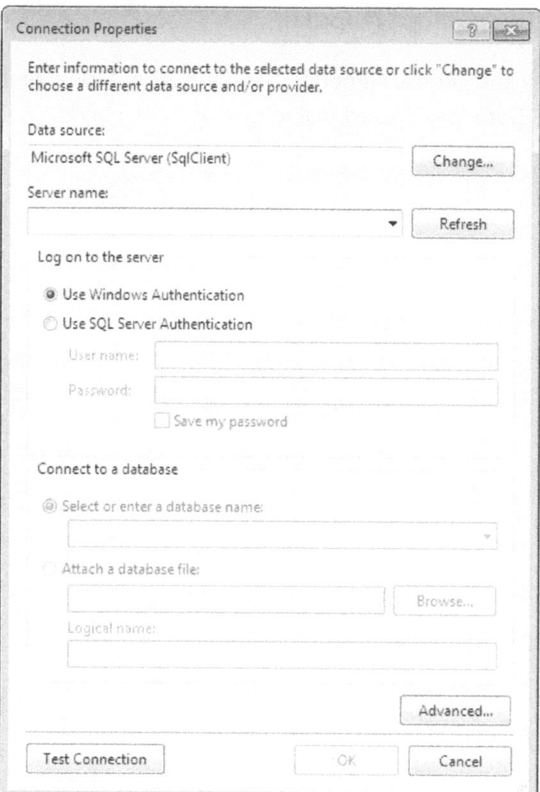

Note If you plan to work with other database managers, make sure you clear the Always Use This Selection check box. Doing so ensures that Visual Studio displays this dialog box each time so that you can choose which database manager you want to use.

4. Choose the name of the server you want to use in the Server Name drop-down list box.
5. Type **TestCustomer** in the Select Or Enter A Database Name field.

Note If you click Test Connection at this point, you should see an error message stating the database doesn't exist. That's because Visual Studio hasn't created it yet. The database will exist after these steps are complete.

6. Click OK. You'll see a dialog box telling you that the database doesn't exist. Visual Studio asks permission to attempt to create the database for you.

7. Click Yes. Visual Studio creates the new database for you. This is a blank database—it doesn't contain any tables, views, indexes, or anything else normally associated with a database. You'll return to the Generate Database Wizard dialog box. However, now the connection information is filled in.

8. Click Next. The Generate Database Wizard creates the Data Definition Language (DDL) script required to create everything in the model you designed, as shown here. You can scroll through this script to see the SQL statements used to make your model a real database and associated table.

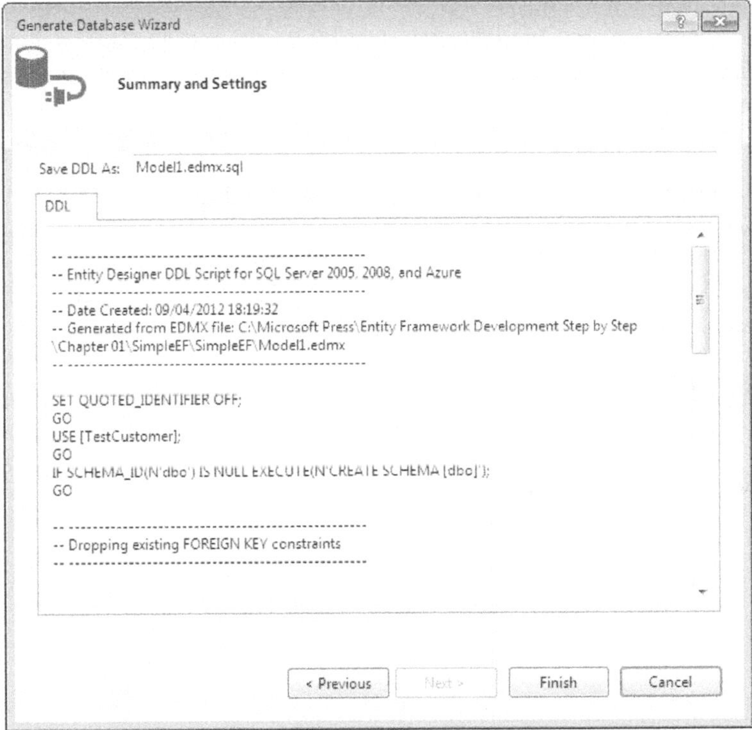

9. Click Finish. You'll see the script, Model1.EDMX.sql, open. It hasn't executed yet. All that the Generate Database Wizard has done is create the script required to make your database model functional.

10. Choose SQL | Transact-SQL Editor | Execute. You'll see a connection dialog box where you can enter the information required to connect to the SQL Server instance you've selected.

11. Enter any required credentials and click Connect. Visual Studio connects to the database manager and executes the SQL script it created. At this point, your database is ready for use. Notice that you didn't have to access the database manager yourself or create any scripts by hand.

Using the resulting framework to display data

Now that you have a database to use—a database generated from a model you created—you might want to see the database in action. There are a number of ways to accomplish the task, but for this first sample, it's probably best to try something easy. The one piece of information you absolutely need to know before you start is that the model you created earlier also generated code. Part of this code is the creation of a container that you use to access the database. The container class always starts with the name of the model, followed by the word *container*. For this example, this means that the name of the container class is *Model1Container*.

Nothing else you do with the Entity Framework is going to be outside your experience if you've worked with collections in the past. The following steps create a simple application that will test just a few of the features that this model provides. Chapter 2, "Looking more closely at queries," will help you start performing more complex tasks.

Creating an application based on the *TestCustomer* database

1. Add four buttons to the Windows Forms application you created at the outset of this example, and name them *btnCount*, *btnAdd*, *btnDelete*, and *btnQuit*. Here's an example of the simple form as it appears in the downloadable source:

2. Right-click the Form1.cs entry in Solution Explorer and choose View Code from the context menu. You'll see the Code Editor. Add a reference to the model container and instantiate it in the form's constructor, as shown here:

```
// Define a container to hold the database information.
Model1Container ThisContainer;

public Form1()
{
   InitializeComponent();

   // Instantiate the container.
   ThisContainer = new Model1Container();
}
```

ThisContainer contains a reference to all of the elements found in the model. In this case, the model only contains a reference to one table, *Customers*. However, in a production application, you could use *ThisContainer* to access every table, view, index, or other feature in the database.

3. Double-click Count. Visual Studio creates an event handler for you. Add the following code to the event handler:

```
private void btnCount_Click(object sender, EventArgs e)
{
   // Display the number of database records.
   MessageBox.Show("There are " +
      ThisContainer.Customers.Count().ToString() +
      " Records.");
}
```

   The container for all of the database elements is found in *ThisContainer*. Within the container is a table named *Customers*. The *Count()* method outputs the number of records in the specified table.

4. Double-click Add and add the following code to the resulting event handler:

```
private void btnAdd_Click(object sender, EventArgs e)
{
   // Create a new record.
   Customer ThisCustomer = ThisContainer.Customers.Create();

   // Add some random data.
   Random ThisValue = new Random(DateTime.Now.Millisecond);
   ThisCustomer.FirstName = ThisValue.Next().ToString();
   ThisCustomer.LastName = ThisValue.Next().ToString();
   ThisCustomer.AddressLine1 = ThisValue.Next().ToString();
   ThisCustomer.AddressLine2 = ThisValue.Next().ToString();
   ThisCustomer.City = ThisValue.Next().ToString();
   ThisCustomer.State_Province = ThisValue.Next().ToString();
   ThisCustomer.ZIP_Postal_Code = ThisValue.Next().ToString();
   ThisCustomer.Region_Country = ThisValue.Next().ToString();

   // Add a new record.
   ThisContainer.Customers.Add(ThisCustomer);
   ThisContainer.SaveChanges();

   // Inform the user.
   MessageBox.Show("Added " + ThisCustomer.CustomerID.ToString());
}
```

   The example begins by creating a new *Customer* record, *ThisCustomer*. It then fills the fields with random numeric values. The content is simply there to make it easy to view the record information later.

   In order to add the new record to the database, the example calls the *ThisContainer.Customers.Add()* method. This method requires a *Customer* object as input. The changes won't take effect until the application calls *ThisContainer.SaveChanges()*. You need to make sure your code calls the *SaveChanges()* method regularly; otherwise, you risk losing application data. Finally, the application shows the record number added to the application.

5. Double-click Delete and add the following code to the resulting event handler:

```
private void btnDelete_Click(object sender, EventArgs e)
{
   // Obtain the first record.
   Customer ThisCustomer = null;
   if (ThisContainer.Customers.Count() > 0)
      ThisCustomer = ThisContainer.Customers.First();
   else
   {
      // Display an error message if there are no records to delete.
      MessageBox.Show("No Records to Delete");
      return;
   }

   // Delete it.
   ThisContainer.Customers.Remove(ThisCustomer);
   ThisContainer.SaveChanges();

   // Inform the user.
   MessageBox.Show("Deleted " + ThisCustomer.CustomerID.ToString());
}
```

A production application would have a lot more checks than this one does, but the code begins by checking whether there are any records to delete in the *Customers* table. If not, the event handler exits after providing an error message.

There are a number of ways to obtain a record from the *Customers* table. For that matter, you might simply want to search for a particular record based on some criterion and delete all those that match. In this case, the code uses the *ThisContainer.Customers.First()* method to obtain a copy of the first record in the table. The code then calls *ThisContainer.Customers.Remove()* to remove the record and *ThisContainer.SaveChanges()* to make the changes permanent. The code then informs the user about the deletion and displays the ID of the customer it deleted.

6. Double-click Quit and add the following code to the resulting event handler:

```
private void btnQuit_Click(object sender, EventArgs e)
{
   // Save the database.
   ThisContainer.SaveChanges();

   // End the program.
   Close();
}
```

One task you should always perform before you exit the application is to save the database changes one more time—just to ensure that none of the changes are lost. After the code calls *ThisContainer.SaveChanges()*, it exits by closing the form.

7. Click Start and try some of the buttons. For example, click Count and you'll see the current record count (0 if there are no records). Click Add and you'll see the identifier of the customer that the application has added. Likewise, click Delete and you'll see the identifier of the customer that the application has deleted. Make sure you end up with at least one record in the database.

8. Choose View | Server Explorer. You'll see the Server Explorer window shown here:

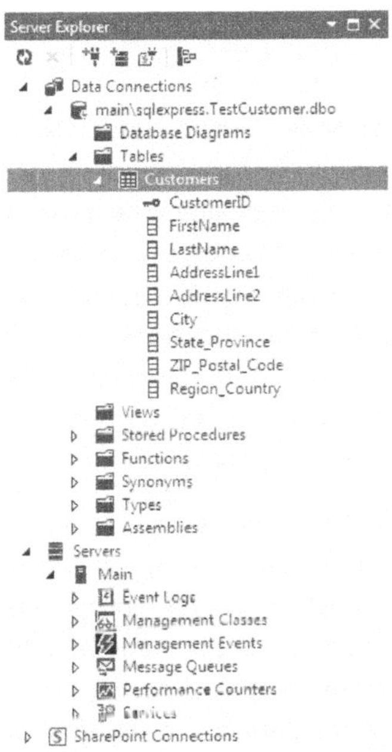

9. Drill down into the TestCustomer.dbo\Tables\Customers entry, as shown in the preceding image. Notice that the complete table structure is precisely as you designed it.

10. Right-click Customers and choose Show Table Data from the context menu. You'll see a new window appear with the data from the table as shown here (your data will most definitely differ from mine because the data is randomly generated in this application):

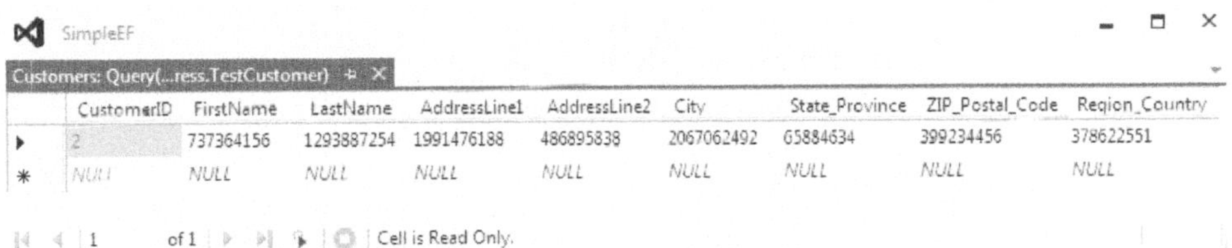

This environment is fully interactive, so you can use it to check the results of your database experiments. More importantly, you can use it to modify the data as necessary to meet test requirements.

11. Click Quit to end the application. You can always experiment with this application later.

Getting started with the Entity Framework

The Entity Framework makes it possible to write database applications using less manually written code because the Entity Framework relies on the content of the conceptual model, storage model, and mapping model files to automatically generate classes that an application can use to access the database reliably. The use of the Entity Framework makes developers more productive and generally reduces application errors. In addition, the automation that the Entity Framework provides helps ensure that the application remains up to date. Changes made by the developer or DBA are automatically reflected in the application.

This chapter has introduced you to the Entity Framework. Make sure you understand the three layers—conceptual model, storage model, and model mapping—before you proceed to Chapter 2. Also take time to create the sample application and view the files it creates. The more time you spend interacting with the data that the Entity Framework creates and manages, the better. Of course, all of the work of creating classes is done for you in the background, but it's still a good idea to know the source of the automation and have an idea of how it works for those situations where the automation doesn't quite produce the results you expected. As part of working with this chapter, try creating your own project based on data that you already have in a sample database on your system. (Please don't work with any production data until you're proficient with the Entity Framework.)

Chapter 2 takes the next natural step in working with the Entity Framework. Instead of simply creating a project and viewing the resulting files, you're going to begin working with some data by making queries. After all, data stored in a database isn't useful until you can get it out and display it to an end user in a useful form. Once you complete Chapter 2, you may want to come back to this chapter and use the techniques described here to view the files that the sample in that chapter creates. You'll see some differences because now you'll be interacting with the data in a meaningful way. Viewing the differences will add to your knowledge of how the Entity Framework interacts with the database and generates XML to model it.

Chapter 1 quick reference

To	Do this
See how the application views the database	Open the .CSDL or .EDMX file and view its content.
See how the database manager views the database	Open the .SSDL or .EDMX file and view its content.
Determine how the Entity Framework resolves differences between the application view and the database manager view of the database	Open the .MSL or .EDMX file and view its content.
Create a new conceptual model	Click Add New Data Source in the Data Source window and choose Empty Model when prompted.
Add entities to the new conceptual model	Drag and drop an *Entity* object from the Entry Framework folder of the toolbox to the Entity Data Model Designer.
Generate a physical database based on your design	Right-click the entity you want to work with and choose Generate Database From Model on the context menu.
Generate the tables and other elements in your model	Choose SQL | Transact-SQL Editor | Execute.
Use the new database in an application	Create a reference to the model container, such as *Model1Container ThisContainer = new Model1Container();*, where *Model1* is the name of the model you want to use.

CHAPTER 2

Looking more closely at queries

After completing the chapter, you'll be able to

- Perform a basic query against a database.
- Use special query mechanisms to create specific queries.
- Combine and summarize data as needed.
- Group data to make it easier to see relationships.

The most natural act when you have a data store of some type is to ask it a question. This activity doesn't necessarily require a database. Knowledgeable people are asked lots of questions by those who want to know something. Someone long ago decided to call this activity a *query* when it comes to computers, but the concept is precisely the same. When you store data with a computer, you want to be able to ask the computer questions about that data later—otherwise, the data is useless. That's what this chapter is about—asking the computer questions to gain information about the data store in the database you create.

Just as there are many ways to ask human experts questions, there are many ways to ask a computer questions. For example, you could simply create a SQL *Query* object to perform the task. Some questions become quite complex though, and asking them using a SQL query may prove difficult for some developers. That's when you start relying on other techniques, such as Language-Integrated Query (LINQ), which uses a SQL-like syntax, but greatly simplifies the method used to actually ask the question. Of course, you can use standard methods that you use with any collection as well. You can even ask for the information found in a specific record number, assuming you know what that record number is.

Presentation is large part of understanding data. When you ask a human expert a question, the expert might provide an answer that would require even more knowledge to understand, or might provide a simplified answer that anyone can understand. Likewise, when you ask computers questions, you want to get output that's understandable by the viewer. Part of making the answer understandable is combining the data in specific ways, so that the viewer sees an overview of the information, rather than drowning in detail. In addition, grouping information in certain ways can help viewers make associations that aren't obvious from the raw data. In short, presentation quality can make the answer to a question either easier or harder to understand, depending on the presentation you use. This chapter discusses presentation issues as they relate to working with data directly.

Defining a basic query

A basic query is one in which the person asking the question needs straightforward results without any special formatting. A basic query could be as simple as obtaining a specific record from a single table in the database and viewing the raw data it provides. Sometimes a user needs only basic information, so it's important to know how to make a basic query to reduce the time and effort required to obtain the information. The following sections describe how to create and run a basic query. You can find the code for this example in the \Microsoft Press\Entity Framework Development Step by Step\Chapter 02\GetUserFavorites folder of the downloadable source code.

Note You can download the source code for this book from the publisher's site at Provide URL Here. It's an exceptionally good idea to download the book's source code so that you can see how the examples should look as you work through them. In addition, if you make a mistake, you can always use the downloaded source code to locate the error and make corrections to your code. If you choose not to type everything in by hand, the downloadable source makes it possible for you to participate in the rest of the book's material.

Creating the model

Chapter 1, "Getting to know the Entity Framework," showed you how to create a basic entity, convert it to a database, and then use it within an application. This example begins with a simple entity that consists of a user name (type *String*), favorite number (type *Int32*), favorite color (type *Int32*), and birth date (type *DateTime*), as shown here:

Notice that the key property is named *UserId* and that the entity is named *UserFavorites*. Besides providing a simple dataset to work with for your first query, this example also exposes you to some new data types so that you can get a better understanding of how they work in the Entity Framework. To start this example, you will create a Microsoft Windows Forms project and then add a class library to it. The following procedure will get you started.

Defining the project and model

1. Choose File | New | Project. You'll see the New Project dialog box.
2. Select the Windows Forms Application template.

3. Type **TestBasicQuery** in the Name field and **GetUserFavorites** in the Solution field. Click OK. Microsoft Visual Studio creates a new project for you.
4. Right-click *TestBasicQuery* in Solution Explorer and choose Add | New Item from the context menu. You'll see the Add New Item dialog box.
5. Select the Data folder in the left pane and the ADO.NET Entity Data Model template in the center pane, as shown here:

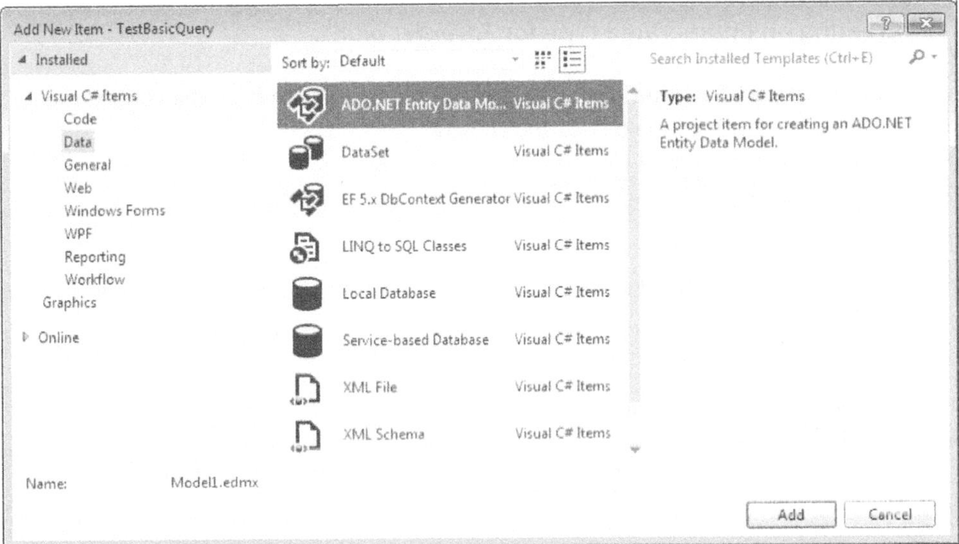

6. Type **UserFavoritesModel** in the Name field and click Add. You'll see the Entity Data Model Wizard appear.
7. Select Empty Model and click Finish. You'll see a blank diagram.
8. Use the techniques you used in the "Using the Entity Data Model Designer" section of Chapter 1 to create the model shown earlier in this chapter. Start with the UserFavorites entity, rename the key value to **UserId**, and then add the required scalar values. Change the *Type* property for each of the scalar values as needed to match the description of the model.

Working with enumerations

This example is going to show how to perform a new technique with *FavoriteColor*. The first question you must have asked when creating the entity is why *FavoriteColor* is an *Int32* type, rather than a *String*, since colors are normally presented as human-readable names. You don't actually want the user to be able to input all sorts of odd colors. If you let the user enter a string name, you might end up with several hundred shades of blue, many of which won't actually use the word *blue* in their name. This is a situation where an enumerated type is going to work well. You can still allow a number of colors from which the user can select, but you also make it possible to search for specific colors. The following procedure tells how to convert an *Int32* type into an enumerated type.

Note The ability to work with enumerated types is new to Entity Framework 5. This feature is really useful for all sorts of data needs. For example, in a production application, you could use an enumerated type to limit the methods for shipping products to those allowed by the organization. Entity Framework 5 also makes working with entities quite easy, as you'll see in this chapter.

Creating an enumerated type for *FavoriteColor*

1. Right-click FavoriteColor and choose Convert To Enum from the context menu. You'll see the Add Enum Type dialog box shown here:

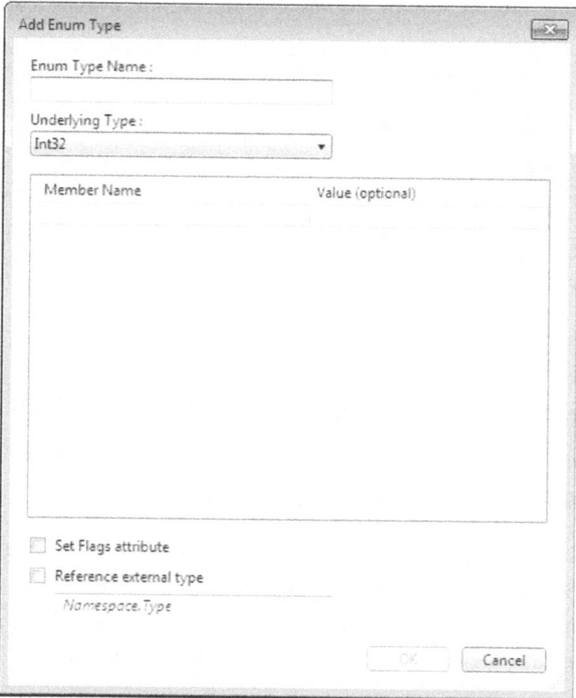

2. Type **ColorNames** in the Enum Type Name field. This is the name that the application will use to access the enumerated type. You'll also use it within your code to access the enumerated members.

3. Type **Red** in the first Member Name field entry and press Enter. The entry point will automatically advance to the next blank entry in the list.

4. Add in turn Blue, Green, Orange, Yellow, Purple, Pink, Black, and White. You should end up with a number of color entries like the ones shown here:

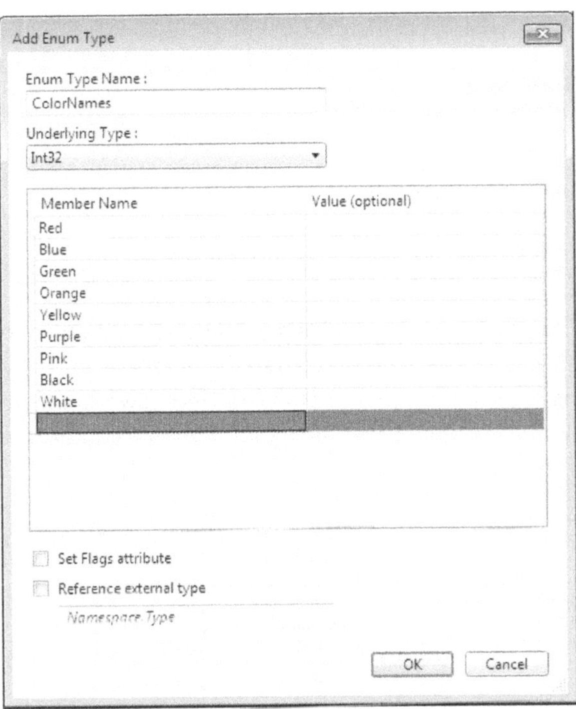

5. Click OK. *FavoriteColor* is now an enumerated type. It doesn't look any different, but if you look in the Properties window, you'll see that the *Type* property value has changed to *ColorNames*.

At this point, you can generate the database from the model using precisely the same technique that you did in Chapter 1. Give the database a name of *UserFavoritesData*.

Obtaining an application data source

If you look at the Data Sources window now, you'll see that it still doesn't contain a data source listed in it, despite the fact you started there to create the *UserFavorites* entity. You used the model, *UserFavoritesModel*, to create the database. However, you can't use *UserFavoritesModel* to interact with the database through the application without writing code. If you wanted to use the coded approach, you'd write something like this to start:

```
// Create the database connection.
var UserFavoritesContext = new UserFavoritesModelContainer();
```

At this point, *UserFavoritesContext* provides a connection to the database that you can use to interact with it. After you create an object like *UserFavoritesContext*, you'd access database functionality, such as adding a new record, by using code like this:

```
// Create a new record.
UserFavorites NewRecord = new UserFavorites();

// Fill in the record data.
NewRecord.Name = "Mark Hassall";
NewRecord.FavoriteNumber = 22;
NewRecord.FavoriteColor = ColorNames.Red;
NewRecord.Birthday = new DateTime(1990, 7, 10);

// Add the record to the database.
UserFavoritesContext.UserFavorites.Add(NewRecord);

// Save the record to the physical database.
MessageBox.Show(UserFavoritesContext.SaveChanges().ToString() + " records changed.");
```

When you run this code opens a window showing the data you just added to the table. Here are typical results for the code, the application adds a new record to the database. In fact, you can verify it by opening the connection to the database in Server Explorer, drilling down to the *UserFavorites* table, right-clicking the table entry, and choosing Show Table Data from the context menu. Visual Studio presented in this short example:

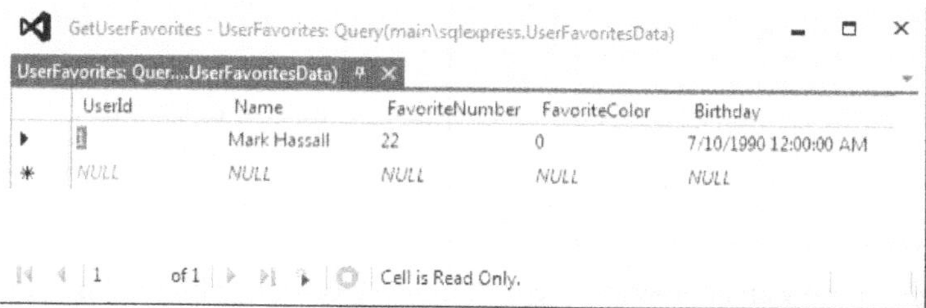

There's nothing wrong with hand-coding the specifics of the database interface, especially when you need to create an application that performs a special task. Fortunately, there's an easier way to work with the database when you perform common tasks that doesn't involve writing a lot of code by hand. It begins with creating an object data source you can use to interact with the model you created earlier in an easier way than writing code for it. The following procedure describes how to create the object data source you use for this example.

Defining an application data source

1. Click Add New Data Source in the Data Sources window. You'll see the Data Source Configuration Wizard shown here:

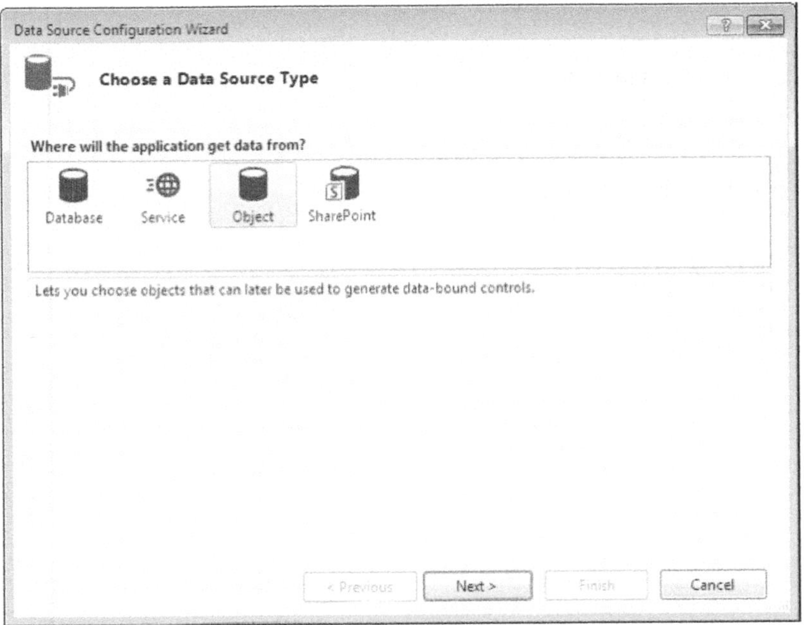

It's essential to remember what sort of connection you need to create when working with the Entity Framework. What you want is a connection to an object that will help you create the application. The connection already exists as part of the model you created earlier. In some cases, developers become lost when thinking about the connection, rather than the goal, which is to make the data visible to the end user.

2. Select Object and click Next. The Data Source Configuration Wizard asks you to select a data object. You know from the code shown earlier in this section that the *UserFavoritesModelContainer* provides access to the connection and the underlying data. However, if you select it, in this case, you'll find that you miss the goal of creating the user interface needed to interact with the data. What you really need to do is to drill down to the *UserFavorites* object, as shown here, and select it:

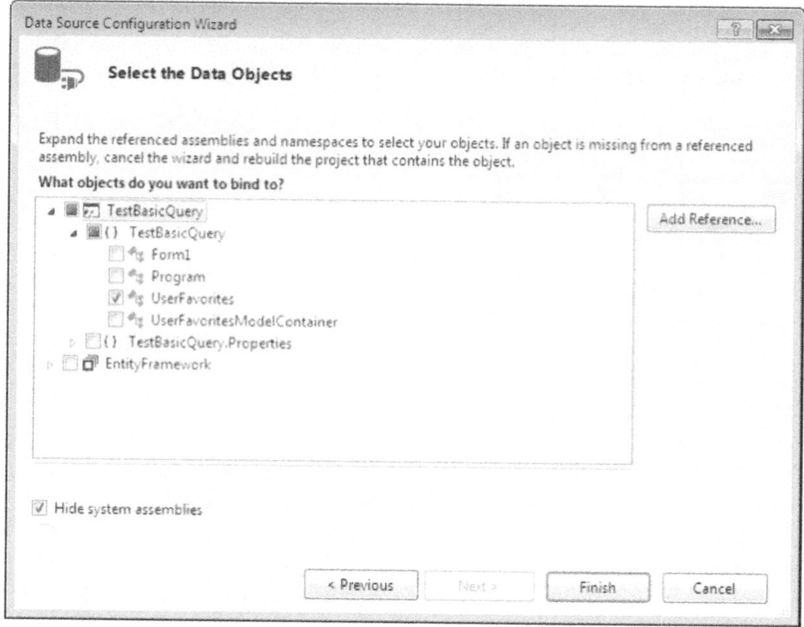

3. Check the UserFavorites box and click Finish. Visual Studio creates the required data source, as shown here:

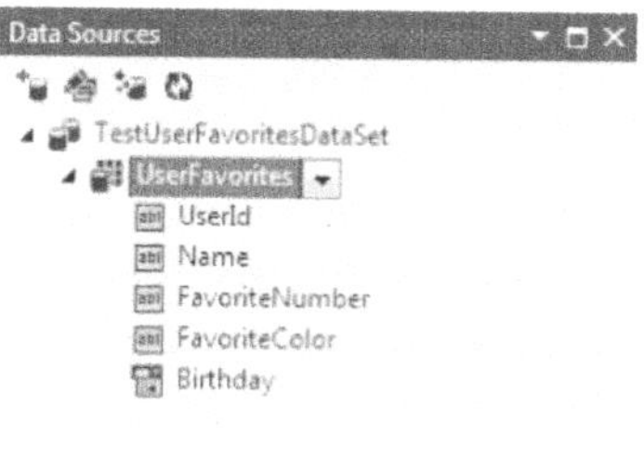

Creating the test application

At this point, you have a data source you can use to create an application. The data source is configurable—you can define how each object should appear when dropped onto a form. For example, you can change UserId from a text box to a label. The following steps help you define the data source configuration and then create a test application using it.

Creating an application from a data source

1. Highlight UserFavorites. You'll see a drop-down list box. (Some developers don't realize that these list boxes are available; they contain configuration options for specific objects.) In this case, you want to see the records one at a time, so you need to change the configuration from grid view to details view.

2. Select Details from the drop-down list. Notice that the UserFavorites icon changes to reflect the change in configuration. Some of the individual fields also require configuration. For example, you don't want to allow the user to change the *UserId* field because this field value is automatically generated by the database.

3. Highlight UserId and choose Label from the drop-down list box. Notice that the icon changes to match the new field configuration.

4. Highlight FavoriteColor. Remember that *FavoriteColor* has an *Integer* data type, but you want it to appear as an enumerated value. This means a little extra configuration at the outset. Choose Customize from the drop-down list box, and you'll see the Options dialog box shown here:

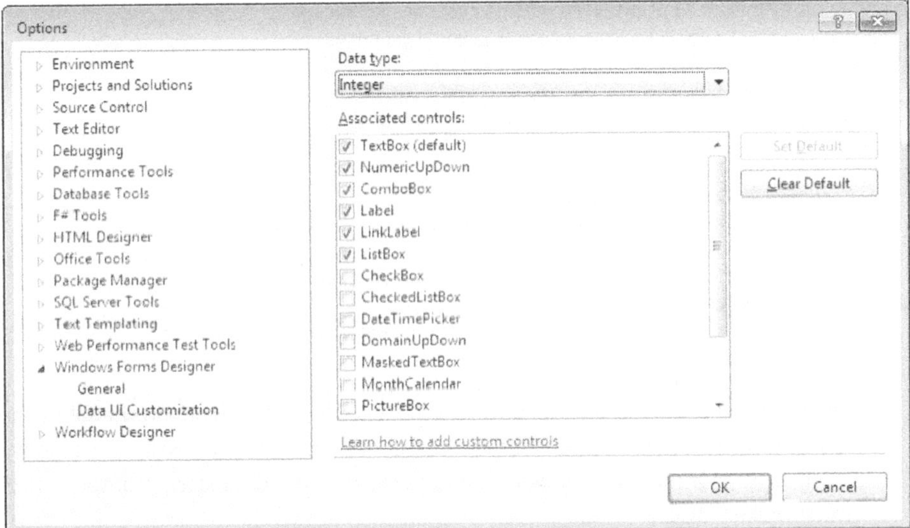

5. Choose the Enum option in the Data Type field and then click OK. This changes the data type, but not the field type.

6. Choose ComboBox from the drop-down list box. The FavoriteColor field icon changes to match the new configuration.

7. Drag and drop *UserFavorites* onto *Form1*. Visual Studio automatically creates a form-based application for working with the database you created earlier, as shown here:

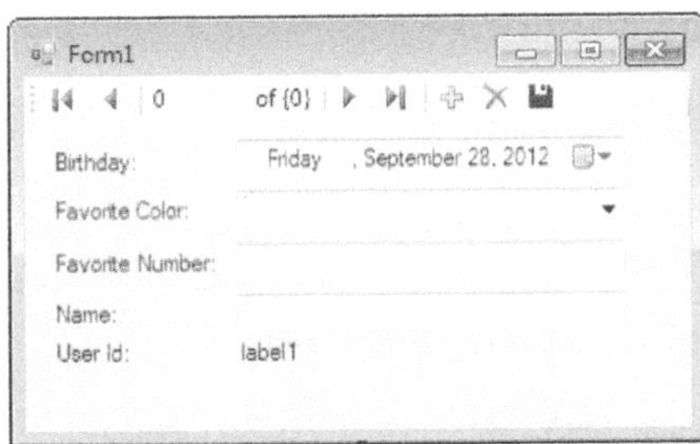

Normally, you'd take time to make this form look pretty and organize it a bit differently from what Visual Studio has provided, but for the sake of simplicity (and getting to the meat of the application faster), just leave things as-is for now. This setup will work just fine for your tests. The application won't work just yet; you do need to make a few additional changes to it.

Notice that Visual Studio also creates two components, *userFavoritesBindingSource* and *userFavoritesBindingNavigator*. These two components perform many of the tasks that you'd normally hand-code automatically. In fact, you'll be amazed at how much work they do for you.

8. Add code to create and initialize the database content and load the records needed by the application. Right-click Form1 in Solution Explorer and choose View Code from the context menu. The code you need to add appears in bold.

```
// Define the context used to access the database.
UserFavoritesModelContainer UserFavoritesContext;

public Form1()
{
   InitializeComponent();

   // Initialize the database context.
   UserFavoritesContext = new UserFavoritesModelContainer();

   // Query the database for the records you want.
   var dbQuery =
      UserFavoritesContext.UserFavorites.Where(id => id.UserId >= 0).ToArray();
}
```

This code begins by creating a database context, just as the code in the first example in the first part of the chapter did. The database context provides access to the data that you defined with your model. However, that data exists in the database. In order to use it locally, you must make a query.

The query code requests every record where the *UserId* field has a value greater than 0, which is all of the records in the table, since they start with a value of 1. Making a call to *ToArray()* actually loads the records from the database to a local variable called *Local*. You'll see how the *Local* variable works in the next step.

9. Double-click Form1 to create a *Load()* event handler. This event handler configures the display elements every time the form loads. Here's the code needed for this task:

```
private void Form1_Load(object sender, EventArgs e)
{

   // Assign a local copy of the queried records to the
   // binding source.
   userFavoritesBindingSource.DataSource =
      UserFavoritesContext.UserFavorites.Local;

   // Fill the Favorite Colors list with acceptable colors and
   // choose a default.
   favoriteColorComboBox.DataSource = Enum.GetValues(typeof(ColorNames));
```

```
    favoriteColorComboBox.SelectedItem = ColorNames.Red;
}
```

By setting the *userFavoritesBindingSource.DataSource* property to *UserFavoritesContext.UserFavorites.Local*, you make it possible for the application to access a local copy of the data from the database. Using a local copy greatly increases application speed. This local copy tracks any changes to the data as the reader works with it. Consequently, when the changes are completed, the user can save them as a batch to the database, improving overall application efficiency.

The application must also configure the *favoriteColorComboBox* to provide access to the standard list of colors that you've defined. The example code shows how to perform this task and then define the default selection. In order to make *favoriteColorComboBox* a little more bulletproof, you need to set the *DropDownStyle* property to *DropDownList*.

10. Select the Save button (the last one on the toolbar) and set its *Enabled* property to *True*. Now you need to add some code to actually make the Save button do something.

11. Double-click the Save button. Visual Studio will create a new event handler for it. Here's the code you need to save the data to disk:

```
private void userFavoritesBindingNavigatorSaveItem_Click(object sender, EventArgs e)
{
    UserFavoritesContext.SaveChanges();
}
```

In a production application, you'd attach this code to the *Closing()* event to ensure that all of the user's changes are saved. The example uses the Save button as a convenience for experimentation purposes, so you can choose not to save changes you've made.

12. Compile the application. It's ready to run.

Running the basic query

When you run the application the first time, you won't see any records. Click the yellow plus icon (Add New) to add a new record to the database. Type some data in the form, press Tab after the last field you enter to ensure it's been accepted, and then click Save Data. Here's what a typical record will look like:

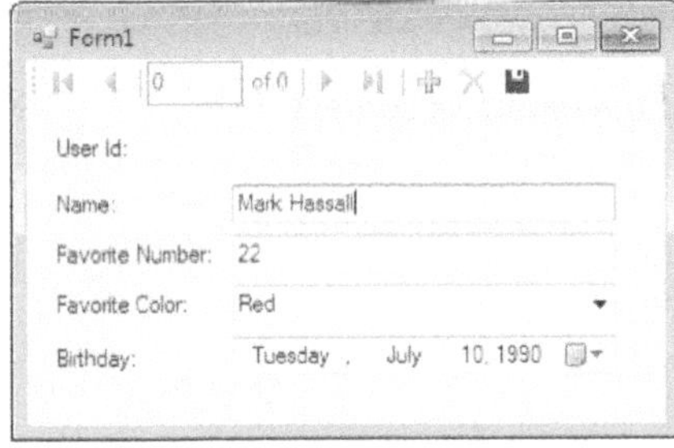

Add several more records to the database. Make sure you click Add New between each record and press Tab after the final field. You'll eventually have a number of records to use in the sections that follow. Table 2-1 shows the data entries that the examples will use (the user ID is added automatically).

TABLE 2-1 Example data entries

Name	Favorite number	Favorite color	Birthday
Mark Hassall	22	Red	July 10, 1990
Kim Abercrombie	15	Blue	August 12, 1991
Yossi Banai	7	Green	January 22, 1970
Andrew Rath	17	Red	July 22, 1989
Corinna Bolender	11	Red	November 30, 1985
Charlie Keen	7	Blue	May 15, 1976
Julia Ilyina	3	Orange	October 5, 1990

Note You can also load these values using a script. Choose File | Open in Visual Studio. Navigate to the \Microsoft Press\Entity Framework Development Step by Step\Chapter 02\SQL Data folder and open the UserFavorites Data.SQL file. Right-click the open file and choose Execute Script from the context menu. When you see the Connect To Server dialog box, make sure the connection settings are correct for your system and click Connect. The script will execute and add the required rows to the *UserFavorites* table you created earlier.

After you enter the records, make sure you click Save Data. Otherwise, the records will only appear in the *Local* property, not in the database itself. The controls at the top of the application let you perform all of the standard database tasks. For example, you can use the controls to move between records. Any change you make to a record will end up in the host database as long as you click Save Data afterward. You can also delete records. All of this functionality comes without much in the way of programming that you've done. The following are the most important tasks to remember when creating an application this way:

- Create the database context.
- Perform a query to load the *Local* property with data.
- Use the *Local* property as the data source for the *BindingSource* control.
- Save changes using the *SaveChanges()* method of the database context.

Creating specific queries

The *GetUserFavorites* application obtains all of the records that the database contains by using a general query in the form of the following lambda expression: *id => id.UserId >= 0*. The query will obtain all of the records because the automatic numbering starts *UserId* with a value of 1. You can't add a record with a value less than 1, so this query always obtains every record.

There are times when you don't want to obtain all of the records. For example, you may decide that you want to see only the people who like the color red or the people born in 1990. The queries you create can also accommodate these needs. In order to accommodate queries, you need to modify the previous example using the procedure that follows. You can find the code for the examples in these sections in the \Microsoft Press\Entity Framework Development Step by Step\Chapter 02\SpecificQueries folder of the downloadable source code.

Adding a button to a toolbar

1. Click the down arrow next to the new item icon on the toolbar, as shown here. You'll see a series of potential controls you can add to the toolbar.

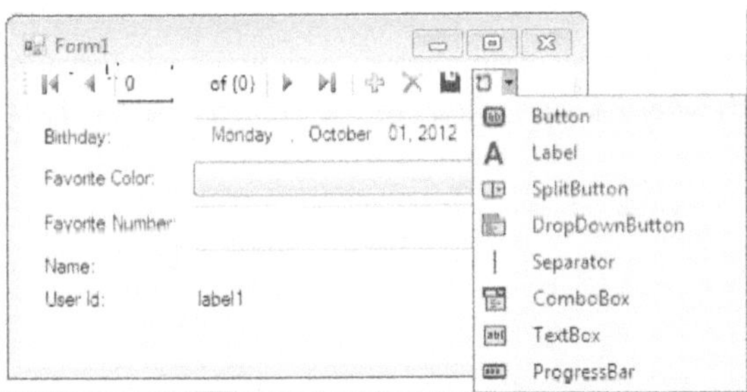

2. Select the Button control. Visual Studio adds a generic button, as shown here:

3. Double-click the button. Visual Studio creates a *toolStripButton1_Click()* event handler for it.

The button you've just added will provide a means for experimenting with various query types. The following sections describe how to create queries that will obtain certain records.

Using literals

Most people are familiar with using literals to create a query. The use of any absolute value defines a literal query. For example, you can ask the application which users like red as a color. The literal value is *Red* in this case. Use the following procedure to see how a literal query works with the example.

Testing for literal values in LINQ

1. Type the following code (shown in bold) into the *toolStripButton1_Click()* event handler:

```
private void toolStripButton1_Click(object sender, EventArgs e)
{
   // Define and perform the query.
   var Results = UserFavoritesContext.UserFavorites.Where<UserFavorites>(
      color => color.FavoriteColor == ColorNames.Red);

   // Create and display the output.
   StringBuilder Output = new StringBuilder();
   foreach (UserFavorites Result in Results)
      Output.Append(Result.UserId + "\t" + Result.Name + "\r\n");
   MessageBox.Show(Output.ToString());
}
```

   In this case, the query places the output of the query in *Results*. The actual query consists of a lambda expression that compares each of the entries in the database with the *ColorNames.Red* literal value. After the application has the records it needs, it uses a *for* loop to place the results in *Output*, and then displays Output on screen.

2. Start the application. You'll see the new button in place in the toolbar.
3. Click toolStripButton1. You'll see the application output, as shown here. The application has indeed found all of the records where a user prefers red, which you can verify by viewing each of the records individually.

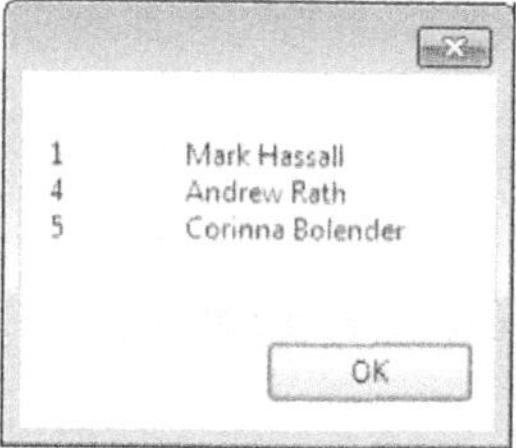

4. Click OK to close the dialog box.
5. Verify that records with the *UserId* values of 1, 4, and 5 do indeed like the color red.
6. Stop the application.

Using operators, properties, and methods

Careful creation of literal queries will address a number of needs. You can even combine literal query values to obtain specific results. Queries that you create for the Entity Framework have access to the same operators that you can use for any other kind of programming need. The following procedure helps you explore the use of operators, properties, and methods when working with queries.

Using operators in LINQ

1. Modify the *toolStripButton1_Click()* event handler code as shown here to rely on operators to create complex queries:

   ```
   private void toolStripButton1_Click(object sender, EventArgs e)
   {
      // Define and perform the query.
      var Results = UserFavoritesContext.UserFavorites.Where<UserFavorites>(
         query => ((query.FavoriteColor == ColorNames.Red || query.FavoriteNumber < 10)
            && (query.Name.Length < 15)));

      // Create and display the output.
      StringBuilder Output = new StringBuilder();
      foreach (UserFavorites Result in Results)
         Output.Append(Result.UserId + "\t" + Result.Name.Length + "\t" +
            Result.FavoriteColor.ToString() + "\t" + Result.Name + "\r\n");
      MessageBox.Show(Output.ToString());
   }
   ```

   This query relies on operators to complete the task. Any record that has a *FavoriteColor* value of *Red* or has a *FavoriteNumber* value less than 10 qualifies at the outset. However, the *Name* field must also have a length that's less than 15 characters long. You can combine elements in any number of ways in order to produce the desired logic. This example relies on both logical AND (&&) and logical OR (||) elements, plus it uses object properties as part of the query.

   To make it easier to verify that the output is correct, this example also modifies the output string. In this case, it adds the name length and the favorite color so you can see them as part of the output.

2. Start the application and click toolStripButton1. The application displays the results of the query, as shown here:

   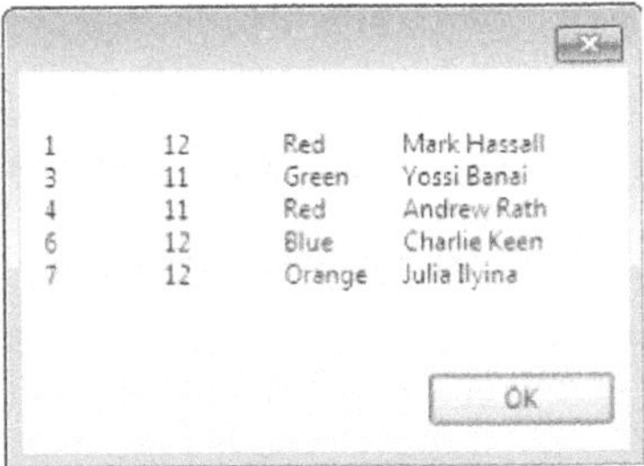

3. Click OK to close the dialog box.

4. Verify that the chosen records do indeed meet the selection criteria. For example, you should try to determine why the record with a user ID of 5 wasn't chosen. After all, the user likes red in that case.

5. Stop the application.

Combining and summarizing data

Most users don't want all of the data that a database contains. The term *information overload* applies to most enterprise data because there's simply too much for any one person to work with effectively. In order for users to make sense of the data you provide, you must initially filter it to provide only the records the user needs. However, large databases still offer more information than the user can use, in most cases, so you have two other choices for getting the information under control:

- Combine data to create aggregate information, such as a list of users who like the color red, but without listing anything but the names.
- Summarize data to provide an overview of the information, such as the total number of users who like the color red, without listing any of the data.

The example in this section shows the effect of combining and summarizing data to obtain specific results. You can find the downloadable code for this example in the \Microsoft Press\Entity Framework Development Step by Step\Chapter 02\CombineAndSummarize folder. Before you begin, add two buttons to the application using the "Adding a button to a toolbar" procedure found in the "Creating specific queries" section of the chapter. The following procedure shows how to create and use this example.

Combining and summarizing data with LINQ

1. Select toolStripButton1 and change its *Text* property to read "Combine."
2. Select toolStripButton2 and change its *Text* property to read "Summarize."
3. Modify the *toolStripButton1_Click()* event handler to perform a type of combine operation, as shown here:

```
private void toolStripButton1_Click(object sender, EventArgs e)
{
   // Define and perform the query.
   List<String> Results = UserFavoritesContext.UserFavorites.Where<UserFavorites>(
      query => query.FavoriteColor == ColorNames.Red).
      Select<UserFavorites, String>(item => item.Name).ToList<String>();

   // Create and display the output.
   StringBuilder Output = new StringBuilder();
   foreach (String Result in Results)
      Output.Append(Result + "\r\n");
   MessageBox.Show(Output.ToString());
}
```

   In this case, the data is first filtered using a query. After that, the names are separated from the rest of the data, combined into a list, and displayed on screen.

4. Modify the *toolStripButton2_Click()* event handler to perform a type of summarize operation, as shown here:

```
private void toolStripButton2_Click(object sender, EventArgs e)
{
   // Summarize the data.
   var Results = UserFavoritesContext.UserFavorites.Count(
      query => query.FavoriteColor == ColorNames.Red);

   // Display the result.
   MessageBox.Show(String.Format(
      "The number of users who like Red is {0}.", Results));
}
```

LINQ provides access to a number of statistical methods, such as *Count()*, *Min()*, and *Max()*. You can combine these methods with queries in order to obtain specific results and then summarize them for the user. In this case, the application provides a summary count of the number of users who like the color red.

5. Start the application and click Combine. The application displays the names of users who like the color red.

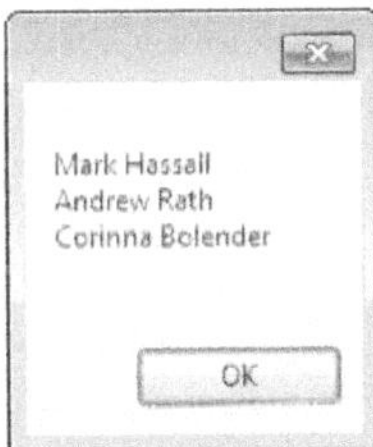

6. Click OK to close the dialog box.
7. Click Summarize. The application displays the number of people who like the color red, as shown here:

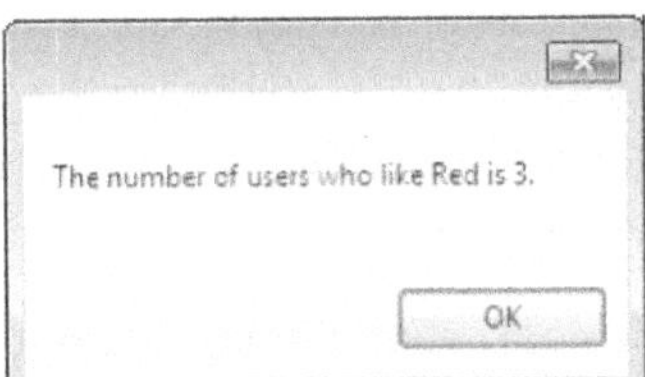

8. Click OK to close the dialog box.
9. Stop the application.

Grouping data

The presentation of data in an order the user understands is an essential part of creating useful database applications. Users sometimes can't see patterns because of the wealth of data. By creating applications that help the user see patterns where they exist, you make it possible for the user to obtain more information than the data itself presents. With this in mind, add a button to the application using the "Adding a button to a toolbar" procedure found in the "Creating specific queries" section of the chapter. The following procedure describes how to create the code required to demonstrate data grouping. You can find the downloadable code for this example in the \Microsoft Press\Entity Framework Development Step by Step\Chapter 02\GroupData folder.

Grouping data with LINQ

1. Modify the toolStrip*Button1_Click()* event handler to group the data by user color choices, as shown here:

```
private void toolStripButton1_Click(object sender, EventArgs e)
{
   // Create a grouped query.
   var Results = UserFavoritesContext.UserFavorites.GroupBy(
      group => group.FavoriteColor);

   // Work through each group.
   StringBuilder Output = new StringBuilder();
   foreach (var Group in Results)
   {
      Output.Append(Group.Key + "\r\n");

      foreach (UserFavorites UserList in Group)
      {
         Output.Append("\t" + UserList.Name + "\r\n");
      }
   }

   // Display the result.
   MessageBox.Show(Output.ToString());
}
```

   It's important to understand that you end up with a list of group objects, and within those group objects is a key and a list of *UserFavorites* objects. In order to display the data, you must work through each group first, and then through the list of *UserFavorites* within the group. The *Key* property contains the key value for this particular group.

2. Start the application and click toolStripButton1. The application displays the results of combining the data, as shown here:

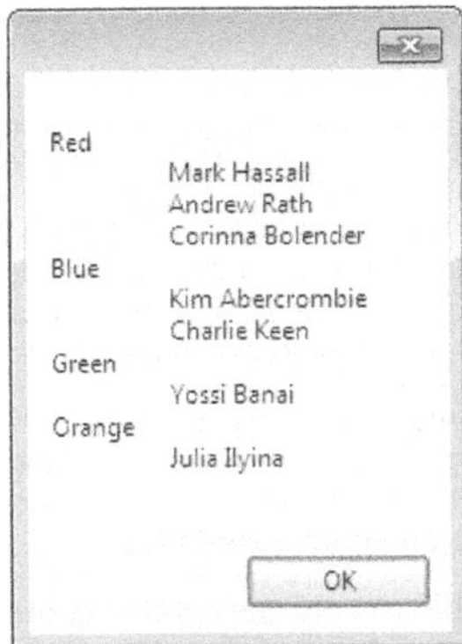

3. Click OK to close the dialog box.
4. Stop the application.

Getting started with the Entity Framework

This chapter has focused on creating queries that help you get the most out of the data that the Entity Framework helps you access and manage. In this case, you created a model, defined a database based on that model, developed an application to manage the database, and finally filled the database with data to test it. The remainder of the chapter explored various techniques for interacting with the data, such as creating complex queries, and summarizing, combining, and grouping the data. The point is that the Entity Framework makes it possible to create flexible applications that contain very little code and yet perform a number of interesting tasks.

Getting the right output so that the user can see how the data is related is an important part of any application development experience. When working with the Entity Framework, it's important to optimize the way in which your application interacts with the database. Remember that there's a local copy of the data that requires local system resources and network bandwidth to download. The better you define a query to obtain only the data the user actually requires, the faster your application will run and the fewer resources it uses. With this in mind, try creating a few queries on your own based on the queries you've already worked with in this chapter. For example, try to discover how many people were born in 1990. Use the techniques shown in this chapter to count the number of output records and also group them by color choice.

The Entity Framework actually supports a number of workflow models, and this chapter shows only one of them. The design-first approach will appeal to a lot of developers because using it means that you don't have to go outside the Visual Studio IDE, yet you can be assured of the correct result from the outset (assuming you spend the time required to create a useful database design). Chapter 3, "Choosing a workflow," shows all three workflow models—database first, design first, and code first—so that you can choose the appropriate workflow for a given situation and use it effectively.

Chapter 2 quick reference

<table>
<tr><th>To</th><th>Do this</th></tr>
<tr><td>Add a new named model to your project</td><td>Right-click the project entry in Solution Explorer, choose Add | New from the context menu, and then select the ADO.NET Entity Data Model template. Type the name of the model you want to create in the Name field.</td></tr>
<tr><td>Create an enumerated type</td><td>Start with an Int32 data type and then use the Add Enum Type dialog box (accessed by right-clicking the property and choosing Convert To Enum from the context menu) to change it to an enumerated type.</td></tr>
<tr><td>Define a model context</td><td>Create a variable to hold the context contained in the model container. For example, if the model is called UserFavoritesModel, you could create a variable to hold the context like this:
<code>var UserFavoritesContext = new
UserFavoritesModelContainer();</code></td></tr>
<tr><td>Save changes made locally to the host database</td><td>Call the SaveChanges() method of the context variable. For example, if you had created a context variable named UserFavoritesContext, then you'd call the following:
<code>UserFavoritesContext.SaveChanges()</code></td></tr>
<tr><td>Fill the Local property with data for use in your application</td><td>Create a LINQ query that describes which data to use in the application. For example, in the sample application, you fill the Local property with all of the records in the database by calling this:
<code>UserFavoritesContext.UserFavorites.Where(id =>
id.UserId >= 0).ToArray();</code></td></tr>
<tr><td>Create complex queries</td><td>Combine logical elements in a single lambda expression. For example, you can use the && and || operators to produce complex results. In addition, you can access the methods and properties of each object element to further define the query.</td></tr>
<tr><td>Obtain additional information about the data</td><td>Rely on object-specific properties and methods. For example, you can use the Length property to determine the size of objects such as strings.</td></tr>
<tr><td>Combine the data</td><td>Create queries that filter the data, extract the pertinent information, and then create an aggregate output of just the information the user needs.</td></tr>
<tr><td>Summarize the data</td><td>Use statistical methods such as Count(), Min(), and Max(), along with filtering queries, to produce specific output that presents the user with an overview of the data.</td></tr>
<tr><td>Group the data</td><td>Use the GroupBy() method to group the data by specific fields. Remember that each group is a hierarchy consisting of a key and the underlying data associated with that key.</td></tr>
</table>

CHAPTER 3

Choosing a workflow

After completing the chapter, you'll be able to

- Describe the code-first workflow approach.
- Describe the model-first workflow approach.
- Describe the database-first workflow approach.
- Define the differences between the workflow choices and make an appropriate choice based on the situation.
- Create an application using the code-first approach.
- Create an application using the model-first approach.
- Create an application using the database-first approach.

Getting work done quickly, efficiently, and accurately depends, in part, on creating an ordered work environment where tasks are performed in a certain way with predictable results. That may sound quite boring, but boring is good when it comes to performing work tasks without a lot of headaches. No one needs or wants drama when working. One of the most important tools in creating an ordered work environment for developers is defining a workflow. Workflows provide an ordered means for accomplishing tasks. They define a procedure where one step follows another in an ordered and timely fashion. The emphasis of a workflow is on the flow part of the equation—one step should naturally flow into the next. When working with the Entity Framework, there are three common workflows: code first, model first, and database first. You use each of these workflows to meet specific needs and under specific conditions. However, the point of the workflow is to make the work easier and more predictable so that you can focus on the database and code more, and the process for creating the application less.

Because understanding the workflow is so important, this chapter begins by reviewing each of the workflows and helping you understand how they work. After you understand the workflows, you'll discover when to use each of the workflows to obtain a desired result from the Entity Framework. In fact, the chapter provides a table that describes how each of the workflows differs and compares them in a way that helps you choose the right workflow for a particular situation.

The chapter ends by showing you an example of each workflow in action. You'll create a simple application that relies on that particular workflow to obtain a desired result. In a production environment, you'll find that understanding the workflows and knowing when and how to use each of them saves you considerable time and makes using the Entity Framework a lot easier. The examples in this chapter will all work with essentially the same database, but each example will highlight how you would interact with that database using that particular workflow. For example, when working with the code-first workflow, you define the database structure using code and then rely on the Entity Framework automation to create the database for you based on the code you provide. Likewise, when working with the model-first workflow, you create a graphical presentation of the database, and then rely on the Entity Framework automation to create the database and underlying classes that you require. The database-first example will actually start with the database you create using the model-first approach.

Considering the user's focus

Most business applications interact with data in some way. The purpose of the application is to help the user manage the data in an efficient and ordered manner. From the user's perspective, the focus is on the data, and the application should be invisible. The more invisible you can make the application, the better the user can focus on the data and complete a desired task. Obviously, an application can't disappear completely, but you can make it appear that way. Here are some things to keep in mind as you work with the Entity Framework to develop your application.

- **Keep it simple** An essential part of making the application disappear is to hide complexity whenever possible. In some cases, hiding complexity literally means hiding aspects of the application that the user won't need very often. However, in other cases it means making specific choices, such as creative use of controls. It's much easier to get a user to check a box or select an option than it is to have the user type specific information. More importantly, the need to keep things simple will affect the model you create with the Entity Framework to some extent. Simplify the model and you'll usually simplify the user interface as well.
- **Make it fun** The more fun you can make the application, the less the user will pay attention to the fact that the application is designed to do work. For example, creative use of what-if scenarios helps users see how application choices affect output. Most users will try to game the application to obtain a specific output, and in the process forget completely about the work aspect of the application. As a result, the user sees a game that manipulates data, rather than an application designed to do work.
- **Create a flow** Most data entry has a flow to it. For example, when you ask a user to enter a person's name, most users find it more natural to enter the first name, middle name, and last name—in that order. When the flow is disrupted by illogical data entry choices, the user becomes more aware of the application and less aware of the data. When creating a new application, track how users currently enter data and use the same flow for your application.

The reasons you need to consider the user's focus is that it will sometimes affect your workflow when interacting with the Entity Framework. For example, the code-first workflow can help you focus on the user's needs first, and then form the database around the user's needs. This approach doesn't always work, however, especially when you must meet specific business or legal requirements. The idea, though, is to find a balance that helps the user focus attention on the data without breaking any rules in the interim.

Understanding the code-first workflow

The code-first workflow (introduced in Entity Framework 4.1) is commonly used when you have an existing application (or existing code) that models a database-like structure. The code consists of one or more classes that define the data model, and then relies on additional code to define how the classes interact. For example, you might create a class called *Book* that defines the properties for identifying a book in a collection; these properties then define the database model, as shown here:

```
public class Book
{
   // Define the fields used for the database.
   public Int32 BookID { get; set; }
   public String Name { get; set; }
   public String Author { get; set; }
   public String ISBN { get; set; }
   public Int32 PageCount { get; set; }
   public DateTime LastRead { get; set; }
}
```

You could use this class in an application without ever creating a database. By adding some additional code, you could store the data from this class on disk as an XML file if desired, or you could continue to use it as an in-memory database for experimentation purposes. However, as your application becomes more complex, you might decide that storing the information in a database really is necessary. This is the point at which the code-first workflow comes into play, because you can use the code you have already created and developed to define the database automatically. The developer doesn't worry about the details of the database and instead focuses on the code that models the database.

Note It's important to note that this class has a field with *ID* in the name as type *Int32*. The automation used with the code-first workflow requires that you provide an *ID* field to use as a key for the database. Anything with *ID* in the name, such as the *BookID* field shown here, will work just fine. You could map another field, such as *ISBN*, as the key field, but that requires some additional programming that isn't discussed in this chapter. Later chapters will discuss various mapping strategies, along with techniques you can use to specify things like the database name. For now, think only about the automation presented in this chapter.

The code-first workflow was created after the model-first and database-first workflows by Microsoft for developers who want to write code, rather than work with a designer. You create the object model for your application using standard Common Language Runtime (CLR) objects with a technique that involves using Plain Old CLR Object (POCO) classes. This workflow is code-centric, rather than designer-centric. When working with this model, you begin with objects that have no relationship with the Entity Framework—you don't need to think or worry about the Entity Framework at all. Once the classes you want to use are in place, you use tools that infer the database model from the design of the classes. After the tools complete their work, you can go back and tweak the model so that it works precisely as you intend it to.

Note An important difference between Entity Framework 5 and previous versions of the Entity Framework is that your classes become the model. When working with earlier versions of the Entity Framework, the developer had the option of generating POCO classes. However, it was the developer's responsibility to maintain the relationship between the generated classes and the Entity Data Model XML (.EDMX) file containing the designer model. If these two sources got out of sync, the results were unpredictable. As a result, developers using earlier versions of the Entity Framework ended up making changes in two places when using a code-first workflow—once in the code and again in the designer. Obviously, this approach led to errors.

Microsoft Visual Studio isn't clairvoyant. You need to tell it to create the database. This doesn't mean you need to change anything about your existing classes, but you do need to create at least one class that tells the application to create the database automatically for you. To start the process, you must tell your application to use Entity Framework 5 using a wizard, which you'll see in action in the "Adding Entity Framework 5 support" section later in this chapter. After that, you add a reference to *System.Data.Entity*. You then add the following *using* statement:

```
using System.Data.Entity;
```

The class must inherit from *DbContext*. However, the code you create to define the database requirement is simple. Here's a minimalistic approach to the previous class example:

```
public class BookContext:DbContext
{
   // Create a database context.
   public DbSet<Book> BookCollection { get; set; }
}
```

The Entity Framework defines a number of methods for interacting with the database without really caring anything about it. For example, you can add records to the database without knowing any details about the connection. You don't even need to know the name of the database. Here's an example of code you could use to add a record to a Microsoft SQL Server database with the information you have so far:

```
private void btnAdd_Click(object sender, EventArgs e)
{
   // Create a new record.
   Book NewBook = new Book();
   NewBook.Author = "John Paul Mueller";
   NewBook.Name = "Professional IronPython";
   NewBook.ISBN = "978-0-470-54859-2";
   NewBook.PageCount = 458;
   NewBook.LastRead = DateTime.Now;

   // Define the database context.
   BookContext context = new BookContext();

   // Create the database, add the record to it, and save
   // the changes.
   context.BookCollection.Add(NewBook);
   context.SaveChanges();
}
```

This code is a bit simplistic, but it clearly shows how you use this workflow. Of course, you can control every aspect of the database transaction if you desire. This example uses the maximum amount of automation and still produces perfectly acceptable results—at least for a small application. Later chapters will delve into some of the details of customizing the code-first workflow to meet specific needs.

Understanding the model-first workflow

The model-first workflow (introduced in Entity Framework 4) is designed to make it easy to create new applications that require database support without having to use the DBMS tools to do it. Every task is performed directly in the Visual Studio IDE. You've already seen this workflow in action in Chapter 2, "Looking more closely at queries." In this case, you create a list of a user's favorite number and color, along with the user's birth date. The workflow begins when you design the database. However, in this case, you use a graphical environment, rather than code, to describe the database design. The result is the same—you end up with a database that contains the data you want in the form you want it, without a lot of extra work or knowledge of the inner workings of the database.

Note Some developers wonder why there was no Entity Framework 2 or 3. Microsoft decided to renumber the Entity Framework versions to match the corresponding .NET Framework. When Entity Framework 4 shipped, it shipped with .NET Framework 4. However, Microsoft is now releasing Entity Framework versions out of band through NuGet, which means there isn't a good reason for the Entity Framework and the .NET Framework version numbers to match any longer. You can see a summary of the changes in each version of the Entity Framework at *http://msdn.microsoft.com/data/jj574253*.

As with the code-first workflow, interacting with the database revolves around a context. In fact, the actual database interaction is the same whether you use model first or code first. You follow the same sequence in both cases:

1. Create the record you want to add to the database.
2. Define a database context.
3. Add the record to the database using the context.
4. Save the changes to the database.

Understanding the database-first workflow

The database-first workflow (introduced in the original Entity Framework) was the original reason to use the Entity Framework. Developers often need to write new applications for existing data. However, databases tend to become complex rather quickly, and trying to create a model that developers can understand is hard. Harder still is the whole concept of using the model to write code that interacts with the database in a safe manner.

In many respects, the database-first workflow is the reverse of the model-first workflow. The database already exists, so the developer must know where the database is located and also have information about the database name. However, the developer need not understand the inner workings of the database—the Entity Framework still hides the inner workings from view.

Considering the need for Entity Framework–aware providers

In order to access a database from the Entity Framework, the database vendor or a third party must create an Entity Framework–aware provider. The provider marshals data and instructions between the Entity Framework and the DBMS. Visual Studio natively ships with the SqlClient provider that lets you access most newer SQL Server versions: the full or Express edition of SQL Server 2005 and the full or Express edition of SQL Server 2008. Starting with Visual Studio 2010, Microsoft dropped support for SQL Server 2000. You can learn more about this provider at *http://msdn.microsoft.com/library/bb896309.aspx*.

It's even possible to build an application that accesses SQL Server Compact. However, this provider has some strict limitations, such as an inability to support schemas with duplicate constraint names. Make sure you understand the limitations before you begin writing an application in this case. SQL Server Compact support isn't shipped with Visual Studio, but you can obtain it from Microsoft. Read more about SQL Server Compact support at *http://msdn.microsoft.com/library/cc835494.aspx*.

You can also access a number of third-party database products, but only if you install the appropriate provider on your system. Third-party providers currently include MySQL, Oracle, Progress, VistaDB, Devart, OpenLink, several IBM products, SQL Anywhere, Sybase, SQLite, Synergex, Firebird, and PostgreSQL (through the Npgsql provider). The list of providers is constantly growing, so it's important to check with your vendor to determine whether there's a provider to fit your need. Review the third party options at *http://msdn.microsoft.com/data/dd363565.aspx.*

Missing from the list of providers is support for Microsoft's Access database. According to Microsoft, there's no Entity Framework support for Access now and none planned for the future. You'll also find that the Entity Framework doesn't support older technologies and access techniques, such as Open Database Connectivity (ODBC). In order to obtain Entity Framework support for a particular database, you must have an Entity Framework–aware provider for it. Microsoft does make it possible for third parties to create new providers, and you can learn about this capability at *http://blogs.msdn.com/b/adonet/archive/tags/sample+provider/.* (Microsoft requires that you sign in using Microsoft Windows Live ID to access MSDN content.) The technique for creating an Entity Framework provider is outside the scope of this book, so this is the last time you'll see it mentioned. To reduce complexity, all of the examples in this book rely on the native SqlClient provider that comes with Visual Studio.

The database workflow begins with a database. In fact, you can use several databases as sources for a single model when desired. An Entity Framework model can theoretically span as many databases as necessary, and the database need not even use the same DBMS. The only requirement is that the databases all have an Entity Framework–aware provider that can translate between instructions and data that the Entity Framework understands and the instructions and data that the DBMS understands. With the proper provider, the Entity Framework can create a model that combines all data sources in a way that a developer can understand.

Once the model is in place, you use the Entity Framework to interact with the objects defined by the model as you would with either the code-first or model-first strategy. This means creating a context and then using that context to perform all of the required tasks. Behind the scenes, the context provides everything needed to manage the data as an object, rather than individual tables within the individual databases.

Defining the workflow choices

Workflow patterns describe a pure approach to completing work. For example, when you start an application from scratch, you might employ the model-first workflow to ensure that your application works as anticipated from the outset. However, many work environments are anything but pure, which is why you need to make choices about the individual workflow or combinations of workflows that you use to complete a project. A project may begin with an existing application where you use the code-first workflow to get started. However, once you have the starting application moved to the

Entity Framework, you might employ the model-first workflow instead in order to create new application elements. In short, the preliminary sections of this chapter examined pure environments, but you typically need to mix and match workflows in a real-world environment. Table 3-1 helps you understand the choices a little better.

TABLE 3-1 Selecting an Entity Framework workflow

Database type	Design preference	Workflow type	Description
New database	Designer centric	Model first	When you need to create a new database and want to see the design in graphical form, using the model-first workflow works best. In the model-first workflow ■ You create the model using the .EDMX designer. ■ You tell the Entity Framework to create the database based on your design. ■ The Entity Framework automatically generates the classes required to interact with the database.
Existing database	Designer centric	Database first	When you have an existing database and want to see the design for it in graphical form, using the database-first workflow works best. In the database-first workflow ■ You tell the Entity Framework to reverse engineer the existing database to create the .EDMX model. ■ The Entity Framework automatically generates the classes required to interact with the database.
New database	Code centric	Code first	When you need to create a new database and want to see the design for it in code form, using the code-first workflow works best. In the code-first workflow ■ You define classes that specify the data for e``ach table in the database using code. ■ You define mapping by creating classes that use the tabular class definitions. ■ You optionally define any special conditions for creating the database and its connection. ■ The Entity Framework automatically generates the database at run time.
Existing database	Code centric	Code first (code second)	Microsoft doesn't have a good method for interacting with an existing database when you want to see the design in code form. Many developers call the approach used in this case *code second* because you are creating code after the database is already in existence (even though Microsoft associates it with the code-first workflow). When working with the code-first workflow in this way ■ You reverse engineer classes that specify the data for each table in the database using code. ■ You reverse engineer mapping by creating classes that use the tabular class definitions. Microsoft does provide tools to assist in reverse engineering the database. You need to download the Entity Framework Power Tools. These tools will reverse engineer the database for you and generate at least some of the code automatically. You can then tweak the code as needed to define the model precisely. This book doesn't cover this particular technique because it's time-consuming and most developers won't use this approach. You can read more about this technique at *http://www.infoq.com/news/2011/05/EF-CodeFirst-PowerTools*.

Creating a code-first example

Reading previous sections of the chapter tells you that the example in this section will rely on classes you create in code to define the database. In this case, you'll work through an example that shows two tables in a one-to-many relationship. Even though this example is a little more complex than the one shown in the "Understanding the code-first workflow" section, you'll find that it isn't really any more difficult to create.

Creating a project

Many of the applications in this book will start in the same way. You'll create a project that demonstrates how the example works. Rather than repeat that material an absurd number of times, in this section you'll learn how to create a basic project once, and then you can refer back to this section as needed when creating the other examples. The following procedure gets you started creating a basic project.

Creating a basic project

1. Start Visual Studio 2012. The examples in this book don't work with the Express edition—you must have one of the paid versions. You can download a free trial of any version of Visual Studio 2012 at *http://www.microsoft.com/visualstudio/downloads*. If you register your copy of the trial, you can extend it for 90 days.
2. Choose File | New | Project. You'll see the New Project dialog box shown here:

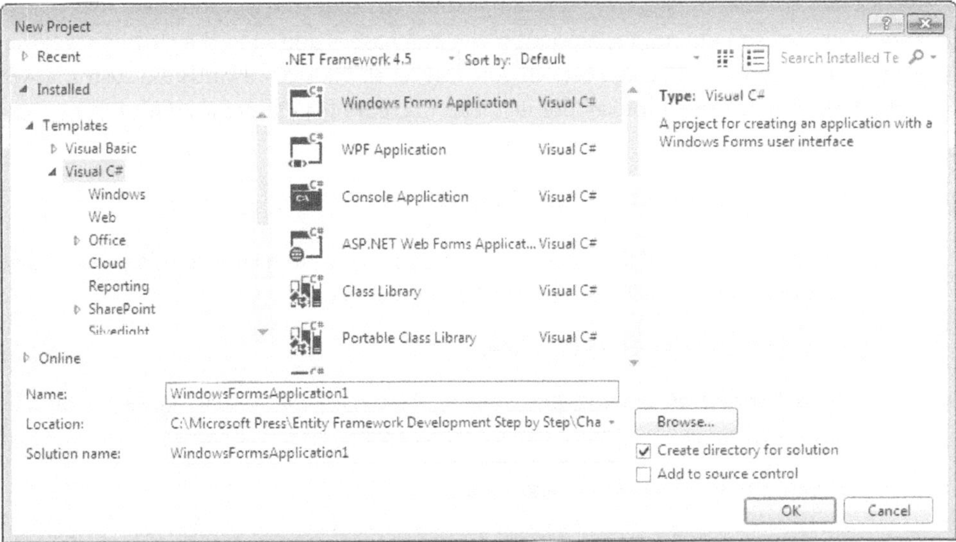

3. Select the Templates\Visual C# folder in the left pane and Windows Forms Application in the middle pane.

4. Check Create Directory For Solution if it isn't already checked.
5. Type **TestCodeFirst** in the Name field.
6. Choose a location to store the application. The example uses C:\Microsoft Press\Entity Framework Development Step by Step\Chapter 03.

> **Note** All of the example code for this book will appear in the Microsoft Press\Entity Framework Development Step by Step\ folder of the downloadable code, organized by chapter. Therefore, all the examples for this chapter appear in the Microsoft Press\Entity Framework Development Step by Step\Chapter 03 folder. You can locate the particular example file, which is CodeFirst in this case, and use the example code provided, rather than type everything yourself. Using the downloadable code will make your learning experience easier, but following the procedures will help you learn more.

7. Type **CodeFirst** in the Solution Name field.
8. Click OK. Visual Studio creates a Windows Forms application you can use to test the output of this example.

Defining the initial classes

In order to define the database, you must create a class that describes it. In this case, you have a one-to-many relationship to consider, so you need two classes. The first will contain the details, while the second will contain the parent. The example uses customers in a store. Every time a customer visits and purchases something, the amount of the purchase is added to the customer's Rewards account. When the customer achieves a certain purchase level, the store awards the customer with a reward of some type. The following procedure tells how to create the classes used for this example.

Creating the customer and purchases classes

1. Right-click the CodeFirst entry in Solution Explorer and choose Add | New Project from the context menu. You'll see the New Project dialog box.
2. Choose the Class Library template.
3. Type **CodeFirstClasses** in the Name field and click OK. Visual Studio creates a new class library for you.
4. Delete the existing *Class1* class code.

5. Type the following code to define the classes used for this example:

```
public class Customer
{
   // Identify the individual customer.
   public Int32 CustomerId { get; set; }
   public String CustomerName { get; set; }

   // Provide linkage to the Purchase class.
   public virtual List<Purchase> Purchases {get; set;}
}

public class Purchase
{
   // Define the individual purchase entries.
   public Int32 PurchaseId { get; set; }
   public DateTime PurchaseDate { get; set; }
   public Decimal Amount { get; set; }

   // Store the customer's identifier for this record.
   public Int32 CustomerId { get; set; }
}
```

The example code simply defines a customer and associated purchases. Each customer has a name and customer ID. The customer ID is used as a key field (for the *Customer* table) that the Entity Framework generates for you later. In addition, there's a link to a list of *Purchase* entries associated with the customer. Notice that this link is a virtual *List<Purchase>* object. You don't actually include a copy of the purchase with the customer data—you only need to create a link to it.

The *Purchase* class contains a purchase ID, which is used to identify the particular purchase, because the customer could make more than one purchase on a particular day. It also contains the date of the purchase and the amount of that particular purchase. The class doesn't contain any particulars about the purchase because you don't need them for the purpose of giving the customer a reward. Notice, however, that the class does include *CustomerId*, which is field that contains the identifier of the customer that made the purchase.

Warning The field name of the key field in the primary class—*Customer* in this case—must match the foreign key field in the secondary class—*Purchase* in this case—or else the Entity Framework won't create the foreign key field properly. Yes, you'll see a foreign key defined, but it won't match an actual column in the table. In this case, the *Customer* key field, *CustomerId*, matches the *Purchase* foreign key field, *CustomerId*.

Adding Entity Framework 5 support

Whenever you hand-code items for the Entity Framework, you need to add Entity Framework support before you can start adding Entity Framework–specific code. However, you need to do more than simply add a reference. In this case, you must actually install the Entity Framework support. The following procedure tells how to perform this task (a task that you perform somewhat often in this book, so I'll be referencing this procedure again later).

Adding Entity Framework 5 support to a file

1. Right-click the CodeFirstClasses entry in Solution Explorer and choose Manage NuGet Packages from the context menu. You'll see the Manage NuGet Packages dialog box shown here (the first part of the title bar will always contain the name of the file that will receive the support you install):

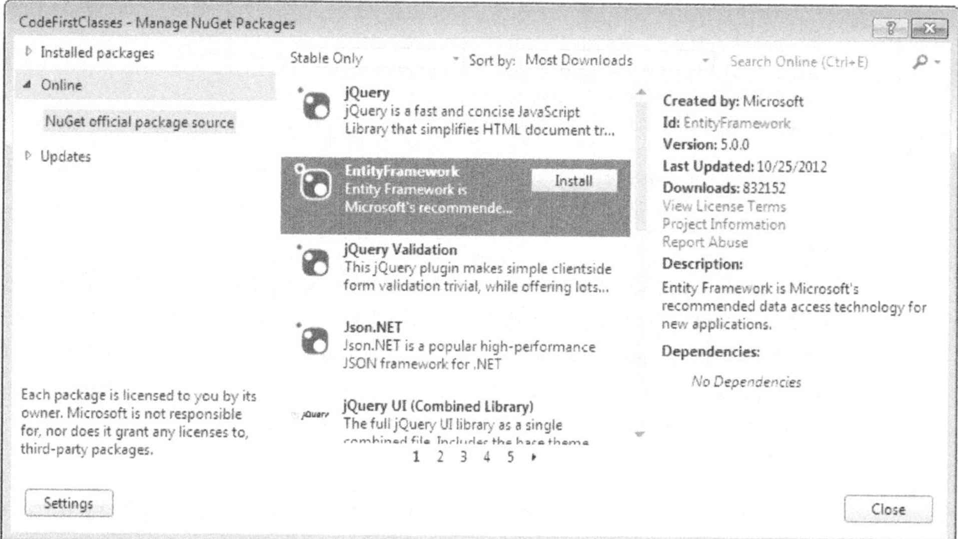

2. Select EntityFramework, as shown in the figure. Notice that the right pane shows the version number of the EntityFramework support you're installing. Make sure you install version 5.0.0 for the examples in this book as a minimum.

3. Click Install. You'll see a License Acceptance dialog box.

4. Click I Accept. Visual Studio installs the required support for your application.

5. Click Close. Visual Studio closes the Manage NuGet Packages dialog box.

6. Add the following *using* statement to the top of the code file:

```
using System.Data.Entity;
```

Creating a code-first context

Adding Entity Framework support to *CodeFirstClasses* automatically provides references to the classes you need. In this case, you definitely need access to *System.Data.Entity,* but this support is added automatically for you (check the References folder to see for yourself). However, Visual Studio doesn't know how to create a database context for you, so you need to perform that task manually using the following procedure.

Creating the *RewardsContext* class

1. Add the following database context class to the Class1.cs file:

```
// Create a context to the database.
public class RewardsContext:DbContext
{
   // Specify the name of the database as Rewards.
   public RewardsContext()
      : base("Rewards")
   {
   }

   // Create a database set for each of the data items.
   public DbSet<Purchase> Purchases { get; set; }
   public DbSet<Customer> Customers { get; set; }
}
```

   This code will actually create two connections to the database. The first will be a table named *Purchases*, which holds the purchase records for each customer; and the second will be a table named *Customers*, which holds the customer information. A number of examples online appear to show that you only need to interact with the parent table, which would be *Customers* in this case, but you need both entries and you need to interact with both of them to create a complete transaction with the database.

   Notice the constructor with the *base()* entry. This entry defines the name of the database. If you don't specify this value, then you get a database that uses the name of the application and context, which probably isn't what you want.

2. Choose Build | Build Solution. Visual Studio builds the application for you.
3. Verify that the solution compiles without error.

Adding a record

At this point, you have the classes and the context required to interact with a database that doesn't even exist yet. Just creating the classes doesn't actually do anything with the database. The Entity Framework creates the database when you add a record to it. With this in mind, the following procedure completes this example by showing how to use the classes you created earlier to add a record to the database. The example won't do anything fancy—it's only intended to add a record for you.

Creating and adding a database record using the code-first approach to the database

1. Add Entity Framework support to *Form1* using the procedure found in the "Adding Entity Framework 5 Support" section of this chapter.

2. Add a *Button* control to *Form1* and place it in the upper-right corner of the dialog box.

3. Change the *Button* name to *btnAdd* and change its *Text* property value to *&Add*.

4. Double-click *btnAdd* to create a *Click()* event handler for it. You'll see the *btnAdd_Click()* event handler.

5. Right-click the References folder in Solution Explorer and choose Add Reference. You'll see the Reference Manager dialog box shown here:

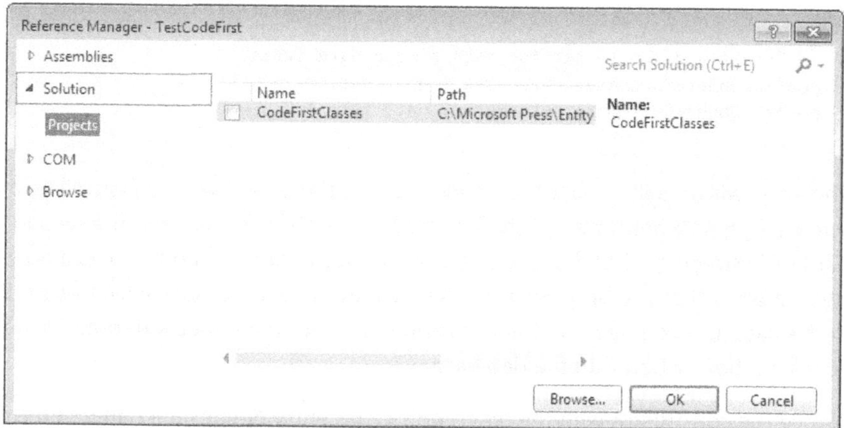

6. Select the Projects folder. Check the CodeFirstClasses option and click OK. Visual Studio adds the required reference for you.

7. Add the following *using* statement to the top of the Form1.cs file:

```
using CodeFirstClasses;
```

8. Type the following code in the *btnAdd_Click()* event handler:

```
private void btnAdd_Click(object sender, EventArgs e)
{
    // Create a new purchase.
    Purchase NewPurchase = new Purchase();
    NewPurchase.Amount = new Decimal(5.99);
    NewPurchase.PurchaseDate = DateTime.Now;

    // Create a new customer and add the purchase.
    Customer NewCustomer = new Customer();
    NewCustomer.CustomerName = "Josh Bailey";
```

```
    // Create the context.
    RewardsContext context = new RewardsContext();

    // Add the record and save it.
    context.Customers.Add(NewCustomer);
    context.Purchases.Add(NewPurchase);
    context.SaveChanges();

    // Display a success message.
    MessageBox.Show("Record Added");
}
```

The code begins by creating a new purchase and associated customer. You'd need to perform these actions no matter how you used the classes, so there's nothing unusual here.

At this point, the code creates a *RewardsContext* object, *context*, and uses it to add the new items to the *Customers* and *Purchases* tables. The code then calls the *Add()* method for each of the tables and adds the new entries to them. Calling *SaveChanges()* makes the changes to the database permanent. In this case, calling *SaveChanges()* also creates the database. The code ends with a simple message box telling you that the record has been added.

9. Click Start or press F5. The application compiles and runs.
10. Click Add. You'll see a message box saying that the record has been added.
11. Close the application. At this point, the *Rewards* database has a new record in it.

Viewing the results

The previous sections helped you create a code-first application. Of course, the question now is whether it produced the desired results. The following procedure will help you view the results of this application. You'll use the same steps, with a different database name, to view the results of other examples in the book.

Viewing the application output

1. Open Server Explorer by choosing View | Server Explorer or by pressing Ctrl+Alt+S. You'll see the Server Explorer window shown here:

2. Right-click Data Connection and choose Add Connection from the context menu. You'll see the Choose Data Source dialog box shown here:

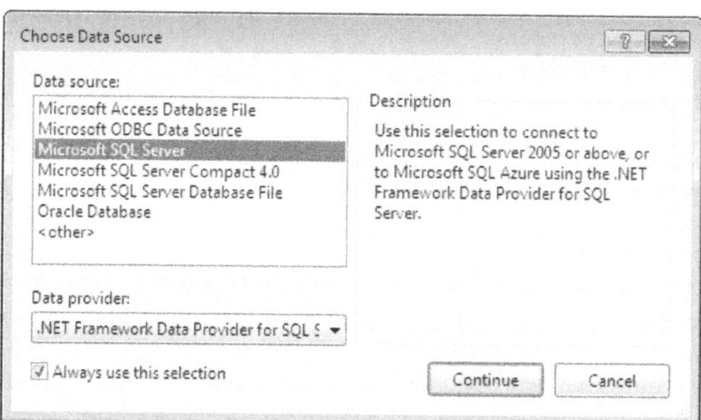

3. Choose Microsoft SQL Server and click Continue. You'll see an Add Connection dialog box like the one shown here:

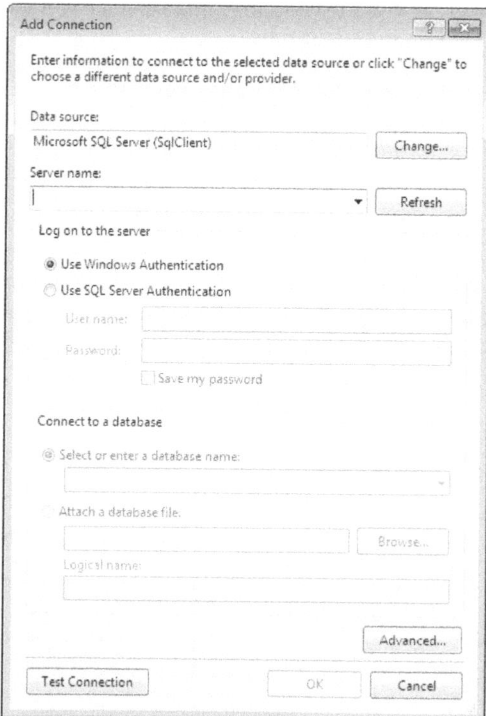

4. Select the SQL Server installation on your local machine in the Server Name field.

5. Select the Rewards database in the Select Or Enter a Database Name field and click OK. Visual Studio creates the connection for you, automatically opens it, and places the cursor on the connection so that you can work with it.

6. Drill down into the *Rewards* database. You'll see that it contains two tables, *Customers* and *Purchases*, as expected, and that those two tables have the expected columns, as shown following. Of course, there's more to these tables than this view shows. For one thing, you need to verify that there's a foreign key set up between the *Purchases* and *Customers* tables. The *Purchases* table should have a foreign key to the *Id* field in the *Customers* table. Fortunately, Visual Studio provides the means to drill down further into the tables as needed.

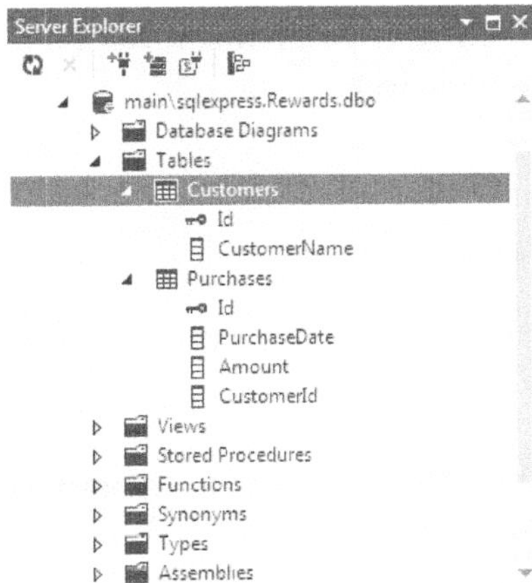

7. Right-click the *Purchases* table and choose Open Table Definition from the context menu. You'll see the dbo.Purchases: Table window, which shows the details for each of the columns in the table. For example, you can determine that none of the columns will allow *Null* value entries.

8. Choose Table Designer | Relationships. You'll see the Foreign Key Relationships dialog box shown here:

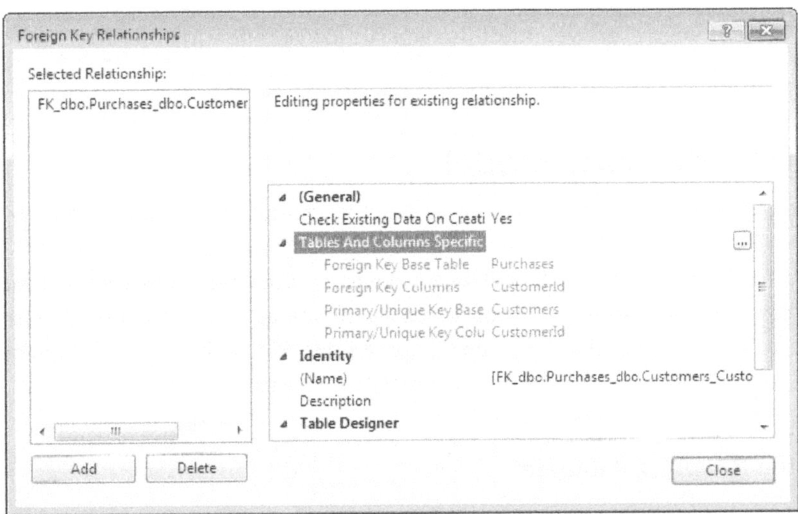

9. Drill down into the Tables And Columns Specific category. You'll see that the foreign key is based on the *CustomerId* fields in both the *Purchases* and *Customers* tables. At this point, you know that the database and tables are configured correctly. Of course, you can review any of the other database and table properties as needed to verify the correct output from this example.

10. Click Close to close the Foreign Key Relationships dialog box.

11. Right-click the *Customers* table and choose Show Table Data from the context menu. You'll see that the table contains the expected data, as shown here:

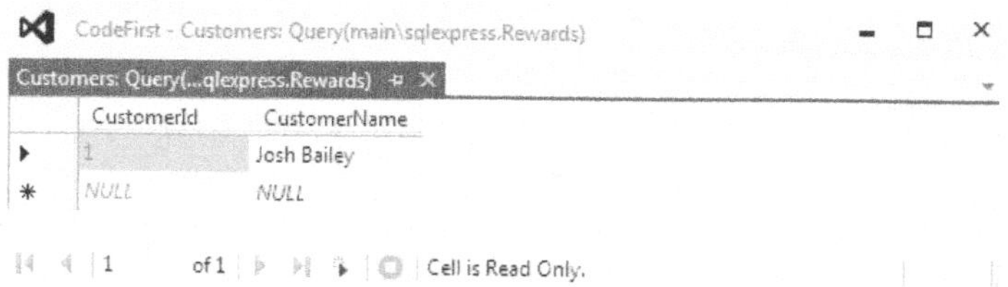

12. Right-click the *Purchases* table and choose Show Table Data from the context menu. You'll see that this table also includes the expected information.

Creating a model-first example

Remember that model-first design techniques let you create the design of the database graphically before you actually create the database. The model-first example described in the sections that follow replicate the results of the code-first example described in the "Creating a code-first example" section of the chapter. The only difference will be the name of the database. Using this approach lets you compare techniques to help you determine which method of creating a database you prefer. Of course, there are times where you must use a particular workflow in order to obtain the desired results.

Defining the database model

If you followed the previous example, you know that the example will contain two tables: *Customers* and *Purchases*. The *Customers* table contains two columns: *Id* and *CustomerName*. The *Purchases* table contains four columns: *Id*, *PurchaseDate*, *Amount*, and *CustomersId* (there's a reason this field is plural in this case—the IDE generates it automatically for you as part of the model definition process). There's a one-to-many relationship between *Customers* and *Purchases*. With this in mind, use the following procedure to create a model for the *Rewards2* database.

Defining the *Rewards2* database

1. Use the procedure found in the "Creating a project" section earlier in this chapter to create a Windows Forms project named *TestModelFirst* and a solution named *ModelFirst*.

2. Right-click the *TestModelFirst* entry in Solution Explorer and choose Add | New Item from the context menu. You'll see the Add New Item dialog box shown here:

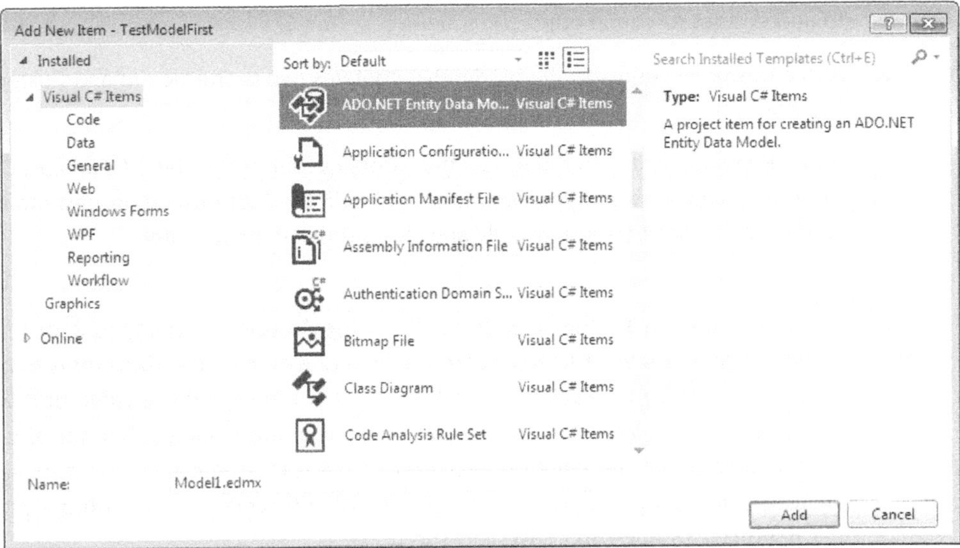

3. Select the ADO.NET Entity Data Model entry. You'll see the project described in the right pane.

4. Type **Rewards2Model.EDMX** in the Name field and click Add. Visual Studio starts the Entity Data Model Wizard, as shown here:

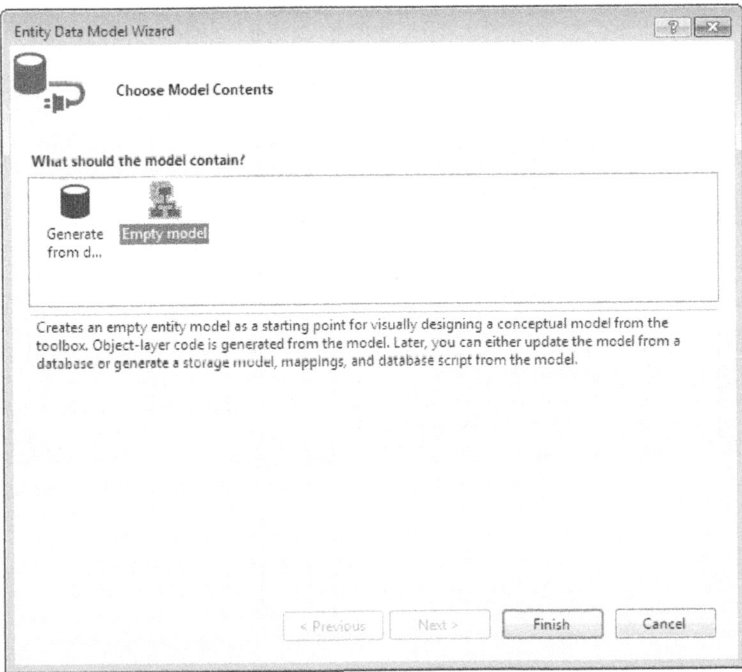

5. Choose the Empty Model option and click Finish. Visual Studio adds the new model to your project. Like the example shown in the "Using the Entity Data Model Designer" section of Chapter 1, "Getting to know the Entity Framework," you use the *Entity* control in the toolbox to add entities to your model.

6. Add a *Customers* entity to the model that contains two properties: *Id* and *CustomerName* (type *String*).

7. Add a *Purchases* entity to the model that contains four properties: *Id*, *PurchaseDate* (type *DateTime*), and *Amount* (type *Decimal*). Don't add the *CustomersId* property to the *Purchases* entity—Visual Studio automatically adds this property for you later.

Note You must set the *Scale* property of the *Amount* property to 2, or Visual Studio will assume you want to have zero decimal places. Because *Amount* is a monetary value, two decimal places will work fine, but you must set the value or it won't work properly. If you want to limit the size of the monetary values that a user can input, you can also set the *Precision* property to the total number of numbers you want to store. For example, if you set *Precision* to 18 and *Scale* to 2, the integer portion of the entry can have up to 16 places in it.

8. Right-click the *Customers* entity and choose Add New | Association from the context menu. You'll see the Add Association dialog box shown here:

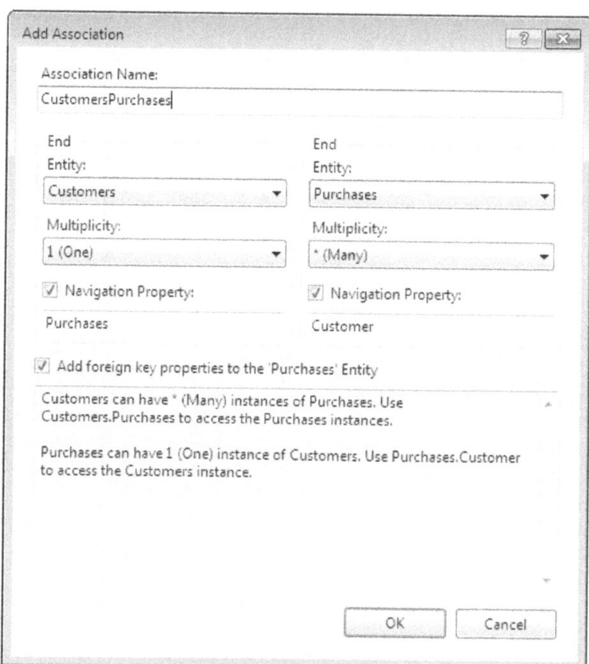

Notice that the dialog box automatically fills in the needed information. For example, because you added *Customers* first and *Purchases* second, it assumes a one-to-many relationship between *Customers* and *Purchases*. In some cases, you need to modify the content of this dialog box, but often, the IDE will automatically determine the correct settings for you.

9. Click OK. Visual Studio creates a one-to-many relationship for you. In addition, it automatically generates the *CustomersId* property for you in the *Purchases* entity. At this point, your model is complete, and it should look like the one shown here:

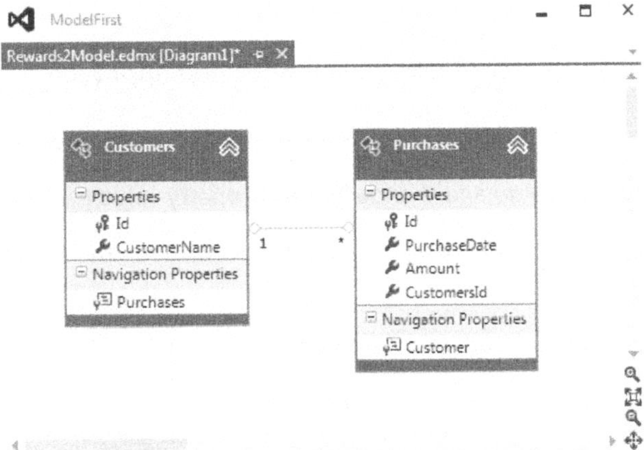

10. Use the procedure in the "Working with the mapping details" section of Chapter 1 to generate the database. Give your database a name of *Rewards2*.

11. Choose Build | Solution. Visual Studio saves all of the changes that you've made to the project and then compiles the application. Most importantly, it automatically generates a *DbContext* class for you use to access the database.

Note You'll notice as the book progresses that more and more of the procedures from earlier chapters are referenced to reduce the complexity of the current procedure. The Entity Framework makes it possible to perform many tasks exclusively with wizards and routine procedures, which takes a lot of guesswork out of the entire process. Workflows should be consistent, repeatable, and most of all, reliable. So, the reuse of procedures from earlier chapters simply makes sense. Doing so allows you to focus on the new information at hand, rather than get bombarded by information you already know.

Adding a record and viewing the results

Unlike the code-first approach, where you must create everything by hand-coding it, the model-first approach includes a certain amount of automation. It even creates the code required to access the database using a context. In addition, you already have the required Entity Framework 5 support added to your application, so there's no manual process involved in this case. Chapter 2 shows how to access the database using a data source. The following procedure shows how to access the database using a context. You'll find that the technique is similar to the one used in the code-first technique, but you don't have to generate any of the code by hand—it is done automatically for you.

Creating and adding a database record using the model-first approach

1. Add a *Button* control to *Form1* and place it in the upper-right corner of the dialog box.
2. Change the *Button* name to *btnAdd* and change its *Text* property value to *&Add.*
3. Double-click btnAdd to create a *Click()* event handler for it. You'll see the *btnAdd_Click()* event handler.
4. Type the following code in the *btnAdd_Click()* event handler:

```
private void btnAdd_Click(object sender, EventArgs e)
{
   // Create a new purchase.
   Purchases NewPurchase = new Purchases();
   NewPurchase.Amount = new Decimal(5.99);
   NewPurchase.PurchaseDate = DateTime.Now;

   // Create a new customer and add the purchase.
   Customers NewCustomer = new Customers();
   NewCustomer.CustomerName = "Josh Bailey";

   // Create the context.
   Rewards2ModelContainer context = new Rewards2ModelContainer();

   // Add the record and save it.
   context.Customers.Add(NewCustomer);
   context.Purchases.Add(NewPurchase);
   context.SaveChanges();

   // Display a success message.
   MessageBox.Show("Record Added");
}
```

This code is similar to the code-first example, but there's one important difference. As with the code-first example, the code begins by creating a new purchase and associated customer.

At this point, the code creates a *Rewards2ModelContainer* object, *context*, and uses it to add the new items to the *Customers* and *Purchases* tables. You may not realize at first that the *Rewards2ModelContainer* is all you need to access the database, but it is. Open the *Rewards2Model.Context.cs* file in the IDE, and you'll see it contains essentially the same code that you used to hand-code the *DbContext* class earlier, in the "Creating a code-first example" section of the chapter.

As before, the code then calls the *Add()* method for each of the tables and adds the new entries to them. Calling *SaveChanges()* makes the changes to the database permanent. In this case, calling *SaveChanges()* also creates the database. The code ends with a simple message box telling you that the record has been added.

5. Click Start or press F5. The application compiles and runs.
6. Click Add. You'll see a message box saying that the record has been added.
7. Close the application. At this point, the *Rewards2* database has a new record in it.
8. Use the technique shown in the "Viewing the results" section earlier in this chapter to verify that the database contains the expected contents.

Creating a database-first example

Many developers start with an existing database. The Entity Framework has this need covered. In fact, working with existing databases was the initial purpose in creating the Entity Framework. You use the database-first workflow to address this requirement in a graphical environment (theoretically, you can also use the code-first approach, but in this case, writing the code first seems like a hard way to do things). The following sections describe how to reverse engineer an existing database and add a new record to it.

Note This example relies on the *Rewards* or *Rewards2* database created in the "Creating a code-first example" or "Creating a model-first example" section of this chapter. You can use either database. The steps assume you're using the *Rewards* database, but the *Rewards2* database is precisely the same and will work just as well.

Reverse engineering the database model

The first step in using the database-first workflow is to reverse engineer an existing database. The database can exist on any server that provides Entity Framework support. For that matter, you can actually use multiple sources in your model, and the sources need not use the same DBMS. A model simply defines how the various sources interact. In the interest of simplicity, though, the example in the following procedure relies on the *Rewards* (or *Rewards2*) database created earlier in this chapter.

Reverse engineering an existing database

1. Use the procedure found in the "Creating a project" section of this chapter to create a Windows Forms project named *TestDatabaseFirst* and a solution named *DatabaseFirst.*
2. Right-click the *TestDatabaseFirst* entry in Solution Explorer and choose Add | New Item. You'll see the Add New Item dialog box.
3. Select the ADO.NET Entity Data Model entry. You'll see the project described in the right pane.
4. Type **RewardsModel.EDMX** in the Name field and click Add. Visual Studio starts the Entity Data Model Wizard.
5. Choose Generate From Database and click Next. The wizard asks you to choose a database connection, as shown here:

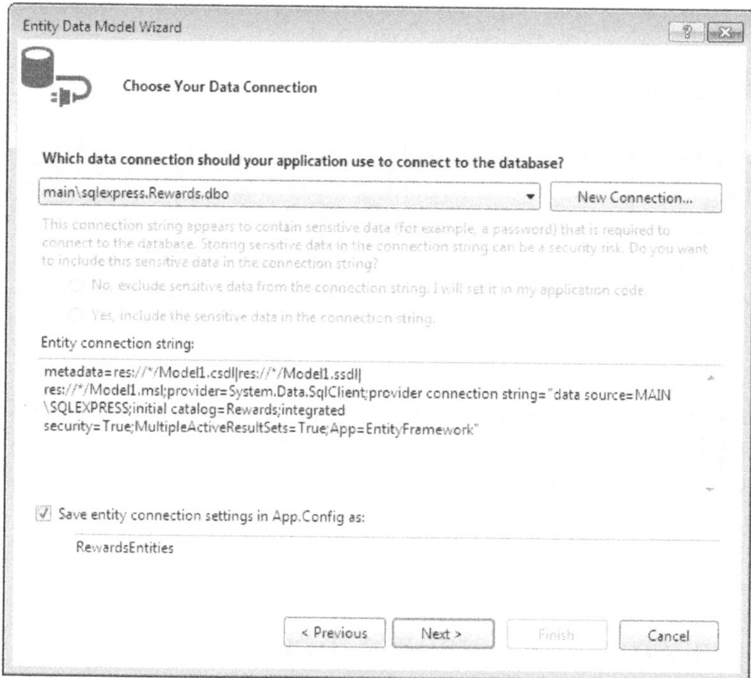

In this case, you already have a connection to use. The example will work fine with either the *Rewards* or *Rewards2* database. If you didn't have an existing connection to use, you'd click New Connection and follow the same steps you used in the "Viewing the results" section of this chapter to create a connection to the database.

6. Choose either the *Rewards* or *Rewards2* database connection and click Next. (The example uses the Rewards *database,* and the screen shots will reflect that fact, but your screen shots will look similar, even if you use the *Rewards2* database.) Visual Studio retrieves the database information. After a moment, the wizard asks you to choose the database elements you want to use in your application, as shown here:

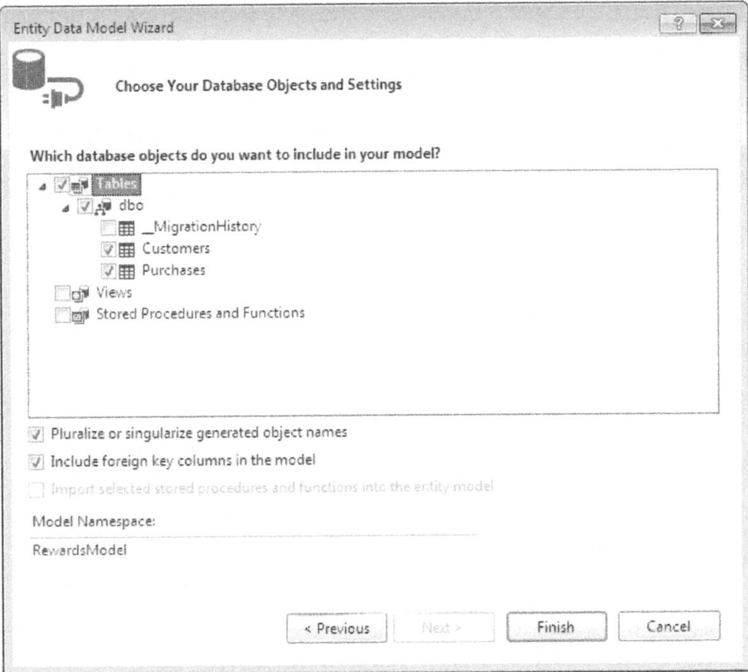

7. Drill down into the *Tables* object by clicking the right-pointing arrows next to each entry. You'll see the tables that make up the example database, as shown in the screen shot.

8. Check the *Customers* and *Purchases* table entries and click Finish. Visual Studio reads the information from the database. After a few moments, you'll see the model generated from the database. The resulting model should look similar to the output of the procedure in the "Defining the database model" section earlier in this chapter. The only difference should be the fact that the entity names are singular, rather than plural, if you used the *Rewards* database.

9. Choose Build | Solution. Visual Studio saves the changes you've made and then compiles the application. You shouldn't see any error messages.

Adding a record and comparing results

There's already a record in this database, so you're adding another record to it in this section. The new record appears in the database you're working with (*Rewards* or *Rewards2*). In many respects, the process for adding the record is the same as adding a record in the model-first example. You can use the procedure found in the "Adding a record and viewing the results" section of the chapter to add a record to the database. There are some differences in the code shown in step 4 of that procedure, but they're small.

```
private void btnAdd_Click(object sender, EventArgs e)
{
   // Create a new purchase.
   Purchase NewPurchase = new Purchase();
   NewPurchase.Amount = new Decimal(5.99);
   NewPurchase.PurchaseDate = DateTime.Now;

   // Create a new customer and add the purchase.
   Customer NewCustomer = new Customer();
   NewCustomer.CustomerName = "Carole Poland";

   // Create the context.
   RewardsEntities context = new RewardsEntities();

   // Add the record and save it.
   context.Customers.Add(NewCustomer);
   context.Purchases.Add(NewPurchase);
   context.SaveChanges();

   // Display a success message.
   MessageBox.Show("Record Added");
}
```

As previously mentioned, the table names are singular when working with the *Rewards* database, so you need to use that form when working with that database. The *DbContext* class name also differs. In this case, you type **RewardEntities** instead. However, if you open the *RewardsModel.Context.cs* file, you'll find that the code is almost exactly the same as the other two workflows. What you should take away from this third example is that each of the workflows produces similar results. In fact, except for some naming differences, each workflow produces precisely the same result. That's the point. You can work the way you need to work with the Entity Framework and be assured that you'll get the same result every time.

Getting started with the Entity Framework

This chapter has emphasized the need for all three workflows that you typically use when working with the Entity Framework. The essential idea to take away from this chapter is that the Entity Framework is designed to work with you, to help you achieve success with a minimum of effort. The three workflows described in this chapter—code first, model first, and database first—are the ones most commonly used. Nothing says that you have to strictly adhere to them or create a workflow of your own that better serves your needs. Consider the content of this chapter as a starting place for your own efforts. What you really need to do is consider how you work and then optimize your efforts around the way you naturally do things. Always remember that the key part of a workflow is the flow—things should move along smoothly without surprises.

Now that you've had some exposure to the various workflows, think about some of the application scenarios you might experience personally. Try to work out which workflows or workflow combinations you'd use to address these application requirements. Part of discovering the usefulness of the Entity Framework is seeing how it can apply to your particular situation. You won't get the most out of the Entity Framework until it becomes part of your work environment (rather than a new technique that's simply bolted on).

The next part of the book discusses how to perform basic tasks using the Entity Framework. Chapter 4, "Generating and using objects," begins by helping you understand how to interact with objects better. The applications to this point have been relatively simple. The examples you see in the next part of the book are a little more complex and better model what you might do in a real-world situation. Don't worry that you'll suddenly become buried in detail, though—Chapter 4 is just one step up from what you've done so far.

Chapter 3 quick reference

To	Do this

Create a context	Define a class that inherits from the *DbContext* class. In this class, you must create a *DbSet* object to access the database in a way that reflects the application view of the database. A context will typically look like this:
	`public DbSet<ApplicationClass>`
	`LocalCollectionObject { get; set; }`
	where the *ApplicationClass* is a class that defines the database structure that resides in your application, and *LocalCollectionObject* is a *List()* object that provides local memory storage of the database content. A context helps you perform standard tasks, such as adding, editing, and removing records.

Move your existing application to the Entity Framework	Employ the code-first workflow and then modify the model that the IDE generates for you to match the actual database requirements completely.
Create an application from scratch	Employ the model-first workflow to create the database model, generate the database from the model, and then create the application based on both the model and physical database.
Use an existing database in a new application	Employ the database-first workflow to create a model based on the existing database, and then create the application based on both the model and physical database.
Develop new features in an existing application	Use a combination of workflow approaches that matches the scenario for your application. For example, use the code-first workflow for existing code where no database currently exists and the model-first workflow for new features.

PART II

Completing basic tasks

The first part of this book introduced you to the Entity Framework and the workflows it supports. Now that you have a better idea of what the Entity Framework is, it's time to see how you can use it to perform basic tasks. This part of the book shows how to perform basic tasks at two levels. In Chapter 4, "Generating and using objects," you begin by gaining knowledge of the Entity Framework objects and how they're used to perform tasks such as querying data and modifying it (including the three basic tasks of adding, editing, and deleting records). The chapter then moves on to the more advanced topics of using Query Builder methods and working with extension methods.

Chapter 5, "Performing essential tasks," builds on what you've learned in Chapter 4. The chapter begins by showing you how to refine the rough management methods in Chapter 4 so that you can build more refined applications that query, add, edit, and delete records. You'll then see how to perform tasks such as saving data to the database safely. The examples, up to this point, have examined the parent-child relationship from an overview perspective—now you'll begin to build on this knowledge to create applications that can manipulate records with relationships more safely. When you finish Chapter 5, you should be able to create a basic application—one that can work with multiple tables at some level. You won't have the knowledge required to work with truly complex datasets, but you'll know enough to build simple applications that manage data safely.

CHAPTER 4

Generating and using objects

After completing the chapter, you'll be able to

- Describe the basic *Entity* objects and how they're used.
- Make a query using an object.
- Modify data using an object.
- Use Query Builder methods.
- Create and use extension methods.

Previous chapters in the book have hinted at the sorts of things you can do when working with objects. You know that you can use a class that inherits from *DbContext* to create a context to a specific database and access its tables. This chapter begins to go beyond these really simple ideas by introducing you to a new query language, Entity SQL. It helps you understand the Entity Framework objects at greater depth and begin to use them to perform more complicated tasks. This new knowledge will help you make queries on datasets and let the user view the data in a form that makes sense. You'll also discover how to manipulate data safely (the previous chapters simply showed how to get the task done in the easiest manner possible).

Early query examples in this chapter show how to work with Entity SQL, which is a language for working with the Entity Data Model. Working directly with Entity SQL can be cumbersome, so, as with many things in programming, there's a shortcut: using Query Builder methods. These methods use a syntax similar to Language Integrated Query (LINQ) to help you to create queries easily. (If you haven't worked with LINQ in the past, don't worry, this chapter will show everything you need to know.) Underneath it all, Microsoft Visual Studio creates an Entity SQL statement that queries the database for you. This chapter is only an introduction to the Query Builder methods—you'll use them often throughout the book.

This chapter also provides a brief introduction to extension methods. You use extension methods to add functionality to built-in .NET classes, so that they behave more as you need them to behave in order to perform useful work with a minimum of code. Using extension methods makes it possible to reduce the amount of repetitive coding you perform. In short, you really aren't changing the .NET class; you simply add to it to meet a specific coding need in your application. Because many coding sequences in the Entity Framework become repetitive, using extension methods can reduce the code you need to provide and also reduce the work required to fix bugs in your application. However, the main impact is that you end up with a class that saves you time and effort—it's more a matter of convenience than necessity, and you could easily skip this section if desired.

Understanding the Entity objects

Entity objects serve an important purpose—they provide access to the entities in your model. The entities, in turn, provide access to properties, associations, and other model features. The purpose of the Entity Framework is to make it easy for the developer to understand the data that the application modifies. In order to do this, the Entity Framework presents the elements of the model you create as objects that you can access within your application. By accessing these objects, you affect the underlying database. You can make changes to the data within the database, modify the database structure, and perform other tasks without really knowing anything about the database (or databases) involved. All you need to know is how to interact with the Entity Framework. In short, the purpose of the *Entity* objects is to provide a consistent means to work with data in your applications no matter what the source of that data might be. With this in mind, the following sections explore *Entity* objects in more detail before you begin working with them as part of an application programming example.

Considering object services

The Entity Framework is composed of a number of layers. The topmost layer, the Entity Data Model, provides the required access to object services. Using object services meets the following needs:

- It reduces the amount of code needed to create applications.
- It makes it possible to program against familiar objects, rather than unfamiliar database constructs.
- It creates an environment where the developer can access data from any source.

Object services also provide access to the lower layers of the Entity Framework. You can use them to obtain various sorts of access, including the following:

- Specific type information
- Relationship information
- Basic data readers and writers

The combination of hiding complexity, yet providing access to details of the underlying model, makes it possible for developers to become more productive with fewer errors and with less knowledge of the actual database functionality. Using object services helps you perform a number of tasks, including the following:

- Creating queries using Entity SQL or Query Builder methods (theoretically, you can also use LINQ)
- Performing Create, Read, Update, and Delete (CRUD) operations against data

- Managing state
- Performing lazy loads (where data needed to perform a task is automatically loaded into the context as needed)
- Managing inheritance
- Navigating relationships

There are, in fact, a host of tasks that object services help you perform that you'll see throughout this book. The important thing to remember is that object services don't simply allow you to perform CRUD operations, as some developers might expect. The overall goal of object services is to create a robust environment that scales to any size application and any size data source, as needed, while providing full error handling, data access, and data layer support. A large part of this chapter is devoted to the query portion of object services, but it's important to know that you'll ultimately do more with object services as the book progresses.

Considering the base classes

The majority of the classes you need to consider when working with the Entity Framework reside in the *System.Data.Entity* namespace. This namespace contains the classes that provide Entity Framework functionality. No matter what kind of application you create, you'll always find at least three of these classes automatically added to your application:

- ***DbContext*** Defines a framework in which an application can create connections to a database as required to perform CRUD tasks. All changes to the database are gathered and grouped within the content and then saved to the database as a batch operation. You can perform tasks such as validating the changes before they're sent to the database, which makes your application faster and more efficient.
- ***DbModelBuilder*** Creates a map between Common Language Runtime (CLR) classes and the database schema. This particular class is associated with the code-first workflow. However, you also see it used with the *DbContext.OnModelCreating()* method to signal an error that occurs when an application has generated a context in the database-first or model-first workflows, and then tries to use that context in code-first mode.
- ***DbSet/DbSet<TEntity>*** Represents the entity set that's actually used to perform CRUD operations. The *System.Data.Entity* namespace offers access to both untyped and typed versions of this class. The untyped version is used when the type of the entity isn't known at build time.

This namespace also contains a number of other classes that you might encounter while working with the Entity Framework. These other classes all help you create the infrastructure required to implement CRUD functionality in your application.

- ***CreateDatabaseIfNotExists<TContext>*** Creates a new database when the database doesn't exist and optionally seeds the database with data. In order to add default records to the database, you must derive a class from this base class and override the *Seed()* method.

- ***Database*** Provides access to the database underlying an Entity Framework model. You can use the methods associated with this class to create or delete the database, check for its existence, or execute a SQL command. You can also use the static methods of this class to delete a database or check for its existence based solely on a standard connection.
- ***DbExtensions*** Defines a number of useful static methods that you can use to interact with queries. For example, you can define which objects to return in a query result. It's also possible to return a query without caching the result in either the *DbContext* or *ObjectContext* objects.
- ***DbModelBuilderVersionAttribute*** Sets the version of the *DbContext* and *DbModelBuilder* conventions that the application should use when building a model from code. The *DbModelBuilderVersion* enumeration described at *http://msdn.microsoft.com/library/system.data.entity.dbmodelbuilderversion.aspx* tells which versions are available.
- ***DropCreateDatabaseAlways<TContext>*** Creates a new database in all situations and optionally seeds the database with data. In order to add default records to the database, you must derive a class from this base class and override the *Seed()* method. If the database already exists, it's automatically dropped before creating the new database.
- ***DropCreateDatabaseIfModelChanges<TContext>*** Creates a new database only when the model changes and optionally seeds the database with data. In order to add default records to the database, you must derive a class from this base class and override the *Seed()* method. If the database already exists, it's automatically dropped before creating the new database.
- ***MigrateDatabaseToLatestVersion<TContext, TMigrationsConfiguration>*** Migrates an existing database to the latest version of the database model using code-first migrations. You can see an example of code-first migrations at *http://msdn.microsoft.com/en-us/data/jj591621*.

The Entity Framework also requires support classes to perform tasks such as exception handling. These support classes appear as part of the *System.Data.Entity.Infrastructure* namespace. The one class that's always added to your application is *UnintentionalCodeFirstException*, and it's used to signal an error in the way a workflow is used. Essentially, this type of error occurs when an application generates a context in the database-first or model-first workflow, and then tries to use that context in the code-first mode. This namespace also includes a number of other classes (as described at *http://msdn.microsoft.com/library/system.data.entity.infrastructure.aspx*) that are used as needed to provide support to the Entity Framework model.

Working with an *EntityCollection*

In reviewing the *Rewards* and *Rewards2* databases created in Chapter 3, "Choosing a workflow," you see that each entry in the *Customer* table can have one or more entries in the *Purchase* table. A customer must make a purchase before appearing in the *Customer* table, so you know that the customer has at least one entry in the *Purchase* table, but it's likely that each customer will have multiple *Purchase* table entries. When working with records, then, it's quite possible to work with an individual customer, but it's likely that you'll have to handle a collection of purchases. The entries will appear as part of an *EntityCollection* object.

Warning It's important to note that the Entity Framework uses an *EntityCollection* object that has nothing to do with the classes in the *System.Collections* namespace. In fact, the *EntityCollection* class doesn't implement the *ICollections* interface. Therefore, even though the basic principle behind an *EntityCollection* is the same as any other collection you've used, it isn't compatible with the classes found in the *System.Collections* namespace. Trying to make the two work side by side won't work.

The *EntityCollection* class is part of the *System.Data.Objects.DataClasses* namespace. This namespace provides the following:

- Classes for types that are defined as part of the Entity Data Model
- Base classes for types that are returned as part of navigation properties
- Classes that define attributes that map CLR objects to conceptual model types

When viewing the *EntityCollection* class role within the namespace, you see the method used to define properties that point to a collection of records in a one-to-many relationship. Look again at the *Rewards2* database model used with the *ModelFirst* example in Chapter 3.

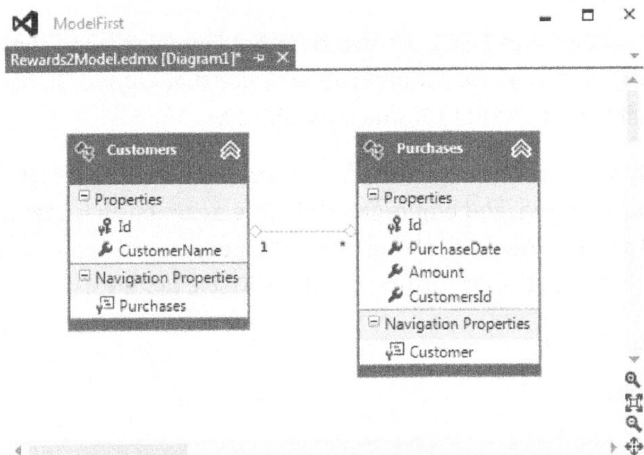

The *Purchases* navigation property found in the *Customers* entity points to a one to many relationship with the *Purchases* entity. In most cases, you'd expect this property to derive from *System.Collections.ICollection*. However, it actually derives from *System.Data.Objects.DataClasses.EntityCollection*—the two classes aren't interchangeable. You can see the one-to-many relationship in the *Multiplicity* property of the *Properties* window when you view the *Purchases* navigation property, as shown here:

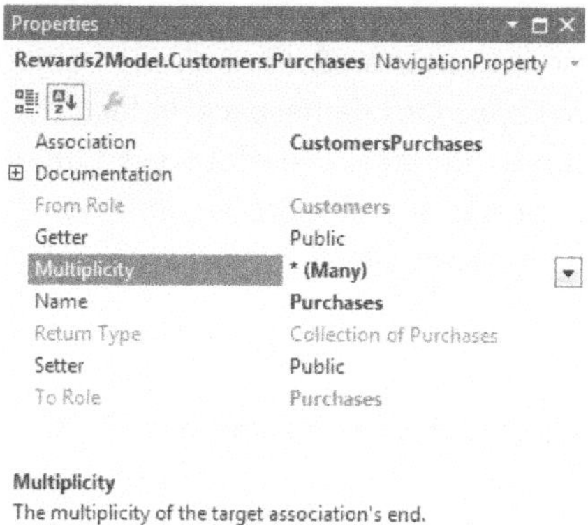

Understanding the role of Entity SQL

The Entity Framework provides a number of methods for interacting with the objects that represent a database. Many developers will already have experience working with T-SQL (Transact-Structured Query Language) or a similar SQL-based language and will want to use that knowledge when working with the Entity Framework. The Entity Framework does work entirely with objects, but it also provides a SQL-like language named Entity SQL that these developers can use to interact with those objects.

It's important to remember that Entity SQL and T-SQL are two different languages, and they're intended for two different purposes. Most developers will immediately notice that Entity SQL has some specific differences that are related to its use with Entity Framework objects:

- **Selections only** You can only select data using Entity SQL. Languages such as T-SQL provide elements that also allow adding, deleting, and editing records. The assumption is that the Entity Framework features will address these other requirements. Because there are only selections, you'll also find that Entity SQL lacks support for these T-SQL features:
  - Data Manipulation Language (DML)
  - Data Definition Language (DDL)
  - Imperative programming
  - Grouping functions
  - Analytic functions
  - Hints
- **Support for collections** An Entity SQL statement can use collections. These collections can appear as part of the *FROM*, *IN*, *EXISTS*, *UNION*, *INTERSECT*, and *EXCEPT* keywords. In addition, you can use collections as part of join operations.

- **Support for expressions** Unlike T-SQL, which has both *subqueries* and expressions, the level of collection support in Entity SQL requires that everything be treated as an expression. This treatment has a significant benefit in that every expression can appear everywhere.
- **No batch queries** It isn't possible to perform batch queries using Entity SQL.
- **No stored procedures** Entity SQL also lacks support for stored procedures. However, you can use functions when their only use is to select data.
- **Logical table and row focus** When working with Entity SQL, you're still using the conceptual model that the Entity Framework creates. This means that any queries you create focus on that conceptual model, rather than the underlying database, and that the mapping layer is still in place between the two.
- **No support for the * operator** It's possible to obtain the same effects as using the * operator, but you need to use the language in a different manner. For example, instead of the *count(*)* aggregate, you use *count(0)* instead. The examples later in this chapter help you understand how the loss of the * operator is fully compensated for as part of the Entity SQL language.
- **Dot syntax differences** When working with T-SQL, you use dot syntax to access the column of a row of a table. Entity SQL extends this notation to allow referencing of properties using dot syntax.
- **Built-in functions and operators** Entity SQL supports only a subset of the built-in functions and operators that T-SQL supports. You can see a description of the function support at *http://msdn.microsoft.com/library/bb738525.aspx*. A list of operators and their precedence appears at *http://msdn.microsoft.com/library/bb387132.aspx*.

These are the highlights of the differences between Entity SQL and T-SQL. You can find a more detailed list of differences at *http://msdn.microsoft.com/library/bb738573.aspx*. The essential concept to remember is that Entity SQL is a SQL-like language, but not SQL itself.

Making queries using objects

In order to be useful, any data system requires some means of retrieving the data it stores. In fact, data retrieval is the main task of most data systems. People spend far more time querying the data than modifying it. Consequently, it pays to have a system in place that's easy for the developer to understand and program, and both easy and flexible for the user to use. The reliance on objects in the Entity Framework makes working with the complex data found in most data systems considerably easier. The following paragraphs describe the objects of interest when working with the Entity Framework. Of course, .NET provides a considerable array of other objects, and you'll encounter a number of them in later chapters.

Considering the role of lambda expressions

Before going any further, it's essential to clarify the concept of a lambda expression, because many developers find it confusing (if you don't find it confusing, simply skip this first paragraph). A lambda expression is an anonymous function (one that doesn't have a specific name) that you use to create delegates or expression trees. The goal behind a lambda expression is to simplify the task of expressing abstractions within an application. Essentially, lambda expressions make it possible to express a concept as a statement. The lambda expression uses the lambda operator, =>, to create the expression. On the left side of the operator you find any arguments used to provide input to the expression. On the right side of the operator is the code used to manipulate the input. Consequently, the expression *x => x * x* means that the lambda expression accepts a value, *x*, as input and provides the square of that value as output. This short description should help you better understand the material that follows. If you still find lambda expressions confusing, check out the article at *http://blogs.msdn.com/b/ericwhite/archive/2006/10/03/lambda-expressions.aspx* for further clarification. You first saw a form of lambda expression used in the "Creating the test application" section of Chapter 2, "Looking more closely at queries." The lambda expression is used to perform a test of a condition and return a Boolean result, as shown here:

```
var dbQuery =
   UserFavoritesContext.UserFavorites.Where(id => id.UserId >= 0).ToArray();
```

In this case, the query will return only those values where *id.UserId* is greater than or equal to 0. Trying to express this concept in some way other than using a lambda expression would be difficult to say the least. As you can see, the left side contains the input argument, *id*, which Visual Studio will help you work with on the right side of the expression (in this case, gaining access to the *UserId* property).

Lambda expressions are typically used within Entity Framework method calls and as part of Entity SQL to perform selections, determine how to group data, and perform other tasks where the criterion is better expressed as a function. Many of the examples in this book rely on lambda expressions to perform specific tasks, so you'll see them used (and explained) relatively often.

Creating a basic query using Entity SQL

The best way to begin understanding Entity SQL is to use it. The syntax is relatively straightforward, but you can see an overview of the syntax at *http://msdn.microsoft.com/library/bb738683.aspx*. This example begins with the *ModelFirst* example you created in the "Creating a model-first example" section of Chapter 3. Use the following procedure to create an Entity SQL statement that obtains a customer record from the database, along with the purchases that the customer has made.

Making an Entity SQL query

1. Copy the *ModelFirst* example you created in Chapter 3 to a new folder and use this new copy for this example (rather than the copy you created in Chapter 3).

2. Add a new button to *Form1*. Name the button *btnQuery* and set its *Text* property to *&Query*.

3. Double-click *btnQuery* to create a new click event handler.

4. Type the following code for the *btnQuery_Click()* event handler:

```
private void btnQuery_Click(object sender, EventArgs e)
{
    // Create the context.
    EntityConnection conn =
        new EntityConnection("name=Rewards2ModelContainer");
    ObjectContext context = new ObjectContext(conn);

    // Define a command string for making the query.
    String EntitySQLCmd =
        "SELECT VALUE CustomerList " +
        "FROM Rewards2ModelContainer.Customers " +
        "AS CustomerList";

    // Create a query object.
    ObjectQuery<Customers> Query =
        new ObjectQuery<Customers>(EntitySQLCmd, context);

    // Execute the query.
    List<Customers> Result = Query.Execute(MergeOption.NoTracking).ToList();

    // Display the customer name on screen.
    MessageBox.Show(Result[0].CustomerName);
}
```

The example begins by creating a connection to the database and then using that connection to create a context. Notice that you must provide the name of the connection to use, which is *Rewards2ModelContainer* in this case.

After creating the connection, the code defines a query string using Entity SQL. This is a simple query, but it serves to show that the syntax is much like the SQL statements you've used in the past. Again, notice that you must reference *Rewards2ModelContainer* to gain access to the *Customers* object. The use of *CustomerList* replaces the * that would normally appear after the *SELECT* keyword.

In order to use the query, you must create an *ObjectQuery* object, *Query*, and then call *Execute()* on that object. The output is a *List* (*Result* in this case). You have several options for creating usable output with the query. The first customer name is displayed on screen.

5. Add the following two *using* statements to the beginning of the file:

```
using System.Data.Objects;
using System.Data.EntityClient;
```

6. Click Start or press F5. The application compiles and runs.

7. Click Query. You'll see the customer's name, Josh Bailey, displayed.

Creating a basic query using LINQ

Most developers rely on LINQ when making queries. LINQ is significantly easier to use and shorter as well. It also has a SQL-like syntax; albeit, not quite as closely attuned to SQL as Entity SQL is. The following procedure shows how to create a query using LINQ and the *ModelFirst* example you created in the "Creating a model-first example" section of Chapter 3.

Making a LINQ query

1. Copy the *ModelFirst* example you created in Chapter 3 to a new folder and use this new copy for this example (rather than the copy you created in Chapter 3).
2. Add a new button to *Form1*. Name the button *btnDisplay* and set its *Text* property to *&Display*.
3. Double-click *btnDisplay* to create a new click event handler.
4. Type the following code for the *btnDisplay_Click()* event handler:

```
private void btnDisplay_Click(object sender, EventArgs e)
{
    // Create the context.
    Rewards2ModelContainer context = new Rewards2ModelContainer();

    // Obtain the first customer.
    var ThisCustomer =
        (from cust in context.Customers
         select cust).First();

    // Place the customer name in the output.
    StringBuilder Output = new StringBuilder(
        ThisCustomer.CustomerName + " has made purchases on: ");

    // Add each of the customer purchases to the output.
    foreach (Purchases ThisPurchase in ThisCustomer.Purchases)
        Output.Append("\r\n\t" + ThisPurchase.PurchaseDate);

    // Display the result on screen.
    MessageBox.Show(Output.ToString());
}
```

The example begins by creating a context, much as the previous example did to add a record to the database. It then creates the first Entity SQL statement for this chapter. If you're familiar with LINQ or SQL, you can see how this statement works to an extent. The *var* keyword defines a variable, *ThisCustomer*, of an unknown type. The compiler ascertains the correct type during the build process. Theoretically, you could also assign a specific type in this case, but using *var* works just fine and reduces the potential for errors during the compilation process.

The Entity SQL statement selects the values from *context.Customers* and places them in *cust*. The *from cust* part of the statement says that the output is taken from the temporary variable *cust*. The data source is specified by *context.Customers*. The actual query is specified by *select cust* (you could modify this part of the statement to change the output if desired). If you were to include a *where* clause, you could choose specific records in the database. However, in this case, all of the records are selected. The output from this Entity SQL statement is then modified by a call to *First()*, which returns just the first record and places it in *ThisCustomer*.

The code now has access to a single record from the database. It places the customer's name in *Output*. At this point, *ThisCustomer.Purchases* points to all of the purchases the customer has made. The code uses a *foreach* statement to place the purchase date for each purchase in *Output*. The end result is that *Output* contains the customer's name and all of the dates of purchase associated with that customer.

5. Click Start or press F5. The application compiles and runs.
6. Click Display. You'll see the result shown here (assuming that you ran the example from Chapter 3 and didn't modify the code from that example):

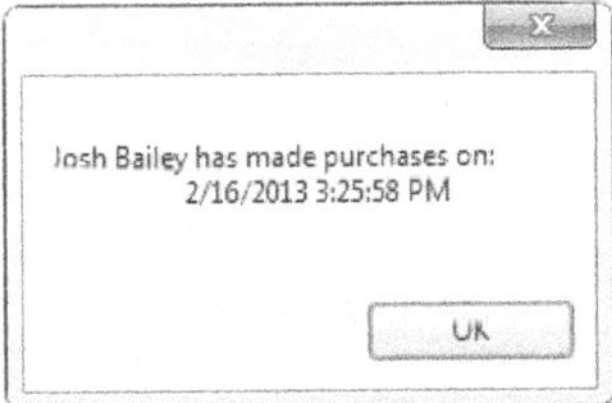
Josh Bailey has made purchases on:
2/16/2013 3:25:58 PM
OK

Note Most of the information you see in the dialog boxes in this chapter will match those on your system. However, you'll encounter a few differences, such as dates. In addition, the application dialog boxes may not match precisely. These small differences won't make any difference in the performance of the example applications.

Modifying data using objects

Querying data is an essential part of applications and it's indeed the task that users perform most often; but at some point, you'll need to add new records, update existing records, and delete old records. This section discusses techniques for performing all three tasks using objects. In this case, you'll work with the *ModelFirst* example you created in the "Creating a model-first example" section of Chapter 3 to add, update, and delete purchases that Josh Bailey has made as a customer of your company. However, before you can get to the code for handling these tasks, you need to add a couple of forms to the example. The following sections describe how to perform all of these tasks.

Adding the forms

In order to make it easier for the user to perform the required tasks, you need two forms: one to display a list of purchases that the user can use to select records to update and delete, and another to provide spaces for adding or updating data. The following procedure begins by adding the selection form. The selection form provides a simple list of purchases made by Josh. All the user needs to do is select the appropriate entry and click a button to use it.

Adding the selection form

1. Copy the *ModelFirst* example you created in the "Creating a basic query using LINQ" section of this chapter to a new folder, and use this new copy for this example (rather than the copy you created earlier). This example relies on the Display button you created earlier to show the results of tasks you perform.

2. Right-click the *TestModelFirst* project entry in Solution Explorer and choose Add | Windows Form from the context menu. You'll see the Add New Item dialog box.

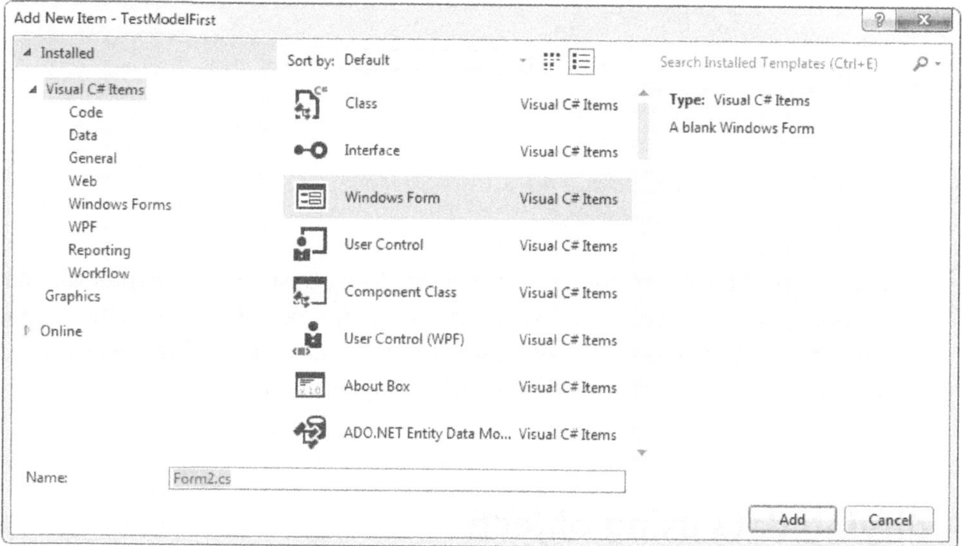

3. Type **frmSelection** in the Name field and click Add. Visual Studio adds the new form to your project.

4. Add two buttons (*btnSelect* and *btnCancel*), a label (*lblPurchases*), and a list box (*lstPurchases*) to the form, as shown here:

5. Set the *DialogResult* property for *btnSelect* to *OK*, the *DialogResult* property for *btnCancel* to *Cancel*, and the *Modifiers* property for *lstPurchases* to *Public*.

Now that you have the selection form in place, you need a second form for modifying the data. In this case, the form provides fields for each of the data fields for the *Purchases* table. The following procedure shows how to add this form.

Adding the data form

1. Right-click the *TestModelFirst* project entry in Solution Explorer and choose Add | Windows Form from the context menu. You'll see the Add New Item dialog box.

2. Type **frmData** in the Name field and click Add. Visual Studio adds the new form to your project.

3. Add two buttons (*btnModify* and *btnCancel*), four labels (*lblID, lblPurchaseDate, lblAmount,* and *lblCustomerID*), three text boxes (*txtID, txtAmount,* and *txtCustomerID*), and a *DateTimePicker* (*dtpPurchaseDate*), as shown here:

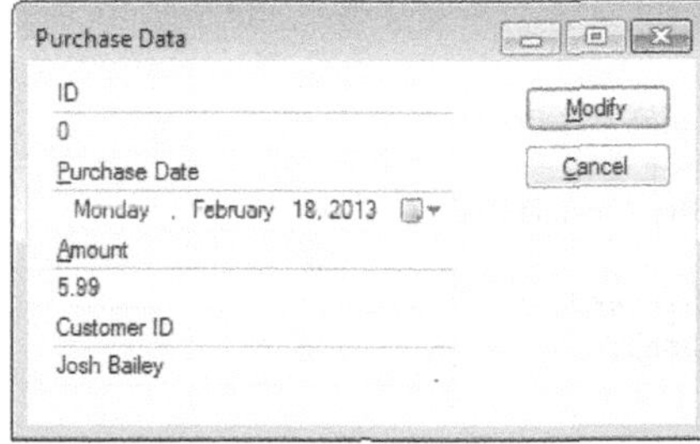

4. Set the *DialogResult* property for *btnModify* to *OK*, the *DialogResult* property for *btnCancel* to *Cancel*, the *Modifiers* property for *txtID, dtpPurchaseDate, txtAmount,* and *txtCustomerID* to *Public*, and the *ReadOnly* property for *txtID* and *txtCustomerID* to *True*.

Adding purchases

A good first step for updating this application is to create a method for adding purchases. In this case, all you need to do is display a form for adding the data. The example will continue to use Josh Bailey's customer record for the sake of simplicity. Use the following procedure to add the code required to add new purchase records.

Adding a *Purchase*

1. Add a new button to *Form1*. Name the button *btnAddPurchase* and set its *Text* property to *Add &Purchase.*
2. Double-click *btnAddPurchase* to create a new click event handler.
3. Type the following code for the *btnAddPurchase_Click()* event handler:

```
private void btnAddPurchase_Click(object sender, EventArgs e)
{
    // Create the form and display it.
    frmData AddData = new frmData();
    DialogResult Result = AddData.ShowDialog(this);

    // Check the dialog result.
    if (Result == DialogResult.Cancel)
        return;

    // Create the context.
    Rewards2ModelContainer context = new Rewards2ModelContainer();

    // Obtain the customer record.
    var ThisCustomer =
        (from cust in context.Customers
         select cust).First();

    // Create a new purchase.
    Purchases NewPurchase = new Purchases();
    NewPurchase.Amount =
        Convert.ToDecimal(AddData.txtAmount.Text);
    NewPurchase.CustomersId = ThisCustomer.Id;
    NewPurchase.PurchaseDate = AddData.dtpPurchaseDate.Value;

    // Add the purchase to the customer record.
    ThisCustomer.Purchases.Add(NewPurchase);
    context.SaveChanges();

    // Display a success message.
    MessageBox.Show("Record Added");
}
```

The code begins by displaying the form. When the user clicks Modify, the code returns and creates a new context. It then obtains the record for Josh Bailey. At this point, the code can use a combination of the data from Josh Bailey's record and *frmData* to create a new purchase object. Notice that the code adds the new purchase directly to Josh Bailey's record. As a final step, the code saves the changes made to the context and displays a message saying the record was added.

4. Click Start or press F5. The application compiles and runs.

5. Click Add Purchase. You'll see the Purchase Data dialog box.

6. Change the value in the Amount field to **6.99** and click Modify. The application adds the new record to the database. Of course, you'll want to verify the addition.

7. Click Display. You'll see the result shown here (assuming that you ran the example from Chapter 3 and didn't modify the code from that example):

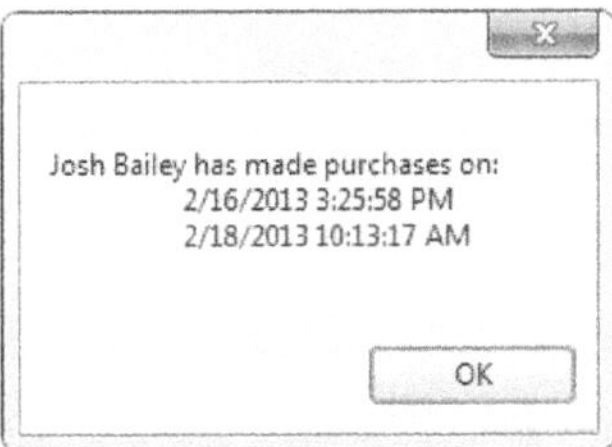

Updating purchases

When users aren't viewing data, they spend considerable time updating it. This part of the example continues using Josh Bailey's record to keep things simple. In order to make a change, the user must select an existing record and then modify the content of that record, so this part of the example uses both of the forms that you created earlier. The following procedure shows how to perform this task.

Updating a *Purchase*

1. Add a new button to *Form1*. Name the button *btnUpdatePurchase* and set its *Text* property to *&Update Purchase*.

2. Double-click *btnUpdatePurchase* to create a new click event handler.

3. Type the following code for the *btnUpdatePurchase_Click()* event handler:

```
private void btnUpdatePurchase_Click(object sender, EventArgs e)
{
    // Create the context.
    Rewards2ModelContainer context = new Rewards2ModelContainer();

    // Obtain the customer record.
    var ThisCustomer =
        (from cust in context.Customers
         select cust).First();

    // Fill the selection form with data.
    frmSelection RecSelect = new frmSelection();
    foreach (Purchases ThisPurchase in ThisCustomer.Purchases)
```

```
        RecSelect.lstPurchases.Items.Add(ThisPurchase.PurchaseDate);

    // Obtain a record selection.
    DialogResult Result = RecSelect.ShowDialog(this);
    if (Result == DialogResult.Cancel)
        return;

    // Obtain the desired purchase record.
    var UpdatePurchase =
        from purchase in ThisCustomer.Purchases
        where purchase.PurchaseDate ==
          (DateTime)RecSelect.lstPurchases.SelectedItem
        select purchase;

    // Create the update form and add data to it.
    frmData ChangeData = new frmData();
    ChangeData.txtAmount.Text =
        UpdatePurchase.First().Amount.ToString();
    ChangeData.txtID.Text =
        UpdatePurchase.First().Id.ToString();
    ChangeData.dtpPurchaseDate.Value =
        UpdatePurchase.First().PurchaseDate;

    // Display the form and wait for changes.
    Result = ChangeData.ShowDialog(this);
    if (Result == DialogResult.Cancel)
        return;

    // Update the purchase record.
    UpdatePurchase.First().Amount =
        Convert.ToDecimal(ChangeData.txtAmount.Text);
    UpdatePurchase.First().PurchaseDate =
        ChangeData.dtpPurchaseDate.Value;
    context.SaveChanges();

    // Display a success message.
    MessageBox.Show("Record Updated");
}
```

This example starts by obtaining a context to the database and using it to populate the entries in *frmSelection*. The code then displays the resulting object, *RectSelect*, to the user, who can select one of the purchase entries based on the date.

When the user selects a date, the code uses the information to obtain the specific purchase record from the database. It then creates a *frmData* object, *ChangeData*; uses the information from the purchase record, *UpdatePurchase*; and displays it on screen. The user can now modify the data.

After the user closes the dialog box, the code updates the purchase record using *UpdatePurchase*. You don't actually have to work directly with the context or the actual customer object, *ThisCustomer*. A call to *SaveChanges()* saves the information to the database.

4. Click Start or press F5. The application compiles and runs.

5. Click Update Purchase. You'll see the list of purchases made by the user, as shown here:

6. Highlight the second date—the one you added in the "Adding purchases" section of the chapter—and click Select. You'll see the Purchase Data dialog box. This dialog box will automatically contain all of the data for this specific record, as shown here:

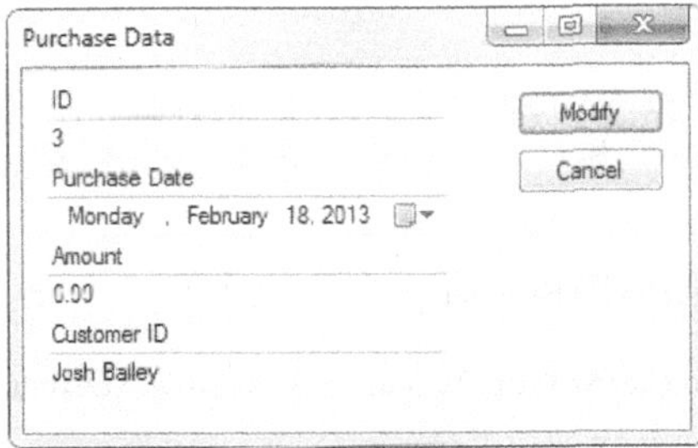

7. Choose the previous day's date in the Purchase Date field and click Modify. The application modifies the record and displays a success message. Of course, you'll want to verify the addition.

8. Click Display. The dialog will display the changed purchase date for you.

Deleting purchases

Deleting records is something that users perform the least often of all of the activities discussed so far. In fact, there are database applications that don't allow deletions, for legal and other reasons. Deleting a record means selecting the entry you want to remove and then signifying you want it gone. As with the other examples, this one relies on Josh Bailey's record. The following procedure shows how to delete a purchase entry from the database.

Deleting a *Purchase*

1. Add a new button to *Form1*. Name the button *btnDeletePurchase* and set its *Text* property to *&Delete Purchase*.
2. Double-click *btnDeletePurchase* to create a new click event handler.
3. Type the following code for the *btnDeletePurchase_Click()* event handler:

```
private void btnDeletePurchase_Click(object sender, EventArgs e)
{
    // Create the context.
    Rewards2ModelContainer context = new Rewards2ModelContainer();

    // Obtain the customer record.
    var ThisCustomer =
        (from cust in context.Customers
         select cust).First();

    // Fill the selection form with data.
    frmSelection RecSelect = new frmSelection();
    foreach (Purchases ThisPurchase in ThisCustomer.Purchases)
        RecSelect.lstPurchases.Items.Add(ThisPurchase.PurchaseDate);

    // Obtain a record selection.
    DialogResult Result = RecSelect.ShowDialog(this);
    if (Result == DialogResult.Cancel)
        return;

    // Create a purchases object the matches the record to remove.
    Purchases RemoveThis =
        ThisCustomer.Purchases.ElementAt(RecSelect.lstPurchases.SelectedIndex);

    // Use the record selection to remove the record from the list.
    context.Purchases.Remove(RemoveThis);
    context.SaveChanges();

    // Display a success message.
    MessageBox.Show("Record Deleted");
}
```

Much of this code should look familiar from the other sections of the chapter. The difference is in the selection of a record to delete. The user selects this record, and the record is placed in *RemoveThis* via the use of the *ElementAt()* method with the selection as the index. The code calls *Remove()*, which deletes the selected record, and then updates the database. Notice that the code uses the *Purchases* table object directly, rather than trying to remove the record using *ThisCustomer.Purchases*. A message box shows successful completion.

Note When working with record deletions, you must interact with the table that holds the data, rather than through a foreign key. If you attempt to remove the record through the foreign key, the application displays an error message.

4. Click Start or press F5. The application compiles and runs.

5. Click Delete Purchase. You'll see the list of purchases made by the user.

6. Highlight the second date—the one you added in the "Adding purchases" section of the chapter—and click Select. The application deletes the record and shows a success dialog box.

7. Click Display. You'll see that the customer now has only one available purchase.

Working with Query Builder methods

Both Entity SQL and LINQ methods of working with data require a little extra effort on the part of the developer in knowing how to build the required statements. Entity SQL takes a strong SQL statement approach, while LINQ uses an approach that more closely matches the object dot syntax that developers are used to using. Query Builder methods are a bit more verbose than either of the other methods, but do have an advantage in making the creation of a successful statement easier and the implications of that statement clearer to others viewing the code. The procedure in this section demonstrates the use of Query Builder methods. This example relies on the *ModelFirst* example you created in the "Creating a model-first example" section of Chapter 3.

Making a Query Builder query

1. Copy the *ModelFirst* example you created in Chapter 3 to a new folder and use this new copy for this example (rather than the copy you created in Chapter 3).

2. Add a new button to *Form1*. Name the button *btnBuildQuery* and set its *Text* property to *&Build Query.*

3. Double-click *btnQuery* to create a new click event handler.

4. Type the following code for the *btnQuery_Click()* event handler:

```
private void btnBuildQuery_Click(object sender, EventArgs e)
{
    // Create the context.
    Rewards2ModelContainer context = new Rewards2ModelContainer();

    // Create the query.
    List<Customers> ThisCustomer =
        context.Customers
        .Where(name => name.CustomerName == "Josh Bailey")
        .ToList();

    // Place the customer name in the output.
    StringBuilder Output = new StringBuilder(
        ThisCustomer[0].CustomerName + " has made purchases on: ");
```

```
        // Add each of the customer purchases to the output.
        foreach (Purchases ThisPurchase in ThisCustomer[0].Purchases)
            Output.Append("\r\n\t" + ThisPurchase.PurchaseDate);

        // Display the result on screen.
        MessageBox.Show(Output.ToString());
    }
```

The code begins by creating a context similar to the one used for the LINQ example. It then creates a query. The query actually results in an *ObjectQuery* output, but the example casts the output to a standard *List* by calling *ToList()* on the output. Using a *List* makes the output easier to enumerate. One of the things that you'll notice as you build the query is that the IDE is quite helpful in providing aid in constructing a usable statement. There are no text-specific inputs where you have to guess what to provide.

The output part of this example is much like the LINQ example. The code relies on a *foreach* statement to parse through the purchases and output them to the screen.

5. Click Start or press F5. The application compiles and runs.
6. Click Build Query. You'll see the same result shown in the "Creating a basic query using LINQ" section of the chapter.

Getting started with the Entity Framework

This chapter has helped you understand the Entity Framework objects at a basic level. In addition, you've learned a little about Entity SQL and about using Query Builder methods to construct Entity SQL statements quickly and easily. Even though the section on extension methods is short, what you need to take away is the fact that it's possible to extend Entity Framework (or any other .NET) classes to meet specific needs. The idea isn't so much to create a new sort of class, but to reduce the work of the class when you work with it. The most important thing you can take away from this chapter is that working with Entity SQL and Query Builder methods is similar to working with T-SQL and LINQ, but that there are differences, and you need to work with both of these technologies to begin to truly understand them.

Now that you have a basic understanding of the *Entity* objects and can use both Entity SQL and Query Builder methods, you need to practice a bit with them. Try changing some of the queries in the examples to obtain different results. For example, try creating a query that obtains every customer who has a purchase in the amount of $5.99. Try creating the query using both Entity SQL and Query Builder methods. Compare the two methods and determine which works better for you—especially which method is easier to understand.

Chapter 5, "Performing essential tasks," builds on the information found in this chapter. Now that you have the basics down, you need to see how to use these techniques to perform more complex tasks than the ones you've performed to date. For example, you need to know how to ensure that your database maintains referential integrity and that the database doesn't end up with duplicates of specific customer records. This second goal will require a modification of the existing *Rewards* database. Since this is the first time you make a model change, this part of Chapter 5 is especially important.

Chapter 4 quick reference

To	Do this
Perform selection or computational tasks easily	Create a lambda expression, ensuring that the left side of the lambda operator, =>, contains the variables you want to use, and the right side contains an expression that outputs the desired result.
Work with datasets when the type isn't known at build time	Rely on the *DbSet* class, rather than the generic *DbSet<TEntity>* class.
Create a lambda expression	Supply a set of variables, add the => operator, and then provide an expression that performs a task with those variables. For example, *x => x * x* returns the square of the input value, *x*.
Select a record using Entity SQL	Create a connection, and then a context from that connection. Define a query using SQL-like statements, such as *SELECT VALUE CustomerList FROM Rewards2ModelContainer.Customers AS CustomerList*. Execute the query and output it as a *List* or other easily enumerated object.
Select a record using LINQ	Write a statement that includes the *from*, *in*, and *select* clauses. Add a variable to hold the temporary data from the query and provide the data source as part of the in clause. For example, *from cust in context.Customers select cust* will obtain all of the customer records in the current context.
Select a record using Query Builder	Create a query that relies on methods called on objects supplied by the context you create. You use lambda statements to define how the query should define the data output. A typical statement will include a number of linked method calls such as *context.Customers.Where(name => name.CustomerName == "Josh Bailey").ToList()*.
Add a record	Create the new content, and then call the *Add()* method on either a foreign key (navigation property) or table object. Call *SaveChanges()* to save the new record to the database.
Update a record	Gain access to the required record, change the contents of the individual properties, and then call *SaveChanges()* to save the content to the database.
Delete a record	Gain access to the required record and then call *Remove* on the table object. Call *SaveChanges()* to make the deletion permanent.

CHAPTER 5

Performing essential tasks

After completing the chapter, you'll be able to

- Specify how the Entity Framework makes viewing, saving, inserting, and deleting data easier.
- Make and save changes to a database.
- Add objects to a database.
- Work with parent/child data.
- Remove objects from the database.

Every application you create will perform a number of essential tasks. Chapter 4, "Generating and using objects," introduced you to these four tasks: querying (viewing) data, adding new records, making changes to existing records, and deleting old records. Even though database applications can become quite complex, the tasks they perform boil down to one of these four activities at some point. For example, the act of printing requires that the application perform a query first, and then send the data it finds to the printer. The Entity Framework makes it easier than ever to perform these four tasks, even when the database itself becomes relatively complex. In addition, using the Entity Framework makes changes less painful. You still have to change some code, but overall, you'll find that you spend less time working through changes, and the changes will contain fewer errors that you'll have to debug later.

Besides discussing the four essential tasks at a greater level of detail, this chapter also explores the parent/child relationship in more depth. You'll also see how changes to database design can (and will) affect both the model and your code. All of these sorts of tasks are part of an essential core of skills that you need to build to use the Entity Framework effectively. The goal when you complete this chapter is to be able to work through most basic Entity Framework tasks without problems, even when the supporting database becomes relatively complex. Of course, future chapters will help you with many of the nuances of working with databases, such as using stored procedures to perform common tasks.

Defining the essential tasks

As part of working through a design using the Entity Framework, you need to consider the tasks that the application will perform. Previous sections of this book have referred to the four basic tasks as follows: making a query, adding new records, modifying existing records, and deleting old records.

It's important to define these essential tasks as part of creating a design. The following sections take a slightly different view of the four tasks in that they discuss the four tasks in view of how they're used within the application. For example, making a query is a specific task, but this task is used in more than one way. In order to add a record, you must first query the database to ensure the record doesn't exist. When adding a child record, you must first query the database to obtain the parent record that the child record will reference.

Viewing the data

When designing your Entity Framework model, you must consider everything that will transpire when a user views the data. It's important to remember that users view data far more often than performing any other tasks. Consequently, viewing the data is a critical path for your application—the act must be both fast and reliable. Of course, the act of viewing the data means making queries to the database.

However, the act of viewing data is far more than simply making a query. The application must retrieve and verify user input in order to make the query. This means accessing tables that contain additional information required for automation (see the "Considering the effects of automation on database design" sidebar for details). In addition, once the query is made, the server must perform any required postprocessing and send the processed data to the client, and then the client must present the information on screen in a usable and pleasing format.

Considering the effects of automation on database design

Something that most tomes on database design leave out is that users anticipate and rely on certain levels of automation in the flow of data from the server to the client application and back. The design you create must include functionality for these requirements. In some cases, this means adding tables to support user needs. Other design decisions may include flattening a table out, rather than attempting to achieve pure referential design, in the interest of making the application faster and more efficient by reducing the number of queries. Following are the five levels of automation that you need to consider as part of your database design:

- **User preferences** Users find it annoying when an application always starts in a default state, which necessitates configuration before each session can begin. The use of various application strategies, such as a mix of desktop and browser-based applications, makes it easier to store user preferences at the server and then automatically configure the user interface when the application starts—no matter which version of the application the user is employing at a given time.
- **Data input** Input errors are a major concern for database developers. Some errors are seemingly small, yet loom large in their effect. For example, simple misspellings or differences in capitalization can cause serious data-flow problems. Anything you can do to automate the data input, such as providing predefined values, reduces errors and increases user efficiency—making tasks easier and faster to perform.

- **Distinguishing between client and server processing** Many applications perform all processing at the client or at the server, rather than distinguishing between the two environments and using the best location for a particular task. Any user input should be validated at the client before being sent to the server, in order to reduce the number of network transmissions and shorten the time required for a user to discover there's an error in input. The user expects to know that an error has occurred in input before moving to the next field of a form so that the application doesn't report back with a number of errors that have nebulous error information provided with them. However, performing calculations and other sorts of intensive tasks that have nothing to do with the user on the client system needlessly burdens the client, creates a throughput bottleneck, and causes the application to work more slowly than it should. A simple way to look at the problem is to consider each network transmission and ask whether the trip is really necessary. In addition, consider whether a task is user oriented (requiring client-side processing) or processing oriented (requiring server-side processing).
- **Output presentation** After a user completes a given task, it's important to provide some sort of feedback so that the user knows the task has completed successfully. Many applications rely on a one-size-fits-all approach for output presentation. The output may work well for a desktop application, but not very well at all when displayed on a smartphone. An application must detect and format the output for the device that the user is utilizing for a given task, especially in this age of Bring-Your-Own-Device (BYOD). In many cases, making this work means storing predefined settings on the server to ensure the presentation is correct.
- **Error resolution** One of the toughest types of automation to provide, error resolution, is possibly the most important. Every user shows specific patterns in making errors during data input. Word processors are an example of modern applications that detect and store these patterns for use in correcting user input. This is a kind of automation that your application should provide in order to resolve errors quickly. When a user has to think through the same error every time it occurs, it becomes annoying and the user begins wasting time in frustration. Storing common user errors for specific users, along with the error resolution that applies to that user, can save a significant amount of time and ensure that some errors are resolved automatically for the user.

Automation takes a considerable number of forms in applications today, but you can group all forms of automation into one of these five categories. Planning the database design to accommodate these forms of applications will help you create more robust applications that are significantly more pleasant to use.

Saving changes

After viewing data in various ways, users change existing information relatively often. The act of saving these changes requires a specific data flow that affects how you design your database using the Entity Framework. A user commonly saves changes under the following circumstances:

- Adding a new record
- Making updates to an existing record
- Modifying application preferences (see the "Considering the effects of automation on database design" sidebar for details)
- Creating specific kinds of output, such as printed reports
- Performing data analysis
- Correcting input or other kinds of user-specific errors

The act of saving a change means verifying that the change occurs successfully and appears in every affected location. For example, some developers will flatten a database so that an application performs more quickly. When an application uses a flattened dataset that appears in a single table—rather than using multiple related tables, as would occur in relational databases—data redundancies can occur, which will affect your application design. Part of the reason to use the Entity Framework models is to help you best decide how to configure the data sources within your application.

Note It's beyond the scope of this book to discuss when and how to flatten datasets to provide specific application benefits. You can find a discussion of dataset–flattening techniques at *http://msdn.microsoft.com/library/windows/desktop/ms716948.aspx*. The example at *http://msdn.microsoft.com/library/windows/desktop/ms713681.aspx* is especially helpful. You should also note that a flattened dataset isn't the same as a flat-file database, where a single table is used to store all information. A flattened dataset is only used for performance enhancement and to reduce the complexity of the application used to manage the data.

Inserting new values

Initially, a database receives a considerable amount of new input. However, as the dataset grows, the new input is replaced by data updates and data queries as primary uses. In fact, there are situations where all data input by common users stops and new entries are made only by highly trusted and skilled personnel. Historical databases may not receive any new input at all. Just how the dataset ages will depend on the kind of data stored in it. Common reasons for inserting new values include the following:

- Adding a new record
- Deleting an existing record

- Logging database or application events
- Creating a new set of user preferences (see the "Considering the effects of automation on database design" sidebar for details)
- Defining changes to the overall database structure

Most modern database applications don't actually delete data. The reasons are many and often complex in nature. Whatever the reason for not wanting to delete the data, a record that's no longer useful is often moved to an archive database and stored offline. So, the very act of deleting a record may mean adding a record to an archive. There's no concept of moving data when it comes to database management. The data is usually added to the new location and then deleted in the old location, rather than moved.

All of the changes to a database are usually tracked in some way. Many DBMS managers provide some sort of automatic logging for database changes, but you may have a requirement to track changes made by the user as well in the form of application events. Each of these events will result in a new record in the tracking table. Rather than add such functionality late in the design process (or after the application has already gone into production), you need to consider adding these features to the initial database model.

New values—those that have never appeared in the database before—represent a major upheaval to the database in some cases. For example, a change to a law could require a company to store additional information about customers, which will require changes to the database structure and the insertion of new values for each customer. When designing a database using the Entity Framework, you must consider how these changes will affect the existing data, as well as the overall structure of the associated application. In addition, you must consider how elements such as the user interface are affected.

Deleting old values

Deleting, rather than archiving, data is becoming a somewhat rare event in database management. The issue is one of accountability. Without a record of what has happened, it's impossible to determine how a specific set of actions caused a particular result. Consequently, many organizations archive all data that's removed from a database in some form. However, deletions do occur; here are the most common reasons for deleting data:

- Deleting an existing record
- Removing user preferences (see the "Considering the effects of automation on database design" sidebar for details)
- Optimizing a dataset for performance reasons

Creating a master/detail form

Many data manipulation tasks fall into a *master/detail* format, where a single parent record points to one or more child records. This is the case with the *Rewards* and *Rewards2* databases that you originally created in Chapter 3, "Choosing a workflow." A single *Customer* table record points to multiple *Purchase* table records. In the past, creating a master/detail form required at least some amount of code—some of which was error prone. Fortunately, Microsoft Visual Studio can perform a great deal of the required work for you when you use the graphical interface to your advantage. The example described in the sections that follows begins with the *ModelFirst* example you created in the "Creating a model-first example" section of Chapter 3.

Note This example creates a new user interface for the *ModelFirst* application. Before you begin working through this example, you should remove the Add button found on *Form1*, along with its associated event handler. Make sure you start with a clean form before working through the example.

Creating the data source

The *ModelFirst* example provides a model of the database, but not an actual connection to it. Before you can do anything else, you need to create a data source that you can use to access the application data. You could write code to perform this task, as was done in previous chapters. However, in this example, you use the IDE to perform all of the heavy lifting. The following procedure shows how to create a data source for a master/detail form.

Creating the master/detail data source

1. Copy the *ModelFirst* example you created in Chapter 3 to a new folder and use this new copy for this example (rather than the copy you created in Chapter 3).
2. Delete *btnAdd* from *Form1*, along with its associated event handler, *btnAdd_Click()*.
3. Choose View | Other Windows | Data Sources to open the Data Sources window. You'll see the Data Source window. It shouldn't currently contain any data sources.
4. Click the Add New Data Source link. You'll see the Data Source Configuration Wizard shown here:

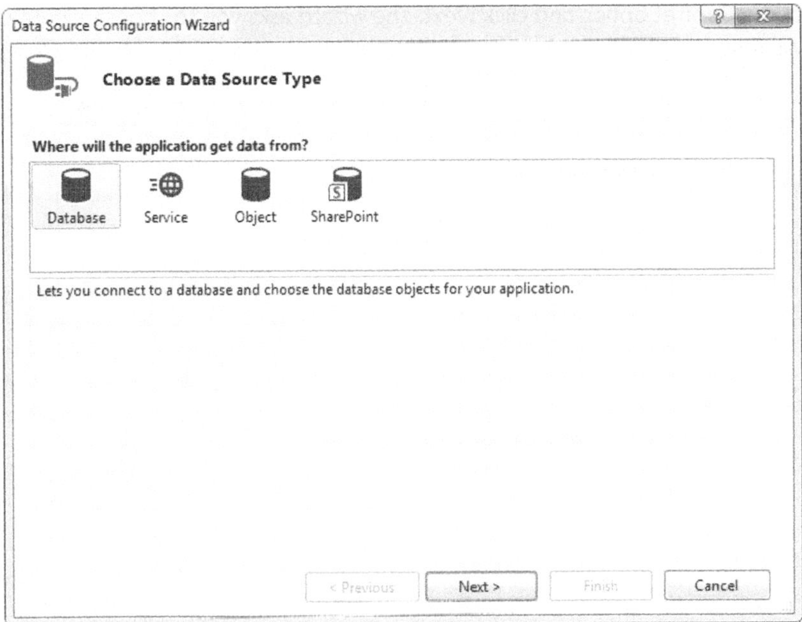

5. Select the Database option and click Next. The wizard asks you to choose a database model, as shown here:

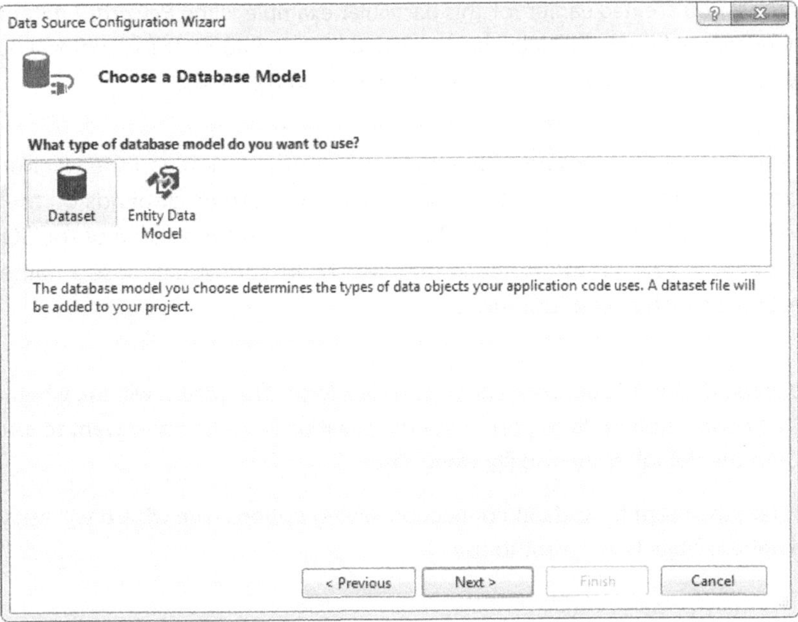

6. Select the Dataset option and click Next. The wizard asks you to choose a data connection, as shown here:

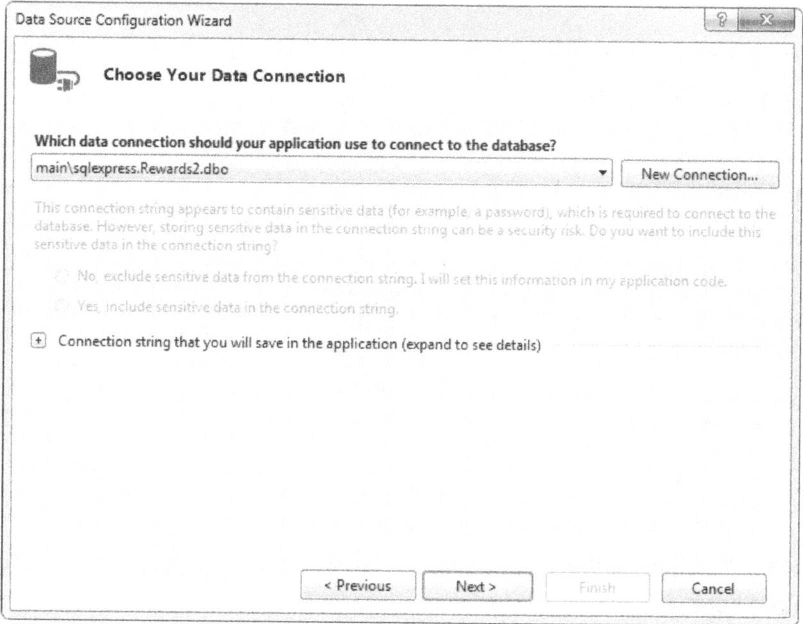

The model you created earlier for this particular example is the *Rewards2* database, so that's the data connection you should choose as well. Depending on the workflow you use, you generally maintain the model and data source in the same project.

Note The precise wording of the connection information you see will likely vary from the wording shown in the screen shot. The wording depends on the name of the machine hosting Microsoft SQL Server (main) and the name of the SQL Server connection, which is *sqlexpress* in this case. Make sure you choose a name that reflects your system configuration.

7. Choose the *Rewards2* data connection and click Next. The wizard will ask whether you want to save the connection name as part of your application. You definitely want to save the connection, and the default name usually works fine.

8. Click Next to accept the default connection-saving options. The wizard will ask you to choose the database objects you want to use.

9. Check the Tables option, as shown here:

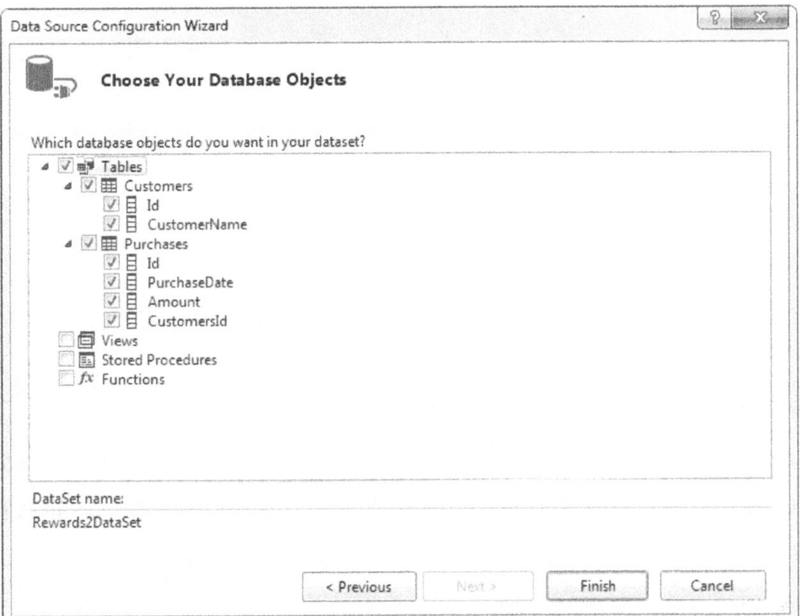

Checking this option will allow access to all of the tables found in the *Rewards2* database. Notice that the dialog box also contains a DataSet Name field. Using the default name normally works fine.

10. Click Finish. The new data source appears in the Data Source window. Before you can use the data source, however, you need to configure it for this application.

Configuring the data source

You have a source for data. However, the data source isn't configured so that you can use it effectively to create a master/detail application. The following procedure helps you perform the configuration required to allow the automation provided by the IDE to work better.

Configuring the master/detail data source

1. Expand the data source entries by clicking the right-pointing arrow next to Rewards2DataSet. Choose Details in the drop-down list for Customers, as shown here:

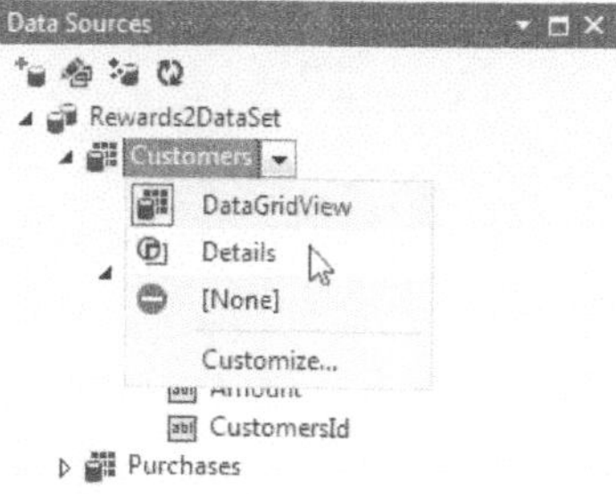

Using the Details option presents a single record at a time so that the user can focus on a single customer and the purchases for that particular customer.

2. Choose Label in the *Id* field for Customers.

3. Expand the Purchases entry under the Customers entry. Choose Label in the *Id* field.

4. Choose None in the *CustomersId* field. Your configuration should look like the one shown here:

Adding and configuring the controls

At this point, you've created and configured a data source to use for the application. The next step is to add and configure the controls. This procedure shows how to add the *Customers* and *Purchases* tables to the form.

Adding and configuring the master/detail controls

1. Drag and drop the *Customers* table from the Data Sources window to the form. Visual Studio creates the required controls for you. Notice that the Id field is a label, while the Customer Name field is a text box. Visual Studio also adds a *BindingNavigator* to the form so that you can easily move between records.

2. Drag and drop the *Purchases* table from the Data Sources window to the form. Visual Studio creates a data grid that contains the fields used to hold purchase information.

3. Arrange the controls for a pleasing appearance, as shown here:

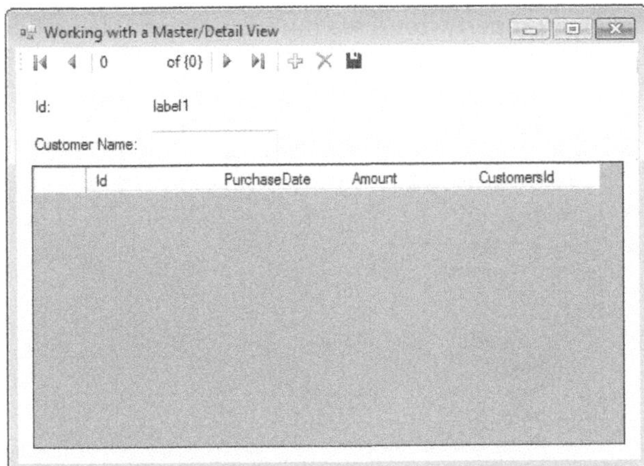

If you started the application now, you'd see all of the purchases for all of the customers in the data grid, which isn't acceptable. The next step describes how to create a relationship between the customer information and the purchases.

4. Select *purchasesDataGridView*. You'll see the properties for this control in the Properties window.

5. Locate the *DataSource* property. The drop-down list shows an entry for *FK_CustomersPurchases*, as shown here:

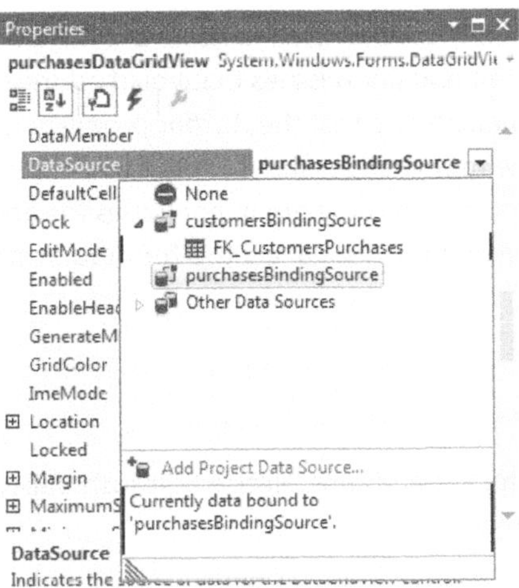

Using the *FK_CustomersPurchases* data source will link the customer data with the purchases data in the data grid.

6. Choose *FK_CustomersPurchases*. Visual Studio automatically generates a new *BindingSource* control named *fKCustomersPurchasesBindingSource*. One of the annoying features of the IDE is that it doesn't always remove columns you don't need. The data grid currently contains the *CustomerId* field, which isn't needed or wanted.

7. Click the ellipses in the *Columns* property. You'll see the Edit Columns dialog box, as shown here:

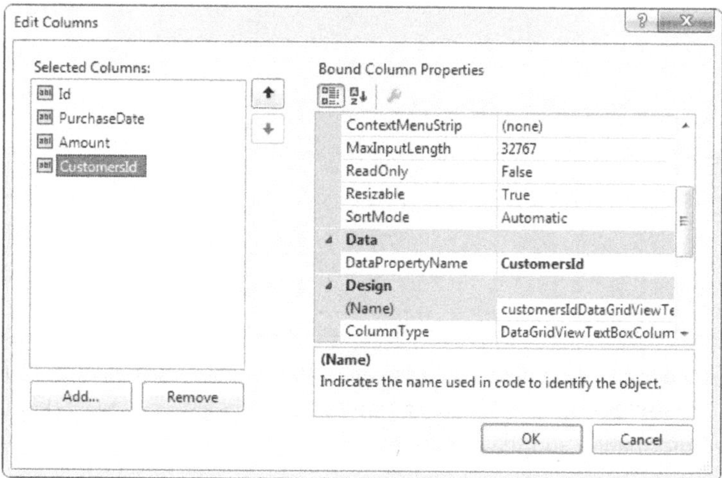

8. Highlight the *CustomersId* entry in the Selected Columns list and click Remove. Click OK. Visual Studio removes the offending column from the data grid.

Testing the result

There's more work you could do with the application, but the essential tasks are finished, and the result is ready for a first test. There are a number of fit and finish issues that you'd address in a production application. For example, you would want to make sure that the *Anchor* property is set correctly for the data grid so that it sizes properly when the user changes the form size. Modifying the field names so that they look nice would be another touch, but these are minor issues for now. The following procedure helps you test the basic application and provides a few tips for modifications you may want to try on your own.

Testing the master/detail view

1. Click Start or press F5. The application compiles and runs. Notice that Josh Bailey's record appears with the one purchase that he has made.

2. Click in the second row of the data grid to create a new purchase record. Type **2/19/2013** in the PurchaseDate field and **7.99** in the Amount field. Click Save Data (the icon that looks like a floppy disk). The application saves the new purchase. Notice that the *Id* field of the data grid changes from –1 to the next number in line (most likely 3 or 4) when you click Save. This is an indicator that the record is actually saved.

Note One change that would be nice is an automatic update of the database. Each time a change occurs, the data should be saved to the database. The user is unlikely to know that clicking Save Data is required.

3. Click Add New (the yellow plus sign). The application adds a new master record.
4. Type **Christian Hess** in the Customer Name field and then click Save Data. The Id field changes from –1 to the next number in line (most likely 2). Again, this is an indicator that the record has been saved.

Warning If you attempt to add both a new customer and an associated purchase without clicking Save Data between operations, the application will experience an error. The automation provided by the IDE doesn't handle this particular situation. One of the changes you would need to make is to provide some means of saving the customer data first, and then provide a means of saving the new purchase for that customer behind the scenes. A user is unlikely to make the changes one at a time.

5. Click in the first row of the data grid to create a new purchase record. Type **2/18/2013** in the PurchaseDate field and **6.99** in the Amount field. Click Save Data.
6. Click Move Previous (the left-pointing arrow). Notice that the contents of the data grid change to reflect the purchases made by Josh Bailey.
7. Select the second row (not an individual cell) of the data grid and press Delete (don't press the Delete button on the toolbar; press the actual Delete key on your keyboard). Click Save Data. The application removes the purchase record.

Note It would be nice if the Delete button could detect where the user has focus and delete the appropriate entry type. As it is now, clicking Delete (the red X) removes the entire record no matter where the insertion point is.

8. Click Move Next (the right-pointing arrow). Notice that the contents of the data grid change to reflect the purchases made by Christian Hess. The essential elements of the application are working, but as you can see, there are fit and finish issues that you'd need to address. Even so, this application can perform all of the required essential tasks.

Getting started with the Entity Framework

The main purpose of this chapter has been to help you understand the four essential tasks that every database application performs at some point. If you feel comfortable with querying data, adding new records, updating record information, and deleting old records, then you've gained the essential information from this chapter. Many database books make things sounds really complex when it really does come down to performing these four tasks well. Everything after these four tasks is simply an addition to the basic four tasks.

This is one chapter you shouldn't leave until you really do understand the material completely, because this chapter provides the basic building blocks for everything that follows. One of the better ways to test your knowledge is to work with the code. Try to change the code so that it performs the task in a different way. Add some of the error trapping and range checking that you'd use in a production application to see how these changes affect the examples. The example code is there for you to experiment with, so that you don't have to experiment with the production code that your business depends upon. The example code is also fully commented and provides a straightforward environment in which to test things—both of which are positives when it comes to the learning curve.

Part III, "Manipulating data using the Entity Framework," begins a new focus on manipulating data in specific ways, rather than simply working with it to perform the four basic tasks. Chapter 6, "Manipulating data using LINQ," begins this transition by exploring Language Integrated Query (LINQ) in more detail. Most developers use LINQ when working with the Entity Framework because it's extremely flexible, terse, and relatively self-documenting. Chapter 6 is especially important because it acquaints you with LINQ functions that can make performing the four basic tasks easier and faster. These functions often provide shortcuts to the longer code examples that you've seen in this chapter.

Chapter 5 quick reference

To	Do this
Design an Entity Framework application properly	Define how the application will perform the four basic tasks: making a query, adding new records, modifying existing records, and deleting old records. Once you've done this analysis, you need to consider how the application will combine the four basic tasks to create a data flow and to ensure that data is successfully managed without error.
Create a robust design that considers user requirements	Design around the five levels of automation that define the user's expectations in today's computing environment: user preferences, data input, client and server processing, output presentation, and error resolution.
View data	Ask for user input, create a query, obtain the requested data from the server, and present the output in a form preferred by the user. Ensure that the user preferences and automation allow for input in a manner that works best with the user's needs.

To	Do this
Save changes	Obtain records that require modification, obtain and verify input from the user at the client level, send the requested changes to the server, perform any required postprocessing on the server, and obtain a change status for the user as output.
Insert new values	Create the requested information template at the client level, obtain and verify input from the user at the client level, send the new information to the server, perform any required postprocessing on the server, and obtain a new input status for the user as output.
Delete old values	Obtain the required deletion information from the user, verify the user request, add the deleted record to an archive database, delete the record from the production database, and obtain a deletion status for the user as output.
Sync a detail view with a master view	Set the detail view *DataSource* property to point to the foreign key of the master dataset.

PART III

Manipulating data using the Entity Framework

Working with data means performing three essential, but different, tasks: viewing (querying), managing, and manipulating the data. Viewing the data means requesting information from the database. You create a query, and the database sends raw data to your application based on that query. Managing the database means performing create, update, and delete tasks that keep the data relevant. Often, the first two tasks are combined into Create, Retrieve, Update, and Delete (CRUD) processes. Manipulating the data means taking raw data and filtering, organizing, or modifying it in some fashion to produce a final result. This part of the book discusses all three of these tasks, but focuses on manipulation.

There are two places to manipulate the data: the client and the server. Chapter 6, "Manipulating data using LINQ," and Chapter 7, "Manipulating data using Entity SQL," discuss methods for manipulating data at the client using Language Integrated Query (LINQ). Of the two, LINQ tends to be easier to understand and work with, while Entity SQL provides greater flexibility and control.

Chapters 8, "Interaction with stored procedures," Chapter 9, "Interaction with views," and Chapter 10, "Interaction with table-valued functions," focus on manipulating data at the server. The most common method for manipulating data is using stored procedures, which is the topic of Chapter 8. However, stored procedures are considered unsafe for certain types of tasks, so Chapter 9 shows how to work with a safer technique: using views. Chapter 10 discusses an entirely new technique for Entity Framework version 5: using Table-Valued Functions (TVFs). Taken together, these three techniques provide a complete server-based solution for manipulating data before presenting it to the end user.

CHAPTER 6

Manipulating data using LINQ

After completing the chapter, you'll be able to

- Describe the basics of LINQ to Entities functionality.
- Specify how LINQ statements are compiled.
- List and use the essential LINQ to Entities functions.

In most cases, developers with a strong C# background, but without an equally strong database background, use Language Integrated Query (LINQ) to query the databases they create and manage using the Entity Framework. LINQ to Entities offers a number of benefits to developers, but the main benefit is simplicity. It's possible to create relatively complex queries without knowing much about the underlying database from a DBMS perspective. Developers can also use syntax that's familiar to make the query, rather than resorting to working with SQL. In addition, the compiler performs part of the work of interacting with the database for the developer, so that the developer can focus on the dataset and not on the language used to access it. In short, the developer gains a considerable efficiency advantage using LINQ to Entities.

This chapter begins by introducing you to LINQ to Entities. You need to know something about how LINQ to Entities works, and you also need to know the syntax so that you can make queries. The chapter won't provide an extensive reference, but you'll have enough information to perform common tasks and a few advanced tasks. The point is that you'll have the information required to get started using LINQ to Entities to perform useful work. The material provided will help you understand the examples better.

Tip There are actually two syntaxes you can use to formulate a LINQ query: query and method based. The *query* expression syntax tends to be easier to understand and clearer, so that's the form used in this book whenever possible. The *method-based* expression syntax is more flexible, and you can perform a few tasks using it that you can't with the query expression syntax, so the book will use this form when necessary to perform complex tasks. Presenting the examples this way will help you better understand when you need to use one syntax over the other. You can also read a comparison of the two syntaxes at *http://msdn.microsoft.com/library/bb397947.aspx.*

As with any LINQ query, LINQ to Entities queries are compiled to determine what they actually mean. The compiler takes the query you create and turns it into something that .NET understands. The next section of this chapter discusses how this process occurs and how it affects the way you use LINQ to Entities. This part of the chapter also provides a few insights into when you need to use the method-based expression syntax to obtain the output you desire.

The final part of the chapter discusses how to use LINQ to Entities with both entity and database functions, which, after all, is the entire point of working with LINQ to Entities in the first place. This section provides you with examples you can use to better understand how LINQ to Entities works. In addition, this material sets the stage for future examples in the book. When you finish this section, you'll have the knowledge needed to move on to the more advanced examples in the book.

Note LINQ to Entities is just one form of a more complex product that appears under the LINQ umbrella. There are, in fact, many different forms of LINQ you can use. However, once you know how to use one form of LINQ, you essentially know how to use them all. That's one of the beauties of a declarative language—you focus on what you need, rather than how to obtain it. You can find a general overview of LINQ as a product at *http://msdn.microsoft.com/library/bb308959.aspx.*

Introducing LINQ to Entities

One of the most important concepts to understand about LINQ to Entities is that it's a declarative language. The focus is on defining what information you need, rather than on how to obtain the information. This means that you can spend more time working with data and less time trying to figure out the underlying code required to perform tasks such as accessing the database. It's important to understand that declarative languages don't actually remove any control from the developer; rather, they help the developer focus attention on what's important.

The sections that follow provide you with a basic overview of LINQ to Entities. You learn about how the LINQ to Entities provider, *EntityClient*, works, discover how to create a basic query, and then move on to some reference information you need later to work with LINQ to Entities in examples. These sections will continue to be useful as a reference as you progress through the book, so keep them in mind as you move on to other topics later.

Considering the LINQ to Entities provider

When working with LINQ to Entities, you rely on a new provider named *EntityClient*. LINQ to Entities transforms your query into *EntityClient* objects and method calls. The *EntityClient* provider then creates an interface between the LINQ to Entities queries and the underlying Microsoft ADO.NET providers through the various layers of the Entity Framework. The *EntityClient* interacts directly with the conceptual model, as shown in the following graphic.

Warning A number of drawings and discussions available online don't mention the need for a database-specific provider. If you're using a DBMS other than Microsoft SQL Server or one of the compatible DBMSs described in Chapter 1, "Getting to know the Entity Framework," then you'll find that your queries won't work. You still depend on ADO.NET to complete tasks.

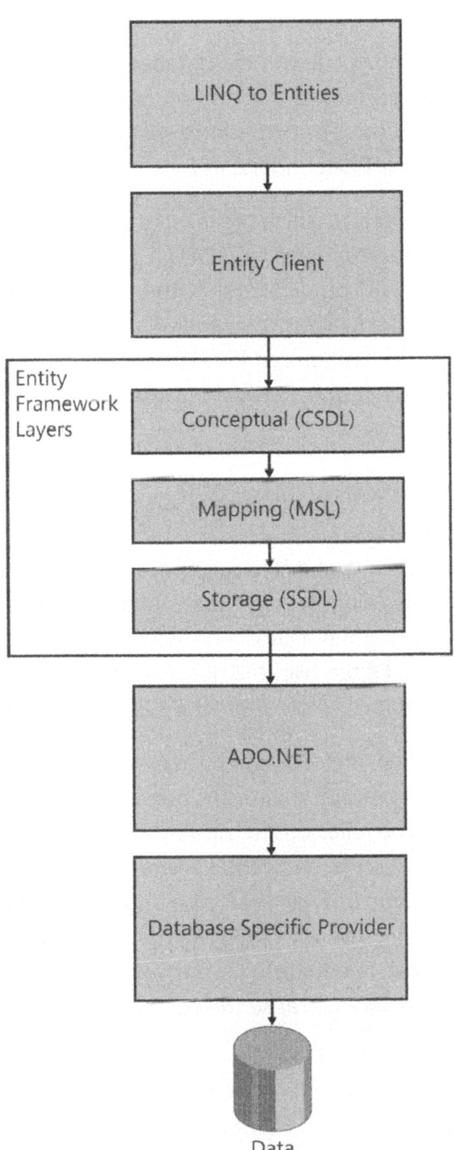

You don't create an *EntityClient* directly. Instead, you indirectly work with the members of the *System.Data.EntityClient* namespace (see *http://msdn.microsoft.com/library/system.data.entityclient.aspx* for details). In order to start a session with a database, the application creates a connection to it with the *EntityConnection* object. It then transmits queries and other requests using an *EntityCommand* and reads the results using an *EntityDataReader*. When you work with LINQ to Entities, the compiler generates the necessary code for you—the focus for you as a developer is the query declaration, rather than the actual code used to make the calls. However, it's important to know what happens in the background.

The standard ADO.NET providers are still used to communicate with the database. However, you don't need to worry about writing all of the code used to perform this communication; *EntityClient* performs this task for you. A simple way to look at *EntityClient* is as a translator that takes your declarative language query and puts it into terms that ADO.NET can understand.

The LINQ to Entities provider interacts with ADO.NET directly, which means that you don't need any other provider to use LINQ to Entities with other databases. However, ADO.NET uses database-specific providers. Microsoft Visual Studio ships with ADO.NET providers for both SQL Server and SQL Server Compact. Of course, there are other databases on the market. You can find a number of ADO.NET providers for other databases at *http://msdn.microsoft.com/data/dd363565.aspx*. If you don't find a suitable provider on MSDN, try other sites, such as Devart (*http://www.devart.com/linqconnect/*) and SQLite (*http://www.sqlite.org/*).

Developing LINQ to Entities queries

There are a number of ways to formulate LINQ queries. The use of different approaches provides developers with flexibility and enables a developer to code using the style that the developer is used to. The first division in LINQ queries is the syntax. A developer has a choice between using the query expression syntax or the method-based expression syntax. Of the two, the query expression syntax is the easiest to understand, while the method-based expression syntax offers the greatest flexibility.

It's also possible to specify precise output type or to allow the compiler to derive the output type based on the query you create (an implicit type). A *precise* output type means providing a specific type, such as *IQueryable<Customers>*. A *derived* output type relies on the *var* keyword (see *http://msdn.microsoft.com/library/bb383973.aspx* for a detailed description of this keyword). The compiler determines the variable type for you. The precise output type provides you with additional control over how the query is made and the results it provides. Using the *var* keyword is necessary at times because you may not be able to determine the precise type. In addition, the *var* keyword makes it more likely that the query will succeed and provide usable data, because the compiler determines the correct type for you.

The query itself requires the use of keywords or methods that reflect those keywords. When using the query expression syntax, a query will use the *select*, *in*, and *from* keywords as a minimum. The best way to see how this works is through an example. The following procedure relies on the *ModelFirst* example you created in the "Creating a model-first example" section of Chapter 3, "Choosing a workflow." (You can find this example in the \Microsoft Press\Entity Framework Development Step by Step\Chapter 06\ModelFirst (LINQ Query) folder of the downloadable source code.)

Creating a LINQ to Entities query

1. Copy the *ModelFirst* example you created in Chapter 3 to a new folder and use this new copy for this example (rather than the copy you created in Chapter 3).
2. Add a new button to *Form1*. Name the button *btnQuery* and set its *Text* property to *&Query*.
3. Double-click *btnQuery* to create a new click event handler.
4. Type the following code for the *btnQuery_Click()* event handler:

```
private void btnQuery_Click(object sender, EventArgs e)
{
    // Create the context.
    Rewards2ModelContainer context = new Rewards2ModelContainer();

    // Obtain the customer list.
    var CustomerList =
        from cust in context.Customers
        select cust;

    // Process each customer in the list.
    StringBuilder Output =
        new StringBuilder("Customer List:");
    foreach (var Customer in CustomerList)
    {
        // Create a customer entry for each customer.
        Output.Append("\r\n" + Customer.CustomerName +
            " has made purchases on: ");

        // Process each purchase for that particular customer.
        foreach (var Purchase in Customer.Purchases)
            Output.Append("\r\n\t" + Purchase.PurchaseDate);
    }

    // Display the result on screen.
    MessageBox.Show(Output.ToString());
}
```

The example begins by creating a context. It's important to remember that you still need to create this connection to the Entity Framework layers in order to access the database. The LINQ query will be translated by the *EntityClient* into a series of commands that will interact with the context to perform the tasks you specify.

The LINQ query comes next. Notice that the example is using the *var* keyword rather than a specific type. The example asks for the list of customers from the context and places each customer in *cust*. It then selects *cust* and places this value in *CustomerList*. Hover the mouse over *CustomerList* in the *foreach* loop that follows, and you'll see that Visual Studio really does assign it a type of *IQueryable<Customers>*, as shown here:

```
// Process each customer in the list.
StringBuilder Output =
    new StringBuilder("Customer List:");
foreach (var Customer in CustomerList)
{                                (local variable) IQueryable<Customers> CustomerList
    // Create a customer
    Output.Append("\r\n" + Customer.CustomerName +
        " has made purchases on: ");
```

Let's say that you decide you want to use *IEnumerable* instead of *IQueryable* (see the "Determining when to use *IEnumerable* in place of *IQueryable*" sidebar for details). In order to use *IEnumerable*, you'd need to rewrite the query like this:

```
// Obtain the customer list.
IEnumerable<Customers> CustomerList =
    from cust in context.Customers
    select cust;
```

This is a master/detail database setup, so the example creates two *foreach* loops to process the data. The first *foreach* loop obtains one Customer from *CustomerList* and processes the customers one at a time. The second *foreach* loop obtains one Purchase from *Customer.Purchases* and processes each purchase for that customer one at a time. The result is an output string that is displayed in a message box.

5. Click Start or press F5. The application compiles and runs.

6. Click Query. You'll see the result shown here (assuming that you ran the example from Chapter 3 and didn't modify the code from that example):

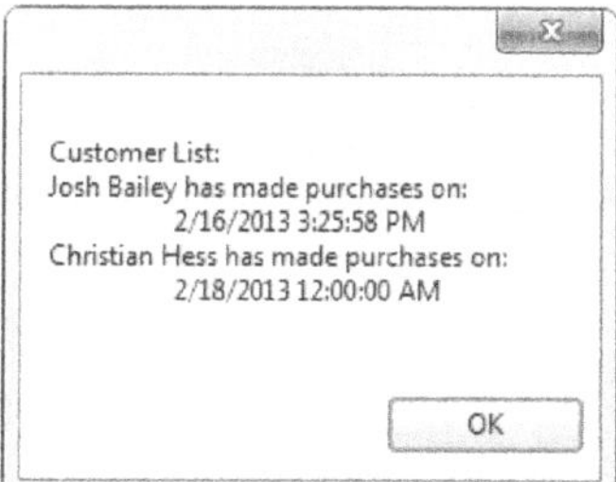
Customer List:
Josh Bailey has made purchases on:
2/16/2013 3:25:58 PM
Christian Hess has made purchases on:
2/18/2013 12:00:00 AM
OK

Note Most of the information you see in the dialog boxes in this chapter will match those on your system. However, you'll encounter a few differences, such as dates. In addition, the application dialog boxes may not match precisely. These small differences won't make any difference in the performance of the example applications.

Determining when to use *IEnumerable* in place of *IQueryable*

When working with LINQ to Entities, some developers assume that you should always use *IQueryable* because it derives from *IEnumerable* and therefore must be superior. Actually, the two interfaces have specific purposes and you should employ the one that works best for your particular need. There are quite a few differences between the two, but here are some general rules of thumb you can follow:

- ***IEnumerable*** Provides a forward-only in-memory presentation of data. Because the query is executed immediately and completely, your application will see a performance boost during the enumeration process when the user is most apt to see the difference. Working with *IEnumerable* means that your application uses *Func* objects that result in the query being executed immediately. You can read more about *Func* objects at *http://msdn.microsoft.com/library/bb534960.aspx*.
- ***IQueryable*** Provides remote access to a database or a web service and allows both forward and reverse iteration. Use this form to enhance the flexibility of your application and its ability to work with remote sources, especially web services. Working with *IQueryable* means that your application uses *Expression* objects that result in the query being executed only when the application requests an enumeration. Because the query is delayed, an *IQueryable* object can perform certain optimizations when using a where or other clause that would throw out some of the results that would normally be processed by an *IEnumerable* object. The tradeoff is that you save memory and some network bandwidth in exchange for longer enumeration times. You can read more about *Expression* objects at *http://msdn.microsoft.com/library/system.linq.expressions.aspx*.

Using the correct object type for the situation can improve the efficiency of your application. It's important to consider how your application works when making the choice. When in doubt, *IQueryable* is the preferred choice because it does offer greater flexibility, and the performance benefits of *IEnumerable* could be outweighed by the amount of data retrieved over high-cost network *connections*. When creating a query that includes a *where* clause, the costs of using *IEnumerable* quickly make *IQueryable* the better choice. *IEnumerable* is almost always a better choice when making a straightforward query, like the one in the example, because the example uses all of the results anyway.

Defining the LINQ to Entities essential keywords

It's important to know the basic keywords used to create a LINQ query. Interestingly enough, there are only a few keywords to remember, but you can combine them in various ways to obtain specific results. The following list contains these basic keywords and provides a simple description of each one (future examples will expand on these definitions for you):

- ***ascending*** Specifies that a sorting operation takes place from the least (or lowest) element of a range to the highest element of a range. This is normally the default setting. For example, when performing an alphabetic sort, the sort would be in the range from *A* to *Z*.
- ***by*** Specifies the field or expression used to implement a grouping. The field or expression defines a key used to perform the grouping task.
- ***descending*** Specifies that a sorting operation takes place from the greatest (or highest) element of a range to the lowest element of a range. For example, when performing an alphabetic sort, the sort would be in the range from *Z* to *A*.
- ***equals*** Used between the left and right clauses of a *join* statement to join the primary contextual data source to the secondary contextual data source. The field or expression on the left of the *equals* keyword specifies the primary data source, while the field or expression on the right of the *equals* keyword specifies the secondary data source.
- ***from* (required)** Specifies the data source used to obtain the required information and defines a range variable. This variable has the same purpose as a variable used for iteration in a loop.
- ***group*** Organizes the output into groups using the key value you specify. Use multiple group clauses to create multiple levels of output organization. The order of the *group* clauses determines the depth at which a particular key value appears in the grouping order. You combine this keyword with *by* to create a specific context.
- ***in* (required)** Used in a number of ways. In this case, the keyword determines the contextual database source used for a query. When working with a join, the in keyword is used for each contextual database source used for the *join*.
- ***into*** Specifies an identifier that you can use as a reference for LINQ query clauses such as *join*, *group*, and *select*.

Warning A common error that some developers make is to confuse the *into* keyword with the *in* keyword. The *into* keyword serves an entirely different purpose, and using it in place of the *in* keyword will cause an error.

- ***join*** Creates a single data source from two related data sources, such as in a master/detail setup. A join can specify an inner, group, or left-outer join, with the inner join as the default. You can read more about joins at *http://msdn.microsoft.com/library/bb311040.aspx*.
- ***let*** Defines a range variable that you can use to store subexpression results in a query expression. Typically, the range variable is used to provide an additional enumerated output or to increase the efficiency of a query (so that a particular task, such as finding the lowercase value of a string, need not be done more than one time).

- ***on*** Specifies the field or expression used to implement a join. The field or expression defines an element that is common to both contextual data sources.
- ***orderby*** Creates a sort order for the query. You can add the *ascending* or *descending* keyword to control the order of the sort. Use multiple *orderby* clauses to create multiple levels of sorting. The order of the *orderby* clauses determines the order in which the sort expressions are handled, so using a different order will result in different output.
- ***where*** Defines what LINQ should retrieve from the data source. You use one or more Boolean expressions to define the specifics of what to retrieve. The Boolean expressions are separated from each other using the *&&* (AND) and || (OR) operators.
- ***select* (required)** Determines the output from the LINQ query by specifying what information to return. This statement defines the data type of the elements that LINQ returns during the iteration process.

Defining the LINQ to Entities operators

The keywords described in the "Defining the LINQ to Entities essential keywords" section of the chapter determine what happens when a query is made using the query expression syntax. Operators determine how the query is made when using the method-based expression syntax. You use operators to modify the output in the following ways:

- **Sort** Modify the natural order of the data returned from the data source. For example, you could create a sorted order of customers based on their last name, even if the database keeps the customer list in a random order.
- **Group** Create an order that is depending on a specific field or expression. For example, you could group a list of customers by the first letter of their last name.
- **Shape** Modify the natural appearance of the data to obtain specific results. For example, you could filter the data so that the output only contains customers whose last name begins with a *G*, or you could determine the average value of the data using aggregation.

The following sections describe a number of common tasks you can perform using LINQ to Entities operators. These are basic operations. Remember that you can combine operators to create almost any data manipulation scenario. Using LINQ to Entities operators makes it possible for you to declare what you want as output, rather than determine how to obtain it. The compiler determines how a particular task is done.

Note LINQ to Entities supports most, but not all, of the standard LINQ methods. For example, you can use a *Select* method with this signature:

```
IQueryable<TResult> Select<TSource, TResult>(
this IQueryable<TSource> source,
Expression<Func<TSource, TResult>> selector
)
```

But you can't use a *Select* method with this signature:

```
IQueryable<TResult> Select<TSource, TResult>(
this IQueryable<TSource> source,
Expression<Func<TSource, int, TResult>> selector
)
```

The difference is subtle. Notice that the second signature includes an *int* as part of the *Func* declaration, which means you can't use the index of the element, as described at *http://msdn.microsoft.com/library/system.linq.enumerable.select.aspx*. You can see a complete list of the supported and unsupported methods at *http://msdn.microsoft.com/library/bb738550.aspx*.

Performing filtering and projection

The main task of any LINQ to Entities expression is to obtain data and provide it as output. The "Developing LINQ to Entities queries" section of this chapter demonstrates the techniques for performing this basic task. However, once you have the data, you may want to project or filter it as needed to shape the data prior to output.

Projection is the act of modifying the output to shape it in a specific way. For example, you can change the case of the characters in a string or perform a calculation on numeric output. It's also possible to use methods to transform the data in a variety of ways that are only limited by your imagination and the requirements of your application. The methods associated with projection are *Select()* and *SelectMany()*.

Filtering is the act of removing undesirable elements from the output. You may only want the names of customers who have achieved a certain number of sales or who live in a particular area. Use the *Where()* method to achieve the desired level of filtering.

Note LINQ to Entities supports all of the common LINQ methods associated with filtering and projection, except for those that require a positional (indexing) argument.

Performing joins

Look again at the example in the "Developing LINQ to Entities queries" section of this chapter. Notice that the example is able to obtain the list of purchases associated with a particular customer because there is a navigable property that is defined as part of the model. It's important to keep this bit of information in mind, especially when you normally work with SQL Server directly by making SQL statements. The join defined by LINQ to Entities is for related tables that have no navigable properties in the model. The result is the same as a standard join, but the purpose of the join is different. Use navigable properties whenever possible to work with related tables.

When performing a join to group like tables together, you use the *Join()* or *GroupJoin()* method. The tables must still possess a common attribute or property that you can exploit to create the relationship. For example, let's say that your in-house database has a table containing a list of products that employ a bar code for identification. However, the description of the product resides on a web service hosted by the supplier. You can use a join on the bar code to obtain a description for the product in your in-house database from the supplier's web service. Because you don't support or own the supplier's database, the database won't appear as part of your model, and you won't have any navigable properties to access it.

Note The LINQ to Entities *Join()* and *GroupJoin()* methods provide full support for all of the standard LINQ overrides, except those that require use of the *IEqualityComparer* interface. This is because LINQ to Entities can't translate the comparer to the source database. You can read more about *IEqualityComparer* at *http://msdn.microsoft.com/library/ms132151.aspx.*

Creating a set

Shaping a result set means defining the set according to specific properties. For example, you might only want the distinct elements from the result set of a query. Even though a particular row in a table is distinct, the result set may not contain the entire row, resulting in duplicates in the output, so you need a way to shape the output so the user only sees unique entries. The methods for creating sets are *All()*, *Any()*, *Concat()*, *Contains()*, *DefaultIfEmpty()*, *Distinct()*, *EqualAll()*, *Except()*, *Intersect()*, and *Union()*.

Note The LINQ to Entities set-related methods provide full support for all of the standard LINQ overrides, except those that require use of the *IEqualityComparer* interface. This is because LINQ to Entities can't translate the comparer to the source database. You can read more about *IEqualityComparer* at *http://msdn.microsoft.com/library/ms132151.aspx.*

Ordering the output

Sorting a result set modifies the order in which the individual records appear so that the user can more easily detect patterns in the output, find a specific output, and look for errors, such as misspellings and duplicate entries. You can combine ordering methods to create a unique output. However, it's an error to provide the same ordering methods more than one time on a result set, and you'll see an exception if you try to do so. The ordering methods are *OrderBy()*, *OrderByDescending()*, *ThenBy()*, *ThenByDescending()*, and *Reverse()*.

When ordering a result set, it's important to realize that LINQ to Entities works against the data source, rather than using an in-memory representation, as would be done when working with the Common Language Runtime (CLR) objects. The data source may have special sort functionality implemented, such as case ordering, kanji ordering, and null ordering. The difference in sort functionality will affect the output you see.

Note The LINQ to Entities ordering-related methods provide full support for all of the standard LINQ overrides, except those that require use of the *IComparer* interface. This is because LINQ to Entities can't translate the comparer to the source database. You can read more about *IComparer* at *http://msdn.microsoft.com/library/8ehhxeaf.aspx*.

Grouping the output

Sorting a result by grouping like items together using a common attribute (such as all customers who live in a particular city) helps users see patterns in the output. When grouping like items together, you use the *GroupBy()* method. It's possible to create multiple levels of grouping by combining multiple *GroupBy()* method calls. Unlike sorting methods, you can create multiple levels of the same *GroupBy()* method calls because each *GroupBy()* method call creates a new level in the output.

When grouping a result set, it's important to realize that LINQ to Entities works against the data source, rather than using an in-memory representation, as would be done when working with the CLR objects. The data source may contain null values that will affect the output in ways that you don't see when performing the same task using CLR objects.

Note The LINQ to Entities *GroupBy()* method provides full support for all of the standard LINQ overrides, except those that require use of the *IEqualityComparer* interface. This is because LINQ to Entities can't translate the comparer to the source database. You can read more about *IEqualityComparer* at *http://msdn.microsoft.com/library/ms132151.aspx*.

Performing aggregation

Shaping the result set by combining or aggregating it in certain ways can help a user see the information in a new way. For example, you might obtain the average of a numeric field so that the user knows when a particular entry is either higher or lower than average. The methods you use to aggregate data are *Aggregate()*, *Average()*, *Count()*, *LongCount()*, *Max()*, *Min()*, and *Sum()*.

There are some significant differences in the way that aggregation occurs when using LINQ to Entities, as contrasted to using the CLR. The most important difference is that the calculations occur on the server, so any loss of precision or type conversions will occur on the server as well. When an error occurs, such as an overflow, the exception is raised as a data source or Entity Framework exception, rather than a standard CLR exception. The errors are only raised when they conflict with the data source assumptions about the data. For example, when working with null values, a CLR calculation will raise an error, but SQL Server won't. Table 6-1 describes how SQL Server handles nulls so that you know what to expect as output.

TABLE 6-1 Techniques SQL Server uses to handle nulls

Method	No data	All nulls	Some nulls	No nulls
Average	Returns null	Returns null	Returns the average of the non-null values in the sequence	Returns the average of all of the values in the sequence
Count	Returns 0	Returns the number of null values in the sequence	Returns the combined number of null and non-null values in the sequence	Returns the total number of values in the sequence
Max	Returns null	Returns null	Returns the maximum of the non-null values in the sequence	Returns the maximum of all of the values in the sequence
Min	Returns null	Returns null	Returns the minimum of the non-null values in the sequence	Returns the minimum of all of the values in the sequence
Sum	Returns null	Returns null	Returns the sum of the non-null values in the sequence	Returns the sum of all of the values in the sequence

Interacting with type

Shaping data by converting its type from one form to another lets you perform additional tasks, such as creating specific output views. For example, it's common to convert data to a string type so that it's possible to use the string methods to manipulate the appearance of the data in certain ways, such as to make the data more aesthetically pleasing to the viewer.

The only types that you can convert or test are those that map to an Entity Framework type. This functionality works at the conceptual level, rather than at the data source, as does some of the other functionality discussed so far. The two common methods for converting and testing data are *Convert()* (primitive types) and *OfType()* (entity types). When working with C#, you can also use the *is()* and *as()* methods.

Tip You can find information about primitive type mapping at *http://msdn.microsoft.com/library/ee382832.aspx*. Entity type mapping information appears at *http://msdn.microsoft.com/library/ee382837.aspx*. Even though the documentation doesn't specifically mention it, you can also use the *OfType()* method with complex types, which are described at *http://msdn.microsoft.com/library/ee382831.aspx*. When working with a DBMS other than SQL Server, you need to find the mapping for that DBMS. For example, the documentation for MySQL appears at *http://www.devart.com/dotconnect/mysql/docs/DataTypeMapping.html*.

Paging the output

Paging methods sort the data by interacting with the rows out of order or shape the data by removing some rows entirely. The output you receive depends on the way in which you use the paging methods in your code. The paging methods are *ElementAt()*, *First()*, *FirstOrDefault()*, *Last()*, *LastOrDefault()*, *Single()*, *Skip()*, *Take()*, and *TakeWhile()*. If you try to use a paging method on a sequence that doesn't contain any entries or contains all null values, the result is null.

> **Note** Not all overrides of all of the paging methods are supported, because there isn't any way to map them to a function at the data source. The functionality you receive from the paging methods depends on the capabilities of the DBMS you work with. Some DBMSs will return a default value for some methods, and this value is always converted to an Entity Framework primitive type result or a reference type with a null default. Unless your ADO.NET provider fully documents the Entity Framework paging method functionality supported, you'll need to test this functionality as part of your application (realizing that it may not work at all).

Summarizing the LINQ operators

LINQ (and by extension LINQ to Entities) supports a number of operators that you access as methods. The following list provides a description of each of these methods; you can use it to determine which to use to perform a specific task:

- ***Aggregate()*** Applies an accumulator function over the elements of a sequence. For example, you might choose to concatenate the individual strings of a series of records together. You can read more about this method at *http://msdn.microsoft.com/library/bb548651.aspx*.
- ***All()*** Determines whether all of the elements in a sequence satisfy a particular condition. You can read more about this method at *http://msdn.microsoft.com/library/bb548541.aspx*.
- ***Any()*** Determines whether a sequence contains any elements. You can read more about this method at *http://msdn.microsoft.com/library/bb337697.aspx*.
- ***Average()*** Computes the average of the elements found in a sequence. You can read more about this method at *http://msdn.microsoft.com/library/bb354760.aspx*.
- ***Concat()*** Adds (concatenates) one sequence to another, so that you end up with a single sequence. You can read more about this method at *http://msdn.microsoft.com/library/bb302894.aspx*.
- ***Contains()*** Looks for the specified element in the specified sequence using the default equality comparator. You can read more about this method at *http://msdn.microsoft.com/library/bb352880.aspx*.
- ***Convert()*** Changes the base type of an element into another base type. You can read more about this method at *http://msdn.microsoft.com/library/system.convert.aspx*.

- ***Count()*** Obtains the number of elements in a sequence. You can read more about this method at *http://msdn.microsoft.com/library/bb338038.aspx*. (See the *LongCount()* method when you want to count a large number of elements.)
- ***DefaultIfEmpty()*** Returns the sequence when there are elements to return. Otherwise, this method returns the default value for the specified sequence, which will likely be an empty or null value. You can read more about this method at *http://msdn.microsoft.com/library/bb360179.aspx*.
- ***Distinct()*** Returns only the unique elements from a sequence. When two elements have the same value, returns just one of the two elements. You can read more about this method at *http://msdn.microsoft.com/library/bb348436.aspx*.
- ***ElementAt()*** Returns the element found at the specified index. You can read more about this method at *http://msdn.microsoft.com/library/bb299233.aspx*.
- ***EqualAll()*** Determines whether two sequences are precisely equal, which means that they must have the same members appearing in the same order. This operator isn't documented as a standard LINQ operator, so Microsoft may restrict its use. You can read more about this method at *http://msdn.microsoft.com/vstudio/bb737910.aspx*.
- ***Except()*** Creates a sequence that contains the elements that don't match between two sequences. The comparison is made using the default comparer. You can read more about this method at *http://msdn.microsoft.com/library/bb300779.aspx*.
- ***First()*** Returns the first element in a sequence. You can read more about this method at *http://msdn.microsoft.com/library/bb291976.aspx*.
- ***FirstOrDefault()*** Returns the first element in a sequence or a default element when no elements exist. You can read more about this method at *http://msdn.microsoft.com/library/bb340482.aspx*.
- ***GroupBy()*** Places the elements in a sequence in groups using the specified key. You can read more about this method at *http://msdn.microsoft.com/library/bb534501.aspx*.
- ***GroupJoin()*** Combines and groups two separate sequences into a single sequence using a common attribute or property. The resulting groups are based upon the same type of expression used to group a single sequence using the *Group()* method. You can read more about this method at *http://msdn.microsoft.com/library/bb534675.aspx*.
- ***Intersect()*** Produces the set intersection of two sequences by using the default comparator. You can read more about this method at *http://msdn.microsoft.com/library/bb460136.aspx*.
- ***Join()*** Combines two separate sequences into a single sequence using a common attribute or property. You can read more about this method at *http://msdn.microsoft.com/library/bb534675.aspx*.
- ***Last()*** Returns the last element in a sequence. You can read more about this method at *http://msdn.microsoft.com/library/bb358775.aspx*.

- ***LastOrDefault()*** Returns the last element in a sequence or a default element when no elements exist. You can read more about this method at *http://msdn.microsoft.com/library/bb301849.aspx.*
- ***LongCount()*** Obtains the number of elements in a sequence and returns that value as a 64-bit number. You use this version of *Count()* when the number of elements is high and you want to avoid a potential overflow condition. You can read more about this method at *http://msdn.microsoft.com/library/bb353539.aspx.*
- ***Max()*** Determines which element contains the maximum value in a sequence. You can read more about this method at *http://msdn.microsoft.com/library/bb335614.aspx.*
- ***Min()*** Determines which element contains the minimum value in a sequence. You can read more about this method at *http://msdn.microsoft.com/library/bb298087.aspx.*
- ***OfType()*** Determines whether an element is of a specific type. You can read more about this method at *http://msdn.microsoft.com/library/bb360913.aspx.*
- ***OrderBy()*** Sorts the elements of a sequence in ascending order using the specified key. You can read more about this method at *http://msdn.microsoft.com/library/bb534966.aspx.*
- ***OrderByDescending()*** Sorts the elements of a sequence in descending order using the specified key. You can read more about this method at *http://msdn.microsoft.com/library/bb534855.aspx.*
- ***Reverse()*** Inverts the order of the elements in a sequence. The elements aren't sorted—merely reversed in order. You can read more about this method at *http://msdn.microsoft.com/library/bb358497.aspx.*
- ***Select()*** Chooses each element of a sequence and optionally modifies its form. You can read more about this method at *http://msdn.microsoft.com/library/bb548891.aspx.*
- ***SelectMany()*** Chooses each element of a sequence, places it in an *IEnumerable* object, and flattens the entire sequence into a single sequence. You can read more about this method at *http://msdn.microsoft.com/library/bb534336.aspx.*
- ***Single()*** Returns the only element in a sequence that satisfies the specified condition and throws an exception if more than one element that satisfies the condition exists. You can read more about this method at *http://msdn.microsoft.com/library/bb155325.aspx.*
- ***Skip()*** Bypasses (skips) the specified number of elements in a sequence and then returns the elements that remain. You can read more about this method at *http://msdn.microsoft.com/library/bb358985.aspx.*
- ***Sum()*** Adds (sums) the individual values of each element in a sequence to create a total. You can read more about this method at *http://msdn.microsoft.com/library/bb298138.aspx.*
- ***Take()*** Returns the specified number of elements in a sequence and then skips (bypasses) the elements that remain. You can read more about this method at *http://msdn.microsoft.com/library/bb503062.aspx.*

- ***TakeWhile()*** Returns the specified number of elements in a sequence while the specified condition remains true, and then skips (bypasses) the elements that remain. You can read more about this method at *http://msdn.microsoft.com/library/bb534804.aspx*.
- ***ThenBy()*** Performs a subsequent sorting of elements in a sequence in ascending order using the specified key. You must precede this method call with either the *OrderBy()* or *OrderByDecending()* method call. You can read more about this method at *http://msdn.microsoft.com/library/bb534743.aspx*.
- ***ThenByDescending()*** Performs a subsequent sorting of elements in a sequence in descending order using the specified key. You must precede this method call with either the *OrderBy()* or *OrderByDecending()* method call. You can read more about this method at *http://msdn.microsoft.com/library/bb534736.aspx*.
- ***Union()*** Produces the set union of two sequences by using the default comparator. You can read more about this method at *http://msdn.microsoft.com/library/bb341731.aspx*.
- ***Where()*** Filters a sequence based on the criterion you provide in the form of an expression. You can read more about this method at *http://msdn.microsoft.com/library/bb534803.aspx*.

Understanding LINQ compilation

LINQ to Entities compiles the queries you create into something that the *EntityClient* can understand. You've seen one example of this compilation in the "Developing LINQ to Entities queries" section of the chapter in the form of bubble help. You were able to hover the mouse over the *CustomerList* object and see its type.

The following sections look at compilation in another way. These procedures take you through the process of using a query with the debugger. It's interesting to see how the debugger handles the query based on the way you create it. In fact, using the debugger as shown in the following procedures will help you gain a much better understanding of the Entity Framework as a whole because you can trace through the tasks it performs in the background for you.

Following an *IQueryable* sequence

The example shown in the "Developing LINQ to Entities queries" section of the chapter uses the *var* keyword to create the *CustomerList* object. The *var* keyword is also used to create *Customer* and *Purchase*. When using the *var* keyword, you allow the compiler to automatically determine which type to use to satisfy a particular need. However, it's nice to see this process in action.

Simply running the example leaves some questions unanswered. For example, you may wonder how and when *Customer* and *Purchase* are created. Working through the example with the debugger helps you answer these kinds of questions.

Tracing through an *IQueryable* example

1. Open the *ModelFirst* example that you worked with in the "Developing LINQ to Entities queries" section of the chapter.

2. Place a breakpoint at the *foreach* line so that it looks like this:

```
// Process each customer in the list.
StringBuilder Output =
    new StringBuilder("Customer List:");
foreach (var Customer in CustomerList)
{
    // Create a customer entry for each customer.
    Output.Append("\r\n" + Customer.CustomerName +
        " has made purchases on: ");
```

3. Click Start or press F5. The application compiles and runs.

4. Click Query. The debugger stops the application at the *foreach* line. There are some interesting things to see at this point.

5. Choose Debug | Windows | Autos. You'll see the Autos window shown here:

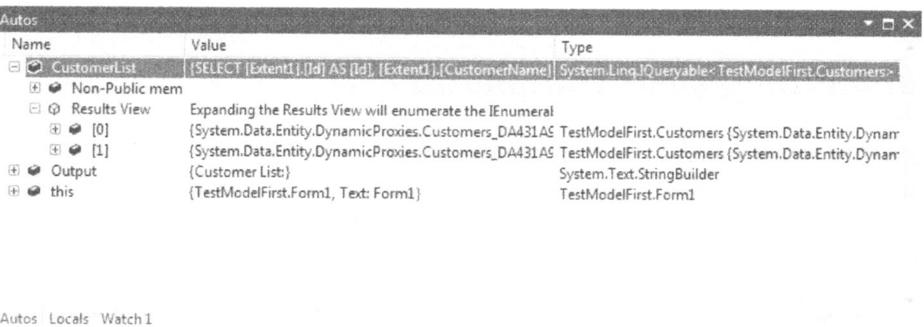

Notice that even though *CustomerList* uses *var* as its type, the actual type is *IQueryable*. The value of *CustomerList* is a form of the query you used.

When you open the Results View, you see that there are two members of type *System.Data.Entity.DynamicProxies*. When working with the Entity Framework, it actually creates a dynamically generated derived type that acts as a proxy for the entity. You can read about these proxies at *http://msdn.microsoft.com/data/jj592886.aspx*. For now, it's important to realize that the *TestModelFirst.Customers* objects don't actually exist.

6. Expanding the Results View has automatically created the customers for you, so click Stop.

7. Perform steps 3 and 4 again to restart the debugger.

8. Click Step Into or press F11 three times. Visual Studio opens a new file, *Customers.cs*, and places the instruction pointer on the constructor for the *Customers* class, as shown here:

Form1.cs   Form1.cs [Design]   Customers.cs

TestModelFirst.Customers   Customers()

```
//------------------------------------------------------------------------------
// <auto-generated>
//     This code was generated from a template.
//
//     Manual changes to this file may cause unexpected behavior in your application.
//     Manual changes to this file will be overwritten if the code is regenerated.
// </auto-generated>
//------------------------------------------------------------------------------

namespace TestModelFirst
{
    using System;
    using System.Collections.Generic;

    public partial class Customers
    {
        public Customers()
        {
            this.Purchases = new HashSet<Purchases>();
        }

        public int Id { get; set; }
        public string CustomerName { get; set; }

        public virtual ICollection<Purchases> Purchases { get; set; }
    }
}
```

100 %

Here, the application is actually creating a *Customers* object. This object includes *Purchases*, as shown.

9. Click Step Into or press F11 four times. The debugger takes you back to the original file and highlights the *in* part of the *foreach* loop, where it verifies that there is another item to process.

10. Click Step Into or press F11. The debugger highlights the *var Customer* part of the *foreach* loop. Choose Debug | Windows | Locals. You'll see the Locals window, as shown here:

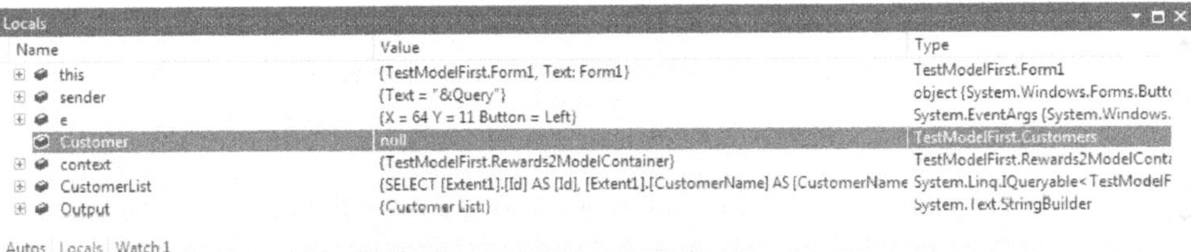

Notice that *Customer* is still null. However, the data type shows that *var Customer* creates a *TestModelFirst*.Customers type. The compiler has automatically chosen the correct type for the variable.

11. Click Step Into or press F11. The value of *Customer* changes to a *System.Data.Entity.DynamicProxies* entry. The type is correct for the kind of information presented, and you see the individual values for *Customer* when you click the plus sign next to it.

12. Click Step Into or press F11 six times. The instruction pointer will end up at the *Output.Append()* line. Notice that the application doesn't create the *Purchase* object as it did the *Customer* object. That's because the *Purchase* object already exists as part of the *Customer* object.

13. Click Step Into or press F11 enough times to take the instruction pointer back to the *in* part of the *foreach* loop. When you click Step Into or press F11 one more time, the debugger reopens *Customers.cs*, and you start the process of creating a *Customers* object again, as described in step 9. You can follow this process at least twice if you created the records described in previous chapters.

14. Click Stop to end the debugging session. At this point, you know that working with the Entity Framework with *IQueryable* means creating objects on demand.

Following a *List* sequence

Working with *IQueryable* produces one result. However, converting the query to a *List* and then processing that *List* produces another. It's interesting to modify the code slightly to see what happens when you use a List to interact with a LINQ to Entities query. The following procedure does just that.

Tracing through a *List* example

1. Modify the query in the *ModelFirst* example so that it looks like this:

```
// Obtain the customer list in list form.
List<Customers> CustomerList =
    (from cust in context.Customers
     select cust).ToList<Customers>();
```

   The result of the query is the same. The only difference is that the output is converted to a *List*.

2. Click Start or press F5. The application compiles and runs.

3. Click Query. The debugger stops the application at the *foreach* line.

4. Click Step Into or press F11 four times. You end up at the opening curly brace for the *foreach* loop. Notice that the debugger didn't open Customers.cs or interact with the constructor in that file. That's because the act of converting the query output to a *List* automatically retrieves the data from the database.

5. Choose Debug | Windows | Locals. You'll see the Locals window shown here:

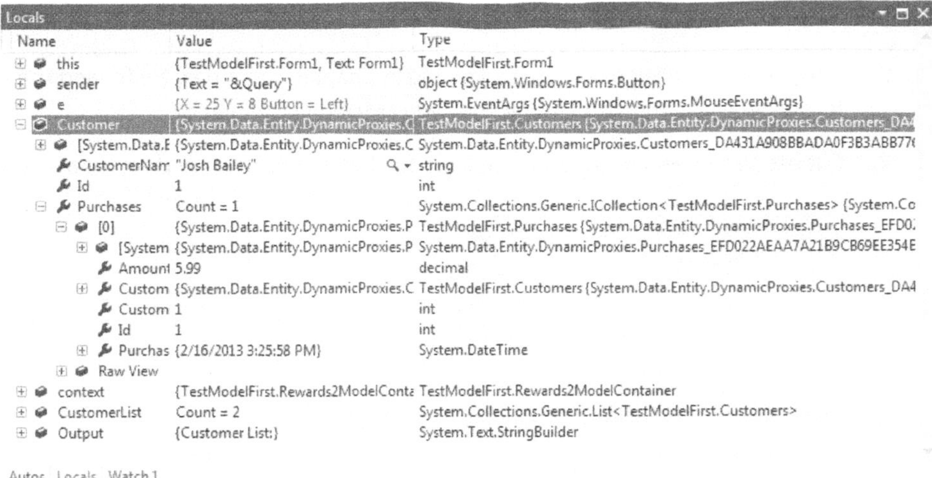

Notice that, even though the *CustomerList* type is not *System.Collections.Generic.List<TestModelFirst.Customers>*, the *Customer* object hasn't changed from before. It's still of type *TestModelFirst.Customers* and contains a *System.Data.Enty.DynamicProxies* value. The only change that using a *List* creates is the fact that the data entries are retrieved immediately, rather than as needed. That said, using a *List* could save time when working with larger datasets. You could always create a thread for the data retrieval process so the user can continue working in the foreground.

6. Click Stop to stop the debugger.

Using entity and database functions

Functions are an important part of modern database applications. You use them to perform a variety of tasks, such as finding the average value of a customer's purchases. Creating and using functions need not be a grueling task. The following sections describe how to create and use functions with the Entity Framework. You can find this example in the \Microsoft Press\Entity Framework Development Step by Step\Chapter 06\ModelFirst (Function) folder of the downloadable source code.

Creating the function

Before you can use a function, you must create it. The following procedure demonstrates one technique for creating functions in SQL Server without leaving the Visual Studio IDE. The procedure relies on the *ModelFirst* example you created in the "Creating a model-first example" section of Chapter 3.

Defining a function using Visual Studio

1. Copy the *ModelFirst* example you created in Chapter 3 to a new folder and use this new copy for this example (rather than the copy you created in Chapter 3).
2. Choose View | Server Explorer. You'll see the Server Explorer window shown here:

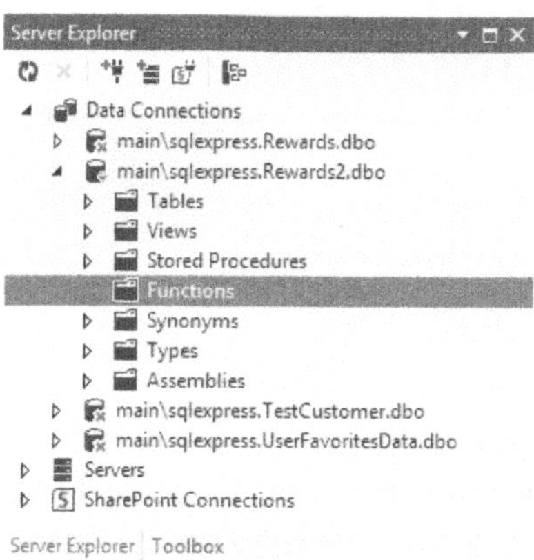

3. Open the Rewards2 connection.
4. Right-click the Functions folder and choose Add New | Table-Based Function. Visual Studio opens a new SQL file for you that contains a basic template for creating table-based functions.
5. Type the following code into the file:

```
USE [Rewards2]
GO

CREATE FUNCTION [dbo].[AveragePurchase]
(
   @CustomerId int
)
RETURNS DECIMAL(3,2)
AS
BEGIN
   DECLARE @Average DECIMAL(3,2)
   SELECT @Average = avg(Amount)
      FROM Purchases
      WHERE CustomersId = @CustomerId;
   RETURN @Average
END
```

   This function begins by selecting the appropriate database for modification. It then creates a function named *AveragePurchase*, which accepts a single input, *CustomerId*. The function creates a variable, *@Average*, of type *DECIMAL*, and uses it as part of an SQL statement that selects the average of the purchases contained in *Amount* from the *Purchases* table, where the *CustomerId* value matches the *@CustomerId* input. The result is the average purchase amount for a single customer.

6. Right-click anywhere in the code window and choose Execute from the context menu. You'll see the Connect To Server dialog box.

7. Provide the required credentials and click Connect. Visual Studio will execute the command for you. You should see "Command(s) completed successfully." on the Message tab that appears when you execute the command.

8. Right-click the Rewards2 entry in Server Explorer and choose Refresh from the context menu. You'll see the new function appear in the Functions folder, as shown here:

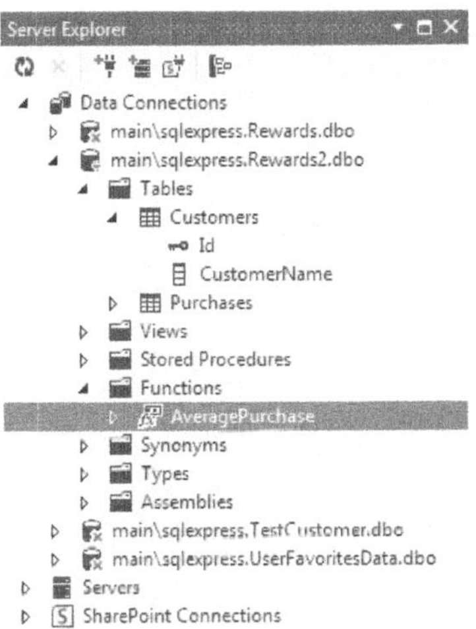

9. Right-click *AveragePurchase* and choose *Execute* from the context menu. You'll see an Execute Function dialog box like the one shown here, telling you the function requires an input value to execute:

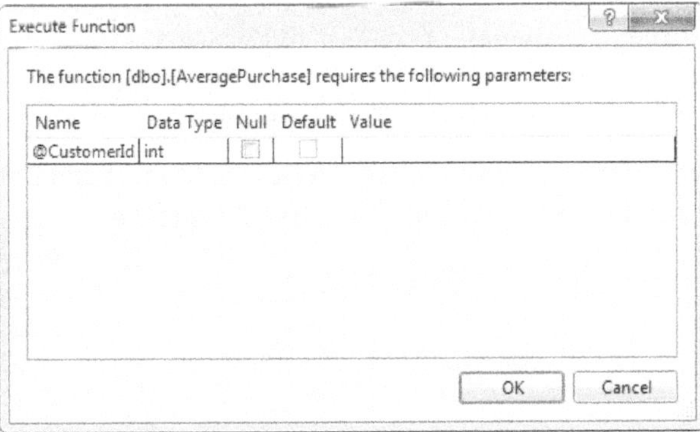

10. Type **1** in the Value field for *@CustomerId* and click OK. Visual Studio automatically creates a new query and executes it. You'll see the output shown here:

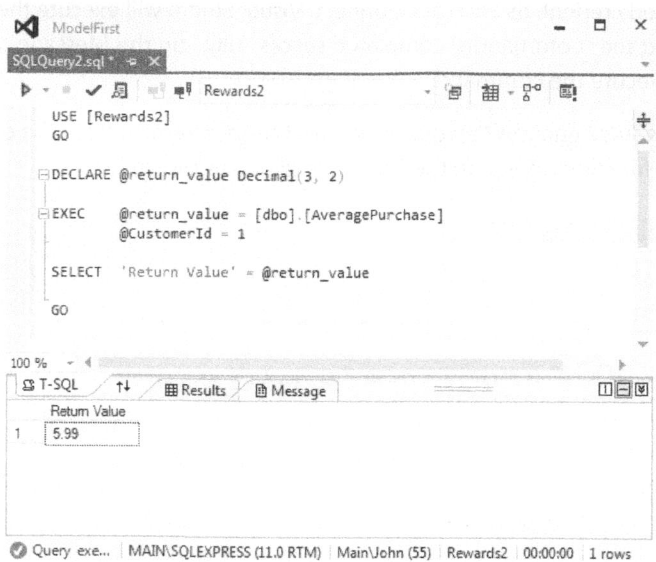

11. Close the SQL file without saving it. The test shows that the query works.

Accessing the function

At this point, you have a database function you can use. You know it works because you tested it. Of course, you have to figure out how to access the function from your code. The following procedure shows how to access the function from within your application.

Tracing through a *List* example

1. Open the Rewards2Model.EDMX file by double-clicking its entry in Solution Explorer.

2. Right-click in any clear area of the designer and choose Update Model From Database from the context menu. You'll see the Update Wizard dialog box shown here:

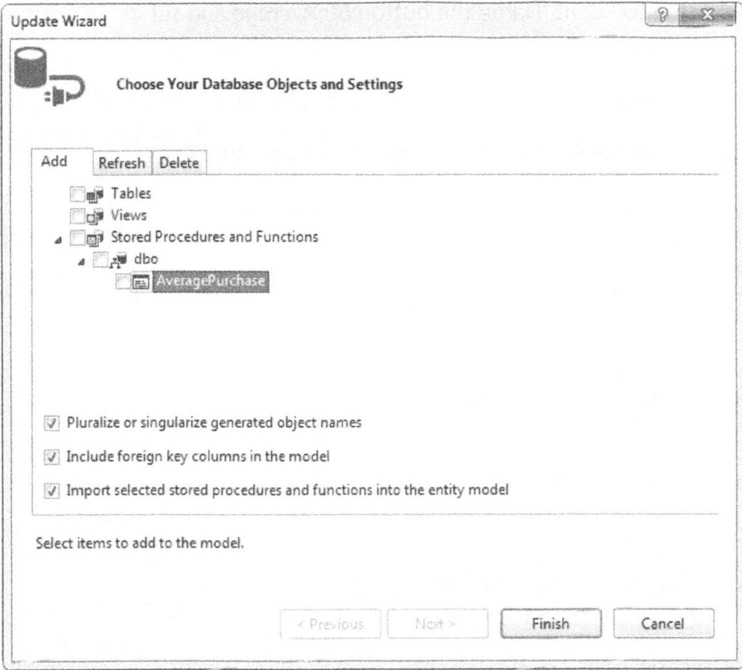

3. Check AveragePurchase and click Finish. It seems as if nothing has happened to your diagram, but the .EDMX file does indeed include a change.

4. Open the Form1.cs file. Add this *using* statement to the beginning of the file:

```
using System.Data.Objects.DataClasses;
```

5. Add this function to the file:

```
[EdmFunction("Rewards2Model.Store", "AveragePurchase")]
public static decimal? AveragePurchase(Int32 CustomerId)
{
   throw new NotSupportedException("Direct calls are not supported.");
}
```

This function requires a little explanation. The *[EdmFunction()]* attribute tells the compiler to look into the .EDMX file in the requested store, which is Rewards2Model.Store in this case, for a function named *AveragePurchase*. You added this entry during the update, even though it doesn't show up in the designer.

The function itself requires an odd format. For one thing, it's a static function, and the return type is *decimal*. Notice the question mark (?) behind the type declaration. You must include it or the function won't work. The function name comes next, along with any arguments the function requires. The only content for the function is the exception shown. The function actually executes at the database.

6. Add a new button to *Form1*. Name the button *btnAverage* and set its *Text* property to *&Average*.

7. Double-click *btnAverage* to create a new click event handler.

8. Type the following code for the *btnAverage_Click()* event handler:

```
private void btnAverage_Click(object sender, EventArgs e)
{
   // Create the context.
   Rewards2ModelContainer context = new Rewards2ModelContainer();

   // Make the query.
   var CustomerList =
      from cust in context.Customers
      select new
      {
         Name = cust.CustomerName,
         Average = AveragePurchase(cust.Id)
      };

   // Create a string to hold the result.
   StringBuilder Output = new StringBuilder();

   // Parse the result.
   foreach (var CustEntry in CustomerList)
      Output.Append(
         CustEntry.Name + " makes an average purchase of "
         + CustEntry.Average + ".\r\n");

   // Display the result on screen.
   MessageBox.Show(Output.ToString());
}
```

The code begins by creating a context. It then creates a LINQ to Entities query based on that context. Notice that the *select* part of the query is different. It creates a new object that contains two entries: *Name* and *Average*. The *Name* entry is directly obtained from *cust.CustomerName*. However, the *Average* entry is actually a call to the *AveragePurchase()* function you created in the database in the "Creating the function" section. What you end up with is a structure-like *IQueryable* object. (Tracing through this example in the debugger is educational, and you should give it a try.)

After the application obtains the names and averages, it creates a string from them using a *foreach* loop. Notice that you access the entries as properties. *CustEntry* is actually an anonymous type. The code ends by displaying the output in a message box.

> **Note** This is an example of an application where you must use *var* instead of either *IQueryable* or *IEnumerable*. The problem is that you're working with an anonymous type—a type that isn't known at design time.

9. Click Start or press F5. The application compiles and runs.

10. Click Average. You'll see the output shown here:

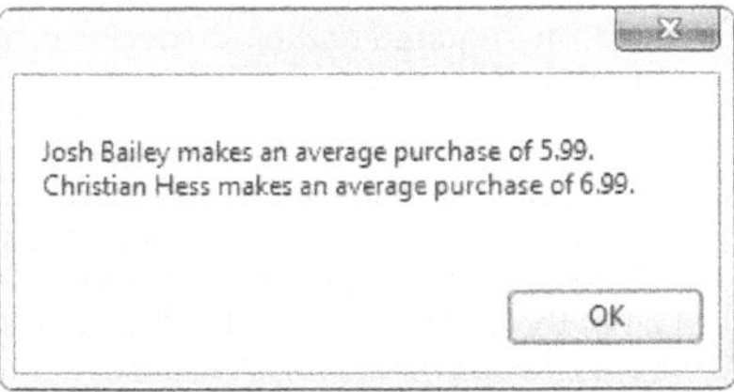

Getting started with the Entity Framework

This chapter has introduced you to LINQ to Entities, which provides a method of querying a database using a simple and straightforward query language. The most important idea to take away from this chapter is that LINQ to Entities makes it possible to focus on the information you need to work with, rather than the method used to obtain it. In order to define what information you need, a declarative language uses a set of keywords and operators that make it possible to tell the compiler what you want. LINQ to Entities queries are compiled into a form that the .NET Framework understands. So, there isn't any hocus-pocus going on—LINQ to Entities simply makes it possible for you to get your work done faster and with fewer errors.

The chapter contains a number of examples. What you need to do at this point is play with those examples to determine how they work. If necessary, single-step through the code using the debugger to determine precisely how the queries work. Once you understand the queries as they appear in the chapter, make changes to them to see how different operators and keywords affect the output. The best way to gain an appreciation of how LINQ to Entities works is to play with it. Spend some time mixing and matching items until you gain a clear understanding of how each item works.

Chapter 7 moves on to another way of interacting with data, using Entity SQL. In this chapter, you gain an in-depth view of working with Entity SQL to perform specific tasks. As in Chapter 6, you start with a basic tutorial of how Entity SQL works, and then move on to examples that demonstrate how to use it. When you finish Chapter 7, you'll be able to compare LINQ to Entities with Entity SQL to determine the strengths and weakness of each approach. You'll also have a better idea of which technology you prefer to use to address a particular need.

Chapter 6 quick reference

To	Do this
Access a non–SQL Server database using LINQ to Entities	Obtain the required database-specific provider to use with ADO.NET.
Create a basic LINQ to Entities query	Combine the *from*, *in*, and *select* keywords to create an expression, and then place the output from this expression into a variable. For example, *var CustomerList = from cust in context.Customers select cust* obtains a list of all of the customers found in the *Customers* table of the specified context named *context*.
Specify that LINQ group the return values in a certain way	Use the *group* keyword to specify that you want grouping and the *by* keyword to define which field or expression to use to perform the grouping task. Place the result of the grouping into a variable by using the *into* keyword.
Specify that LINQ sort the return values in a certain way	Use the *orderby* keyword to specify that you want the output sorted and include a field or expression to use to perform the sorting task. Control the order of the sort using the *ascending* or *descending* keyword.
Output a result set using an in-memory presentation that provides performance benefits during enumeration	Create an output object based on *IEnumerable*.
Output a result set using a remote presentation that provides flexibility	Create an output object based on *IQueryable*.
Project specific output values from the query	Use the *Select()* or *SelectMany()* methods.
Filter the output to remove undesirable elements	Use the *Where()* method.
Join two data sources that lack a navigable property	Use the *Join()* or *GroupJoin()* method to create an inner, group, or left-outer join.
Create a result set that exhibits one or more specific properties	Use the set-related methods: *All()*, *Any()*, *Concat()*, *Contains()*, *DefaultIfEmpty()*, *Distinct()*, *EqualAll()*, *Except()*, *Intersect()*, and *Union()*.
Change the order in which the rows in a result set appear	Use the ordering-related methods: *OrderBy()*, *OrderByDescending()*, *ThenBy()*, *ThenByDescending()*, and *Reverse()*.
Define groups of rows containing the same attribute	Use the *GroupBy()* method.
Define new views of existing data by combining rows	Use the aggregation-related methods: *Aggregate()*, *Average()*, *Count()*, *LongCount()*, *Max()*, *Min()*, and *Sum()*.
Perform type conversion and testing	Use the *Convert()* (primitive types) and *OfType()* (entity types). When working with C#, you can also use the *is()* and *as()* methods.
Access the rows out of order or remove some rows from the sequence depending on position	Use one of the paging methods: *ElementAt()*, *First()*, *FirstOrDefault()*, *Last()*, *LastOrDefault()*, *Single()*, *Skip()*, *Take()*, or *TakeWhile()*.

CHAPTER 7

Manipulating data using Entity SQL

After completing the chapter, you'll be able to

- Describe the basic functionality of Entity SQL.
- Use Entity SQL to select data.
- Employ literals when working with Entity SQL.
- Place data in a specific order.
- Group data by content.

Chapter 4, "Generating and using objects," provides a basic introduction to Entity SQL, but it doesn't explore this method of interacting with the Entity Framework in detail. As described in the "Understanding the role of Entity SQL" section of Chapter 4, this technique of creating queries is focused on making use of SQL language knowledge that developers already possess. That said, Entity SQL provides a considerable array of features that makes it possible to extract data from a database quickly and relatively simply, as long as you know the Entity SQL language (the example in the "Creating a basic query using Entity SQL" section of Chapter 4 shows the barest of examples). It's essential to remember that unlike T-SQL, you can't use Entity SQL to make changes to the database or its data. The first section of this chapter describes other differences that you need to understand before working with Entity SQL.

Working with Entity SQL is about selecting data. However, there are many ways in which to select data, and this chapter explores a number of them. For the most part, you'll use LINQ to Entities, which is described in Chapter 6, "Manipulating data using LINQ," to make queries. However, Entity SQL has some specific advantages, such as the ability to perform dynamic query building. In addition, the SQL-like foundation language makes it easier to transition code that you may already own into a form that works well with the Entity Framework—something that isn't possible when working with LINQ to Entities. (When all is said and done, Entity SQL and LINQ to Entities both allow you to perform most of the same tasks, but by using different strategies and sets of language skills in each case.) The remainder of this chapter will explore these special advantages so that you know they exist and can make use of them when needed.

Understanding Entity SQL

Entity SQL is a SQL-like language you use for creating queries against a database. As mentioned in Chapter 4, the language is SQL-like, not completely compatible with SQL. In addition, the focus isn't on interacting directly with the DBMS, but rather extracting data from the DBMS using a language that's easily translated to a DBMS-specific language. Given an appropriate database-specific provider, it's possible to use Entity SQL to interact with any DBMS, not just Microsoft SQL Server. The following sections help you better understand how Entity SQL works and the ways in which you can use it to create queries against the DBMS.

Considering the Entity SQL data flow

As with LINQ to Entities, Entity SQL relies on *EntityClient* to translate what it does into something the Entity Framework layers can map into database-specific commands through Microsoft ADO.NET and database-specific providers. The entire stack of software is about the same in structure as shown here:

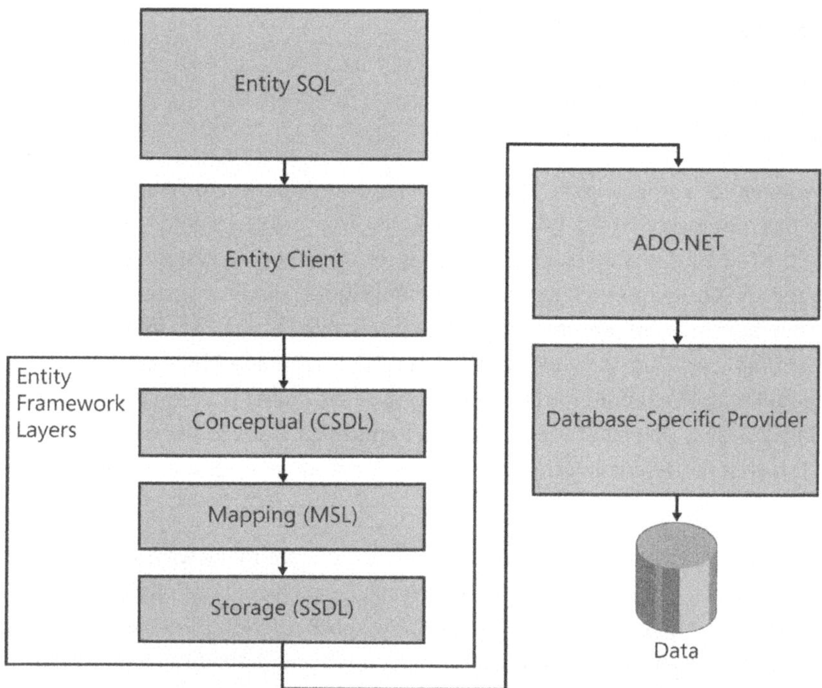

Warning A number of drawings and discussions available online don't mention the need for a database-specific provider. If you're using a DBMS other than SQL Server or one of the compatible DBMSs described in Chapter 1, "Getting to know the Entity Framework," then you'll find that your queries won't work without adding a database-specific provider. You still depend on ADO.NET to complete tasks.

However, the actual functioning of Entity SQL is quite different from LINQ to Entities, even if the path is approximately the same. When working with Entity SQL, you create a command that the *EntityClient* executes against the conceptual model. The process isn't working against the database directly. Rather, the command is mapped by the Entity Framework layers into something ADO.NET can understand and send to the database-specific provider. By the time the DBMS sees the command, it's translated into a form that the DBMS can understand. On the return trip, the results of the DBMS query are mapped into .NET objects, which are sent through the *EntityClient* and reported by Entity SQL as a result.

Commands are created as *EntityCommand* objects. The actual Entity SQL command is stored within the *EntityCommand.CommandText* property. So, this is where the string you construct ends up—as part of an object. In most cases, your application will call the *EntityCommand.ExecuteReader()* method to actually execute the command. This method returns an *EntityDataReader* object you can use to interact with the data from the DBMS. Of course, this data is in a form that works well with .NET—it isn't in its original format. All of these objects (and quite a few others related to Entity SQL) reside in the *System.Data.EntityClient* namespace, described at *http://msdn.microsoft.com/library/system.data.entityclient.aspx.*

Defining the Entity SQL components

Entity SQL most definitely differs from T-SQL, as described in the "Understanding the role of Entity SQL" section of Chapter 4. However, this overview hardly tells you everything there is to know about Entity SQL. The following sections describe the components used to make up Entity SQL—the features that you use to create queries and execute them against the server. After you read this overview, you'll be ready to work through the rest of the chapter, which describes these components in detail and demonstrates them as needed.

SELECT VALUE and *SELECT*

Entity SQL provides two methods for selecting items. Each method has a specific purpose, as described in the following list:

- ***SELECT VALUE*** Provides the means for selecting a single item without constructing a row wrapper around the items. This means you can shape the item more easily because you can access it directly.
- ***SELECT*** Provides the means for selecting multiple items. The return value is a collection of data rows containing one or more fields. This approach is more flexible and allows you to create complex datasets.

Note For the sake of clarity, this chapter will often illustrate Entity SQL statements as pure text, instead of as part of an example. Normally, you always create an Entity SQL statement as a string and assign it to the *EntityCommand.CommandText* property.

To illustrate the difference between *SELECT VALUE* and *SELECT*, begin with the example query from Chapter 4. In this case, the query selects a single item, so it uses *SELECT VALUE*, as shown here:

```
SELECT VALUE CustomerList
FROM Rewards2ModelContainer.Customers
AS CustomerList
```

The result is a single value, which contains the entire dataset. However, you can also return individual members by using *SELECT*. Here's an example of using *SELECT* to obtain just part of the information:

```
SELECT CustomerList, CustomerList.Purchases
FROM Rewards2ModelContainer.Customers
AS CustomerList
```

In this case, the result set includes the customer information and the purchase information as two separate entities that you'd need to process separately. However, using this approach would allow additional flexibility in processing the data that you wouldn't have when working with the single object returned by *SELECT VALUE*. You'll see more examples of how this would work later in the chapter.

Literals

A literal is essentially a kind of string. You can enclose literal values in either single or double quotes in most cases—Entity SQL won't care which delimiter you use. However, there are many types of literals used with Entity SQL, and there are peculiarities in the way you work with them. With this in mind, you want to know how literals work in Entity SQL to ensure that you get the proper results. The following sections discuss literal values and how to format them correctly. (You can find more detailed information on MSDN, at *http://msdn.microsoft.com/library/bb399176.aspx*.)

Warning The problem with Entity SQL literals is that if you don't format them correctly, Entity SQL may raise an exception or the query may simply refuse to provide any return information. If it does provide a return value, the information you receive may not be what you expected. In fact, it could be completely incorrect. It's essential that you format the literals correctly and that you test the results of your queries to ensure you obtain the proper information in return from the DBMS.

String A string literal is a series of characters used to store textual information. There isn't anything mysterious about string literals except in the way you store the characters. It turns out that there are two presentations, Unicode and non-Unicode. The default settings use non-Unicode (8-bit) characters that don't work well with many languages and will most definitely cause problems when making queries against DBMSs that rely on Unicode characters. In order to overcome this problem, you preface the string with an *N*, like this:

```
N"My Unicode string"
```

The *N* must appear next to the string literal without any spaces, and it must be an uppercase *N*. You do have the option of using single or double quotes to enclose the string.

DateTime* and *Time There isn't any literal that's specifically designed to provide a date value. All date values must include both the date and the time. In addition, a date value is independent of locale; it must appear in a specific format regardless of what format is commonly used to denote date and time in that locale. A date and time value is always preceded by the *DATETIME* keyword. Notice that this keyword must appear in uppercase. You can't use mixed case. However, you can place one or more spaces between the *DATETIME* keyword and the literal value, but the *DATETIME* keyword and the literal value must appear on the same line.

To create a date-and-time mixed value, you use the format *DATETIME "2013-03-04 17:53"* where 2013 is the year, 03 is the month, 04 is the day, 17 is the hour, and 53 represents the minutes. You may optionally add seconds and fractional seconds. The fractional seconds can range from 0 to 9999999, but must always consume seven spaces. A value of *DATETIME "2013-03-04 17:53:00:000000000"* is the same as the previous date and time value because the number of seconds is 0 and the fractional seconds value is also 0.

Warning There are no default literal date/time or time values. You must specify a value as part of the literal. The literal must contain all of the required elements. If you leave elements out, Entity SQL will either raise an exception or not return the requested information, even when the information resides in the database.

Entity SQL does provide a time-specific literal value. In this case, you precede the literal value with the *TIME* keyword. Again, you can add one or more spaces between the *TIME* keyword and the literal value. The literal value must contain hours and minutes—seconds and fractional seconds are optional. A time literal value of *TIME "17:53:22"* contains 17 hours (5 P.M.), 53 minutes, and 22 seconds.

Note You can also create a date/time offset value. The Microsoft documentation details how to create this type of literal. Essentially, it's the same as working with a date/time, but with a little added information—the offset.

Integer, real, and decimal Numeric literals aren't enclosed in quotes, but they do have specific formatting requirements. Integer types come in two sizes: *Int32* and *Int64*. The default size is *Int32*. You create an integer value by providing a series of numbers without a decimal or fractional part. For example, *123* is an *Int32* literal value. In order to create an *Int64* literal value, you add an uppercase *L*—for example, *123L*.

Real numbers, both float and double, provide an integer value, decimal point, and fractional value, such as 123.0. In this case, the double (64-bit) value is the default. To create a 32-bit floating-point value, you add a lowercase *f* after the number—for example, *123.0f*.

Decimal values provide added precision for financial calculations. As with real numbers, a decimal value has an integer value, decimal point, and fractional value. However, in this case, you add an uppercase *M* after the number, such as in *123.0M*.

Other In order to provide a complete solution, Entity SQL provides access to a number of other literals. For example, you can use the *null* keyword to create null values of any type. However, when working with null values, you must follow some special rules. For example, you can only use null values in special contexts, as described at *http://msdn.microsoft.com/library/bb387141.aspx*. As described on this page, it would be illegal to use a null value as an argument for a row constructor (theoretically, to create a blank row).

Boolean literals are represented by the keywords *true* and *false*. Even though the documentation doesn't specify case in this instance, it's best to use lowercase *true* and *false*.

Binary strings are a series of hexadecimal digits enclosed in single quotes, preceded by the *BINARY* keyword or the shortcut *X*. You must use single quotes. In this case, you can use either a lowercase or uppercase *X* to represent the binary string. In addition, the hexadecimal digits can be either uppercase or lowercase. When you create a binary string, use an even number of digits. If you don't, Entity SQL will pad the string to produce an even number of digits. You can use any number of spaces between the *BINARY* keyword or the *X* shortcut and the string, but they must appear on the same line. All the following binary strings are acceptable:

```
BINARY '0123456789ABCDEF'
X '0123456789ABCDEF'
x       '0123456789abcdef'
```

It's also possible to create Globally Unique Identifiers (GUIDs) using literals. A GUID relies on hexadecimal digits within single quotes (no double quotes allowed) in a 8-4-4-4-12 pattern. Each group of digits must be separated by a hyphen. You can use any number of spaces between the GUID keyword and the string, but they must appear on the same line. Here's a typical example of a GUID literal:

```
GUID '01234567-89AB-CDEF-0123-456789ABCDEF'
```

Type constructors

Type constructors create objects of a specific type. Entity SQL provides support for row, collection, and named type constructors. The following sections describe each of these types. You can discover additional information about these constructors at *http://msdn.microsoft.com/library/bb386869.aspx*.

ROW You use the row constructor to create anonymous, structurally typed records. The result is a *ROW* type (see *http://msdn.microsoft.com/library/bb399170.aspx* for details) that contains one or more fields, each of which has a type that corresponds to the type of data the field contains. Each field should have an alias associated with it. Even though the Entity Framework will attempt to generate an alias if you don't provide one, providing an alias is always the best way to construct a row type. The following example constructs a row type containing four fields:

```
ROW(1 AS IntValue, 1.5 AS DoubleValue, "ABC" AS StringValue, true as BooleanValue)
```

The constructor begins with the *ROW* keyword. The individual fields appear in parentheses after the *ROW* keyword, and there's no space between the keyword and the opening parenthesis. Each field defines an alias using the *AS* keyword. There are some rules you must follow when working with the row constructor:

- Each field must use a unique alias.
- Expressions in a row constructor can't refer to other expressions in the same constructor.

Collection A collection constructor creates a *MULTISET<T>* object (see *http://msdn.microsoft.com/library/bb387137.aspx* for details) that contains a group of items of the same type that you can access as a list. Every item of type *T* must be mutually compatible. The following example creates a *MULTISET<T>* of strings:

```
MULTISET("One", "Two", "Three")
```

The constructor begins with the *MULTISET* keyword, followed by a list of items to include in the *MULTISET* in parentheses. There isn't any space between the *MULTISET* and the list.

Named type The named type constructor lets you create a conceptual model of an instance, complex, or entity type (see *http://msdn.microsoft.com/library/bb738526.aspx* for details). There's no keyword associated with this type, but you must provide a type alias. Here's an example of an instance type named *Name*:

```
Name("Josh", "Bailey")
```

Notice that the alias is a single term and that the type definition includes two strings. You can use any valid Entity SQL type as content. Here's an example of a complex type named *Customer.Id*:

```
Customer.Id(5, "Josh", "Bailey")
```

The difference, in this case, is that there's a type, *Customer*, that has a property, *Id*, that contains three fields: one integer and two strings. A complex type can have other properties, and you can nest types within each other, like this:

```
Customer.Id(5, "Josh", "Bailey", Customer.Purchase(5, 6.99M))
```

In this case, there's a *Customer* type that has one level that contains *Id* information, and a second level that contains a *Purchase*. The *Id* consists of an integer and two strings. The *Purchase* consists of an integer and a decimal value. An entity type describes an entire entry for a particular model, like this:

```
Model.Customer(5, "Josh", "Bailey", Customer.Purchases(Purchase(5, 6.99M), Purchase(6, 6.99M)))
```

The essential fact to remember is that named types can vary in complexity and purpose. You can use them to model an instance, a complex type, or an entire entity, as needed. Named types are also returned from a number of the method calls you use with Entity SQL, as will become clearer as the chapter progresses.

References

Entity SQL provides access to a number of reference operators that you use to interact with foreign keys in an entity set. The operators react to the foreign key reference as a type of pointer. The following list describes each of the reference operators. You'll see them used in other areas of the chapter. Each list entry also provides a reference to further information, should you want to explore these operators in greater detail.

- ***CREATEREF*** Creates a reference to an entity within an entity set (essentially creating a foreign key). You can read more about this operator at *http://msdn.microsoft.com/library/bb386880.aspx.*
- ***DEREF*** Dereferences a reference pointer so that you can work with the entity pointed at by the reference. You can read more about this operator at *http://msdn.microsoft.com/library/bb386885.aspx.*
- ***KEY*** Extracts the key used to create a reference or entity expression. You can read more about this operator at *http://msdn.microsoft.com/library/bb399756.aspx.*
- ***NAVIGATE*** Provides the means for navigating over the relationship created between entities. The result is a *Ref<T>* object when working with a one-to-one relationship or a *Collection<Ref<T>>* object when working with a one-to-many relationship. The navigation occurs through the conceptual model, rather than against the DBMS. You can read more about this operator at *http://msdn.microsoft.com/library/bb387146.aspx.*
- ***REF*** Returns a reference to an entity instance that consists of the entity key and the entity set name. You can read more about this operator at *http://msdn.microsoft.com/library/bb399743.aspx.*

Functions

Working with functions makes it easier to perform some tasks, especially when the tasks require complex computations or repetition. When working with Entity SQL, you can use following:

- **User-defined functions** As with the user-defined function described in the "Using Entity and database functions" section of Chapter 6, most Entity SQL functions you use are performed against the conceptual model. Entity SQL also provides the means to define functions inline, as part of the query.
- **Canonical functions** The Entity Framework provides a number of built-in functions that you can use with Entity SQL. The database-specific provider you use will normally support these functions, but you need to check the vendor documentation to be certain. When a canonical function isn't supported, the Entity SQL query fails and usually generates an exception.

However, since these functions are consistent across all vendors, Microsoft recommends using them over provider-specific functions.

- **Provider-specific functions** A vendor can choose to implement functions as part of the database-specific provider. These functions are unique to a particular provider and may not even work across all versions of a particular DBMS. Because these functions are unique to a particular database-specific provider, they aren't discussed in this book—you need to consult the documentation that comes with the database-specific provider to learn more.

The following sections help you better understand how to work with functions when using Entity SQL. It won't surprise you to know that even though the techniques for doing so are different than when working with LINQ to Entities, the sources and results of the functions are the same. In addition, the rules for working with functions follow those established for .NET functions in general.

User-defined functions Most developers associate user-defined functions with functions created within the database. You access these functions to perform specific tasks. To create such a function, you rely on a SQL query. You can see an easy method for creating such a function in the "Creating the function" section of Chapter 6. In fact, you'll see an example of accessing this function later in the chapter.

One of the ways in which Entity SQL excels when compared to LINQ to Entities is in the way it lets you dynamically create functions inline. You perform this task using the *FUNCTION* operator, as described at *http://msdn.microsoft.com/library/dd490947.aspx*. An inline function exists only for the time that the query executes. Dynamically creating functions in this way provides you with additional flexibility without clogging the database with functions that you don't intend to use regularly.

Note An Entity SQL query can actually contain multiple functions. In addition, the functions can have the same name as long as they have a unique signature. See the "Working with overloaded functions" section later in the chapter for details on how Entity SQL manages multiple functions with the same name.

Aggregate functions You can think of an aggregate as a method of combining various parts into a cohesive whole. That's what happens when you work with aggregates in Entity SQL. The function combines a collection of records into a single value of some sort. For example, you might choose to count the number of records in a collection or locate the maximum record. Aggregate functions come in two forms, collection functions and group functions, as described in the following list:

- **Collection functions** Functions that you can use anywhere in an expression to aggregate a collection into a scalar value. (A *scalar value* is one that has a specific value or magnitude, such as a number or a string.) This includes using the functions within predicates and as part of projections. These functions include the following (you can find detailed information about them at *http://msdn.microsoft.com/library/bb399163.aspx*):
  - ***AVG*** Determines the average value of a collection.
  - ***CHECKSUM_AGG*** Calculates the checksum of the values in a collection.

- ***COUNT/COUNT_BIG*** Returns the number of items in a collection. When using *COUNT*, you receive an *Int32* value. Using *COUNT_BIG* returns an *Int64* value.
- ***MAX*** Determines the maximum value in a collection and returns that value.
- ***MIN*** Determines the minimum value in a collection and returns that value.
- ***STDEV*** Returns the standard deviation of all of the values in a collection.
- ***STDEVP*** Returns the standard deviation for the population of all of the values in a collection.
- ***SUM*** Calculates the total value of all of the values in a collection.
- ***VAR*** Returns the variance of all of the values in a collection.
- ***VARP*** Returns the variance for the population of all of the values in a collection.

- **Group functions** Functions that appear as part of a *GROUP BY* clause in a query. The aggregate is calculated on all of the members of a particular group, and the scalar value of each group is placed in an output collection. You can modify these functions using the *DISTINCT* and *ANY* keywords. You can use the same functions as with a collection, but the result is based on groups, not the collection as a whole.

Note Entity SQL also allows the use of user-defined aggregate functions. A discussion of user-defined aggregates is outside the scope of this book. However, you can find a discussion of them at *http://msdn.microsoft.com/library/ms190678.aspx*.

Working with overloaded functions You can create multiple functions with the same name in Entity SQL as long as each function has a unique signature. In other words, Entity SQL must be able to determine which function to use based on the criteria used to determine a unique signature. When working with multiple functions that have the same name, Entity SQL uses these rules to find a unique signature in the order presented:

- Number of parameters
- Types of input arguments
- Subtypes of input arguments
- Types or subtypes of promoted input arguments (where arguments are cast to another type)

When Entity SQL can't make a clear determination of which function to use based on these criteria, then the expression is ambiguous, and Entity SQL can't execute it. You'll receive an exception that specifies the ambiguity. Even if Entity SQL can determine that a single function matches the signature of the call, the input arguments may not precisely match the required parameters. In this case, Entity SQL will raise an exception.

Namespaces

Just as you use namespaces to avoid naming issues with the .NET Framework, you can use them with Entity SQL to avoid naming problems with type names, entity sets, functions, and other elements. In fact, the use of namespaces in Entity SQL is similar to the use of namespaces in the .NET Framework. Importing a namespace can take two forms, as shown here:

```
USING System.Data;
USING tsql = System.Data;
```

Essentially, Entity SQL searches namespaces for functions and other elements needed to perform a query, much as the .NET Framework does (there's a discussion of the topic at *http://msdn.microsoft.com/library/bb399361.aspx*). However, unlike the .NET Framework, you can't use partially qualified namespaces with Entity SQL. Namespaces can be used over the *DbCommand* and *DbConnection* objects used to create, manage, and execute queries.

Paging

A query can rely on paging to obtain just part of the result set of a query. Using part of the result set means that the query will take less time and use fewer resources, improving overall application performance. The technique is called *paging* because it's typically used to display one page of results at a time in output where the results would normally require multiple pages. You can also use paging to limit the results to those matching a numeric limitation.

Entity SQL implements paging as part of the *ORDER BY* clause of a query. There are three keywords associated with paging: *SKIP*, *LIMIT*, and *TOP*. You can use *SKIP* and *LIMIT* together to create certain effects. *TOP* is always used by itself. The following list describes these keywords:

- ***SKIP*** Skips the specified number of rows in the result set. For example, if you specify *SKIP 5*, then the output would begin with the sixth record in the result set. You can read more about *SKIP* at *http://msdn.microsoft.com/library/bb738680.aspx*.
- ***LIMIT*** Returns just the number of rows specified from the result set. For example, if you specify *LIMIT 5*, then the output would contain just five records. You can read more about *LIMIT* at *http://msdn.microsoft.com/library/bb738635.aspx*.
- ***SKIP/LIMIT*** When used together, *SKIP* and *LIMIT* create a record range. For example, if you specify *SKIP 10 LIMIT 5*, the output would begin with record number 11 and end with record number 15 from the result set.
- ***TOP*** Returns the specified number of rows from the beginning of the result set. For example, if you specify *TOP 50*, then records 1 through 50 from the result set will appear in the output. You can read more about *TOP* at *http://msdn.microsoft.com/library/bb738522.aspx*.

Grouping

Creating groups of like rows from a collection is an important part of creating many queries. Entity SQL accomplishes this task using the *GROUP BY* clause. Unlike using LINQ to Entities, you must follow SQL-like rules when creating a *GROUP BY* clause in Entity SQL. The most important of these rules is that every expression in the *SELECT* clause must be accounted for in the *GROUP BY* clause or wrapped in an aggregate. You'll see examples of how this works in the "Grouping data" section later in the chapter. You can read about other requirements of using the *GROUP BY* clause at *http://msdn.microsoft.com/library/bb399764.aspx.*

Navigation

Navigation is the process of using a reference to access another entity from the current entity. For example, when you access a list of purchases from a customer's records (as you did in earlier chapters, and you'll do again in this one), you're using navigation to move from the customer record to its associated purchases. Navigation can also work in the other direction, as shown by the model for the examples in this book. When working with a *Purchases* record, you can access the associated *Customer* record using navigation, as shown here:

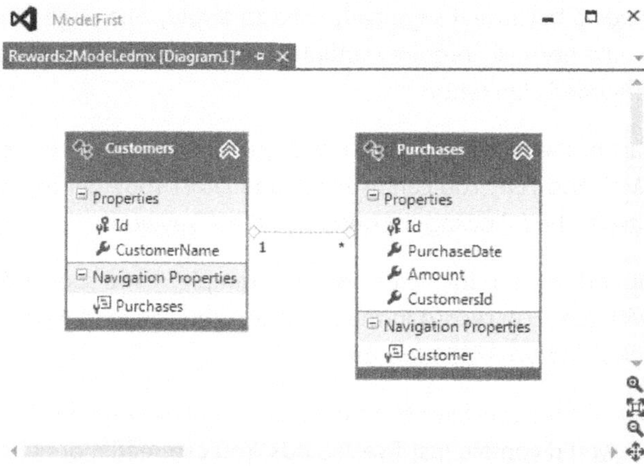

The purpose of the Navigation Properties section of the model is to show you the navigation you can use to relate one record to another. Of course, this is at the entity level. Interestingly enough, you can use the navigational properties for other tasks. For example, you can use them to help filter and sort the query based on the relation of a record in one table to a record in another table.

CASE expression

SQL provides a *CASE* statement that many developers find useful. Fortunately, Entity SQL provides an equivalent in the form of the *CASE* expression. The *CASE* expression provides the means for performing tasks based on the result of one or more Boolean expressions. It takes the following form:

```
CASE
   WHEN Boolean_expression THEN result_expression
   [ ...n ]
```

```
    [
      ELSE else_result_expression
    ]
END
```

The Boolean expression determines whether the *result_expression* is executed. An optional *ELSE* clause provides the means of performing some other actions when the Boolean expression is false. For example, you might check a customer's name and do something about it, like this:

```
CASE
   WHEN Customers.CustomerName == "Josh Bailey"
   THEN "Good Customer!"
   ELSE "Watch this one."
END
```

In this case, when the customer's name is Josh Bailey, the *CASE* expression returns a value of *Good Customer!* However, when the customer's name is something else, the *CASE* expression returns *Watch this one.* This expression is useful in making decisions as part of a query so that you can gain additional flexibility in creating useful output.

Note The flexibility provided by the *CASE* expression is another area in which Entity SQL excels in relation to LINQ for Entities. A few people have tried to come up with equivalents for LINQ to Entities. For example, you can find one method at *http://sankarsan.wordpress.com/2010/05/16/case-statement-equivalent-in-linq/.* In most cases, you'll find that the LINQ to Entities equivalents tend to be complex and a bit hard to understand.

Selecting data

As described in the "*SELECT VALUE* and *SELECT*" section earlier in the chapter, there are actually two methods for selecting data using Entity SQL. The "Creating a basic query using Entity SQL" section of Chapter 4 shows how to use the *SELECT VALUE* method for obtaining the data. The procedure in this section adds a second method that relies simply on *SELECT* to obtain data, using the Chapter 4 example as a starting point.

Creating a *SELECT* query

1. Copy the *ModelFirst (Display - Entity SQL)* example you created in Chapter 4 to a new folder and use this new copy for this example (rather than the copy you created in Chapter 4).
2. Add a new button to *Form1*. Name the button *btnQuery2* and set its *Text* property to *Query &2*.
3. Double-click *btnQuery2* to create a new click event handler.

4. At the top of the file, you need to add the following *using* statement to provide access to the *DbDataRecord* class:

```
using System.Data.Common;
```

5. Type the following code for the *btnQuery2_Click()* event handler:

```
private void btnQuery2_Click(object sender, EventArgs e)
{
    // Create the context.
    EntityConnection conn =
        new EntityConnection("name=Rewards2ModelContainer");
    ObjectContext context = new ObjectContext(conn);

    // Define a command string for making the query.
    String EntitySQLCmd =
        "SELECT CustomerList.Id, CustomerList.CustomerName " +
        "FROM Rewards2ModelContainer.Customers " +
        "AS CustomerList";

    // Create a query object.
    ObjectQuery<DbDataRecord> Customers =
        context.CreateQuery<DbDataRecord>(EntitySQLCmd);

    // Display the customer name on screen.
    MessageBox.Show(Customers.First()["CustomerName"].ToString());
}
```

The code begins by creating a context. It uses precisely the same technique as the example in Chapter 4.

The next step is to create the command string. Notice that this example retrieves the *Id* and *CustomerName* fields from the database separately, so you don't include the *VALUE* clause. In all other respects, the command string is the same. For example, you still retrieve the data from *Rewards2ModelContainer.Customers*.

The *ObjectQuery* object, *Customers*, uses a different approach in this example. In this case, the code creates an instance of *DbDataRecord*, which provides some useful functionality for moving between records. You can read more about this class at *http://msdn.microsoft.com/library/system.data.common.dbdatarecord.aspx*. This class will also appear in a number of examples in this chapter so you can see it at work.

The final task is to display the customer name on screen, just as the example from Chapter 4 does. The *First()* method obtains the first record from the list of records retrieved by the query. You can use either a string or integer index to retrieve a specific field from the record. Using a string is more readable, but using an integer provides a small performance boost. The field data is an object, so you need to convert it to a string using the *ToString()* method, as shown.

6. Click Start or press F5. The application compiles and runs.

7. Click Query 2. You'll see the customer's name, Josh Bailey, displayed.

Working with literals in Entity SQL

Literals are used in a number of ways in Entity SQL. You've seen a number of uses for them so far in the chapter. However, one of the easiest ways to experiment with literals is to create queries that use them to perform some specific task. The following sections discuss the literals by overall type and show you examples of their use within a query.

Using the standard literals

The standard literals include Boolean, integer, float, double, and string types. These are the types you use most often to perform queries that rely on the *WHERE* clause. The following procedure describes how to use a string literal to select a specific record from the *Customers* table of the sample database.

Creating a standard literals query

1. Add a new button to *Form1*. Name the button *btnQuery3* and set its *Text* property to *Query &3*.
2. Double-click *btnQuery3* to create a new click event handler.
3. Type the following code for the *btnQuery3_Click()* event handler:

```
private void btnQuery3_Click(object sender, EventArgs e)
{
    // Create the context.
    EntityConnection conn =
        new EntityConnection("name=Rewards2ModelContainer");
    ObjectContext context = new ObjectContext(conn);

    // Define a command string for making the query.
    String EntitySQLCmd =
        "SELECT CustomerList.Id, CustomerList.CustomerName " +
        "FROM Rewards2ModelContainer.Customers " +
        "AS CustomerList " +
        "WHERE CustomerList.CustomerName='Josh Bailey'";

    // Create a query object.
    ObjectQuery<DbDataRecord> Customers =
        context.CreateQuery<DbDataRecord>(EntitySQLCmd);

    // Create an output string.
    StringBuilder Output =
        new StringBuilder("Customer Data:");
    DbDataRecord ThisRecord = Customers.First();
    for (int i = 0; i < ThisRecord.FieldCount; i++)
        Output.Append("\r\n\t" + ThisRecord.GetName(i) +
            ": " + ThisRecord[i].ToString());

    // Display the customer name on screen.
    MessageBox.Show(Output.ToString());
}
```

This example works similarly to the one in the "Selecting data" section of the chapter. However, notice that the query now includes a *WHERE* clause. The query is specifically designed to locate the record of Josh Bailey. The name is enclosed in single quotes as a string literal. This is commonly how you see string literals in queries in your code.

The act of obtaining the data from the DBMS is the same. However, notice that this example obtains and displays the individual field values for the first record in the *DbDataRecord* collection. In some cases, you do need to obtain the actual field names, which are retrieved using the *GetName()* method.

4. Click Start or press F5. The application compiles and runs.
5. Click Query 3. You'll see the output shown here:

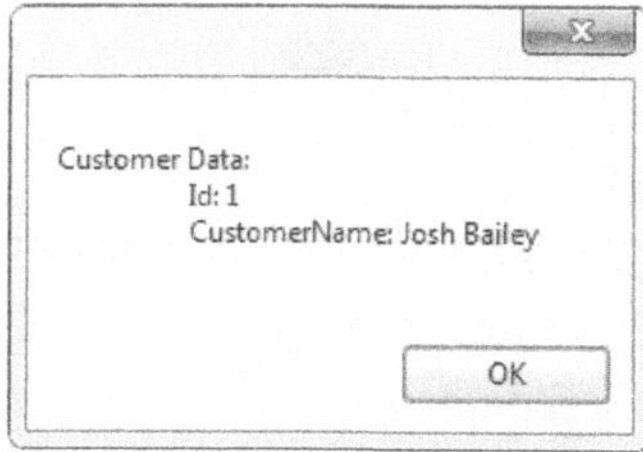

Adding some additional data

It would be helpful to have a few additional records for testing purposes. The procedure in this section uses what you discovered in the "Using the standard literals" section to add some new purchase records to the existing customers. These records will be helpful in working with other examples in this chapter.

Adding records using a *SELECT*

1. Add a new button to *Form1*. Name the button *btnNewPurchases* and set its *Text* property to *&New Purchases*.
2. Double-click *btnNewPurchases* to create a new click event handler.
3. Type the following code for the *btnNewPurchases_Click()* event handler:

```
private void btnNewPurchases_Click(object sender, EventArgs e)
{
    // Create the query context.
    EntityConnection conn =
        new EntityConnection("name=Rewards2ModelContainer");
    ObjectContext context = new ObjectContext(conn);

    // Define a command string for making the query.
    String EntitySQLCmd =
        "SELECT CustomerList.Id, CustomerList.CustomerName " +
        "FROM Rewards2ModelContainer.Customers " +
```

```
        "AS CustomerList";

    // Create a query object.
    List<DbDataRecord> Customers =
        context.CreateQuery<DbDataRecord>(EntitySQLCmd).ToList();

    // Create the management context.
    Rewards2ModelContainer management = new Rewards2ModelContainer();

    // Create new purchases for Josh Bailey.
    Purchases NewPurchase1 = new Purchases();
    NewPurchase1.CustomersId = Convert.ToInt32(Customers[0][0]);
    NewPurchase1.Amount = new Decimal(10.99);
    NewPurchase1.PurchaseDate = new DateTime(2013, 3, 20);
    management.Purchases.Add(NewPurchase1);

    Purchases NewPurchase2 = new Purchases();
    NewPurchase2.CustomersId = Convert.ToInt32(Customers[0][0]);
    NewPurchase2.Amount = new Decimal(3.99);
    NewPurchase2.PurchaseDate = new DateTime(2013, 3, 14);
    management.Purchases.Add(NewPurchase2);

    // Create new purchases for Christian Hess.
    Purchases NewPurchase3 = new Purchases();
    NewPurchase3.CustomersId = Convert.ToInt32(Customers[1][0]);
    NewPurchase3.Amount = new Decimal(0.99);
    NewPurchase3.PurchaseDate = new DateTime(2013, 3, 18);
    management.Purchases.Add(NewPurchase3);

    Purchases NewPurchase4 = new Purchases();
    NewPurchase4.CustomersId = Convert.ToInt32(Customers[1][0]);
    NewPurchase4.Amount = new Decimal(15.99);
    NewPurchase4.PurchaseDate = new DateTime(2013, 3, 19);
    management.Purchases.Add(NewPurchase4);

    // Save the purchases to the database.
    Int32 NumRecords = management.SaveChanges();

    // Display a success message.
    MessageBox.Show(NumRecords.ToString() + " New Records Added!");
}
```

There are a few tricks you should note in this example. The first is the technique used to convert the query to a *List* immediately. Using *List* objects can have some definite advantages when working with Entity SQL. In this case, notice that you can access the customer's *Id* field by using simple array references, such as *Customers[0][0]* for Josh Bailey.

Even though you can create a query using Entity SQL, you can never use it to manage database data. That's why this example creates a second context, *management*, to provide this functionality. The *management* content provides the means for adding the new records.

Each record must appear in a unique object if you plan to save all of the changes at one time to improve application performance. If you try to reuse an existing object, the changes you make will overwrite any previous changes. Consequently, this example uses *NewPurchase1* through *NewPurchase4* to hold the new records.

When you do save the changes, you can retrieve the total number of changes as output from the *SaveChanges()* method call. That's how this example is able to tell you how many records are added to the *Purchases* table.

4. Click Start or press F5. The application compiles and runs.
5. Click New Purchases. The application displays a dialog box telling you it has added four new records.

Using a date or time literal

Many user searches focus on date and time. When something happened is as important as what happened in many situations. You may want to know that a customer spent a certain amount of money on a specific date—any other purchases are immaterial at the time of the search. The procedure in this section looks at the use of a date literal to choose specific records from the example database.

Creating a date literal query

1. Add a new button to *Form1*. Name the button *btnQuery4* and set its Text property to *Query &4*.
2. Double-click *btnQuery4* to create a new click event handler.
3. Type the following code for the *btnQuery4_Click()* event handler:

```
private void btnQuery4_Click(object sender, EventArgs e)
{
    // Create the context.
    EntityConnection conn =
        new EntityConnection("name=Rewards2ModelContainer");
    ObjectContext context = new ObjectContext(conn);

    // Define a command string for making the query.
    String EntitySQLCmd =
        "SELECT PurchaseList, PurchaseList.Customer.CustomerName " +
        "FROM Rewards2ModelContainer.Purchases " +
        "AS PurchaseList " +
        "WHERE PurchaseList.PurchaseDate > DATETIME '2013-02-17 00:00'";

    // Create a query object.
    ObjectQuery<DbDataRecord> Purchases =
        context.CreateQuery<DbDataRecord>(EntitySQLCmd);

    // Create an output string.
    StringBuilder Output =
        new StringBuilder("Purchase Data:");

    // Process the individual purchase records.
```

```
    foreach (var Purchase in Purchases)
    {
        // Add the customer name.
        Output.Append("\r\n\t" + Purchase[1]);

        // Obtain access to the purchase information.
        var PurchaseInfo = Purchase[0] as Purchases;

        // Add the purchase information.
        Output.Append(" spent " + PurchaseInfo.Amount +
            " on " + PurchaseInfo.PurchaseDate + ".");
    }

    // Display the customer name on screen.
    MessageBox.Show(Output.ToString());
}
```

This example begins in the same way that others in this chapter begin, by creating a context and a query. There are several points of interest in this query. The first thing you should notice is that this *SELECT* query selects the entire *Purchases* table in the first element, and the *CustomerName* field from the *Customer* reference in the *Purchases* table as the second entry. It's absolutely essential that you not confuse the reference with the table. When this query is made, the customer information will correspond to the individual purchase.

The second thing you should notice is that the *WHERE* clause uses the *PurchaseDate* field as a comparison. However, the comparison operator is a greater-than symbol, not an equal symbol. The reason is that dates must be precise—they include time information as well as the date. If you want to obtain a specific day, you must perform a range comparison from midnight of that day to 11:59 in the evening. Also note how the *DATETIME* keyword is used and the date is formatted.

Working with the data is different in this example as well. A *foreach* loop provides the means to view all of the records retrieved by the query. The *foreach* loop retrieves an individual return, which includes both the *Purchases* table as the first element and the *CustomerName* field as the second element. To add the *CustomerName* field value to the output, all you need to do is place *Purchase[1]* into *Output*.

The code uses a two-step process to obtain the purchase information. The *PurchaseInfo* obtained retrieves the entire *Purchases* table content for a single record from *Purchase*. It then selects specific fields from that record to add to *Output*.

4. Click Start or press F5. The application compiles and runs.
5. Click Query 4. You'll see the output shown here:

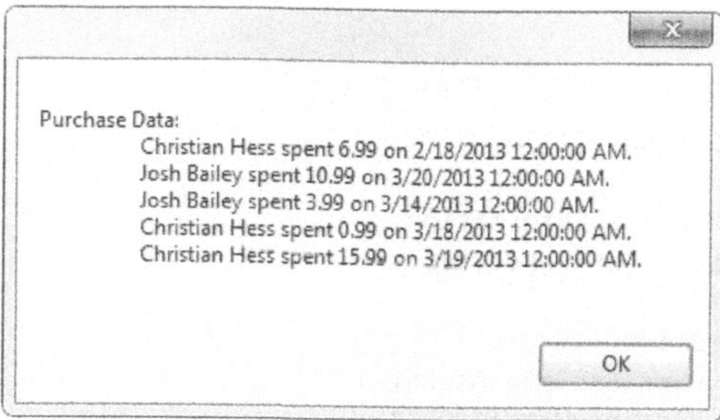

Purchase Data:
Christian Hess spent 6.99 on 2/18/2013 12:00:00 AM.
Josh Bailey spent 10.99 on 3/20/2013 12:00:00 AM.
Josh Bailey spent 3.99 on 3/14/2013 12:00:00 AM.
Christian Hess spent 0.99 on 3/18/2013 12:00:00 AM.
Christian Hess spent 15.99 on 3/19/2013 12:00:00 AM.
OK

Interacting with a decimal literal

Searching for monetary values in a database is also a big concern for users. Locating entries based on monetary values could help a user find customers who need additional incentives to buy more or help a manager find departments that are spending too much. The procedure in this section helps you create a query based on a decimal literal.

Creating a decimal literal query

1. Add a new button to *Form1*. Name the button *btnQuery5* and set its *Text* property to *Query &5*.
2. Double-click *btnQuery5* to create a new click event handler.
3. Type the following code for the *btnQuery5_Click()* event handler:

```
private void btnQuery5_Click(object sender, EventArgs e)
{
    // Create the context.
    EntityConnection conn =
        new EntityConnection("name=Rewards2ModelContainer");
    ObjectContext context = new ObjectContext(conn);

    // Define a command string for making the query.
    String EntitySQLCmd =
        "SELECT PurchaseList, PurchaseList.Customer.CustomerName " +
        "FROM Rewards2ModelContainer.Purchases " +
        "AS PurchaseList " +
        "WHERE PurchaseList.Amount > 1.00M " +
               "&& PurchaseList.Amount < 10.00M";

    // Create a query object.
    ObjectQuery<DbDataRecord> Purchases =
        context.CreateQuery<DbDataRecord>(EntitySQLCmd);

    // Create an output string.
    StringBuilder Output =
        new StringBuilder("Purchase Data:");

    // Process the individual purchase records.
    foreach (var Purchase in Purchases)
```

```
        {
            // Add the customer name.
            Output.Append("\r\n\t" + Purchase[1]);

            // Obtain access to the purchase information.
            var PurchaseInfo = Purchase[0] as Purchases;

            // Add the purchase information.
            Output.Append(" spent " + PurchaseInfo.Amount +
                " on " + PurchaseInfo.PurchaseDate + ".");
        }

        // Display the customer name on screen.
        MessageBox.Show(Output.ToString());
    }
```

This example uses the same approach as the example in the "Using a date or time literal" section of the chapter. However, there are some differences you should notice. First, this query uses a range check to obtain records that appear between a specific starting and ending point. Second, notice the addition of the *M* after the monetary amount. If you leave this letter off, the query will fail because a double won't match a decimal value.

4. Click Start or press F5. The application compiles and runs.
5. Click Query 5. You'll see the output shown here:

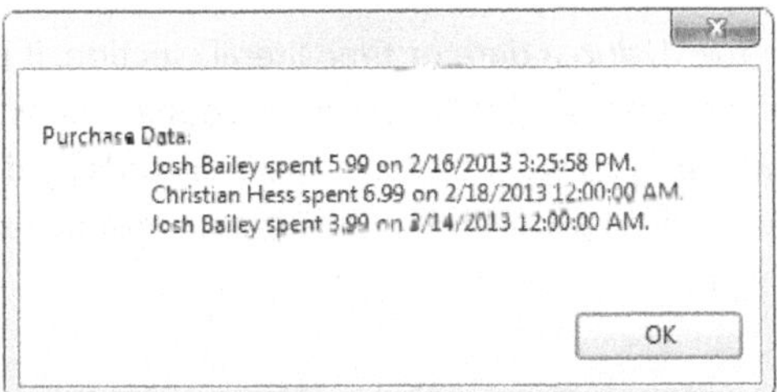
Purchase Data:
Josh Bailey spent 5.99 on 2/16/2013 3:25:58 PM.
Christian Hess spent 6.99 on 2/18/2013 12:00:00 AM.
Josh Bailey spent 3.99 on 3/14/2013 12:00:00 AM.
OK

6. Close the application. Remove the *M* from either (or both) of the decimal values.
7. Click Start or press F5. The application compiles and runs.
8. Click Query 5. You'll see the error message shown here:

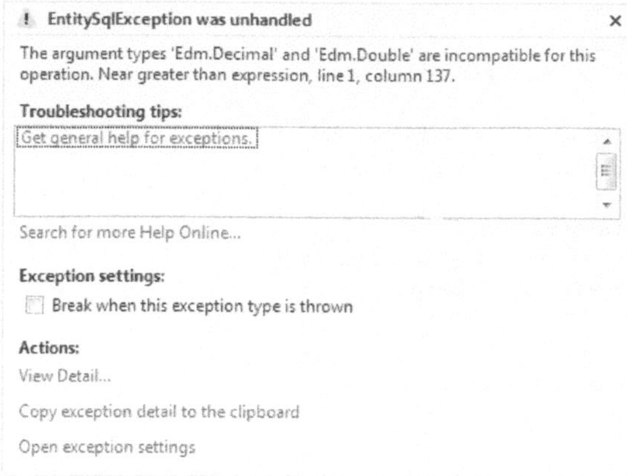

9. Click Stop Debugging to end the debugging process.

10. Close the application.

11. Add the *M* back to the decimal values. Choose Build | Build Solution to make the change permanent.

Ordering data

When viewing the output of the example in the "Using a date or time literal" section, it probably occurred to you that the data would be better viewed in a specific order. Of course, you want all of the records for a specific customer together, and then you want to order those records by date, so the example actually requires two levels of ordering. The procedure in this section examines a technique for ordering data to make it easier to work with.

Ordering purchases by *CustomerId* and *PurchaseDate*

1. Add a new button to *Form1*. Name the button *btnQuery6* and set its *Text* property to *Query &6*.

2. Double-click *btnQuery6* to create a new click event handler.

3. Copy the code from the *btnQuery4_Click()* event handler and modify the query string so that it looks like this:

```
// Define a command string for making the query.
String EntitySQLCmd =
    "SELECT PurchaseList, PurchaseList.Customer.CustomerName " +
    "FROM Rewards2ModelContainer.Purchases " +
    "AS PurchaseList " +
    "WHERE PurchaseList.PurchaseDate > DATETIME '2013-02-17 00:00' " +
    "ORDER BY PurchaseList.CustomersId, " +
    "PurchaseList.PurchaseDate";
```

Notice that this query relies on the *ORDER BY* clause. You specify the ordering criteria in the order in which you want to see the data ordered. Reversing the two *ORDER BY* criteria in this case would change the output. Each *ORDER BY* criterion is separated by a comma, as shown in this example.

4. Click Start or press F5. The application compiles and runs.
5. Click Query 6. You'll see the output shown here:

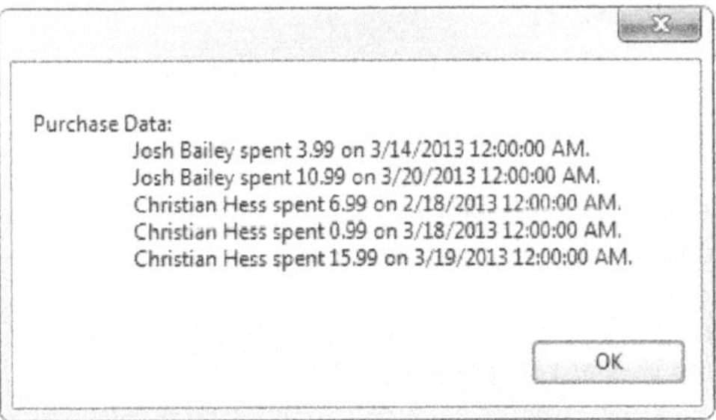

Purchase Data:
Josh Bailey spent 3.99 on 3/14/2013 12:00:00 AM.
Josh Bailey spent 10.99 on 3/20/2013 12:00:00 AM.
Christian Hess spent 6.99 on 2/18/2013 12:00:00 AM.
Christian Hess spent 0.99 on 3/18/2013 12:00:00 AM.
Christian Hess spent 15.99 on 3/19/2013 12:00:00 AM.
OK

Grouping data

Data often lends itself to grouping. Creating a group makes it possible for users to see patterns with greater ease and generally makes the data a bit neater. The procedure in this section shows how to create groups of data and display them in a logical manner on screen.

Creating a decimal literal query

1. Add a new button to *Form1*. Name the button *btnQuery7* and set its *Text* property to *Query &7*.
2. Double-click *btnQuery7* to create a new click event handler.
3. Type the following code for the *btnQuery7_Click()* event handler:

```
private void btnQuery7_Click(object sender, EventArgs e)
{
    // Create the context.
    EntityConnection conn =
        new EntityConnection("name=Rewards2ModelContainer");
    ObjectContext context = new ObjectContext(conn);

    // Define a command string for making the query.
    String EntitySQLCmd =
        "SELECT Grouping.CustomersId, " +
        "  (SELECT PurchaseList, PurchaseList.Customer.CustomerName " +
        "   FROM Rewards2ModelContainer.Purchases " +
        "   AS PurchaseList " +
        "   WHERE PurchaseList.CustomersId = Grouping.CustomersId " +
        "   ORDER BY PurchaseList.Amount) " +
```

```
            "FROM Rewards2ModelContainer.Purchases " +
            "AS Grouping " +
            "GROUP BY Grouping.CustomersId";

    // Create a query object.
    ObjectQuery<DbDataRecord> CustomerData =
        context.CreateQuery<DbDataRecord>(EntitySQLCmd);

    // Create an output string.
    StringBuilder Output =
        new StringBuilder("Purchase Data:");

    // Process the data records.
    foreach (var Customer in CustomerData)
    {
        // Obtain the list of customer data as a List.
        var CustomerList = (List<DbDataRecord>)Customer[1];

        // Add the customer's name.
        Output.Append("\r\n\t" + CustomerList.First()[1]);

        // Process each purchase in the list.
        foreach (var Purchase in CustomerList)
        {
            // Add the purchase data.
            var PurchaseData = (Purchases)Purchase[0];
            Output.Append("\r\n\t\t" + PurchaseData.Amount);
            Output.Append(" on " + PurchaseData.PurchaseDate);
        }
    }

    // Display the customer name on screen.
    MessageBox.Show(Output.ToString());
}
```

The focus of this example is on the query and then the processing of the output data. The query is actually in two parts. First, there's the query that groups all of the records by the *CustomersId*. Second, there's a nested query that obtains the data for each of these groups from the database, along with the *CustomerName* data using navigation. You saw a similar approach in the "Ordering data" section of the chapter. The difference is that now the data is ordered by *Amount* and the data is also grouped by *CustomersId*.

Of course, if you simply make the query and subquery without any sort of linkage, you'd see every purchase for every customer, which is not what you want. The *WHERE* clause is exceptionally important in this query. Notice that the only records selected are those where the *CustomersId* value matches in each of the queries. The *WHERE* clause must make a match on fields that are actually selected as part of the *GROUP BY* clause in the first query.

Processing the data also takes a somewhat different form this time. There are two *foreach* loops: one for the first query and one for the second. The first query selects individual customer IDs. However, you don't want to display a customer ID on screen—what you really want to display is the *CustomerName* field. The problem is that *CustomerData* returns two objects—the first contains the *CustomersId* value, and the second contains the combination of the *Purchases* table record and the *Customer* reference used for navigation. To obtain the *CustomerName*, you must first cast the second object in *Customer* to a *List<DbDataRecord>*. You can then extract the first record of that list and obtain the *CustomerName* from it as shown.

The second *foreach* loop works exclusively with the *Purchases* table record. Again, you must cast the data in *Purchase* to the correct type. Obtaining the data from *PurchaseData* is simply a matter of accessing the field value at that point.

4. Click Start or press F5. The application compiles and runs.
5. Click Query 7. You'll see the output shown here:

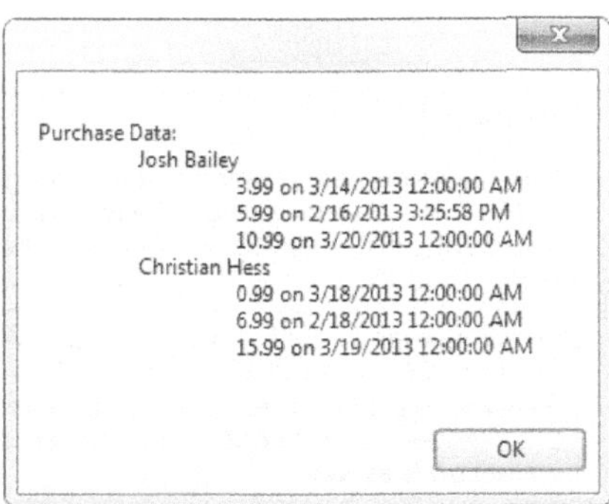

Getting started with the Entity Framework

This chapter has helped you explore Entity SQL in some depth. You've discovered that you can perform a considerable number of tasks using this SQL-like language. If you are familiar with SQL, you've no doubt also noticed a considerable number of differences between Entity SQL and standard SQL or T-SQL. If you take one thing away from this chapter, though, it's that Entity SQL is its own language and not specifically associated with SQL or T-SQL. In fact, you can use Entity SQL against any DBMS for which you have the appropriate database-specific provider, much as you can use LINQ to Entities against any DBMS under the same circumstances. The choice comes down to which form of communication works best for you as a developer.

The only way to learn a language such as LINQ to Entities or Entity SQL is to play around with it. It's important to use the language and see what it can do. This chapter contains a number of Entity SQL examples that you could easily modify just to see what happens. That's the essence of play when it comes to learning language fundamentals—to tweak and see what happens. Try working with the examples in both Chapter 6 and this chapter to see which language—LINQ to Entities or Entity SQL—works best for you in particular situations. If you're like some developers, you may find that one solution works best most of the time, but the other solution has advantages for specific needs. That's why knowing both techniques will prove handy.

Chapter 8, "Interaction with stored procedures," moves back to LINQ to Entities to work with stored procedures. Using stored procedures can help you leverage code that a Database Administrator (DBA) has already created to perform certain tasks directly on the DBMS. In addition, you'll find that there are performance benefits in using stored procedures instead of local code to perform certain tasks. Of course, to use a stored procedure, you must know the language of the host DBMS, which is going to be some form of SQL most of the time. In this case, you rely on the Entity Framework to call the stored procedure, send it any required data, and receive the result, but the stored procedure actually performs the task for you.

Chapter 7 quick reference

To	Do this
Create a Unicode string	Place an uppercase *N* in front of the string, such as *N"This is my Unicode string."* The *N* must be uppercase, and there can't be any spaces between the *N* and the string.
Create a date/time value	Create a string in the following format: *DATETIME "2013-03-04 17:53"*, where 2013 is the year, 03 is the month, 04 is the day, 17 represents the hours, and 53 represents the minutes. You may optionally add seconds and milliseconds as well.
Create a time value	Create a string in the following format: *TIME "17:53"*, where 17 represents the hours and 53 represents the minutes. You may optionally add seconds and milliseconds as well.
Define a 64-bit integer value	Add an uppercase *L* after the number, such as *123L*.
Define a 32-bit real value	Add a lowercase *f* after the number, such as *123.0f*.
Define a decimal value	Add an uppercase *M* after the number, such as *123.0M*.
Define a null value	Use the *null* keyword.
Define a Boolean value	Use the *true* or *false* keyword.
Generate a binary string	Use the *BINARY* keyword or *X* (or lowercase *x*) shortcut, followed by the string in single quotes, such as *BINARY '0123456789ABCDEF'*.
Generate a GUID	Use the *GUID* keyword followed by a string that has the proper format in single quotes, such as *GUID '01234567-89AB-CDEF-0123-456789ABCDEF'*.
Create an anonymous, structurally typed record	Employ the row constructor using the *ROW* keyword and aliased fields, like this: *ROW(1 AS IntValue, 1.5 AS DoubleValue, "ABC" AS StringValue, true AS BooleanValue)*.
Define a multiset	Employ the collection constructor using the *MULTISET* keyword and a list of items with the same type, such as *MULTISET("One", "Two", "Three")*.
Specify a named type	Create a conceptual model of an instance, complex, or entity type using a type alias and type content such as *Customer.Id(5, "Josh", "Bailey")* for a complex type.
Work with references that allow you to interact with foreign keys in an entity set	Use one of the reference keywords (*CREATEREF, DEREF, KEY, NAVIGATE*, or *REF*) to perform the required task.

To	Do this
Combine an entire collection into a single scalar output	Use one of the aggregate collection functions: AVG, CHECKSUM_AGG, MAX, MIN, STDEV, STDEVP, SUM, VAR, or VARP.
Combine like groups of records within a collection into a single scalar output	Use one of the aggregate group functions, AVG, CHECKSUM_AGG, MAX, MIN, STDEV, STDEVP, SUM, VAR, or VARP, with the GROUP BY clause in a query. As part of this aggregate use, you can combine the GROUP BY clause with the DISTINCT or ANY keyword.
Overload a function name	Vary the number of parameters, types of input arguments, subtypes of input arguments, or types or subtypes of promoted input arguments. The signature of two functions with the same name must differ in some unambiguous manner, or Entity SQL will raise an exception.
Add a namespace	Start with the USING keyword, followed by the namespace you want to add, such as USING System.Data.
Select ranges of records within a query	Use the paging-related keywords—SKIP, LIMIT, or TOP—to select a specific record range. You may combine the SKIP and LIMIT keywords to specify a nonzero output range. For example, if you specify SKIP 10 LIMIT 5, the output would begin with record number 11 and end with record number 15 from the result set. You can't use TOP with the other keywords.
Group records with a like value in a specific field	Use the GROUP BY clause and provide the key you want to use for grouping. Remember that every expression in the SELECT clause must be accounted for in the GROUP BY clause or wrapped in an aggregate.

Make choices within a query based on an expression	Use the CASE statement. Provide the expression within the WHEN clause and the output in the THEN clause. You may optionally include an ELSE clause that provides output when the expression is false. A typical CASE statement looks like this:
	
	`CASE`
	`   WHEN Customers.CustomerName == "Josh Bailey"`
	`   THEN "Good Customer!"`
	`   ELSE "Watch this one."`
	`END`

Create record-based output from a query	Use the DbDataRecord class as the input to the ObjectQuery object.

CHAPTER 8

Interaction with stored procedures

After completing the chapter, you'll be able to

- Describe what a stored procedure is and how it affects the Entity Framework.
- Create a stored procedure as part of your database model.
- Describe how to develop an application that uses a stored procedure.
- Create an application that uses a stored procedure.

Stored procedures provide a means of storing data management code directly on the server in the SQL language. Unlike other forms of application code described in this book, a stored procedure is accessible by anyone who has access to the server and the required security privileges. It doesn't matter what language you're using outside of Microsoft SQL Server, or whether you're using another language at all. In short, stored procedures provide the best general-purpose method of creating data management code that everyone can access.

Using stored procedures provides a certain level of continuity between applications and ensures that every application performs a specified task in precisely the same manner (increasing reliability and reducing the potential for error). Of course, there are downsides to using stored procedures as well, not the least of which is that developers have to learn the SQL language. This chapter explores using stored procedures as part of your Entity Framework solution. It begins by providing an overview of stored procedures in the first section (and you can easily skip that section if you've used stored procedures extensively).

Note Knowing how to use stored procedures with the Entity Framework is important. Many organizations have policies in place that restrict direct access to the database for security or legal reasons. The only method of access allowed is through the use of stored procedures. In fact, some organizations go further and allow queries only through views (a topic discussed in Chapter 9, "Interaction with Views,"), so there's no chance of accidentally modifying the data.

Understanding what a stored procedure is and how to use it from the Entity Framework are two different things. The chapter will discuss and demonstrate the techniques used to create and add stored procedures to your Entity Framework model. Following this, you can use the example stored procedure in your application to perform various tasks, just as anyone else will use the stored procedure as part of an application solution. The effect is similar to the one demonstrated for functions in the "Using Entity and database functions" section of Chapter 6, "Manipulating data using LINQ."

Understanding stored procedures

At its simplest level, a stored procedure is simply a kind of macro that contains the steps that a Database Administrator (DBA) would normally perform to accomplish a task. When you review many stored procedures, what you see is a series of steps. These steps are often modified with the use of parameters that provide additional data to the stored procedure, but the overall simple view is that you're simply recording a series of task-related steps for later playback. The goal is to automate repetitive steps so the DBA doesn't have to perform them. However, some stored procedures can become quite complex, and they're used for more than simple automation. No matter what sort of stored procedure you're using, they all have some essential characteristics that are discussed in this section of the chapter.

Note It's outside the scope of this book to provide you with a complete tutorial about stored procedures. Most books about SQL Server take entire chapters to even scratch the surface. What this chapter provides is a light overview—enough information so that you'll be able to follow the examples in the rest of the chapter. If you find yourself getting lost, there's an excellent stored procedure tutorial at *http://www.mssqltips.com/sqlservertutorial/160/sql-server-stored-procedure/*.

You've already worked with stored procedures in a couple of places in the book. For example, when generating the database from a model, you create a .SQL file first that contains the same sort of code found in a stored procedure, and then you right-click that file and choose Execute from the context menu to create the database (see the "Working with the mapping details" section of Chapter 1, "Getting to know the Entity Framework," as an example). You could also add data to a database using the SQL script found in UserFavorites Data.sql in the "Running the basic query" section of Chapter 2, "Looking more closely at queries." In short, you already have a little experience using stored procedure–like scripts. They both use the same language—a stored procedure simply adds a little to the basic functionality of scripts found in .SQL files.

A stored procedure starts simply. All you need is a task to perform, such as a query. For example, you might decide that you want to obtain a list of customers from the *Rewards2* database. In this case, your query might be this:

```
SELECT * FROM Rewards2.dbo.Customers
```

This query selects all of the fields for all of the customers from the *Rewards2 Customers* table. The abbreviation *DBO* stands for "database owner." It usually appears in lowercase as *dbo* to represent the owner in resources found in the database. In order to create a stored procedure, you simply tell SQL Server to create it using the following:

```
CREATE PROCEDURE GetCustomers
```

This command simply says to create a stored procedure named *GetCustomers*. There are all sorts of naming conventions that organizations follow, but any unique name will do. You connect the command to create the stored procedure with the query you want the stored procedure to perform with the *AS* keyword. A command often ends with the keyword *GO*, which means to perform the task immediately, rather than waiting for a number of commands to pile up to perform in batch mode. So, the entire script for creating a simple stored procedure is as follows:

```
CREATE PROCEDURE GetCustomers
AS
SELECT * FROM Rewards2.dbo.Customers
GO
```

Stored procedures can also accept arguments as input. The arguments always appear with an @ (at) sign in front of them, and you supply a value to the argument as part of making the query. For example, you could specify a query like this one:

```
SELECT * FROM Rewards2.dbo.Customers WHERE CustomerName = @Name
```

The need for the variable is expressed as part of the *CREATE PROCEDURE* syntax. So, you'd add @ *Name* to it and create a statement like this one:

```
CREATE PROCEDURE GetCustomers @Name NVarChar(30)
AS
SELECT * FROM Rewards2.dbo.Customers WHERE CustomerName = @Name
GO
```

The *NVarChar(30)* part of the *CREATE PROCEDURE* statement defines the type (Unicode variable length character string) and length (30 characters maximum). You must define the type as a minimum and some types, such as *NVarChar*, require further definition for their length.

Note SQL Server queries are case insensitive. This book relies on case to help make the query easier to understand. By convention, the keywords appear in uppercase and variable information in mixed (Pascal) case. However, you can use whatever case your organization requires to make the queries clear and understandable without any loss of functionality.

There's a logical process to creating and managing stored procedures. This chapter won't focus on that topic, but you'll work with simple stored procedures like those shown in this section. You'll also see how to create stored procedures without using the SQL Server tools—the chapter will use Server Explorer to perform the task instead. When you view the database in either Server Explorer or SQL Server Management Studio, you'll see the stored procedures in a Stored Procedures folder, as shown here. (When working with SQL Server Management Studio, this folder resides under the Programmability folder for the database in question.)

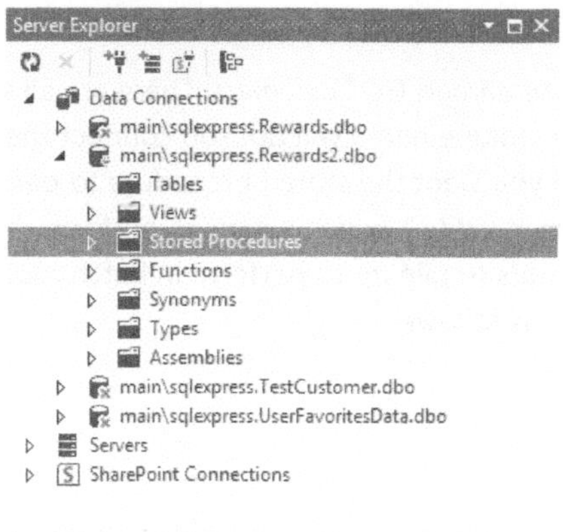

Using stored procedures vs. views to select data

Many developers wonder about the differences between stored procedures and views. They're actually quite different in concept and functionality. Stored procedures are flexible and they can do more than simply select data—you can use them to perform the create, read, update, and delete (CRUD) operations that reflect the sum of tasks you perform with a database. In addition, stored procedures accept parameters (arguments), and you can use control logic within them to determine the output based on environment, user rights, parameter data, and other forms of input.

A view, on the other hand, is a stored query. It accepts no parameters and doesn't rely on any sort of control logic. The output from a view remains consistent. You get the same columns and the same type of result set. The only thing that varies is the data in the database. The data that a view works with ultimately controls the variation in data returned by the view. A view works best in situations where you can anticipate the output needed in advance. For example, if an organization requires the same report every week, using a view makes sense because the view will return the data with the least fuss and the smallest potential for damage to the data.

From a SQL perspective, a view is a kind of virtual table, while a stored procedure is a series of statements that return a result. Views have some advantages in that you can use them as you would tables. For example, you can index a view or join it to another view, much as you would join two tables. Stored procedures don't allow indexing or joining, because you're getting a result set back, not a table. Theoretically, a view will perform better because you're returning the same optimized dataset each time. However, there's a lot of debate on the matter, and the optimization that Microsoft provides for stored procedures makes the decision hard.

In general, you want to use stored procedures where flexibility and the ability to perform CRUD operations are concerns. Views work best where security and the ability to treat the output as a table are concerns. As to performance, you'll need to create both a view and a stored procedure form of the same query, and time the results. In most cases, you'll find that the view is faster, but you may also find that a stored procedure works better in cases where SQL Server's ability to optimize the query works to an advantage.

Adding stored procedures to your model

In order to use stored procedures with the Entity Framework, you must have the required stored procedure in the database and then update the model with it. If you work for an organization that requires you to use stored procedures, you probably have a wealth of them available already. However, the first section that follows shows how to create a simple stored procedure that you can use with the examples in this chapter, and also so you know how to do it in the future. The next section demonstrates how to update the model to use the stored procedures. Once you have the update in place, you can use the stored procedure in a manner similar to how you worked with the function in the "Using entity and database functions" section of Chapter 6.

Defining the stored procedure using Server Explorer

Before you can do anything with stored procedures, you need a stored procedure to work with. If you work for an organization that requires the use of stored procedures for all database tasks, you'll undoubtedly have plenty of stored procedures to work with. However, it's good to know how to create stored procedures, and your example database doesn't currently have any stored procedures in it. The following procedure shows how to define a simple stored procedure for use with the examples throughout the rest of the chapter.

Creating a simple stored procedure

1. Open your copy of Microsoft Visual Studio. You don't need to have a project loaded because you're going to be interacting with Server Explorer and SQL Server.

2. Choose View | Server Explorer to open the Server Explorer window if it isn't already open. Under Data Connections, you should see closed connections to the four databases used in the book.

Tip You can easily tell when a connection is closed. The database icon will have a red X in the lower-right corner.

3. Open the connection to the *Rewards2* database by clicking the right-pointing arrow next to it. You'll see a list of folders associated with the database, including the Stored Procedures folder.

4. Right-click the Stored Procedures folder and choose Add New Stored Procedure from the context menu. You'll see a new window appear that has a template for creating a stored procedure in it, like the one shown here:

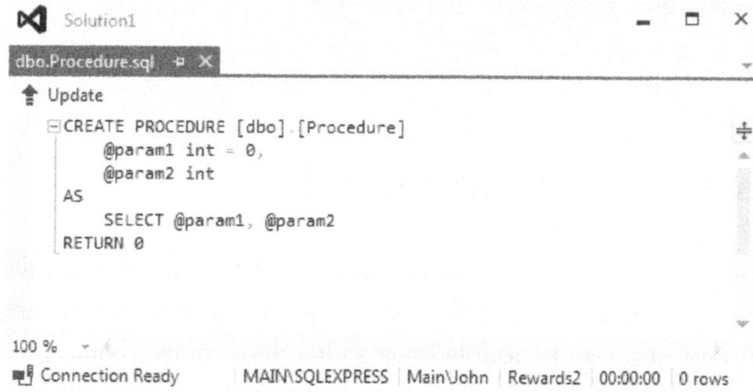

5. Overwrite the template code with the following code:

```
CREATE PROCEDURE ChooseClients
AS
   SELECT * FROM Customers AS C
   INNER JOIN Purchases AS P
   ON C.Id = P.CustomersId
   ORDER BY P.PurchaseDate
```

6. Click the Update button that appears on the left side directly above the editor. Visual Studio prepares the update and displays the following dialog box showing the changes:

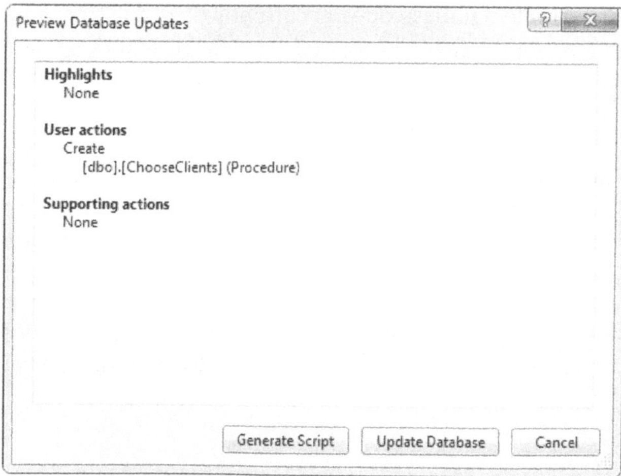

7. Click Update Database. Visual Studio begins the database update. You can follow the progress of the update in the Data Tools Operations window. When the process is complete, you'll see an "Update completed successfully" message like the one shown here:

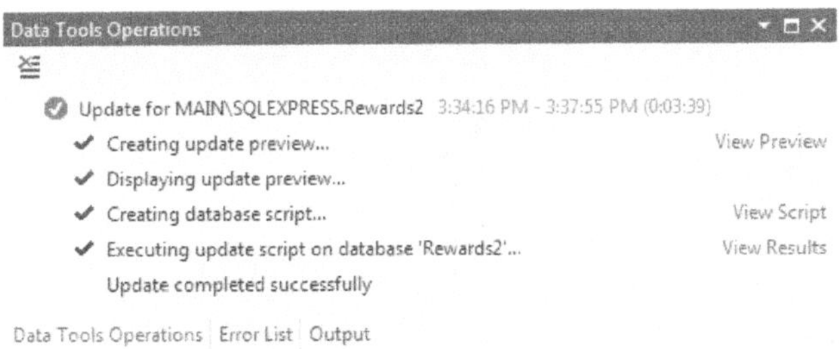

Testing the stored procedure

At this point, you've created a new stored procedure and updated the database with it. Unfortunately, you don't know whether the stored procedure will work properly. Testing the stored procedure now will save you considerable time later. If you know that the stored procedure works, then you can look elsewhere when you encounter problems getting the application to work. The following procedure demonstrates how to test the stored procedure you created in the "Defining the stored procedure using Server Explorer" section of this chapter. Of course, you can use this process any time you have a stored procedure to check.

Testing a simple stored procedure

1. Choose View | Server Explorer to open the Server Explorer window if it isn't already open.
2. Open the Stored Procedures folder, and you should now see the *ChooseClients* stored procedure, as shown here:

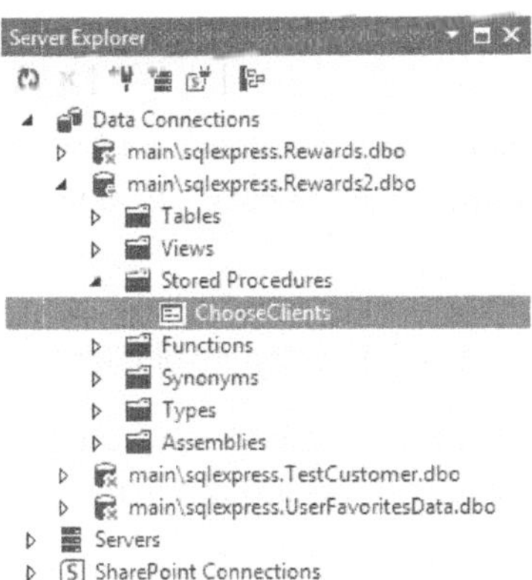

3. Right-click the ChooseClients entry and choose Execute from the context menu. Visual Studio creates and executes a new SQL query. You'll see results similar to the ones shown here:

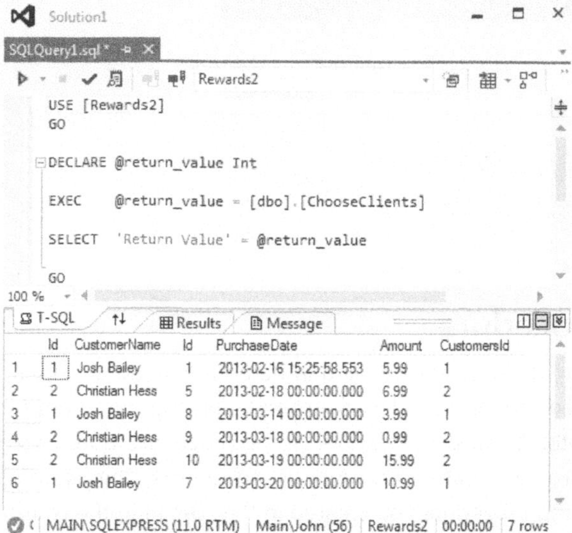

Updating the model

At this point, you have a stored procedure to use and you've tested it. The stored procedure is still inaccessible from your database model, which means you can't use it in an application yet. From an Entity Framework perspective, stored procedures and functions are similar. In fact, stored procedures use a modified form of the same entries that functions do. With this in mind, the following procedure will look similar to the one that you used to update the model with a function in Chapter 6.

Updating the model to use stored procedures

1. Copy the *ModelFirst* example you created in Chapter 3, "Choosing a workflow," to a new folder, and use this new copy for this example (rather than the copy you created in Chapter 3).
2. Open the copied solution in Visual Studio.
3. Open the Rewards2Model.EDMX file by double-clicking its entry in Solution Explorer.
4. Right-click in any clear area of the designer and choose Update Model From Database from the context menu. You'll see the Update Wizard dialog box, as shown here:

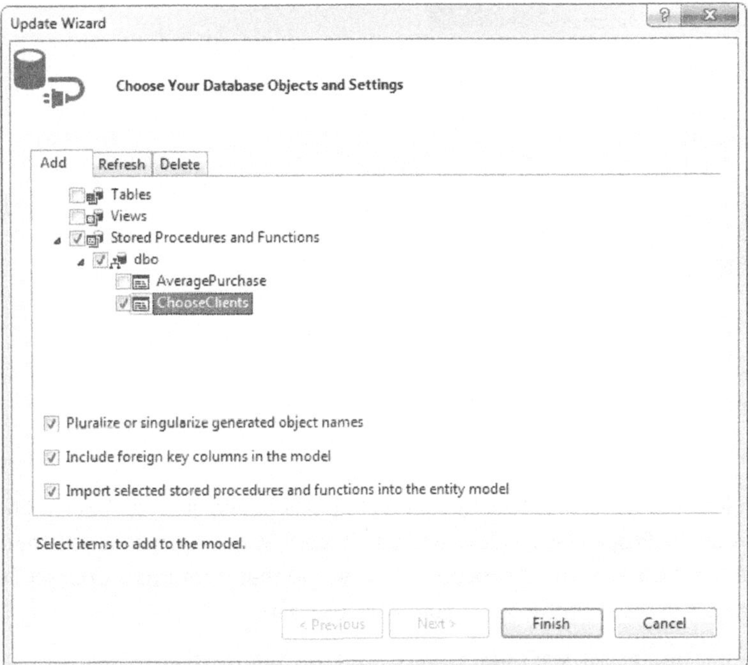

Notice that the wizard groups both stored procedures and functions together. It's essential that you know whether an addition is a stored procedure or a function, so you know how to interact with it later. Review your choices in Server Explorer as needed.

Note The only items you see are those that are either new or updated. The reason the *AveragePurchase* function appears, in this case, is that you're using the Chapter 3 copy of the *ModelFirst* application, which hasn't had this function added to it. Normally, functions or stored procedures that you've already added to an application won't appear in the list.

5. Drill down to the *ChooseClients* stored procedure entry and check it. Click Finish. The wizard completes its task. As with the function, you won't see the addition to the designer view of the model.
6. Choose Build | Build Solution to update the model. At this point, you can see the stored procedure, but you must do something special.
7. Right-click in any open area of the model designer and choose Model Browser from the context menu. You'll see the Model Browser window, as shown here:

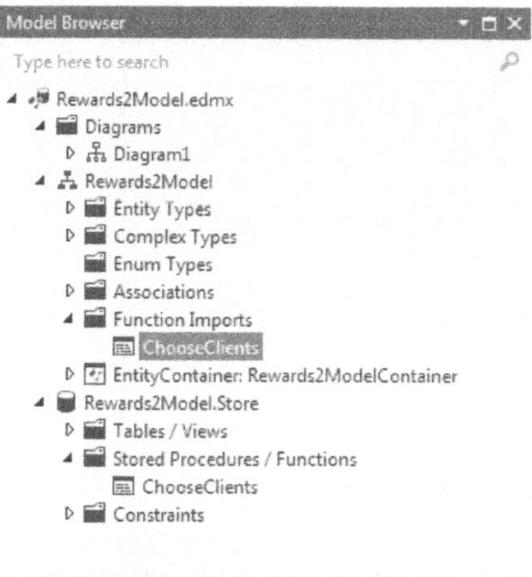

8. Drill down into the Rewards2Model\Function Imports folder, and you'll see a ChooseClients entry. Look at the Properties window, and you'll see that this entry tells you that *ChooseClients* is both the function and stored procedure name, and that it returns a *ChooseClients_Result* type (which is the result of the query you make using it).

9. Drill down into the Rewards2Model.Store\Stored Procedures/Functions folder and you'll see a second ChooseClients entry. This time, the Properties window provides information used by the Entity Framework to interact with the stored procedure. Most of this information isn't changeable.

10. Drill down into the Rewards2Model\Complex Types folder, and you'll see the *ChooseClients_Result* complex type entry. Open this entry, and you'll see a list of fields returned by the query. When you select a particular field, you can see the properties for it. For example, when you select Amount, the query returns a *Decimal* type with a precision of 18 digits and a scale (decimal portion) of 2 digits.

Modifying a stored procedure

Sometimes a stored procedure performs as requested, but new requirements come to light, and you need to modify it so that it performs differently. For example, in the case of the example stored procedure, you may decide that it's important to provide a method for changing the order of the entries. Using the date order of the original stored procedure may not work for your particular needs.

In order to change the ordering, you need to provide a parameter for the stored procedure that allows it to modify the ordering field. Any change to a stored procedure requires that you test it again before using it. Finally, the copy of the stored procedure that's seen by the model isn't the copy that's currently on the server, so you need to perform an update. The following sections perform all of these tasks.

Performing the required update

Stored procedures can be extremely flexible when you put them together correctly. The simple stored procedure you started with for this example performs a single query. However, by adding parameters to the stored procedure, you can make a single piece of code perform quite a few other tasks. The update, in this case, is modest. You'll change the stored procedure so that it can now accept input and change the order in which the output appears.

Updating a simple stored procedure

1. Choose View | Server Explorer to open the Server Explorer window if it isn't already open.
2. Right-click the ChooseClients entry found in the Stored Procedures folder for the Rewards2 database, and choose Open. You'll see an editor open with the code for the stored procedure you created earlier.
3. Change the script so it looks like this:

```
ALTER PROCEDURE ChooseClients
   @OrderBy NVarChar(20)
AS
   SELECT * FROM Customers AS C
   INNER JOIN Purchases AS P
   ON C.Id = P.CustomersId
   ORDER BY
      CASE @OrderBy
         WHEN 'PurchaseDate' THEN P.PurchaseDate
         WHEN 'Amount'       THEN P.Amount
         WHEN 'CustomersId'  THEN P.CustomersId
                             ELSE P.PurchaseDate
      END
```

   The editor will complain about the use of the *ALTER* keyword. However, if you don't use *ALTER*, SQL Server will complain that the stored procedure already exists when you try to execute the script. The script will work fine as shown.

   This example adds an argument, *@OrderBy*, that allows you to define which field to use to order the output. However, you can't pass a field directly to SQL Server, so you have two choices: use a *CASE* statement, as shown in the example, or rely on dynamic SQL. The example uses the *CASE* statement because it's more reliable and secure. The size of *@OrderBy* is also designed to reduce the chance of someone passing data other than the name of a field to the script.

   The *CASE* statement provides the means to sort on several different fields, including the customer's name and ID. Notice that it provides an *ELSE* clause. This approach ensures that even if the caller passes an incorrect value, the output information will still be ordered.

4. Right-click the editor window and choose Execute from the context menu. The script is executed, and you'll see "Command(s) completed successfully" as an output message.

Retesting the stored procedure

Any time you make a change to a stored procedure, you need to test it to ensure that it still works as intended. The problem with updates is that they can appear quite reasonable and well thought out, but then testing shows that they don't (or won't) work as intended. The better you test any stored procedure before you begin using it in your application, the less likely it will be that you'll end up with problems in your application later. The following procedure shows the retesting procedure for this stored procedure.

Retesting a simple stored procedure

1. Choose View | Server Explorer to open the Server Explorer window if it isn't already open.
2. Open the Stored Procedures folder. Right-click the *ChooseClients* stored procedure and choose Execute from the context menu. This time, the stored procedure doesn't execute immediately. What you see is the Execute Stored Procedure dialog box shown here:

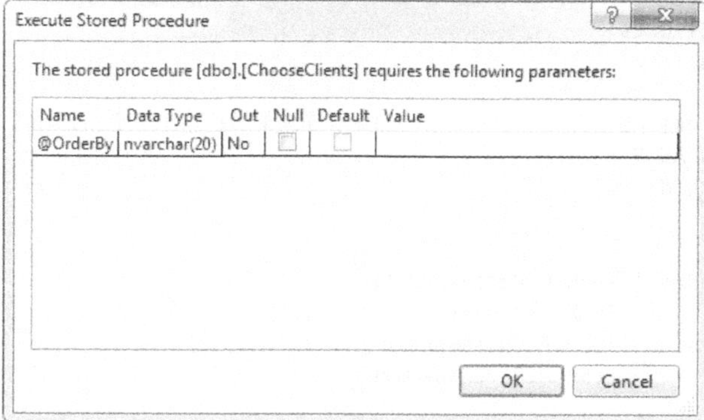

3. Type **Amount** in the Value field and click OK. The output shows the purchases sorted by amount, rather than by purchase date.
4. Repeat steps 2 and 3 for *PurchaseDate* and *CustomersId*. In each case, the stored procedure will output the results in the desired order.
5. Repeat steps 2 and 3 with a value such as *SomeValue*. The stored procedure will output the results in purchase date order.
6. Repeat steps 2 and 3 with a value that's too long, such as *ThisValueIsALittleTooLong*. You won't see an error—the stored procedure will output the results in purchase date order. However, SQL Server will truncate the input string at the 20th letter.

Adding the update to the model

It may seem as if the model should already know about the *ChooseClients* stored procedure, and it does—it knows about the original version that doesn't require any sort of parameter. Every time you update a stored procedure (or other facet) of your database, you need to update the model as well.

There are rare cases when the model doesn't require an update, but in such cases, the Update Wizard will simply not show the feature being available for update. The following procedure shows how to update the model after you make the required changes to the stored procedure.

Updating the model after a stored procedure change

1. Right-click in any clear area of the designer and choose Update Model From Database from the context menu. You'll see the Update Wizard.
2. Drill down into the Stored Procedures and Functions\dbo folder. Notice that the ChooseClients entry isn't there. That's because the entry doesn't exist in the model.
3. Select the Refresh tab. Drill down into the Stored Procedures and Functions\dbo folder and select ChooseClients.
4. Click Finish. Visual Studio generates the required changes to the model. Of course, you want to verify the changes.
5. Choose Build | Build Solution to save the modifications to the model.
6. Right-click in any open area of the model designer and choose Model Browser from the context menu. You'll see the Model Browser window.
7. Drill down into the Rewards2Model\Function Imports folder, and you'll see a ChooseClients entry. Open the ChooseClients entry, and you'll see that there's a new entry for @OrderBy, as shown here. (The same entry appears in the ChooseClients entry in the Rewards2Model.Store\Stored Procedures/Functions folder.)

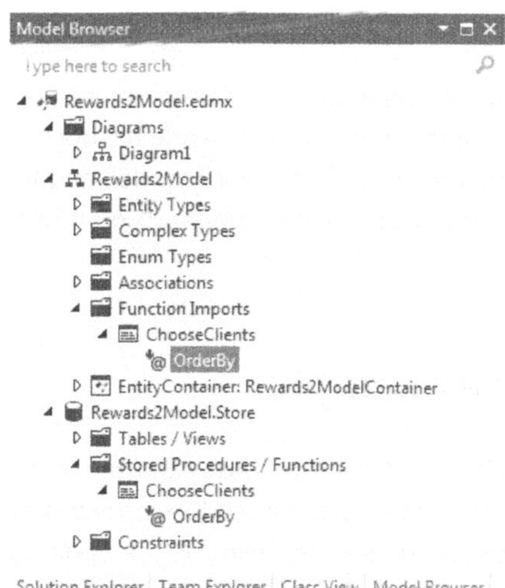

Building an application using stored procedures

All of the examples so far in the book have relied on the Entity Framework to use client-side code to perform all of the Create, Retrieve, Update, and Delete (CRUD) operations required to maintain the database. In this scenario, the client application creates a command and uses Microsoft ADO.NET to pass it to the server. A large part of the processing burden is placed on the client in this scenario. This solution makes the most sense when you're working with fat clients, such as desktop systems, and there are no organizational requirements to use stored procedures for consistency and security reasons.

However, it's entirely possible to use stored procedures for every bit of the processing required by the client application. In this case, the client calls on the stored procedure on the server to perform all of the required work. The client simply passes any required parameters to the server along with the request so that the server has what it needs to fulfill the request. This scenario works best with thin clients because the processing burden is on the server. In addition, it can be more efficient because network traffic is reduced. Instead of sending all of the data to the client for processing, the server sends just the subset that the client actually needs.

It's important to understand that using stored procedures is an option that comes with specific requirements. For example, using stored procedures means that you must have the means to perform four basic tasks:

- Create (Insert)
- Read (select)
- Update
- Delete

These requirements are normally addressed by four separate stored procedures. You must provide this information to the client application in order for the application to work. In short, you must create and test each of the stored procedures, update the Entity Framework model, and then incorporate the changes into the client application. The method of incorporation depends on how the client is configured.

Creating a basic stored procedure example

The stored procedure is ready for use. You can select the list of purchases and the associated customers for each purchase in the database. In addition, the stored procedure provides the means for ordering the output in various ways. The procedure in this section relies on the updated *ModelFirst* example you've been working with throughout the chapter. It demonstrates how to use the stored procedure as part of an application solution.

Developing an application that uses stored procedures

1. Add the following new controls to *Form1*:
   - ***Button*** (Name) *btnQuery, Text &Query*
   - ***Label*** (Name) *lblOrderBy, Text &Order By*
   - ***ComboBox*** (Name) *cbOrderBy, Text PurchaseDate*
2. Click the ellipses in the *Items* property for *cbOrderBy.* You'll see the String Collection editor.
3. Enter the following values, one on each line, in the String Collection editor:
   - *Amount*
   - *CustomersId*
   - *PurchaseDate*
4. Click OK. Visual Studio adds the order-by strings to *cbOrderBy.*
5. Double-click btnQuery to create a new click event handler.
6. Type the following code for the *btnQuery_Click()* event handler:

```
private void btnQuery_Click(object sender, EventArgs e)
{
    // Create the context.
    Rewards2ModelContainer context = new Rewards2ModelContainer();

    // Make the query.
    var PurchaseList =
       from purchase
       in context.ChooseClients(cbOrderBy.SelectedItem.ToString())
       select purchase;

    // Create a string to hold the result.
    StringBuilder Output = new StringBuilder();

    // Parse the result.
    foreach (var PurchaseEntry in PurchaseList)
        Output.Append(
           PurchaseEntry.CustomerName + " ID " +
           PurchaseEntry.CustomersId + " purchased " +
           PurchaseEntry.Amount + " on " +
           PurchaseEntry.PurchaseDate + "\r\n");

    // Display the result on screen.
    MessageBox.Show(Output.ToString());
}
```

This example uses the context object to access the *ChooseClients()* method directly. This method requires string input to define the order of the output, which is supplied by *cbOrderBy* in this case.

After the call is made, *PurchaseList* contains one entry for each purchase in the database. A *foreach* loop provides access to each of the purchases and places them in *PurchaseEntry*. You can access the fields directly, as shown.

7. Click Start or press F5. The application compiles and runs.
8. Select Amount In The Order By field of the example application.
9. Click Query. You'll see the exception dialog box shown here:

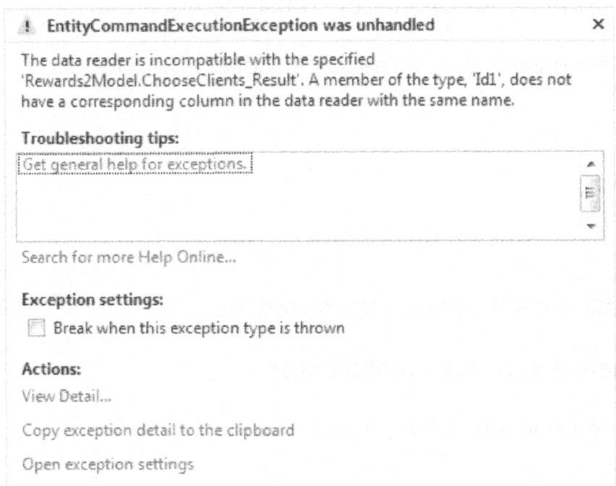

There's no *Id1* column in the model. However, the model does have two *Id* columns, and you can't create a type that has two properties with the same name. You'll encounter this problem at times when working with the Entity Framework. When you use the model-first workflow, you do have the choice of changing the conflicting field name. However, when working with a production system, changing a field name is probably a bad idea. The example shows a second course, which is simply to delete the conflicting property.

10. Select Rewards2Model.EDMX and then open the Model Browser window.
11. Drill down into the Complex Types folder and open the *ChooseClients_Result* complex type. You'll see a list of properties, as shown here:

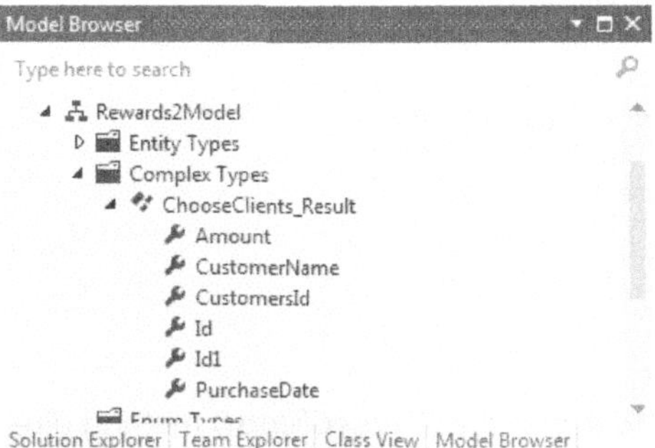

12. Right-click Id1 and choose Delete From Model from the context menu. Visual Studio removes the property.

13. Click Start or press F5. The application compiles and runs.

14. Select Amount in the Order By field of the example application.

15. Click Query. You'll see the output shown here:

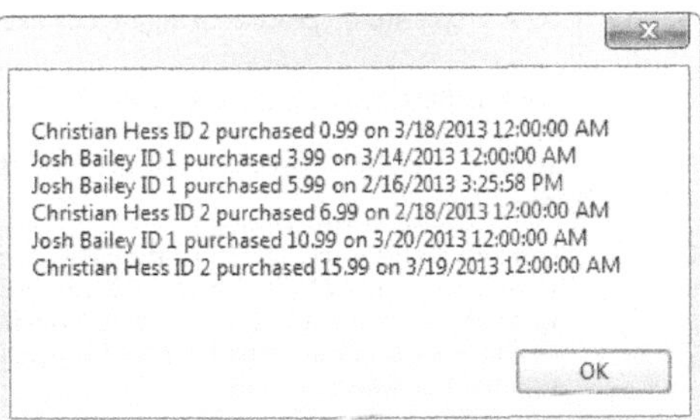
Christian Hess ID 2 purchased 0.99 on 3/18/2013 12:00:00 AM
Josh Bailey ID 1 purchased 3.99 on 3/14/2013 12:00:00 AM
Josh Bailey ID 1 purchased 5.99 on 2/16/2013 3:25:58 PM
Christian Hess ID 2 purchased 6.99 on 2/18/2013 12:00:00 AM
Josh Bailey ID 1 purchased 10.99 on 3/20/2013 12:00:00 AM
Christian Hess ID 2 purchased 15.99 on 3/19/2013 12:00:00 AM
OK

16. Perform steps 14 and 15 for each of the two remaining ordering methods so that you can see how they work.

Getting started with the Entity Framework

This chapter has demonstrated the basics for creating, managing, and using stored procedures with the Entity Framework. Knowing how to work with stored procedures is essential because many organizations don't allow direct database access—they only allow access through stored procedures and views. The most important concept to take away from this chapter is that defining and using stored procedures need not be difficult, and you can perform a considerable amount of work without leaving the IDE. Server Explorer is a great tool for working with stored procedures, and you should spend some time practicing with it.

Now that you have some knowledge of stored procedures, take some time to play around with them for a while. For example, try creating a new stored procedure on your own. This time, start with the *Purchases* table and query it. Try modifying queries and using the modified form in your application. The only way to become proficient with stored procedures is to create, update, and test them in your application. Make sure you spend time working through the steps required to keep the stored procedure and your model in sync. Try working with complex types as needed to fully understand how complex types modify the use of stored procedures.

Views are also an important part of working with the Entity Framework. A view offers a method of obtaining data from the database without actually touching the data. Using views is considered safer than stored procedures because views aren't able to modify the database content in any way. In addition, using views, when you can, enhances application performance. You'll find that your application is faster when using views to make queries. Rely on stored procedures when you need to make complex queries or manage the database in some way (such as adding or deleting records).

Chapter 8 quick reference

To	Do this

Create a stored procedure	Define the stored procedure using the *CREATE PROCEDURE* statement, followed by the word AS, your query, and the word *GO*. A simple stored procedure might look like this:
	
	`CREATE PROCEDURE GetCustomers`
	`AS`
	`SELECT * FROM Rewards2.dbo.Customers`
	`GO`

Allow the stored procedure to access variable input	Add arguments to the stored procedure. You provide the arguments as part of the *CREATE PROCEDURE* statement and again as part of the query. Arguments always begin with an @ sign. Here's an example of a stored procedure that has an argument of *@Name*:
	
	`CREATE PROCEDURE GetCustomers @Name NVarChar(30)`
	`AS`
	`SELECT * FROM Rewards2.dbo.Customers WHERE`
	`CustomerName = @Name`
	`GO`

Create a new stored procedure	Right-click the Stored Procedures folder in Server Explorer and choose Add New Stored Procedure from the context menu.
Test an existing stored procedure	Right-click the entry for the stored procedure in the Stored Procedures folder in Server Explorer, and choose Execute from the context menu.
Update the model so that it knows about the stored procedure	Right-click in any clear area of the designer and choose Update Model from Database from the context menu. Follow the steps provided by the wizard to include the stored procedure in the model (you won't actually see the stored procedure appear in the designer).
See the addition of a function or stored procedure to a model	Right-click in any open area of the model designer and choose Model Browser from the context menu.
Modify a stored procedure	Change the *CREATE* keyword to *ALTER* so that SQL Server modifies the existing stored procedure.

Create a stored procedure that works with multiple field values	Rely on a *CASE* statement to transform an input string into a field value, like this:
	
	`ALTER PROCEDURE ChooseClients`
	`   @OrderBy NVarChar(20)`
	`AS`
	`   SELECT * FROM Customers AS C`
	`   INNER JOIN Purchases AS P`
	`   ON C.Id = P.CustomersId`
	`   ORDER BY`
	`      CASE @OrderBy`
	`         WHEN 'PurchaseDate' THEN P.PurchaseDate`
	`         WHEN 'Amount'       THEN P.Amount`
	`         WHEN 'CustomersId'  THEN P.CustomersId`
	`                             ELSE P.PurchaseDate`
	`      END`

CHAPTER 9

Interaction with views

After completing the chapter, you'll be able to

- Describe what a view is and how it affects the Entity Framework.
- Create a view as part of your database model.
- Create an application that uses a view.
- Develop a writable view.

Views and stored procedures are often confused. The two serve completely different purposes (see the "Using stored procedures vs. views to select data" sidebar in Chapter 8, "Interaction with stored procedures"), and you need to know how to use both of them to develop complete applications with a maximum of both security and reliability. A view, as the name implies, is an actual view of the data—it's a read-only snapshot of the data. It's a type of virtual table you use to obtain access to data. Like tables themselves, you can index views and join views together to create a new perspective of the information. However, views also make it impossible to perform the full set of Create, Read, Update, and Delete (CRUD) operations—all you can do is select (read) the data using a view alone.

This chapter demonstrates the techniques used to create new views, add them to your model, and then use them as part of an application. The flexibility of views will surprise you, and you'll likely find that you use them relatively often, even if company policy does permit you to use client-side code to perform most tasks. The one thing you need to take away from this chapter is that a view on the server is accessible to every application you create, so you only have to define and test the selection criteria one time in order to use it everywhere. That's one of the special features of views—they make it possible for you to reduce your workload.

Note As with many other programming techniques, it's possible to overuse views or use them in the wrong way. Remember that you can't send parameters to views, so views won't be as flexible as stored procedures in some situations. In addition, you should reserve views for those situations where you really do plan to use the same selection criteria across applications. For example, you might need to select specific data for a report that's used everywhere. It's important not to clutter the database with views that are only used once or with a single application.

The final portion of this chapter deals with a special task you can perform with views. It's possible to make views writable by adding stored procedures to the process. (You can also make views writable by fiddling with the model at a low level, but this isn't a recommended approach.) The example in this chapter shows a basic but usable approach to the problem.

Understanding views

Views are used in an entirely different way from functions or stored procedures, and indeed, they're an entirely different kind of strategy. A Database Administrator (DBA) normally creates views as a means for accessing data in a safe manner. The view doesn't allow any changes. All that a user can do with a view is access the data for use in some type of output, such as a report. Because most user activity with a database involves some sort of search—accessing the data to obtain information from it—using views answers many user needs. There's a class of user that never inputs data directly. This group performs searches for information and uses the data for output such as reports, but the input is performed by someone else. For example, consider someone who searches a parts catalog for a specific item. The goal of the search is to find the part. Yes, this same individual may come back later and make a purchase, but the purchase will affect an entirely different database. This person has no need to ever modify the parts catalog, so views work fine.

So far, this book hasn't worked with any views. However, using a view is much the same as working with a stored procedure. It begins with a query such as this one:

```
SELECT * FROM Rewards2.dbo.Customers
```

It's important to remember that the query must be self-contained. You can't pass parameters that will change the query in any way. Consequently, the query you create for a view is static and never changes unless someone actually rewrites the code. For example, if you write a query that needs to be ordered in four different ways, you theoretically require four different views. However, there's a way around this limitation. You can create a more generic view and then perform tasks such as ordering the data at the client—getting the best of both views and local processing.

This query selects all of the records and all of the fields from the *Rewards2 Customers* table. The *dbo* portion stands for "database owner." The use of the asterisk (*) is a wildcard for all fields. To create the query, you use a statement like this one:

```
CREATE VIEW ViewCustomers
```

The first keyword, *CREATE*, defines a new entry in the database. *VIEW* is the kind of entry to create. *ViewCustomers* is the name of the entry. By convention, most DBAs begin views with the word *View* to make their use apparent. It's important to use names that make the purpose and functionality of a view or stored procedure easy to determine. In this case, the query will create a view of the *Customers* table.

You connect the *CREATE* statement to the query with the *AS* keyword, just as you would for a stored procedure. Adding the word *GO* means that the task will be performed immediately, rather than waiting for a number of other tasks to complete in a batch process. So, the resulting script for creating a new view could look like this:

```
CREATE VIEW ViewCustomers
AS
SELECT * FROM Rewards2.dbo.Customers
GO
```

As with stored procedures, you can modify views to incorporate needed changes. For example, you may decide that the view isn't working quite right. A view, like a stored procedure, uses the *ALTER* keyword to signify an alternation instead of a new view. Consequently, a script to alter a view might look like this:

```
ALTER VIEW ViewCustomers
AS
SELECT * FROM Rewards2.dbo.Customers
GO
```

Views are stored in a special location in Server Explorer. To locate the views you create, look in the *Views* folder of the database connection you create in Server Explorer, as shown here. (When working with Microsoft SQL Server Management Studio, there's a Views folder as one of the main entries for the database in question.)

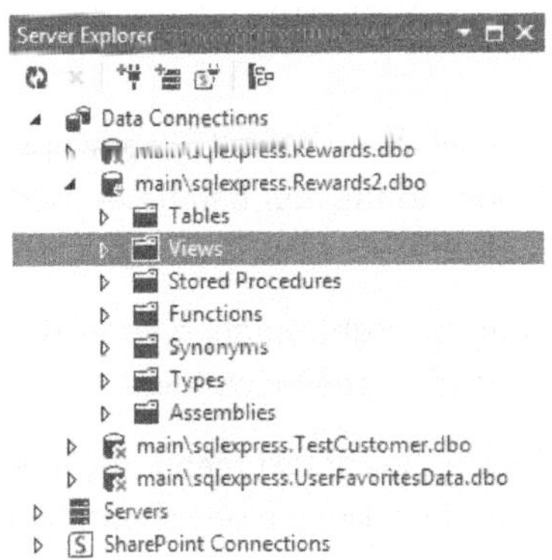

Note This chapter provides only an overview of views to get you through the examples. Like stored procedures, views can become quite complex and incorporate a number of useful and interesting features. For example, you can tell SQL Server to encrypt the results of a view to make unauthorized viewing next to impossible. You can learn more about the *VIEW* syntax at *http://msdn.microsoft.com/library/ms187956.aspx*. Views are also one of the most common and standardized SQL features. There's an excellent generic tutorial for using them at *http://www.w3schools.com/sql/sql_view.asp*.

Adding views to your model

Before you can do anything with a view, you need to have a view to use. As with stored procedures, a production database is likely to have a number of views defined for you by the DBA. However, you need to know how to create and use views, because you can't be sure that there will be a DBA to define them for you, and you also need to create them for test purposes. The following sections show how to create views using Server Explorer, test them, and then update your model to use them. Working with views is somewhat different than working with functions (described in Chapter 6, "Manipulating data using LINQ") and stored procedures (described in Chapter 8), but you'll also notice similarities.

Defining views using Server Explorer

There are a number of different ways to create views using the SQL Server tools. However, most developers will prefer creating a view using Server Explorer because doing so doesn't require leaving the IDE. Fortunately, Microsoft Visual Studio makes the task relatively easy. You can use essentially the same procedure you use to create stored procedures, with a few modifications, as noted in the following procedure.

Creating a simple view

1. Open your copy of Visual Studio. You don't need to have a project loaded because you're going to be interacting with Server Explorer and SQL Server.
2. Choose View | Server Explorer to open the Server Explorer window if it isn't already open. Under Data Connections, you should see closed connections to the four databases used in the book.
3. Open the connection to the *Rewards2* database by clicking the right-pointing arrow next to it. You'll see a list of folders associated with the database, including the Views folder.
4. Right-click the Views folder and choose Add New View from the context menu. You'll see a new window appear that has a template for creating a view in it, like the one shown here:

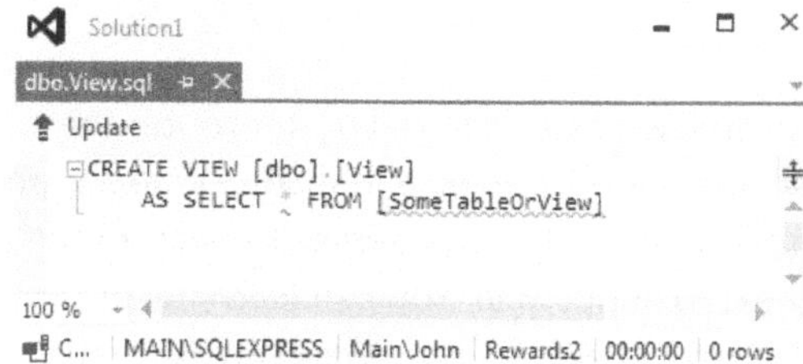

Compare this screen shot with the one in the "Defining the Stored Procedure Using Server Explorer" section of Chapter 8. You'll see some important differences. For example, the template doesn't include parameters because you can't use them with a view. In addition, notice that a view doesn't have a *RETURN* statement by default, because views are virtual tables, not functions. You can't use the *RETURN* statement in a view. The query itself assumes that you're going to work with a table—the stored procedure template query is more generic because you can do other things with it.

5. Overwrite the template code with the following code:

```
CREATE VIEW ViewClients
AS
   SELECT C.CustomerName, P.Id, P.Amount, P.CustomersId, P.PurchaseDate
   FROM Customers AS C
   INNER JOIN Purchases AS P
   ON C.Id = P.CustomersId
```

Tip This query spells out the individual fields that the query should return. Notice that the *C.Id* field is missing from the list. You don't need it to work with the data in this case, so excluding it removes problems with duplicate field names that you might otherwise experience. Using individual field names can save you work and the need for error resolution later.

6. Click the Update button that appears on the left side directly above the editor. Visual Studio prepares the update and displays the following dialog box showing the changes:

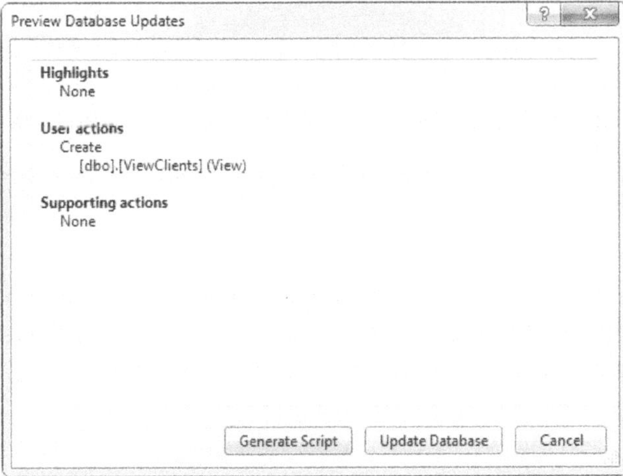

7. Click Update Database. Visual Studio begins the database update. You can follow the progress of the update in the Data Tools Operations window. When the process is complete, you'll see an Update Completed Successfully message like the one shown here:

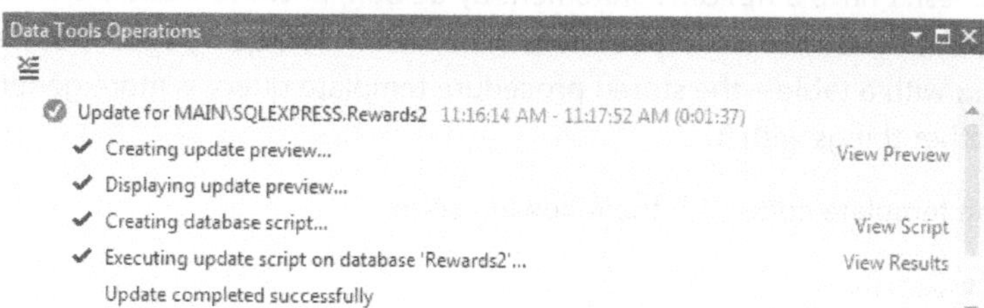

Testing the view

Some developers get the idea that simply because a view doesn't modify data in the database, it requires less stringent testing than a stored procedure or function. However, views, like stored procedures, present plenty of opportunity for errors. The focus is on the client part of the application in this case. You need to ensure that the view provides precisely the results that you expected. If the results differ, you need to find out why. A user will make decisions based on the information that a view provides, so the information needs to be accurate. In addition, an application can use the output from a view as input to a stored procedure. When the view output is less than accurate, the input to the stored procedure is affected as well, potentially causing damage to the database. Consequently, views require the same level of testing that stored procedures do in order to ensure your applications run well. The following steps provide a testing procedure you can use for the example view and modify to meet your view-testing requirements.

Testing a simple view

1. Choose View | Server Explorer to open the Server Explorer window if it isn't already open.
2. Open the Stored Procedures folder, and you should now see the ViewClients view, as shown here.

Note You may have to click the Refresh button in the upper-left corner of Server Explorer to refresh the display if you can't see the ViewClients entry. Server Explorer may not automatically refresh its content to show the new entry.

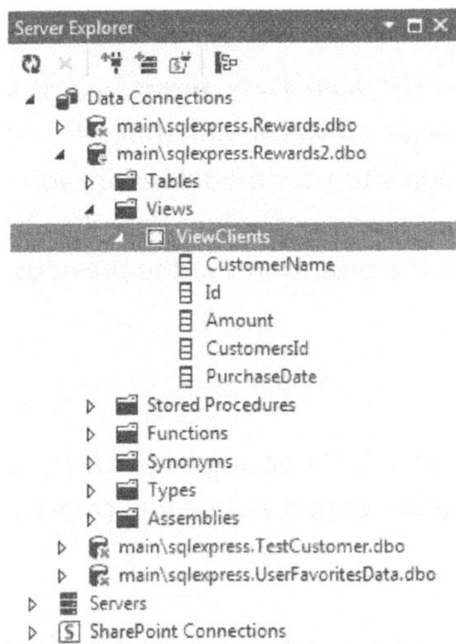

Tip Clicking the right-pointing arrow next to ViewClients also displays the names of fields returned by the view. You can click each field in turn and check its entries in the Properties window to ensure that each field will return the information you need.

3. Right-click the ViewClients entry and choose Show Results from the context menu. Visual Studio displays the view to you. You'll see results similar to those shown here:

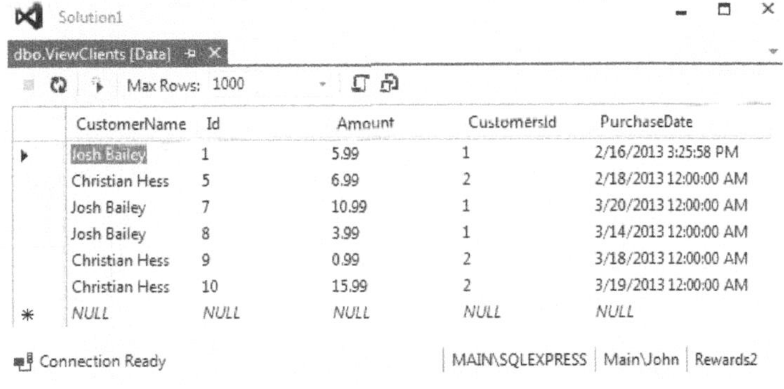

CustomerName	Id	Amount	CustomersId	PurchaseDate
Josh Bailey	1	5.99	1	2/16/2013 3:25:58 PM
Christian Hess	5	6.99	2	2/18/2013 12:00:00 AM
Josh Bailey	7	10.99	1	3/20/2013 12:00:00 AM
Josh Bailey	8	3.99	1	3/14/2013 12:00:00 AM
Christian Hess	9	0.99	2	3/18/2013 12:00:00 AM
Christian Hess	10	15.99	2	3/19/2013 12:00:00 AM
NULL	NULL	NULL	NULL	NULL

Note You should have noticed that the view doesn't execute—it simply returns the data as a table. It's essential to remember that stored procedures and functions execute, while views are virtual tables that you see as tables.

Updating the model

You've already seen that there are significant differences between views and stored procedures, even though both can return data to an application using queries. However, one thing they share in common is that you must add both views and stored procedures to your model before you can successfully use them in an Entity Framework application. The following procedure describes how to add a view to a model after you create and test the view using the procedures in the previous sections.

Updating the model to use views

1. Copy the *ModelFirst* example you created in Chapter 3, "Choosing a workflow," to a new folder, and use this new copy for this example (rather than the copy you created in Chapter 3).
2. Open the copied solution in Visual Studio.
3. Open the Rewards2Model.EDMX file by double-clicking its entry in Solution Explorer.
4. Right-click in any clear area of the designer and choose Update Model From Database from the context menu. You'll see the Update Wizard, as shown here:

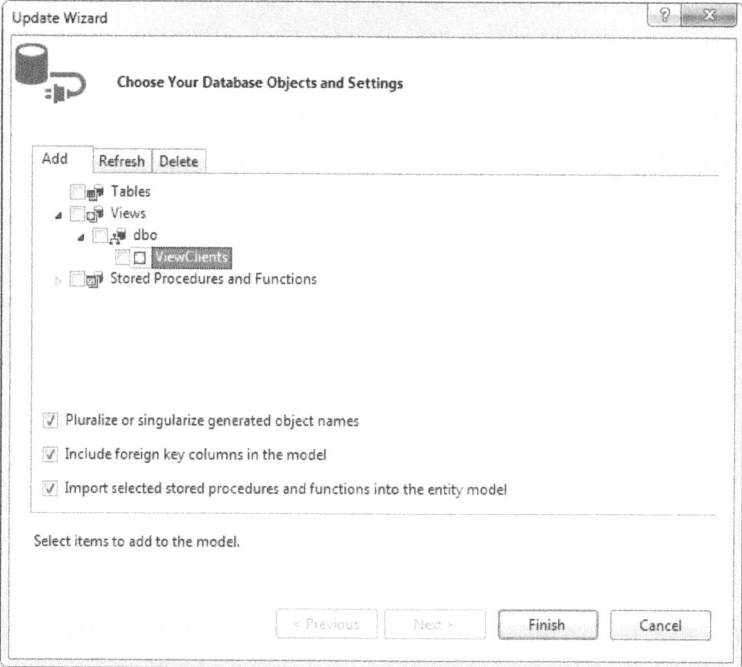

Notice that the wizard places views in a separate Views folder. This is because views are significantly different from stored procedures and functions. The fact that views appear in a separate table should help remind you of this difference.

Views are a kind of virtual table. However, the wizard also keeps them separate from the tables to help enforce the idea that views aren't tables. They can be thought of as virtual tables, but you're still dealing with an entity created from a query.

5. Drill down to the ViewClients view entry and check it. Click Finish. The wizard completes its task. In contrast with stored procedures and functions, in this case the ViewClients view is actually added to the model, as shown here:

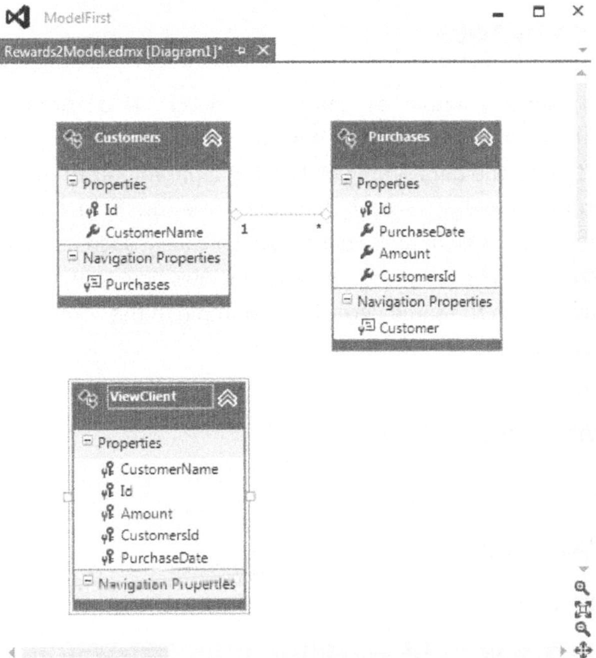

6. Choose View | Output. You'll notice that the Output window contains the result of updating the model with the ViewClients view. Your results will look something like this:

```
The model was generated with warnings or errors.
Please see the Error List for more details. These issues must be fixed before running
your application.
Loading metadata from the database took 00:00:00.4400890.
Generating the model took 00:00:00.9720729.
```

7. Choose View | Error List. You'll see the Error List window, which contains the following error message:

```
The table/view 'Rewards2.dbo.ViewClients' does not have a primary key defined. The key
has been inferred and the definition was created as a read-only table/view.
```

8. Look again at the Rewards2Model.EDMX designer window, and you'll see that the wizard's solution for fixing the problem of not having a key field was to make every field a key field. Obviously, this is a less-than-optimal solution.

9. Right-click CustomerName and click Entity Key to remove the check mark next to it. You'll see that *CustomerName* now uses a standard field icon.

10. Repeat step 9 for the *Amount*, *CustomersId*, and *PurchaseDate* fields. Only the *Id* field should retain the key field icon.

11. Choose Build | Build Solution to update the model.

Creating a basic view example

Using a view in an application is relatively simple compared to working with a stored procedure. All you really need to do is access the context, and most of the work is done for you. However, it's important to remember that you can't order the data simply by passing a parameter to the view. The view will present the data in record order unless you modify the data somehow. In fact, you can consider the data in a view as raw data that results from making a particular query, such as joining two tables together, as is the case in this example. The following procedure shows how to work with a view in such a way as to order the output (much the same way as the example in the "Creating a basic stored procedure example" section of Chapter 8).

Developing an application that uses a view

1. Add the following new controls to *Form1*:
   - ***Button*** (Name) *btnQuery*, *Text* &Query
   - ***Label*** (Name) *lblOrderBy*, *Text &Order By*
   - ***ComboBox*** (Name) *cbOrderBy*, *Text PurchaseDate*
2. Click the ellipses in the *Items* property for *cbOrderBy*. You'll see the String Collection editor.
3. Enter the following values, one on each line, in the String Collection editor:
   - ***Amount***
   - ***CustomersId***
   - ***PurchaseDate***
4. Click OK. Visual Studio adds the order by strings to *cbOrderBy*.
5. Double-click btnQuery to create a new click event handler.
6. Type the following code for the *btnQuery_Click()* event handler.

```
private void btnQuery_Click(object sender, EventArgs e)
{
   // Obtain the context.
   Rewards2ModelContainer context = new Rewards2ModelContainer();
```

```
    // Create a variable to hold the ordered data.
    IOrderedQueryable<ViewClient> OrderedData = null;

    // Determine the data order.
    switch (cbOrderBy.SelectedIndex)
    {
        case 0:
            OrderedData = context.ViewClients.OrderBy(value => value.Amount);
            break;
        case 1:
            OrderedData = context.ViewClients.OrderBy(value => value.CustomersId);
            break;
        case 2:
            OrderedData = context.ViewClients.OrderBy(value => value.PurchaseDate);
            break;
        default:
            OrderedData = context.ViewClients.OrderBy(value => value.PurchaseDate);
            break;
    }

    // Define a variable to hold the output.
    StringBuilder Output = new StringBuilder();

    // Create the application output.
    foreach (var Client in OrderedData)
        Output.Append(Client.CustomerName + " ID " +
            Client.CustomersId + " purchased " +
            Client.Amount + " on " +
            Client.PurchaseDate + ".\r\n");

    // Show the output on screen.
    MessageBox.Show(Output.ToString());
}
```

The example begins by creating a context of type *Rewards2ModelContainer*. It then creates a variable, *OrderedData*, of type *IOrderedQueryable<ViewClient>*, to hold the ordered information. You create a data order much as you would with a stored procedure, by using a field name. The *switch* block performs the actual order selection using the value provided by *cbOrderBy.SelectedIndex*.

Each *OrderBy()* method call uses a different lambda expression to output the data in a particular order. As with stored procedures, you select a sort order using a field name.

Tip An advantage of using a view is that you can create multiple levels of ordering. For example, *OrderedData = context.ViewClients.OrderBy(value => value.CustomersId).OrderBy(value => value.Amount);* would sort the data first by customer ID, and then by the amount of the purchase. You can create any number of levels of ordering desired (with the idea that more levels usually reduce application performance).

The example than creates a *StringBuilder* object, *Output*, to hold the information. It uses a *foreach* loop to obtain the values for each customer and place them in *Output*. Finally, the application displays the content of *Output* in a dialog box.

7. Click Start or press F5. The application compiles and runs.

8. Select Amount in the Order By field of the example application.

9. Click Query. You'll see the output shown here:

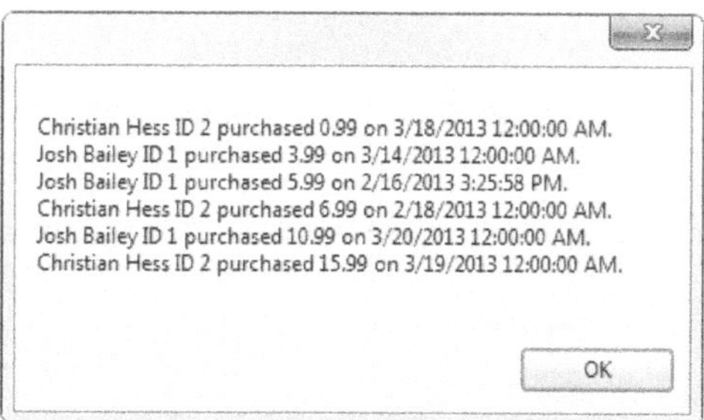
Christian Hess ID 2 purchased 0.99 on 3/18/2013 12:00:00 AM.
Josh Bailey ID 1 purchased 3.99 on 3/14/2013 12:00:00 AM.
Josh Bailey ID 1 purchased 5.99 on 2/16/2013 3:25:58 PM.
Christian Hess ID 2 purchased 6.99 on 2/18/2013 12:00:00 AM.
Josh Bailey ID 1 purchased 10.99 on 3/20/2013 12:00:00 AM.
Christian Hess ID 2 purchased 15.99 on 3/19/2013 12:00:00 AM.
OK

The output from this example is the same as the output of the example in Chapter 8. However, the technique for arriving at this output is different. You have options for creating output using a number of techniques when working with the Entity Framework, and it's a good idea to keep them in mind as you work through various issues. In some cases, you'll find that views excel, while other situations call for a stored procedure.

10. Perform steps 8 and 9 for each of the two remaining ordering methods so that you can see how they work.

Making views writable

There's a technique for creating a writable view. The view itself isn't writable, but the stored procedures you create to go with the view are writable. You can couple views and stored procedures in a manner that creates an application with the best features of both. Access to the database is strictly controlled using methods that are fully controlled and approved by the organization. The following procedure describes how to perform this task.

Developing a writable view

1. Copy the *ModelFirst* example you created in the "Updating the Model" section of this chapter (and updated in the "Creating a Basic View Example" section) to a new folder and use this new copy for this example (rather than the copy you created earlier).

2. Open the copied solution in Visual Studio.

3. Create a new stored procedure named *AddClient* using the techniques shown in Chapter 8.

4. Add the following code to *AddClient*:

```
CREATE PROCEDURE AddClient
   @CustomerName NVarChar(max),
   @PurchaseDate DateTime,
   @Amount       Decimal(18,2)
AS
   /* Determine whether the customer already exists. */
   DECLARE @CustCount Int
   SET @CustCount = (SELECT COUNT(CustomerName) FROM Customers WHERE CustomerName=@
CustomerName)

   /* When @CustCount equals 0, the customer doesn't exist.
      The call to INSERT INTO will add the customer. */
   IF @CustCount = 0
   BEGIN
      INSERT INTO Customers (CustomerName)
      VALUES (@CustomerName)
   END

   /* Obtain the customer's Id value for use in adding a new record to the
      Purchases table. */
   DECLARE @CustId Int
   SET @CustId = (SELECT Id FROM Customers WHERE CustomerName=@CustomerName)

   /* Perform the insertion. */
   INSERT INTO Purchases (CustomersId, Amount, PurchaseDate)
   VALUES (@CustId, @Amount, @PurchaseDate)
```

This stored procedure is a lot more complicated than the stored procedures you used in the past. The stored procedure must actually perform several different tasks to update the two tables, *Customers* and *Purchases*, in the database. First, it must determine whether the customer already exists. When the customer doesn't exist, the stored procedure adds the new customer.

Second, the stored procedure must obtain the customer's *Id* value for use in adding a record to the *Purchases* table. Theoretically, you could ask the client to provide this information, but it's much safer to obtain it directly from the database, as shown.

Third, the stored procedure adds the new purchase to the database. This means adding the customer's ID, the amount, and the purchase date. The purchase ID value is automatically provided by the DBMS.

Note In some cases, the Entity Framework will misinterpret the return type of the stored procedure and map it incorrectly. When this occurs, you'll see a "The data reader returned by the store data provider doesn't have enough columns for the query requested" error message. To fix this error, open the Model Browser window, select the errant function in the Function Imports folder, and verify that the Return Type property is set to (None).

5. Create a new stored procedure named *DeleteClient* using the techniques shown in Chapter 8.

6. Add the following code to *DeleteClient*:

```
CREATE PROCEDURE DeleteClient
   @PurchaseId int
AS
   /* Obtain and save the customer's ID */
   DECLARE @CustId Int
   SET @CustId = (SELECT CustomersId FROM Purchases WHERE Id=@PurchaseId)

   /* Verify that the purchase exists. */
   IF @CustId IS NULL
   BEGIN
      RETURN -1
   END

   /* Delete the purchase from the database. */
   DELETE FROM Purchases WHERE Id=@PurchaseId

   /* Verify there are purchase records left for this
      customer */
   DECLARE @PurchaseCount Int
   SET @PurchaseCount = (SELECT COUNT(*) FROM Purchases WHERE CustomersId=@CustId)

   /* If there are no purchase records left, delete
      the customer record as well */
   IF @PurchaseCount < 1
   BEGIN
      DELETE FROM Customers WHERE Id=@CustId
   END

   /* Return a success value */
   RETURN 0
```

Records are removed from the database based on the purchase ID. However, before the stored procedure can remove the record, it must first save the customer ID associated with that record. If *@CustId* comes up *NULL* after performing a search, it means that the stored procedure received an errant purchase ID, and the stored procedure exits.

When *@CustId* is a valid value, the stored procedure removes the record from *Purchases*. Of course, you also want to remove the customer's record when there are no more purchases associated with that customer. The stored procedure next checks for additional purchases by that customer—when none exist, the stored procedure also removes the customer record from the *Customers* table.

7. Create a new stored procedure named *UpdateClient* using the techniques shown in Chapter 8.

8. Add the following code to *UpdateClient*:

```
CREATE PROCEDURE UpdateClient
   @PurchaseId   Int,
   @CustomerName NVarChar(max),
   @PurchaseDate DateTime,
   @Amount       Decimal(18,2)
```

```
AS
   /* Begin by updating the purchase record. */
   UPDATE Purchases
   SET PurchaseDate=@PurchaseDate, Amount=@Amount
   WHERE Id=@PurchaseId

   /* Obtain the customer's ID. */
   DECLARE @CustId Int
   SET @CustId = (SELECT CustomersId FROM Purchases WHERE Id=@PurchaseId)

   /* Make a customer name change as well. */
   UPDATE Customers
   SET CustomerName=@CustomerName
   WHERE Id=@CustId
```

The update procedure is straightforward. First, the stored procedure updates the *Purchases* table. It then finds the customer ID based on *@PurchaseId* and uses this information to update the *Customers* table as well.

Note Make sure that each of the stored procedures is added to the model so that you can use them in the example. Otherwise, you won't be able to use the stored procedures with the view.

9. Open the Rewards2Model.EDMX file by double-clicking its entry in Solution Explorer.

10. Right-click the ViewClient entry in the designer and choose Stored Procedure Mapping from the context menu. You'll see a Mapping Details window like the one shown here:

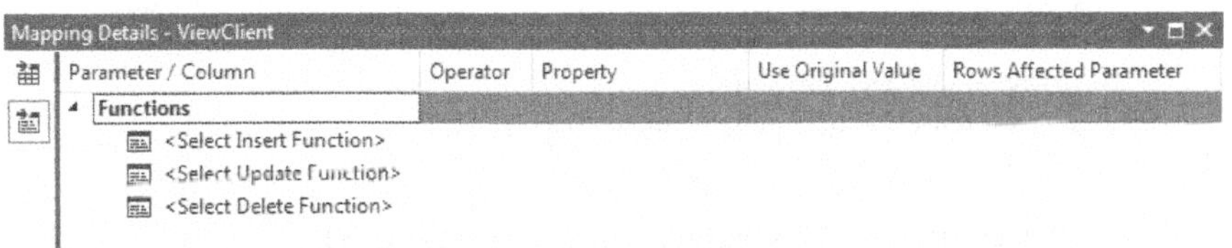

11. Click <Select Insert Function> and choose AddClient from the list. Visual Studio automatically creates the required mapping for you, as shown here:

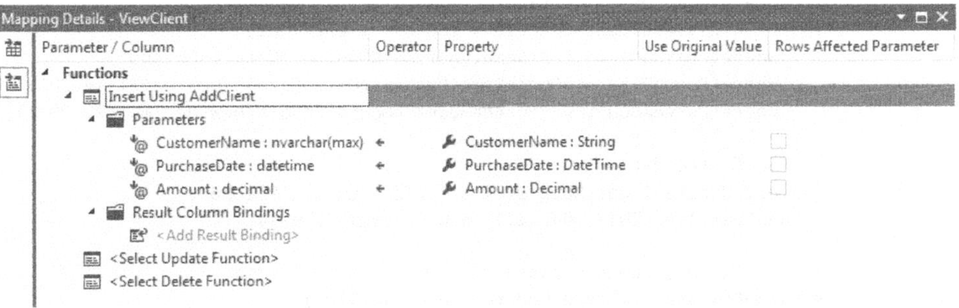

12. Click <Select Update Function> and choose UpdateClient from the list. Visual Studio automatically creates the required mapping. Notice that there isn't any mapping between the *@PurchaseId* parameter and a property. If you don't create a mapping, Visual Studio will raise an error when you try to compile the application.

13. Select Id : Int32 to map *@PurchaseId* to the *Id* field of the *Purchases* table.

14. Click <Select Delete Function> and choose DeleteClient from the list. Visual Studio automatically creates the required mapping. Again, you must manually map the *@PurchaseId* parameter.

15. Select Id : Int32 to map *@PurchaseId* to the *Id* field of the *Purchases* table.

16. Add three buttons to *Form1*:

    - *btnAdd2* with a *Text* property value of *Add &2*
    - *btnUpdate* with a *Text* property value of *&Update*
    - *btnDelete* with a *Text* property value of *&Delete*

17. Add code for the event handlers for each button, as shown here:

```
private void btnAdd2_Click(object sender, EventArgs e)
{
   // Obtain the context.
   Rewards2ModelContainer context = new Rewards2ModelContainer();

   // Add a new record to the database.
   context.AddClient(
      "Carole Poland", new DateTime(2013, 04, 16), new Decimal(20.99));

   // Display a success message.
   MessageBox.Show("Record Added Successfully");
}

private void btnUpdate_Click(object sender, EventArgs e)
{
   // Obtain the context.
   Rewards2ModelContainer context = new Rewards2ModelContainer();

   // Locate the specified record.
   IQueryable<ViewClient> Record = context.ViewClients
      .Where(CustName => CustName.CustomerName == "Carole Poland")
      .Where(PurchDate => PurchDate.PurchaseDate.Equals(new DateTime(2013, 04, 16)))
      .Where(PurchAmount => PurchAmount.Amount.Equals(new Decimal(20.99)));

   // Modify the data.
   context.UpdateClient(Record.First().Id, "Carole Poland",
      new DateTime(2013, 04, 17), new Decimal(25.99));

   // Display a success message.
   MessageBox.Show("Record Updated Successfully");
}
```

```
private void btnDelete_Click(object sender, EventArgs e)
{
   // Obtain the context.
   Rewards2ModelContainer context = new Rewards2ModelContainer();

   // Locate the specified record.
   IQueryable<ViewClient> Record = context.ViewClients
      .Where(CustName => CustName.CustomerName == "Carole Poland")
      .Where(PurchDate => PurchDate.PurchaseDate.Equals(new DateTime(2013, 04, 17)))
      .Where(PurchAmount => PurchAmount.Amount.Equals(new Decimal(25.99)));

   // Modify the data.
   context.DeleteClient(Record.First().Id);

   // Display a success message.
   MessageBox.Show("Record Deleted Successfully");
}
```

In each case, the event handlers obtain a *Rewards2ModelContainer* context, and then use it to access the database. When working with the *AddClient()* stored procedure, all you need to do is provide the required input arguments, which consist of the customer's name, the purchase date, and the purchase amount.

Notice how the *btnUpdate_Click()* and *btnDelete_Click()* event handlers locate a specific record using ganged *Where()* methods. Each *Where()* method has a lambda function that further refines the search criteria using the customer's name, the purchase date, and the purchase amount. The goal of this search is to obtain a purchase ID to use to identify a specific record to the stored procedure. As with record addition, in this case the event handlers call either *UpdateClient()* or *DeleteClient()* using the context and by supplying the required values.

18. Click Start or press F5. The application compiles and runs.
19. Click Add 2.
20. Click Query. You'll see the output shown here:

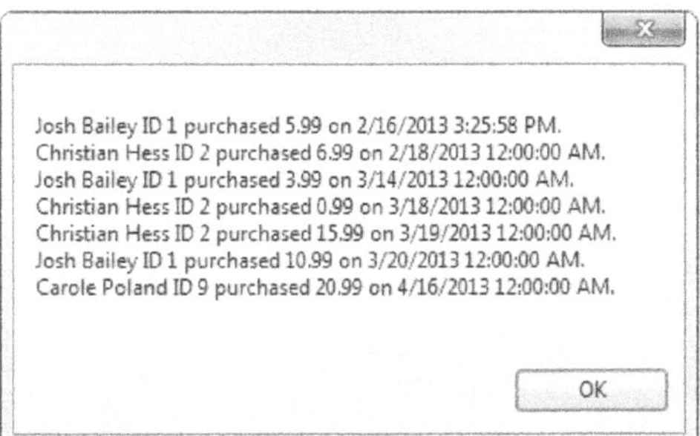

Josh Bailey ID 1 purchased 5.99 on 2/16/2013 3:25:58 PM.
Christian Hess ID 2 purchased 6.99 on 2/18/2013 12:00:00 AM.
Josh Bailey ID 1 purchased 3.99 on 3/14/2013 12:00:00 AM.
Christian Hess ID 2 purchased 0.99 on 3/18/2013 12:00:00 AM.
Christian Hess ID 2 purchased 15.99 on 3/19/2013 12:00:00 AM.
Josh Bailey ID 1 purchased 10.99 on 3/20/2013 12:00:00 AM.
Carole Poland ID 9 purchased 20.99 on 4/16/2013 12:00:00 AM.
OK

21. Perform steps 19 and 20 using the Update button first, and then the Delete button. You should see the expected results each time.

Getting started with the Entity Framework

This chapter has helped you understand how views work and how to incorporate them into your application. View-based applications are quite secure because data doesn't pass from the application directly to the database, and views aren't able to accept parameters that could be used to perform tasks outside the desired range of actions envisioned by the DBA. Many organizations use views whenever possible because the security and reliability features they offer. In addition, you'll find that many users have no need to modify the data in a database—all they really need is the ability to retrieve, search, and order the data for various uses, such as reports. If you take one thing away from this chapter, it's that a view is probably the best way to access data from multiple applications because it also provides a means to create a consistent data source across all applications that the view services.

You've seen a number of view examples in the chapter. As with stored procedures, the best way to become better acquainted with views is to play with them. Take some time to work through the examples and then make modifications to the views to achieve specific results. Remember that you must use the *ALTER VIEW* keywords, rather than the *CREATE VIEW* keywords, to make changes to a view. It's possible to create views of any complexity you need by defining queries that work well in many situations.

Chapter 10, "Interaction with table-valued functions," moves into a new area for the Entity Framework: Table-Valued Functions (TVFs). Developers have wanted access to TVFs for quite some time, and Microsoft finally provided access to them in Entity Framework 5. (You can see a list of other new Entity Framework 5 features at *http://msdn.microsoft.com/data/ee712907*.) The TVF support in the Entity Framework is a little limited. For example, you must use the database-first workflow to use TVFs. While TVFs are similar to stored procedures, they have one specific advantage: the ability to be used as part of a Language Integrated Query (LINQ) query because they're composable (a *composable* entity is one that can be combined with other components to create a desired result, which means that the entity must be both self-contained and stateless). You'll find all the details about TVFs in Chapter 10.

Chapter 9 quick reference

To	Do this

Create a view	Define the view using the *CREATE VIEW* statement, followed by the word *AS*, your query, and the word *GO*. A simple view might look like this:
	`CREATE VIEW ViewCustomers`
	`AS`
	`SELECT * FROM Rewards2.dbo.Customers`
	`GO`

Alter a view	Specify which view to change using the *ALTER VIEW* statement, followed by the word *AS*, your query, and the word *GO*. A simple view alteration might look like this:
	`ALTER VIEW ViewCustomers`
	`AS`
	`SELECT * FROM Rewards2.dbo.Customers`
	`GO`

Create a new view using Server Explorer	Right-click the Views folder under the desired database entry in Server Explorer and choose Add New View from the context menu.
Update the model so it knows about the view	Right-click in any clear area of the designer and choose Update Model From Database from the context menu. Follow the steps provided by the wizard to include the view in the model (you should see the view added to the designer, just as you would a table).
Remove a field from the list of entity keys	Right-click the affected field in the designer and click Entity Key in the context menu to remove the check mark next to it.

Modify the order of table data obtained from a view	Use the *OrderBy()* method and place the result in another variable, such as the following:
	`var OrderedData = context.ViewClients.`
	`OrderBy(value => value.Amount);`
	where *OrderedData* is generally an object of type *IOrderedQueryable<T>*, the context is obtained from the data model, *ViewClients* is the name of a view, and the lambda expression specifies the sort order by providing the name of a field.

CHAPTER 10

Interaction with Table-Valued Functions

After completing the chapter, you'll be able to

- Describe what a Table-Valued Function (TVF) is and how it affects the Entity Framework.
- Create a TVF as part of your database model.
- Interact with a TVF using Entity SQL.
- Interact with a TVF using Language Integrated Query (LINQ).
- Perform entity mapping.

Many developers haven't even heard of TVFs yet because they're a relatively new technology, and organizations are often slow to adopt new technologies. A TVF is a User-Defined Function (UDF) that returns a table instead of a scalar type. The technology has actually been around since Microsoft SQL Server 2005. Any Database Administrators (DBAs) reading this introduction are probably rolling their eyes, but developers usually focus on what is available, and TVFs haven't been available for use until this latest version of the Entity Framework. A TVF mixes some of the best elements of views and stored procedures. For example, as with a view, you can use a TVF to represent a table. However, as with a stored procedure, you can use parameters with TVFs and incorporate a certain level of programmability. The first section of this chapter goes into a little more detail, but that's the essential overview of TVFs if you want to get right into the coding areas.

Note This chapter presents an overview of TVFs that's adequate for working through the examples, and it describes the way they affect the Entity Framework. It doesn't discuss TVFs in detail. You can find a more detailed overview of TVFs at *http://msdn.microsoft.com/library/ms191165.aspx*. There's also an interesting introduction to TVFs from a Common Language Runtime (CLR) perspective at *http://www.mssqltips.com/sqlservertip/2582/introduction-to-sql-server-clr-table-valued-functions/*. Finally, see Chapter 5 of the book *Microsoft® SQL Server®2012 T-SQL Fundamentals*, by Itzik Ben-Gan (Microsoft Press, 2012), which you can obtain here: *http://shop.oreilly.com/product/0790145321978.do*.

The next parts of the chapter show how to create a TVF, test it, and add it to the Entity Framework model. You then create a simple application that relies on the TVF to perform useful work; it's similar to the stored procedure and view examples in Chapter 8, "Interaction with stored procedures," and Chapter 9, "Interaction with views." Using this approach helps you gain a better understanding of just how TVFs differ from both stored procedures and views. Each technology has a particular task to perform and a special place in your developer toolbox.

The final parts of the chapter help you understand various types of mapping you can perform with TVFs to make the data they provide more accessible. Mapping becomes even more important than it was with views because with TVFs, you can map the data in a number of ways. A particular mapping strategy can make the data easier to access and less of a hassle to use in your application. The final part of the chapter describes how to interact with TVFs using recursion.

Understanding TVFs

TVFs are simply UDFs that return a table, as described in the introduction to the chapter. However, they're a bit more than that, and it pays to know as much as you can about TVFs before you start working with them in the Entity Framework. The following sections help you understand TVFs at a more detailed level. If you've already spent considerable time working with TVFs in other environments, you can probably skip the first two sections, but make sure you read the last four sections, because they're Entity Framework specific.

Note If you're not quite sure what UDFs are, you should spend a little time reviewing some material about them. A full discussion of UDFs is outside the scope of this book. You can find an excellent (albeit older) overview of UDFs at *http://msdn.microsoft.com/library/aa175085.aspx* and a more detailed article at *http://www.extremeexperts.com/sql/articles/UDFFunctions.aspx*. There's also an excellent MSDN article that can double as a tutorial at *http://msdn.microsoft.com/magazine/cc164062.aspx*. For people who would prefer to have a tutorial, check out this one on the Techipost site: *http://www.techipost.com/2011/03/16/a-tutorial-on-stored-procedures-and-user-defined-functions/*.

Comparing TVFs to views

TVFs and views have one essential similarity—they're both *composable*. This means that the Entity Framework will treat a TVF as a virtual table. In addition, you can use a TVF as part of a SQL query—just as you would a table. However, TVFs and views have some significant differences that you need to know about:

- TVFs can have multiple *SELECT* statements (views have just one).
- TVFs can contain procedural code, which means that they can do many of the things that stored procedures can do.
- TVFs allow the use of parameters, which means you can pass values to a TVF to modify its behavior.

Comparing TVFs to stored procedures

TVFs are more like stored procedures than views. However, they have some significant advantages over the stored procedures:

- They are allowed anywhere within a query.
- They allow use of filtering.

It may seem at first that you would want to use TVFs in place of stored procedures in all cases. However, stored procedures still have one significant advantage over TVFs: they allow you to return multiple result sets. In addition, a stored procedure can return a scalar type—TVFs always return a table.

Note TVFs are actually used in a number of ways as part of SQL Server. For example, you rely on them to perform tasks such as a full text search (see *http://msdn.microsoft.com/library/cc721269.aspx* for details).

Defining the storage layer

Normally, you don't worry too much about the actual code used to maintain the model. A combination of the designer, Model Browser window, and other Microsoft Visual Studio features makes it quite easy to understand what to do without actually spending time with the underlying XML. However, the XML is important in this case, because the differences are subtle, and the use of TVFs is relatively new

TVFs and functions look much the same in the XML. In Chapter 6," Manipulating data using LINQ," you created a function named *AveragePurchase*. The XML for *AveragePurchase* looks something like this (some attributes have been removed because they have no bearing on this discussion):

```
<Function Name="AveragePurchase" ReturnType="decimal" IsComposable="true" Schema="dbo">
  <Parameter Name="CustomerId" Type="int" Mode="In" />
</Function>
```

Note In previous versions of the Entity Framework, it wasn't possible to set the *IsComposable* attribute to *true* for functions. This is a new feature of Entity Framework 5. In order to use the output of a function as part of a query, it's necessary to set *IsComposable* to *true*.

Notice that the *ReturnType* attribute returns a decimal value. The *AveragePurchase* function is a scalar function—it returns a single value so you can define that value using the *ReturnType* attribute. When working with a TVF, you're dealing with a complex return type, so a simple attribute won't do. Consequently, the TVF uses a fuller XML description, similar to this one:

```
<Function Name="ObtainClients" IsComposable="true" Schema="dbo">
  <Parameter Name="OrderBy" Type="nvarchar" Mode="In" />
  <ReturnType>
```

```
    <CollectionType>
      <RowType>
        <Property Name="RowNo" Type="bigint" Nullable="false" />
        <Property Name="CustomerName" Type="nvarchar(max)" />
        <Property Name="Id" Type="int" />
        <Property Name="PurchaseDate" Type="datetime" />
        <Property Name="Amount" Type="decimal" Scale="2" />
        <Property Name="CustomersId" Type="int" />
      </RowType>
    </CollectionType>
  </ReturnType>
</Function>
```

The changes shown here make the return type a collection of rows. Each of these rows contains five database fields: *CustomerName*, *Id*, *PurchaseDate*, *Amount*, and *CustomersId*. (Don't worry about the *RowNo* field for right now—you'll receive an explanation of how this field works when you create the TVF in the "Defining the TVF Using Server Explorer" section of the chapter.) The mapping between these property values describes the database structure and the resulting output of the function, which uses .NET types. This new feature is called *function mapping*, and it allows the Entity Framework to provide full Create, Read, Update, and Delete (CRUD) support for TVFs in your application.

Defining the mapping layer

When working with any database object, the Entity Framework must provide mapping between the storage layer and the conceptual layer, where the application finally interacts with the entity. A TVF can use two forms of mapping:

- ***Entity*** **type** A template used as the basis for the Entity Framework. Entity types define the top-level structures for any model, including the database definition. The template for an ***Entity*** type accepts these types of information:
  - Unique name (required)
  - Entity key, defined by one or more properties (required)
  - Data, in the form of properties (optional)
  - Navigation properties used to create associations between entities (optional)
- **Complex type** A template designed to provide rich, structured properties in entities or other complex types. Like entity types, complex types can carry a data payload in the form of primitive types or other complex types. Complex types require only a unique name and the data payload in the way of template information, so you can use them for data that has no key. However, complex types have these differences from entity types:
  - Complex types can't exist independently because they lack identities.
  - Complex types can't be part of an association, and therefore aren't usable for navigation properties.

In the creation of the mapping layer, the entity type begins with an *<EntityTypeMapping>* tag, which defines the entity *TypeName* attribute. Likewise, the complex type begins with a *<Complex-TypeMapping>* tag that defines the complex *TypeName* attribute. Both types define a series of *<ScalarProperty>* tags, which define the mapping between the storage layer and the conceptual layer. These tags are precisely the same in both cases. Here's an example of what function mapping might look like for complex type mapping (the default scenario for TVFs):

```
<FunctionImportMapping FunctionImportName="ObtainClients"
                       FunctionName="Rewards2Model.Store.ObtainClients">
  <ResultMapping>
    <ComplexTypeMapping TypeName="Rewards2Model.ObtainClients_Result">
      <ScalarProperty Name="RowNo" ColumnName="RowNo" />
      <ScalarProperty Name="CustomerName" ColumnName="CustomerName" />
      <ScalarProperty Name="Id" ColumnName="Id" />
      <ScalarProperty Name="PurchaseDate" ColumnName="PurchaseDate" />
      <ScalarProperty Name="Amount" ColumnName="Amount" />
      <ScalarProperty Name="CustomersId" ColumnName="CustomersId" />
    </ComplexTypeMapping>
  </ResultMapping>
</FunctionImportMapping>
```

Notice that the mapping begins by defining a relationship between the storage layer function definition and the conceptual layer function definition. The mapping includes a definition of the parameter provided as input (without actually naming the parameter in this case). The result of the call appears within a *<ResultMapping>* tag, followed by a *<ComplexTypeMapping>* tag, and finally the *<ScalarProperty>* tags that define the actual mapping between the storage layer and the conceptual layer.

Defining the conceptual layer

The conceptual layer provides a definition of how the TVF appears to the application. When working with a TVF, the definition is a straightforward description of which types to use to interact with the lower layers. The definition could look like this:

```
<FunctionImport Name="ObtainClients" IsComposable="true"
                ReturnType="Collection(Rewards2Model.ObtainClients_Result)">
  <Parameter Name="OrderBy" Mode="In" Type="String" />
</FunctionImport>
```

The conceptual layer also defines the result type, which relies on a *<ComplexType>* tag that includes the *Name* attribute defining the name of the result type. Within this definition are a number of *<Property>* tags that define the details of each element of the complex type. Here's an example of what a complex type definition might look like:

```
<ComplexType Name="ObtainClients_Result">
  <Property Type="Int64" Name="RowNo" Nullable="false" />
  <Property Type="String" Name="CustomerName" Nullable="true" />
  <Property Type="Int32" Name="Id" Nullable="true" />
  <Property Type="DateTime" Name="PurchaseDate" Nullable="true" Precision="23" />
  <Property Type="Decimal" Name="Amount" Nullable="true" Precision="18" Scale="2" />
```

```
  <Property Type="Int32" Name="CustomersId" Nullable="true" />
</ComplexType>
```

Defining the object layer

Interestingly enough, even though most texts compare TVFs to views and stored procedures because of the way that TVFs work, in practice, TVFs are more related to functions. This means that at the object layer, within your code, you access a TVF in much the same way as you would any other function—by creating a stub function and adding the *[EdmFunction()]* attribute to it. The "Using Entity and Database Functions" section of Chapter 6 details the process for creating and using a function. However, unlike a SQL function, the stub contains meaningful code (as you'll see later in the chapter), rather than simply throwing an exception whenever someone tries to call it. Here's what a TVF stub might look like:

```
[EdmFunction("Rewards2ModelContainer", "ObtainClients")]
public virtual IQueryable<ObtainClients_Result> ObtainClients(string orderBy)
{
    var orderByParameter = orderBy != null ?
        new ObjectParameter("OrderBy", orderBy) :
        new ObjectParameter("OrderBy", typeof(string));

    return ((IObjectContextAdapter)this).ObjectContext.CreateQuery<ObtainClients_Result>(
            "[Rewards2ModelContainer].[ObtainClients](@OrderBy)", orderByParameter);
}
```

It's important to note that you can call this function directly in your code. In addition, this function accepts arguments that it then passes along to the TVF on the server. You also need to consider these issues when working with a TVF:

- The function returns a *DbDataRecord*, which means that the records aren't richly typed—limiting the kinds of tasks you can perform with the output.
- You use the store name with the *[EdmFunction()]* attribute, just as you would with a function, because this is a store function.
- The inclusion of a meaningful body in the function means you can call this function directly from LINQ as needed.
- The stub isn't necessary when working with Entity SQL, because you call the TVF directly in this situation.

Adding TVFs to your model

Before you can use a TVF, you must create one, test it, and then add it to the model. The following sections provide details on performing these essential steps. Not surprisingly, most of the steps look similar to those that you perform for functions, stored procedures, and views, but there are subtle differences, and you need to take care in performing them.

Defining the TVF using Server Explorer

Creating a TVF using Server Explorer is similar to creating a function. The main difference is how the function is created. The following procedure helps you through the process of creating the TVF for this example (and TVFs in general).

Creating a simple TVF

1. Open your copy of Visual Studio. You don't need to have a project loaded, because you're going to be interacting with Server Explorer and SQL Server.

2. Choose View | Server Explorer to open the Server Explorer window if it isn't already open. Under Data Connections, you should see closed connections to the four databases used in the book.

3. Open the connection to the *Rewards2* database by clicking the right-pointing arrow next to it. You'll see a list of folders associated with the database, including the Functions folder shown here:

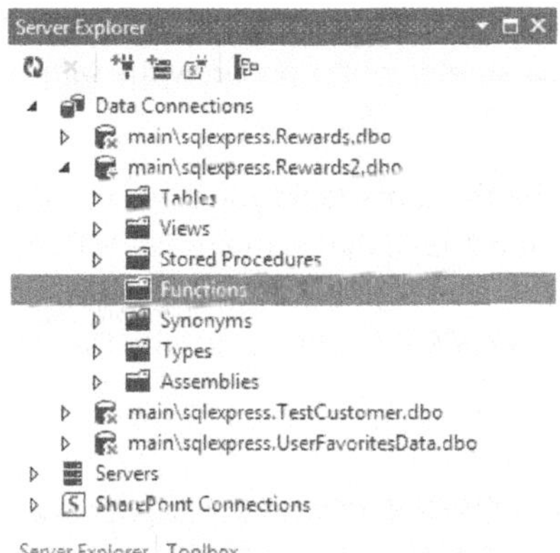

4. Right-click the Functions folder and choose Add New | Table-Valued Function. Visual Studio opens a new .SQL file for you that contains a basic template for creating a TVF.

5. Type the following code into the file:

```
CREATE FUNCTION ObtainClients
(
   @OrderBy NVarChar(20)
)
RETURNS @returntable TABLE
(
   RowNo          BigInt PRIMARY KEY NOT NULL,
   CustomerName   NVarChar(Max),
   Id             Int,
   PurchaseDate   DateTime,
   Amount         Decimal(18,2),
   CustomersId    Int
```

```
)
AS
BEGIN
   INSERT INTO @returntable
   SELECT ROW_NUMBER()OVER(ORDER BY
      CASE @OrderBy
         WHEN 'PurchaseDate' THEN P.PurchaseDate
         WHEN 'Amount'       THEN P.Amount
         WHEN 'CustomersId'  THEN P.CustomersId
                             ELSE P.PurchaseDate
      END
          )RowNo,
          C.CustomerName,
          P.Id,
          P.PurchaseDate,
          P.Amount,
          P.CustomersId
   FROM Customers AS C
   INNER JOIN Purchases AS P
   ON C.Id = P.CustomersId
   RETURN
END
```

The script starts out by defining a parameter, *@OrderBy*, of type *NVarChar(20)*, which you use to define the sort order of the output. This parameter works precisely the same as it did for the stored procedure in Chapter 8.

A TVF returns a table. It may not necessarily be the same table you started with, but it's a table. In this case, you see that *@returntable* is a *TABLE* that contains fields from both *Customers* and *Purchases*. However, the first field is actually new. *RowNo* is a generated field that provides the means to order the output. The *ORDER BY* clause used with the stored procedure in Chapter 9 won't work with a TVF.

Warning Microsoft changed the way that *ORDER BY* works in SQL Server 2012. Even though scripts written for SQL Server 2008 work just fine with the *ORDER BY* clause, they won't work with SQL Server 2012. The script shown in this chapter works with both versions of SQL Server. There's a discussion of this issue on StackOverflow (*http://stackoverflow.com/questions/11222043/table-valued-function-order-by-is-ignored-in-output*) that discusses the details, but the essential bit of information to take away from this chapter is that you must use the generated field to obtain useful results.

Now that the table is defined, the script will *SELECT* data into it. The overall *SELECT* statement looks similar to the one used with the stored procedure, except that it doesn't contain the *ORDER BY* clause. Instead of the ORDER BY clause, you'll see the generated field create by the *ROW_NUMBER()* ranking function (see *http://msdn.microsoft.com/library/ms186734.aspx* for details), which returns the row number of a result set. The *OVER* clause specifies the sequence used to generate the row number. In this case, the row number is generated as the result of an *ORDER BY* clause that's determined by *@OrderBy*.

6. Right-click the Functions folder and choose Refresh from the context menu. You'll see the new function, as shown here (notice this function uses a different icon from the scalar function you added in Chapter 6):

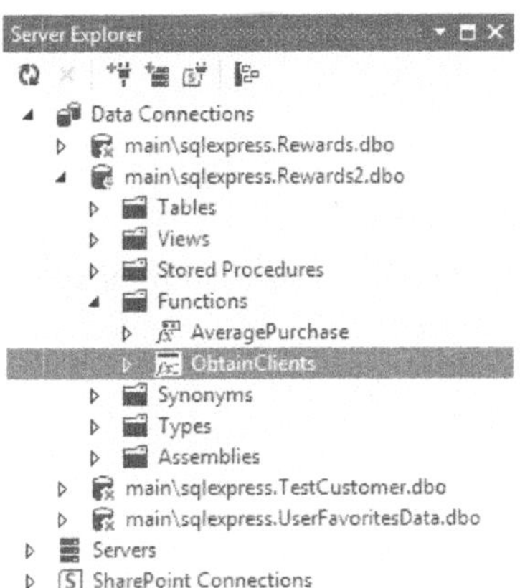

Testing the TVF

You now have a somewhat complex-looking TVF to use, but you have no idea whether it will work (especially given the odd generated field). As with stored procedures and views, it's essential to test a TVF before you begin using it with your application. The following procedure will look somewhat familiar (with a few twists). It helps you test the TVF and ensure that it generates the output that you expect from this example.

Testing a simple TVF

1. Choose View | Server Explorer to open the Server Explorer window if it isn't already open.
2. Open the Functions folder, and you should see the *ObtainClients* TVF.
3. Right-click the *ObtainClients* TVF and choose Execute from the context menu. You'll see the Execute Stored Procedure dialog box shown here:

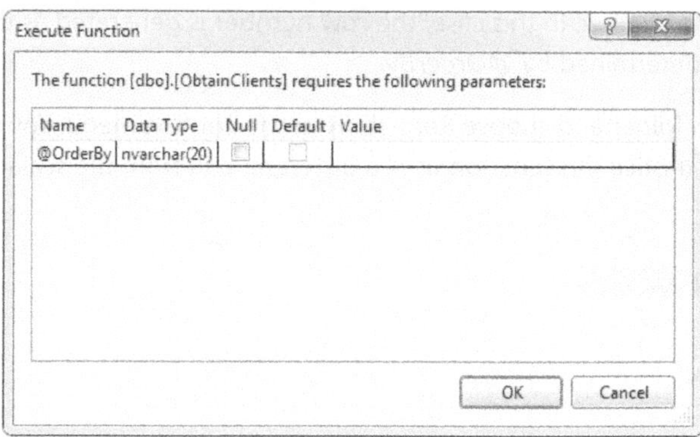

4. Type **Amount** in the Value field and click OK. A new SQL query window appears. The output shows the purchases sorted by amount, as shown here:

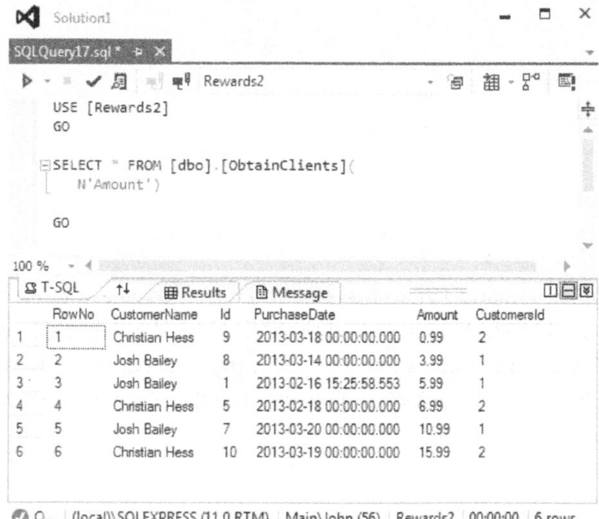

	RowNo	CustomerName	Id	PurchaseDate	Amount	CustomersId
1	1	Christian Hess	9	2013-03-18 00:00:00.000	0.99	2
2	2	Josh Bailey	8	2013-03-14 00:00:00.000	3.99	1
3	3	Josh Bailey	1	2013-02-16 15:25:58.553	5.99	1
4	4	Christian Hess	5	2013-02-18 00:00:00.000	6.99	2
5	5	Josh Bailey	7	2013-03-20 00:00:00.000	10.99	1
6	6	Christian Hess	10	2013-03-19 00:00:00.000	15.99	2

Notice that the output is also sorted by the *RowNo* field. It's important to realize that *RowNo* is the actual sort order. Yes, the output does appear with the *Amount* field sorted, but this is the result of creating the generated *RowNo* field, rather than ordering by the *Amount* field directly.

5. Repeat steps 3 and 4 for *PurchaseDate* and *CustomersId*. In each case, the TVF will output the results in the desired order.

6. Repeat steps 3 and 4 with a value such as *SomeValue*. The TVF will output the results in purchase date order.

7. Repeat steps 3 and 4 with a value that's too long, such as *ThisValueIsALittleTooLong*. You won't see an error. The TVF will output the results in purchase date order. However, SQL Server will truncate the input string at the 20th letter.

Updating the model

Once you're certain that the TVF is ready for use, you need to update the model with it. This step lets you use the TVF in a number of ways to obtain information from the database and present it to the user. The following procedure shows how to add a TVF to the model.

Updating the model to use a TVF

1. Copy the *ModelFirst* example you created in Chapter 3, "Choosing a workflow," to a new folder, and use this new copy for this example (rather than the copy you created in Chapter 3).
2. Open the copied solution in Visual Studio.
3. Open the Rewards2Model.EDMX file by double-clicking its entry in Solution Explorer.
4. Right-click in any clear area of the designer and choose Update Model From Database from the context menu. You'll see the Update Wizard, as shown here:

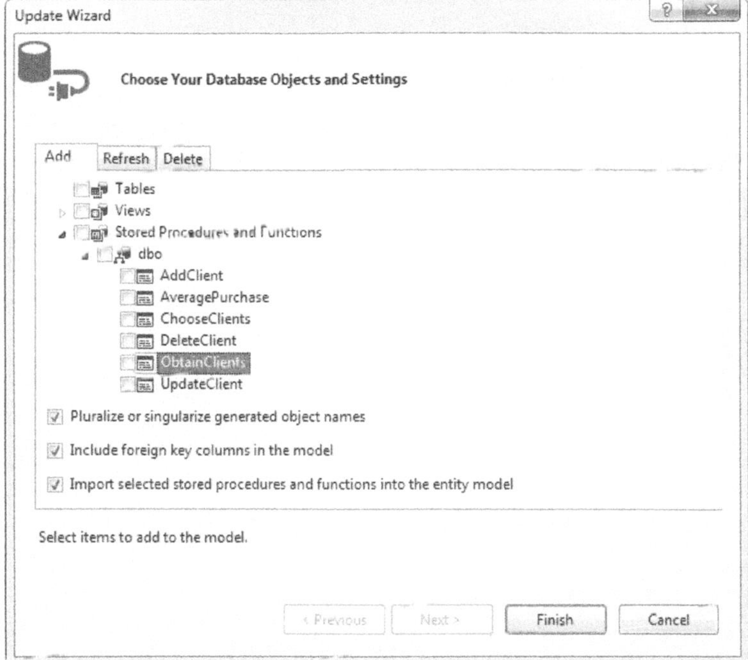

Notice that the wizard groups functions, stored procedures, and TVFs together. It's essential that you know whether an addition is a stored procedure or a function, so you know how to interact with it later. Review your choices in Server Explorer as needed.

Note The only items you see are those that are either new or updated. The reason the functions and stored procedures from previous chapters appear in the list is that you're using the Chapter 3 copy of the *ModelFirst* application, which hasn't had these items added to it. Normally, functions or stored procedures that you've already added to an application won't appear in the list.

5. Drill down to the *ObtainClients* TVF entry and check it. Click Finish. The wizard completes its task. As with both functions and stored procedures, you won't see the addition to the designer view of the model.

6. Choose Build | Build Solution to update the model. At this point, you can see the TVF using the Model Browser.

7. Right-click in any open area of the Model Designer and choose Model Browser from the context menu. You'll see the Model Browser window shown here:

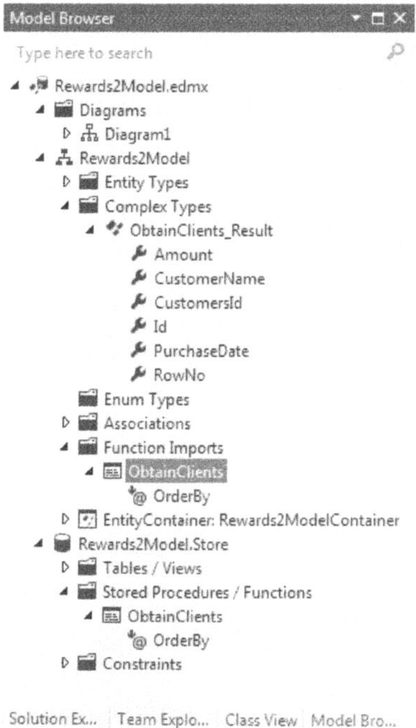

8. Drill down into the Rewards2Model\Function Imports folder, and you'll see an ObtainClients entry. Look at the Properties window, and you'll see that this entry tells you that *ObtainClients* is both the TVF and stored procedure name, and that it returns an *ObtainClients_Result* type (which is the result of the query you make using it).

9. Drill down into the Rewards2Model.Store\Stored Procedures/Functions folder, and you'll see a second ObtainClients entry. This time the Properties window provides information used by the Entity Framework to interact with the stored procedure. Most of this information isn't changeable.

10. Drill down into the Rewards2Model\Complex Types folder, and you'll see the ObtainClients_Result complex type entry. Open this entry and you'll see a list of fields returned by the query. When you select a particular field, you can see the properties for it. For example, when you select Amount, you'll see that it returns a *Decimal* type with a precision of 18 digits and a scale (decimal portion) of 2 digits.

Calling a TVF using Entity SQL

You can use Entity SQL to call a TVF directly once it has been added to your model. The advantage of this approach is that you gain a little flexibility in making calls to the TVF. However, it also has the disadvantage of requiring you to create the query in code. The following procedure shows how to call a TVF directly.

Developing an Entity SQL application that uses a TVF

1. Add the following new controls to *Form1*:
   - ***Button*** (Name) *btnQueryEntitySQL, Text &Entity SQL*
   - ***Label*** (Name) *lblOrderBy*, Text *&Order By*
   - ***ComboBox*** (Name) *cbOrderBy, Text PurchaseDate*
2. Click the ellipses in the *Items* property for *cbOrderBy*. You'll see the String Collection editor.
3. Enter the following values, one on each line, in the String Collection editor:
   - ***Amount***
   - ***CustomersId***
   - ***PurchaseDate***
4. Click OK. Visual Studio adds the order-by strings to *cbOrderBy*.
5. Double-click *btnQueryEntitySQL* to create a new click event handler.
6. Add the following *using* statements to the beginning of the file:

```
using System.Data.Objects;
using System.Data.EntityClient;
using System.Data.Common;
```

7. Type the following code for the *btnQuery_Click()* event handler:

```
private void btnQueryDirect_Click(object sender, EventArgs e)
{
   // Create the context.
   EntityConnection conn =
       new EntityConnection("name=Rewards2ModelContainer");
   ObjectContext context = new ObjectContext(conn);

   // Define a command string for making the query.
   String EntitySQLCmd =
       "SELECT OC " +
       "FROM Rewards2ModelContainer.ObtainClients('" +
       cbOrderBy.SelectedItem + "') " +
       "AS OC";

   // Create a query object.
   ObjectQuery<DbDataRecord> Query =
       new ObjectQuery<DbDataRecord>(EntitySQLCmd, context);

   // Execute the query.
   ObjectResult<DbDataRecord> Result = Query.Execute(MergeOption.NoTracking);

   // Define an output string.
   StringBuilder Output = new StringBuilder();

   // Enumerate the records and add them to the output.
   foreach (var Record in Result)
   {
      // Cast the first item in the record as the proper type.
      ObtainClients_Result ThisRow = (ObtainClients_Result)Record[0];

      // Add the individual items.
      Output.Append(ThisRow.CustomerName + " ID " +
         ThisRow.CustomersId + " purchased " +
         ThisRow.Amount + " on " +
         ThisRow.PurchaseDate + ".\r\n");
   }

   // Display the customer name on screen.
   MessageBox.Show(Output.ToString());
}
```

This version of the example makes a direct query of the TVF using Entity SQL. The code begins by creating a connection to the container and using that connection to create a context. The next steps are to create a query string; use the string to build an *ObjectQuery, Query*; and then execute *Query* to obtain an *ObjectResult, Result*. Notice how the query string is created. It obtains all of the data from the table by using *SELECT OC*, where *OC* is the full output of the call to *Rewards2ModelContainer.ObtainClients()*. Remember that the *ObtainClients()* TVF requires an *@OrderBy* value, which is supplied by *cbOrderBy.SelectedItem* in this case.

Result is an *ObjectResult* that contains a single field holding a materialized data record, *Record[0]*. To make that information useful, you must perform an *ObtainClients_Result* cast on it. This act makes the individual fields readily available. The code uses the information to create a *StringBuilder*, *Output*, which is finally used as input for a message box.

8. Click Start or press F5. The application compiles and runs.
9. Select Amount in the Order By field of the example application.
10. Click Query. You'll see the output shown here:

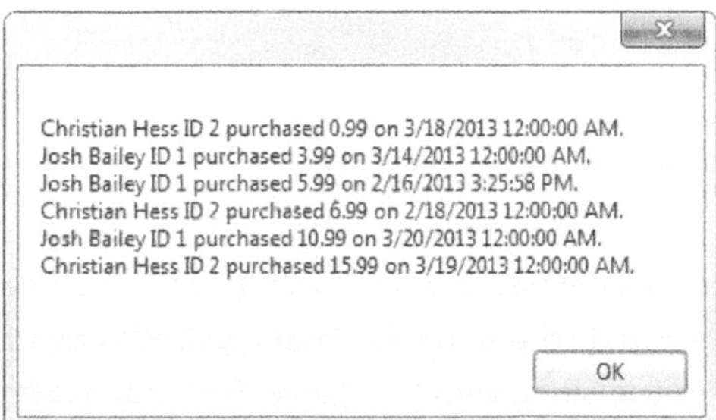
Christian Hess ID 2 purchased 0.99 on 3/18/2013 12:00:00 AM.
Josh Bailey ID 1 purchased 3.99 on 3/14/2013 12:00:00 AM.
Josh Bailey ID 1 purchased 5.99 on 2/16/2013 3:25:58 PM.
Christian Hess ID 2 purchased 6.99 on 2/18/2013 12:00:00 AM.
Josh Bailey ID 1 purchased 10.99 on 3/20/2013 12:00:00 AM.
Christian Hess ID 2 purchased 15.99 on 3/19/2013 12:00:00 AM.
OK

11. Perform steps 9 and 10 for each of the two remaining ordering methods so that you can see how they work.

Calling a TVF using LINQ

Using LINQ to access your TVF is similar to accessing a stored procedure. In fact, you may not actually notice much of a difference. It's important to remember that stored procedures and TVFs are used in different ways, but that the Entity Framework tends to smooth the playing surface from the developer's perspective. Consequently, what may appear to the developer as essentially the same routine is actually much different beneath the surface. With this in mind, the following procedure shows how to use the TVF you created earlier with LINQ.

Developing a LINQ application that uses a TVF

1. Add a new button named *btnQueryLINQ* with a *Text* property of *&LINQ* to *Form1*.
2. Double-click *btnQueryLINQ* to create a new click event handler.
3. Type the following code for the *btnQuery_Click()* event handler:

```
private void btnQueryLINQ_Click(object sender, EventArgs e)
{
   // Create the context.
   Rewards2ModelContainer context = new Rewards2ModelContainer();

   // Make the query.
   var PurchaseList =
      from purchase
      in context.ObtainClients(cbOrderBy.SelectedItem.ToString())
      select purchase;
```

```
    // Create a string to hold the result.
    StringBuilder Output = new StringBuilder();

    // Parse the result.
    foreach (var PurchaseEntry in PurchaseList)
        Output.Append(
            PurchaseEntry.CustomerName + " ID " +
            PurchaseEntry.CustomersId + " purchased " +
            PurchaseEntry.Amount + " on " +
            PurchaseEntry.PurchaseDate + "\r\n");

    // Display the result on screen.
    MessageBox.Show(Output.ToString());
}
```

In this case, the code begins by creating a context. It then uses the context to execute a LINQ query. Notice that the TVF works in precisely the same way that a stored procedure works. You simply pass the order you want to use along with the query. The code enumerates the result of the query and places it in a *StringBuilder*, *Output*, which is then displayed on screen.

4. Click Start or press F5. The application compiles and runs.
5. Select Amount in the Order By field of the example application.
6. Click Query. You'll see the same output as for the Entity SQL example in the "Calling a TVF Using Entity SQL" section of the chapter.
7. Perform steps 5 and 6 for each of the two remaining ordering methods so that you can see how they work.

Mapping a TVF to an entity type collection

There are advantages to using entities, rather than complex types, when working with TVFs. For one thing, entities can have key fields, while complex types can't. The default model update for your TVF is a complex type. You need to perform that update before you can work with the TVF at all. The following procedure takes you to the next step. It shows how to take the example you've already created and map it to an entity collection.

Mapping a TVF to an entity

1. Copy the *ModelFirst* example you initially created in this chapter to a new folder and use this new copy for this example (rather than the copy you created earlier).
2. Open the copied solution in Visual Studio.

3. Open *Form1* and remove *btnAdd*, along with its associated code. Choose Build | Build Solution to make the changes complete.

4. Open the Rewards2Model.EDMX file by double-clicking its entry in Solution Explorer.

5. Right-click in any clear area of the designer and choose Add New | Entity from the context menu. You'll see the Add Entity dialog box shown here:

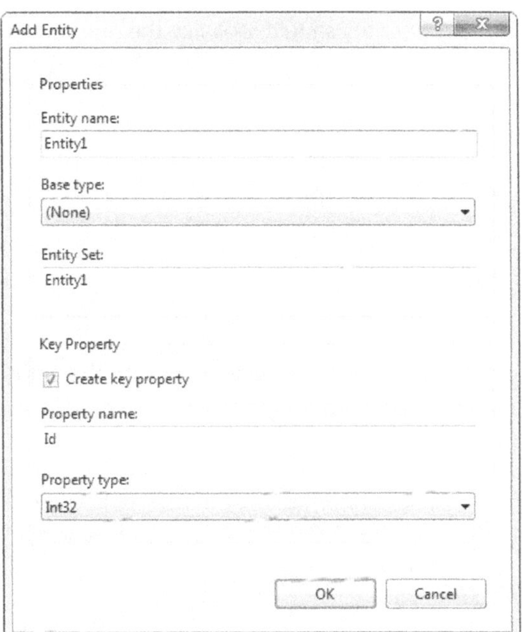

The name you choose for the entity should reflect its use within the application. Unlike a complex type, an entity should have a key property. The temptation would be to use the *Id* field because it's the key property for the *Purchases* table. However, this is a TVF, and the *RowNo* field is actually the key field in this case.

6. Type **ObtainClientsEntity** in the Entity Name field. Notice that the dialog box automatically fills in the Entity Set field name for you.

7. Type **RowNo** in the Property Name field. Choose Int64 in the Property Type field. These two fields define the key field used for this entity.

8. Click OK. Visual Studio creates the entity for you.

9. Right-click the *ObtainClientsEntity* entity and choose Add New | Scalar Property from the context menu.

10. Type **Amount** in the new property entry and press Enter. Visual Studio creates the new scalar property for you.

11. Choose Decimal in the Type property in the Properties window. Because this is a decimal value, type **18** for the *Precision* property and **2** for the *Scale* property.

12. Repeat steps 9 through 11 for *CustomerName* (type *String*), *CustomersId* (type *Int32*), *Id* (type *Int32*), and *PurchaseDate* (type *DateTime* and *precision* 23). At this point, the entity is complete; however, it isn't yet accessible. Your entity should look like the one shown here:

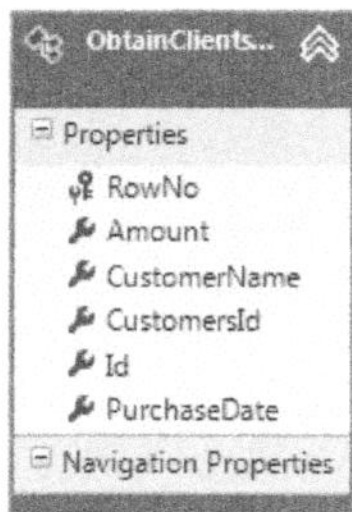

13. Choose Build | Build Solution to create the code required to work with the entity. You'll see an error message, "Error 3027: No mapping specified for the following EntitySet/AssociationSet - ObtainClientsEntities." Don't worry, this is normal.

14. Select the *ObtainClients* entry in the Rewards2Model\Function Imports folder of the Model Browser. You'll see the properties for this entry in the Properties window, as shown here:

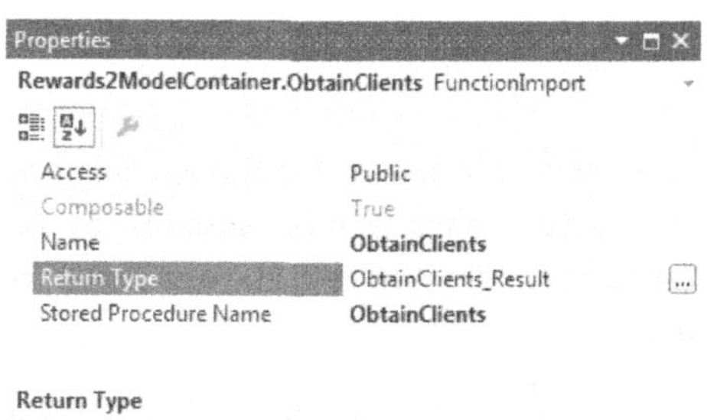

15. Click the ellipses in the Return Type property. You'll see an Edit Function Import dialog box like the one shown here:

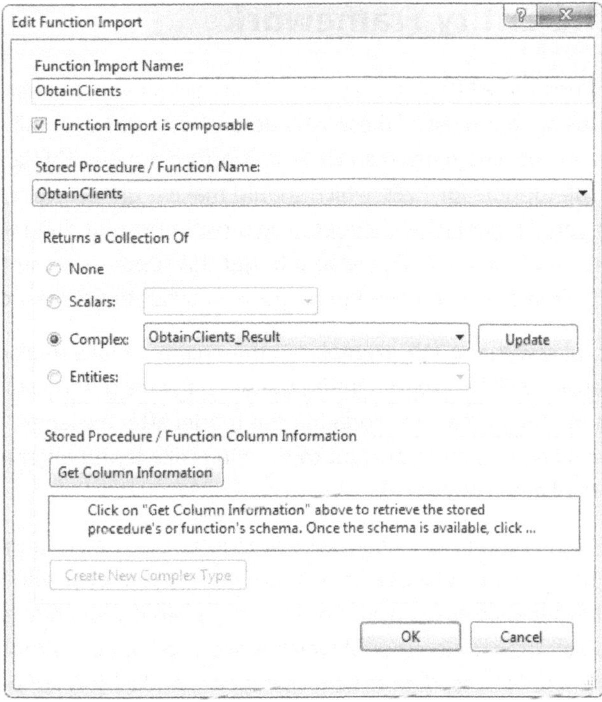

16. Select the Entities option. Choose ObtainClientsEntity from the associated drop-down list box. Click OK. The example is now using entity mapping. However, the code won't compile as-is, because it still relies on complex type mapping. There's actually only one line of code you need to change.

17. Change the line of code in the *btnQueryEntitySQL_Click()* event handler that reads

    ```
    ObtainClients_Result ThisRow = (ObtainClients_Result)Record[0];
    ```

    to read

    ```
    ObtainClientsEntity ThisRow = (ObtainClientsEntity)Record[0];
    ```

18. Click Start or press F5. The application compiles and runs.

19. Select Amount in the Order By field of the example application.

20. Click Query. You'll see the same output as for the Entity SQL example in the "Calling a TVF Using Entity SQL" section of the chapter.

21. Perform steps 5 and 6 for each of the two remaining ordering methods so that you can see how they work.

Getting started with the Entity Framework

This chapter has helped you understand a little more about TVFs by giving you a general overview. A lot of developers find TVFs confusing, but most of those who do understand TVFs really want to use them in their applications. TVFs are nothing more than UDFs that return a table. This latest version of the Entity Framework provides full support for TVFs, which should make it unnecessary to perform any odd workarounds to obtain tabular data when needed. The most important thing to remember is that you must use the latest version of the Entity Framework to get this support—customers who are using older versions of the Entity Framework will need to upgrade in order to use your code.

It would be relatively easy to play with the TVF examples in this chapter. Make small changes at first to see how they work. Because you'll be experimenting quite a bit while getting started with TVFs anyway, make sure you understand the process for updating the model after a change. The newness of TVFs makes them a special challenge, so it's important to do things like trying different data types to see how they're mapped by the Entity Framework.

Chapter 11, "Dealing with exceptions," marks a change in direction. You'll be starting to work through errors that the Entity Framework produces and consider how best to deal with them. Anything as complex as DBMSs will experience errors from time to time, even if your code is perfect and your users input data with absolute accuracy (neither of which is likely to happen). Problems such as server glitches, downed network connections, data stream corruption, and all sorts of other issues that aren't under your control will create errors that you must handle as part of your application code. Chapter 11 marks the starting point for dealing with the most common sorts of errors.

Chapter 10 quick reference

<table>
<thead>
<tr><th>To</th><th>Do this</th></tr>
</thead>
<tbody>
<tr><td>Create a TVF</td><td>Define the TVF using the CREATE FUNCTION statement with any required parameters. You must define the return type as a table using the RETURNS TABLE statement and a table content declaration. This statement can include a variable, such as @returntable. The table declaration is followed by the word AS, an INSERT statement, your query, and the word RETURN. (There are actually many variations of the TVF—this is just one formulation.) A simple TVF might look like this:
<pre><code>CREATE FUNCTION SimpleObtainClients
(
)
RETURNS @returntable TABLE
(
   CustomerName   NVarChar(Max),
   Id   Int,
   PurchaseDate   DateTime,
   Amount   Decimal(18,2),
   CustomersId   Int
)
AS
BEGIN
   INSERT INTO @returntable
   SELECT C.CustomerName,
          P.Id,
          P.PurchaseDate,
          P.Amount,
          P.CustomersId
   FROM Customers AS C
   INNER JOIN Purchases AS P
   ON C.Id = P.CustomersId
   RETURN
END</code></pre></td></tr>
<tr><td>Alter a TVF</td><td>Specify which TVF to change using the ALTER FUNCTION statement, followed by the modifications you want to make. The process is similar to the one you use for creating a TVF and for altering other database elements such as scalar functions, stored procedures, and views.</td></tr>
<tr><td>Create a new TFV using Server Explorer</td><td>Right-click the Functions folder under the desired database entry in Server Explorer and choose Add New | Table-Valued Function from the context menu.</td></tr>
<tr><td>Update the model so it knows about the TVF</td><td>Right-click in any clear area of the designer and choose Update Model From Database from the context menu. Follow the steps provided by the wizard to include the TVF in the model (you should see the view added to the designer, just as you would a table).</td></tr>
</tbody>
</table>

PART IV

Overcoming entity errors

Every application experiences some sort of error from time to time. Even if you have created perfect code (a near impossibility), the libraries and underlying platform that the application uses to execute instructions could be less than perfect. In addition, users can and will create exceptional conditions under which errors occur. You must also consider sources of error due to the local environment and the environment to which the client computer connects. The network is also a source of errors. In short, your application will experience errors of various types, and you need to know how to handle them. That's the focus of this part of the book—dealing with errors of all sorts.

Chapter 11, "Dealing with exceptions," discusses exceptions. An exception is an error that occurs when a condition that the developer couldn't (or didn't) anticipate happens within the application, its network connection, its environment, or the server and its database. Exceptions register exceptional conditions—unanticipated events.

Chapter 12, "Overcoming concurrency issues," moves on to a particular kind of error that occurs in environments where multiple requests overlap and cause problems. *Concurrency* is a kind of error that occurs when the consistency of the output of one component is violated by another component. The result is erroneous data. The data may end up at the client or within the database, but the point is that concurrency issues cause errors that result when components collide in their interactions and cause some sort of damage.

Chapter 13, "Handling performance problems," helps you understand performance as it applies to the Entity Framework. You may not view performance issues as an error, but delivering data to the client at a glacial pace can cause all sorts of problems for the end user. The end user normally responds to slow applications by damaging them and the data they're supposed to protect in some way—usually out of sheer frustration. In short, performance is a significant source of errors that you need to consider as part of creating robust applications.

CHAPTER 11

Dealing with exceptions

After completing the chapter, you'll be able to

- Explain what an exception is.
- Define common exception sources.
- Create code to handle string exceptions.
- Create code to handle query exceptions.
- Develop methods for handling other exception types.
- Define concurrency exceptions.

When you discuss an exception, it's always in regard to something unexpected. For example, an exception to a rule is a situation that the rule couldn't anticipate. You do something different, in such a case, because the rule didn't cover it. Application code encounters the same situation. Even the best developer (or development team) can't anticipate every contingency. Situations will occur that defy even the best efforts at mitigation, causing an error. However, you aren't without resources in dealing with these situations. Handling an exception with code that deals with the exception by doing something different—something special—makes a bad situation better.

There are many situations where exceptions occur. This chapter considers some of the most common sources of exceptions with regard to the Entity Framework. There probably isn't enough room in an entire book to cover every possible exception, but this chapter will help you understand those that happen often enough to cause you real problems with your application.

Note This chapter doesn't cover common .NET application exceptions, except where they overlap with Entity Framework issues. Your application could still encounter other kinds of errors that have nothing to do with the Entity Framework. For example, the failure of your application to find an external configuration file is an application-specific error that this chapter won't discuss. You still need to handle these sorts of error as part of your application code.

If you take nothing else away from this chapter, you should become more aware of the fact that exceptions happen to everyone. You're not a bad developer for experiencing exceptions. The application only becomes poorly designed when it doesn't handle exceptions well enough to recover in most cases. Even users understand that exceptions happen, but users are depending on you to handle those exceptions so they can keep working with the application instead of suffering the consequences of a crash. The focus of this chapter is on understanding exceptions and then determining what you can do to handle them in a safe and succinct manner.

Understanding exceptions

There are many schools of thought regarding exceptions. The best way to view an exception is an event that occurs due to unanticipated or unwanted circumstances. An exception is the response to an exceptional event, such as when a user enters incorrect information or the network connection suddenly fails. Some exceptions, such as incorrect user input, are avoidable. You can perform checks on the incorrect input or you can use controls that don't allow the incorrect input in the first place. Other exceptions, such as a failed network connection, are unavoidable—the best you can hope to do is to handle them when they occur. However, you could still check the network connection before you use it and potentially avoid the problem using that approach.

When working with the Entity Framework, you not only consider the standard exceptions, but also exceptions that are Entity Framework specific. The "Considering exception sources" section of the chapter will provide a detailed view of these exceptions, but for the most part, the main exception that you need to consider is the *System.Data.Entity.EntityException* exception. This is the base class for all entities that are thrown by the *EntityClient* object. Knowing about this class and the classes that inherit from it will help you manage a large percentage of the exceptions that generally occur. However, you do need to consider other sorts of exceptions that can happen (as described later in the chapter).

It's important to realize that exceptions aren't a strange beast in the Entity Framework, much as you may think from reading some posts and articles. An exception works the same no matter the environment in which it appears. To take the mystery out of exceptions, simply consider them a means of informing your application that something unexpected has happened. In some respects, an exception is a sort of specialized event in that it stops the normal application flow, and you use a special structure (the *try...catch* block) to handle the exception. When working with the Entity Framework, as in every other environment, use these best practices to handle exceptions efficiently and successfully:

- Handle small blocks of code If you place a *try...catch* block around a huge number of lines of code, it's difficult to handle the exception because you don't precisely know where the exception occurred or what caused it. Use *try...catch* blocks that focus on individual tasks so that it's more likely that your application will recover from the exception.
- Perform setups outside the ***try...catch*** block To ensure that the exception focuses on the task at hand, rather than the task setup, make sure the setup code resides outside the *try...catch* block. This practice not only reduces the number of lines of code within the *try...catch* block, but it also helps focus your attention on the task, rather than the task setup, when reviewing code for potential sources of error.

- **Use the most specific exception possible** The more precise you can make the exception, the more likely it is that you'll discover the true source of an exception. Using general exceptions is a last ditch effort to keep the application from crashing—not the first line of defense against exceptions. For example, a *System.Data.PropertyConstraintException* is more specific (and therefore a better choice) than a *System.Data.ConstraintException*. Of course, there are situations where you need both, because the *PropertyConstraintException* may not actually catch the exception you need to catch. However, if you catch the *PropertyConstraintException* first, you know that the *ConstraintException* comes from some other source.

- **View all pertinent information** Some exception-handling code that you see only checks the basic information without delving into the details. The detail information, when the code that throws the exception provides it, can help your application recover from the exception in at least some cases, but only if your application is designed to use the information.

- **Rethrow exceptions as needed** If the current code block can't handle an exception, rethrow it so that the next level can attempt to repair the problem. Only when you reach the topmost level of your application should you provide some means of handling, quashing, or ignoring an exception. The last course of action your application should take is to fail gracefully when all other courses of action have failed. Make sure your graceful failure doesn't include data loss.

- **Don't simply log exceptions** A common problem with database applications is that the application logs exceptions that no one ever sees. An error can continue to occur for months before a major data loss event has the administrator actually reviewing the application logs. By the time the administrator looks at the logs your application creates, it's usually too late to correct the problem, and the data is lost. Make sure you provide some positive means of informing the user, administrator, or developer about an exception. The more critical the exception, the greater the need to inform multiple parties about it.

- **Include a *finally* clause with your *try...catch* block** It's important to ensure you don't make a situation worse by creating memory leaks or other problems in your application as the result of an exception. For example, make sure you close and release any resources you may have in use at the level you're using them. The most essential task is to close any file resources to ensure the data is flushed to the file and the application doesn't experience data loss. You can read more about the *finally* clause at *http://msdn.microsoft.com/library/dszsf989.aspx*.

These are the most common best practices you should follow when handling Entity Framework exceptions. All of them could apply to any .NET application you can create (even though some are specifically tweaked for use with the Entity Framework). The reason these best practices are emphasized when working with the Entity Framework is the complex environment that the Entity Framework creates. A lot of activity takes place in the background automatically when you work with the Entity Framework, and you need to ensure that your application properly handles tasks, because the automation may not work as expected when an exception occurs.

Tip You can find a torrent of exceptional-handling advice online. Of course, no one actually has time to read all of that information. A good site to check for a succinct list of great general exception tips for .NET developers is at *http://www.codeproject.com/Articles/9538/Exception-Handling-Best-Practices-in-NET.*

Considering exception sources

The Entity Framework provides a rich computing experience for developers and users alike. This rich computing experience also increases the complexity of the Entity Framework, which in turn creates an environment where exceptions can happen in multiple ways. It's not surprising that there are a number of error sources associated with the Entity Framework. The problem is that these exception sources are spread across a number of namespaces because the Entity Framework covers a lot of ground. The following sections provide a good overview of the kinds of exceptions that you should consider handling in your application to ensure the application has the best possible chance of completing tasks without interruption.

Tip There are a number of cheat-sheet sites that provide lists of exceptions and corresponding short descriptions. For example, you can find one such list at *http://www.mikesdotnetting.com/Article/130/Cheat-Sheet-.NET-Framework-Exceptions*. These exception lists are helpful because they prevent you from having to scour the .NET documentation looking for exceptions in the various namespaces. Using the most precise exception that you can makes it a lot easier to handle the exception and potentially avoid an application crash. Creating your own log of commonly encountered exceptions and how you handled them is also a big help in locating and repairing similar exceptions later.

Dealing with the *System.Data.EntityException*

The *System.Data.EntityException* class acts as the base class for a number of exceptions that occur when working with the *EntityClient* object. These are the classes that you use most often to safeguard your Entity Framework applications. The following list provides a short description of each of the specific exception classes that inherit from *EntityException*:

- ***System.Data.EntityCommandCompilationException*** This exception occurs when you create a command that the compiler isn't able to turn into a command tree. In most cases, it means that the query you created has some problem with it.

- ***System.Data.EntityCommandExecutionException*** This exception occurs when you create a command that the compiler could turn into a command tree, but that the underlying storage provider couldn't execute for some reason. For example, the user may not have the rights required to request that the database manager perform the task.
- ***System.Data.EntitySqlException*** An Entity SQL query passes command text directly to the storage provider. This exception indicates that the command text has a syntactic or semantic rule error in it. In most cases, the error message will tell you the source of the problem, such as a missing or invalid clause.
- ***System.Data.MappingException*** In order to perform a task, the Entity Framework must be able to map an application command into a command that the storage provider understands. You see this exception when there isn't any way to map the request. You could also see errors that indicate that a particular type has been mapped more than once—this error occurs in multithreaded applications with synchronization problems.
- ***System.Data.MetadataException*** The Entity Framework must be able to find the .CSDL, .SSDL, and .MSL files used to describe the underlying database mode. When you see this exception, it means that the application is unable to locate one or more of these files. The location of the files is stored in the application's .CONFIG file—in most cases, in a string that looks like this:

```
connectionString="metadata=res://*/Rewards2Model.csdl|res://*/Rewards2Model.ssdl|res://*/
Rewards2Model.msl;provider=System.Data.SqlClient;provider
```

  The string is part of the *<add>* tag that appears as a child of the *<connectionStrings>* tag. The names and paths of the metadata files must match the actual application configuration. When you see this error, the problem is commonly that the developer has changed the name of the .EDMX file.
- ***System.Data.ProviderIncompatibleException*** This exception occurs when you attempt to use a data provider that isn't compatible with the version of the Entity Framework that you're using. The error can occur even when the data provider worked with a previous version of the Entity Framework, so it's important to test the data provider you plan to use as soon as possible in the application development process. Obtain an updated data provider to fix this particular problem.

Common exceptions that apply to the Entity Framework

There are a number of exceptions that apply to the Entity Framework that are also used in other situations. For example, the Entity Framework will generate a *System.ArgumentException* or *System.InvalidOperationException* when the *EntityConnectionString* object is misconfigured. The *EntityConnectionString* is used whenever you instantiate an *ObjectContext*. The connection string actually appears in the application's .CONFIG file. It will appear as the *<add>* tag in the *<connectionStrings>* section of the *.CONFIG* file. The part of the string you need to look at to resolve this issue is:

```
name="Rewards2ModelContainer"
```

The *name* attribute value must match the name of the entity container. You'll receive an error message, such as "Connection String Can't Be Found or Is Improperly Configured" or "No connection string named 'Container Name' could be found in the application config file," when the two names don't match. Of course, there can be other problems with the *<add>* tag as well, and these other issues can also generate a *System.ArgumentException* or *System.InvalidOperationException*.

Another common exception is *System.NotSupportedException*. You can see this exception in a number of situations. However, in most cases, you see it as the result of making a query that the compiler can understand, but it has no direct mapping to the data store. One such example is the *ToShortDateString()* method used with LINQ. In this case, the compiler understands the method just fine, but when you try to run the application, it generates a somewhat confusing message stating that LINQ to Entities doesn't recognize the method. When you see this sort of error, you know to look at the methods used in the query to ensure the data store actually provides a mapping for them. The workaround is to modify the data after the query returns it to you.

The point is that you need to be prepared to see some common exceptions as part of working with the Entity Framework. In some cases, the source of the exception might not be clear from the accompanying message. The best way to proceed is to begin by checking your query. If the query looks fine, try different formulations to determine whether the source of the exception is an unsupported mapping, such as the *ToShortDateString()* method. After you verify that your query is fine, make sure you check your connection with the database. Of course, you'll also want to recheck any setups you perform to ensure that you're passing valid information to the database. Entity SQL queries are especially prone to problems involving typos and other difficult-to-find issues.

Working through *System.Data* namespace exceptions

You use the *System.Data* namespace to access .NET features that work with the ADO.NET architecture. This namespace includes access to all of the data-specific classes (including *DataSet*, *DataTable*, *DataRow*, and *DataColumn*) that you work with when accessing a database. In most cases, the Entity

Framework hides many of these data access specifics from view. However, just because they're hidden doesn't mean you won't see exceptions generated by them when necessary. Of course, you've already seen a number of these exceptions in the "Dealing with the *System.Data.EntityException*" section of the chapter. The following list provides a short description of the additional (less common) exception classes you see when working with the *System.Data* namespace.

Note Some exceptions are so generic that it's unlikely you'll ever see them, and they don't appear in this list. For example, *System.Data.DataException* acts as the base class for a host of more specific exceptions, including *System.Data.ConstraintException*, *System.Data.DeletedRowInaccessibleException*, *System.Data.Design.TypedDataSetGeneratorException*, *System.Data.DuplicateNameException*, *System.Data.EntityException*, *System.Data.InRowChangingEventException*, *System.Data.InvalidCommandTreeException*, *System.Data.InvalidConstraintException*, *System.Data.InvalidExpressionException*, *System.Data.MissingPrimaryKeyException*, *System.Data.NoNullAllowedException*, *System.Data.ObjectNotFoundException*, *System.Data.ReadOnlyException*, *System.Data.RowNotInTableException*, *System.Data.StrongTypingException*, *System.Data.TypedDataSetGeneratorException*, *System.Data.UpdateException*, and *System.Data.VersionNotFoundException*.

In addition, there are some exceptions that simply don't apply to applications that use the Entity Framework. For example, the *System.Data.InRowChangingEventException* only applies when you provide code for the *RowChanging* event and call the *EndEdit()* method within the associated event handler. Since it's unlikely that you'll create a handler for this event when working with the Entity Framework, the exception doesn't apply. These exceptions don't appear in the following list, but you need to be aware that some truly bizarre circumstance could cause the Entity Framework to throw them.

Just in case you didn't think exceptions were confusing enough, at times it's also possible to find some exceptions that the .NET Framework documents, but doesn't use. For example, the .NET documentation lists the *System.Data.InvalidCommandTreeException*, and then promptly tells you that this exception is never used. This list doesn't include unused exceptions. If it turns out that Microsoft uses them sometime in the future, I'll document them on my blog for this book, at *http://blog.johnmuellerbooks.com/categories/263/entity-framework-development-step-by-step.aspx*. However, just because Microsoft isn't using a particular exception doesn't mean you can't use it in your code.

- ***System.Data.ConstraintException*** Whenever you work with the database, you must adhere to any constraints placed on working with the various tables. In most cases, the model you create also provides support for the constraints associated with the database. However, when the model inadvertently lets you create a query that compromises a constraint, you see this exception. A special form of this exception is the *System.Data.PropertyConstraintException*, which applies specifically to database properties.

- ***System.Data.DeletedRowInaccessibleException*** This exception occurs when you attempt to perform an operation on a row that has been deleted. There are specific causes for this exception, but in general, any task you attempt to perform on the deleted row will throw this exception. The source of the deletion need not be the client application, but could also be from an external source.
- ***System.Data.DuplicateNameException*** Every object you create in a database must have a unique name. This exception is thrown whenever you attempt to create two objects of the same type with the same name. The exception can occur in all sorts of situations. For example, when reading a data source, such as an RSS feed, it's possible to have two columns with the same name. Even though the data file will parse and read correctly, having two columns with the same name will raise this exception. The solution is to verify that the data source is not only well formed, but uses unique names for each column you intend to import.
- ***System.Data.EvaluateException*** A data column can have an expression that's used to filter rows, calculate the values in a column, or create an aggregate column. When the database manager can't evaluate this expression, you see this exception thrown. The exception can also appear when the returned dataset doesn't contain the column in question. Even if a query works, it may not return the results you think it will, which can result in this particular exception.
- ***System.Data.InvalidConstraintException*** Although the Entity Framework makes this exception unlikely, you could create a query that attempts to either define or access a constraint in an invalid manner. For example, if you create a relationship between a parent and a child table, the key field must exist in both tables. Using the model-first or database-first workflow eliminates all possibility of this exception occurring. However, you could possibly see it when using a code-first workflow.
- ***System.Data.InvalidExpressionException*** This is the parent class of *System.Data.EvaluateException* and *System.Data.SyntaxErrorException*. You see it when there's an error in a data column expression, but it isn't either an evaluation or syntax error. Data column expressions are used to filter rows, calculate the values in a column, or create an aggregate column.
- ***System.Data.MissingPrimaryKeyException*** Every table you create must have a primary key. You'll encounter this particular error relatively often when working with the Entity Framework, especially when using the model-first workflow. Fortunately, the designer or compiler will make you aware of the problem long before you actually run the code in most cases.
- ***System.Data.NoNullAllowedException*** This exception is thrown whenever you attempt to place a null value in a column that has its properties set not to allow null values.
- ***System.Data.ObjectNotFoundException*** An object must exist in the model before you can use it. This exception is thrown when you attempt to use an object that doesn't exist. In at least some cases, the cause of the exception could be as simple as a mistyped column name in a query. It's easier to create the conditions required for this exception when using Entity SQL because the query isn't checked at compile time.

- ***System.Data.OperationAbortedException*** A user can choose to abort certain tasks that your application performs. Just which operations can be aborted depends on the configuration and design of your application. Whenever a user does abort an operation (such as a record update), you receive this exception. *Aborting* means that the user chose to prematurely end the operation, as opposed to the operation simply timing out or encountering an error.
- ***System.Data.PropertyConstraintException*** This specifies that a specific kind of constraint exception has occurred. The application has attempted to modify a property in a way that creates referential errors within the database. The parent exception is *System.Data.ConstraintException*.
- ***System.Data.ReadOnlyException*** Any time you try to write data to a database field that's marked read-only for some reason, the Entity Framework will throw this exception. You normally see this exception as the result of a call to *SaveChanges()*. The exception can occur when you try to write a value to an identity field used as a primary key (normally the *Id* field) or when someone has the record locked in a pessimistic concurrency configuration. However, there are a number of other causes for this problem, including the use of multiple contexts when working with a database.
- ***System.Data.StrongTypingException*** This exception is thrown when a strongly typed dataset encounters a *DBNull* value. In fact, the act of calling *IsDBNull()* can cause the exception in some cases, such as checking an *Int32* field for *DBNull*, since an *Int32* can never contain a null value. The exception can also occur during a call to a method such as *ToList()*. If the dataset includes a property or field that contains a null value, and the property or field shouldn't contain such a value, the Entity Framework throws this exception.
- ***System.Data.SyntaxErrorException*** There are a number of situations in which you'll see this exception. The most common is that you actually have an error in the query you created. This error happens most often when using Entity SQL. However, the problem could be one of the provider not understanding a query element. For example, when working with MySQL, it's possible to see an error of this sort under certain circumstances when using a LINQ *Where()* method call. Verify that the query is correct first, and then check to ensure the provider offers full support for the query options you've used.
- ***System.Data.UpdateException*** This is a catchall exception that occurs whenever the Entity Framework can't update a database and no specific error has occurred. A common source of this exception is a shared context. A single update fails within the context for a specific reason, such as a *System.Data.ReadOnlyException*. Because the errant update still resides in the context, any subsequent call to *SaveChanges()* will fail and cause an *UpdateException* because the update didn't fail for a specific reason (other than it couldn't proceed due to the failed exception). The most important way to avoid this exception is to use the Unit of Work pattern, described at *http://blogs.msdn.com/b/adonet/archive/2009/06/16/using-repository-and-unit-of-work-patterns-with-entity-framework-4-0.aspx*.

Working through *System.Data.Common* namespace exceptions

The exceptions that you encounter as part of the *System.Data.Common* namespace are database specific. They normally reflect some problem with the data source, rather than your code. The issue could be as simple as a bad connection, but these exceptions normally reflect something a bit more precise than that. For example, you might see an exception of this sort as the result of a misconfiguration at the data source. There's only one data source exception that you commonly see when working with the Entity Framework:

- ***System.Data.Common.DbException*** You see this exception when the system can't figure out precisely what is wrong with the data source. (Some developers also use this exception when creating code that uses data sources from multiple vendors.) It's more common to see one of the provider-specific exceptions that inherit from this exception, such as the following:
  - ***System.Data.Odbc.OdbcException*** An error has occurred with an Open Database Connectivity (ODBC) data source. Since the Entity Framework doesn't support ODBC, you shouldn't expect to see this particular exception unless you write custom code to support it.
  - ***System.Data.OleDb.OleDbException*** An error has occurred with an Object Linking and Embedding for Databases (OLE-DB) data source. Since the Entity Framework doesn't support OLE-DB, you shouldn't expect to see this particular exception unless you write custom code to support it.
  - ***System.Data.OracleClient.OracleException*** An error has occurred with an Oracle-specific data source.
  - ***System.Data.SqlClient.SqlException*** An error has occurred with a Microsoft SQL Server–specific data source.

Note You may also see exceptions that aren't listed in the .NET Framework documentation. In many cases, these exceptions come from non-Microsoft providers that provide the required Entity Framework support. For example, MySQL provides such support through the connector provided at *http://www.mysql.com/downloads/connector/net*. You can read an article about using this particular provider with the Entity Framework at *http://dev.mysql.com/doc/refman/5.1/en/connector-net-tutorials-entity-framework-winform-data-source.html*. The use of third-party providers is one reason that some developers use the generic *System.Data.Common.DbException*, rather than something more specific.

Working through *System.Data.Linq* namespace exceptions

Although the *System.Data.Linq* namespace documentation says that it's specific to LINQ to SQL usage, it also affects your use of LINQ to Entities when you make LINQ queries and the underlying data source is SQL Server. (It may affect other providers as well, but there isn't any documented evidence to support this idea.) Theoretically, you could see these exceptions when working with Entity SQL queries, but you'll more likely see them when using LINQ queries. The following list describes the exceptions you could see when working with the Entity Framework:

- ***System.Data.Linq.ChangeConflictException*** Whenever you attempt to make a change to a database with optimistic concurrency in place, there's a chance that someone else will have made a change between the time you obtained the record and the time you actually submit any changes. This exception indicates that a change has occurred—someone else has modified the record. Interestingly enough, this exception can occur when performing a left outer join or when working with some controls. One way to avoid this problem is to set the *UpdateCheck* property for all non–primary key fields in the table. It's also important to verify that the database doesn't have triggers that could fire between the time you obtain the record and the time you submit a change. You also need to verify that a field marked nullable in the database is marked as nullable in the model.
- ***System.Data.Linq.DuplicateKeyException*** This exception occurs when you attempt to add an object that passes a key that has already been used by another object to the identity cache. For example, you might try to add a duplicate customer to a customer database. You'll likely find this exception as an inner exception to a *System.Data.UpdateException*. Another potential source of this problem is when you delete an existing object and then create a new object that contains the same key. Even though you delete the existing object first, the Entity Framework may actually attempt to perform the insertion first. To avoid this issue, make sure you call *SaveChanges()* after each unit of work. In other words, you would call *SaveChanges()* after making the deletion to ensure the deletion is actually in place before you attempt the insertion.
- ***System.Data.Linq.ForeignKeyReferenceAlreadyHasValueException*** You see this exception when your application attempts to modify a foreign key after the entity is already loaded into the cache. What this essentially means is that the association properties and the foreign key aren't equal for some reason—possibly as a result of a query you've made. There's a good discussion of this issue at *http://www.faridesign.net/2010/11/linq-to-sql-operation-is-not-valid-due-to-the-current-state-of-the-object/*.

Handling connection string exceptions

A common problem, especially when working on larger projects, is to encounter a problem with an application's connection string. The error could come from a multitude of sources. However, in most cases you can trace the problem down to the application's .CONFIG file. Something in the .CONFIG file is wrong or has changed due to a configuration change in the application itself. The following sections describe how to see the exception and then show how to deal with it.

Seeing the connection string problem

A good technique for working through exception issues is to play with your code to see what sorts of things can go wrong. Connection string issues can (and do) happen when an application resides on a client system and is damaged or misconfigured in some way. The following procedure helps you simulate such a configuration problem so that you can see how it will appear to the end user.

Observing connection string issues

1. Copy the LINQ query version of the *ModelFirst* example you created in Chapter 6, "Manipulating data using LINQ," to a new folder, and use this new copy for this example (rather than the copy you created in Chapter 6).

> **Note** The LINQ version of the *ModelFirst* example in Chapter 6 appears in the *ModelFirst* (LINQ Query) folder of the downloadable source code. If you created your own version of the example, the folder name will probably be different.

2. Open the copied solution in Microsoft Visual Studio.
3. Open the App.CONFIG file found in Solution Explorer.
4. Locate the *<add>* tag within the *<connectionStrings>* tag.
5. Change the following entry:

```
name="Rewards2ModelContainer"
```

   to read:

```
name="BadEntry"
```

6. Click Start or press F5. The application compiles and runs.
7. Click Query. You'll see the InvalidOperationException Was Unhandled dialog box shown here:

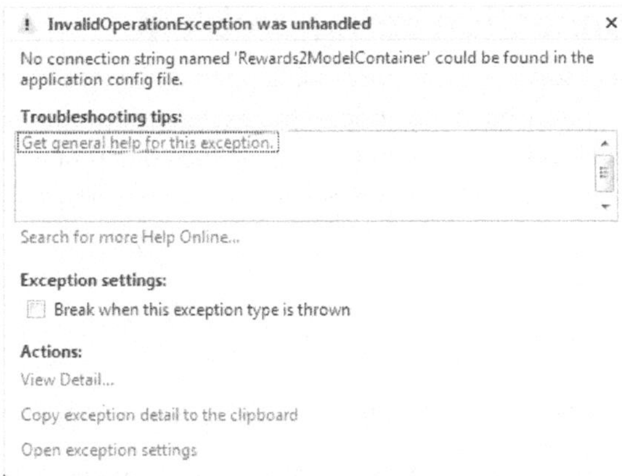

8. Click Stop Debugging. The application stops and the IDE returns to editing mode.
9. Reverse the edit you made in step 5 and run the application to ensure that the change works as expected. Click Query to ensure you see the desired output from Chapter 6.
10. Change the following entry:

```
metadata=res://*/Rewards2Model.csdl
```

to read:

```
metadata=res://*/BadEntry.csdl
```

11. Click Start or press F5. The application compiles and runs.
12. Click Query. You'll see the MetadataException Was Unhandled dialog box shown here:

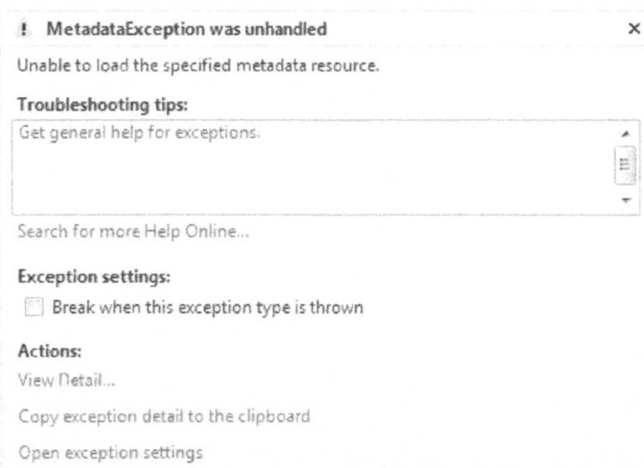

13. Click Stop Debugging. The application stops and the IDE returns to editing mode.
14. Reverse the edit you made in step 10 and run the application to ensure that the change works as expected. Click Query to ensure you see the desired output from Chapter 6.

Creating code for the connection string problem

Now that you have a better idea of what sorts of exceptions will happen and, more importantly, where they'll happen, you can add exception-handling code to the example application. The best way to approach the issue is to create flexible, yet precise, exception-handling code that will deal with the majority of the issues in a succinct manner. The following procedure shows one way to deal with the connection string issues.

Handling a connection string problem

1. Open the *Form1* source code file and locate the *btnQuery_Click()* event handler code.
2. Modify the code so that it now includes exception-handling code, as shown here:

```
// Create the new customer list.
IQueryable<Customers> CustomerList = null;

try
{
   // Obtain the customer list.
   CustomerList =
       from cust in context.Customers
       select cust;
}
catch (InvalidOperationException IOE)
{
   // Show an error message.
   MessageBox.Show("Cannot Create the Connection!\r\n" +
      IOE.Message);

   // Exit the event handler.
   return;
}
catch (MetadataException ME)
{
   // Show an error message.
   MessageBox.Show("Cannot Create the Connection!\r\n" +
      ME.Message);

   // Exit the event handler.
   return;
}
catch (DataException DE)
{
   // Show an error message.
   MessageBox.Show("Unexpected Data Exception!\r\n" +
      DE.GetType().FullName + "\r\n" +
      DE.Message);

   // Exit the event handler.
   return;
}
catch (Exception Ex)
{
```

```
    // Show an error message.
    MessageBox.Show("Unexpected Error!\r\n" +
       Ex.GetType().FullName + "\r\n" +
       Ex.Message);

    // Exit the event handler.
    return;
}
```

The first thing you should notice is that *CustomerList* is now defined separately as *IQueryable<Customers>*. You must perform this step to ensure that *CustomerList* is accessible outside of the *try...catch* structure.

Notice that the two specific errors come first. Always test more specific errors before you test less specific errors. The more precisely you can define an error, the less time you'll spend fixing it. In at least some cases, you'll even be able to recover from the error enough to allow continued application use. In this case, the application continues to work. However, before this call can proceed, you must fix the problem.

A less specific exception, *DataException*, allows you to provide a more detailed message than using a general exception. However, you're still not sure which exception has actually occurred, so this error message returns *DE.GetType().FullName*. This property tells you the actual exception type so that you can add a specific handler for it.

The final exception is the general exception. It doesn't tell you anything about the error except that it happened. As with *DataException*, the error output returns *Ex.GetType().FullName* so that you know what specific exception has happened.

3. Open the *App.CONFIG* file found in Solution Explorer.
4. Locate the *<add>* tag within the *<connectionStrings>* tag.
5. Change the following entry:

   ```
   name="Rewards2ModelContainer"
   ```

   to read:

   ```
   name="BadEntry"
   ```

6. Click Start or press F5. The application compiles and runs.
7. Click Query. This time you'll see the error dialog box shown here:

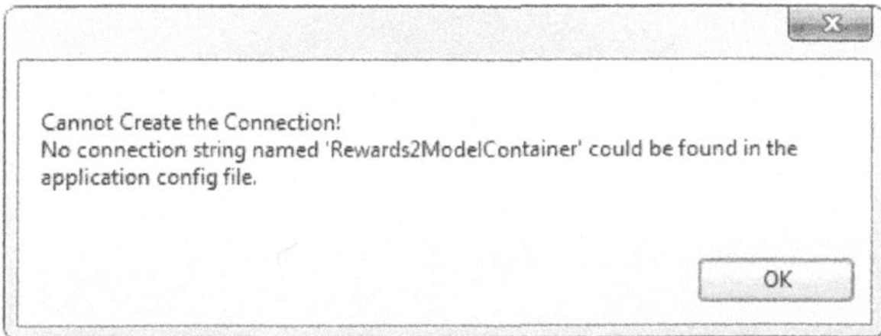

8. Click OK to close the dialog box. Close the application. The application stops and the IDE returns to editing mode.

9. Reverse the edit you made in step 5 and run the application to ensure that the change works as expected. Click Query to ensure you see the desired output from Chapter 6.

10. Change the following entry:

    ```
    metadata=res://*/Rewards2Model.csdl
    ```

    to read:

    ```
    metadata=res://*/BadEntry.csdl
    ```

11. Click Start or press F5. The application compiles and runs.

12. Click Query. Again, you'll see an error dialog box instead of the exception as you did before.

13. Click OK to close the dialog box. Close the application. The application stops and the IDE returns to editing mode.

14. Reverse the edit you made in step 10 and run the application to ensure that the change works as expected. Click Query to ensure you see the desired output from Chapter 6.

15. Change the following entry:

    ```
    metadata=res://*/Rewards2Model.csdl
    ```

    to read:

    ```
    metadata=res://C:/Rewards2Model.csdl
    ```

    This is actually a malformed string. You'll see a correctly formed string for a local drive, but with incorrect information, later in this procedure. An error like this actually happened to someone as the result of a less skilled administrator manually changing the *App.CONFIG* file.

16. Click Start or press F5. The application compiles and runs.

17. Click Query. This error wasn't trapped by any of the specific exceptions. Instead, you receive the general exception shown here (which includes the specific error type, *System.IO.FileLoadException*):

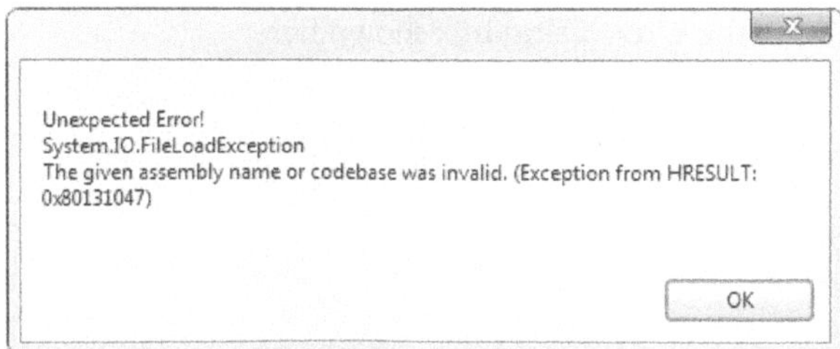

18. Click OK to close the dialog box. Close the application. The application stops and the IDE returns to editing mode.

19. Reverse the edit you made in step 15 and run the application to ensure that the change works as expected. Click Query to ensure you see the desired output from Chapter 6.

20. Change the following entry:

```
metadata=res://*/Rewards2Model.csdl
```

to read:

```
metadata=C:/Rewards2Model.csdl
```

This change shows how you'd reconfigure an application to use a file on a local drive, rather than the embedded copy in the application. Using this approach could help you create a temporary fix to the model. However, you must also supply the required file, which isn't present in this case.

21. Click Start or press F5. The application compiles and runs.

22. Click Query. You'll see the "Cannot Create the Connection!" error message. Notice that the message tells you precisely what is wrong this time. The application can't find the resource it needs on the local drive. Even though the error wasn't anticipated, the exception handling was flexible enough to handle it.

23. Click OK to close the dialog box. Close the application. The application stops and the IDE returns to editing mode.

24. Reverse the edit you made in step 20 and run the application to ensure that the change works as expected. Click Query to ensure you see the desired output from Chapter 6.

Adding another layer of exception handling

Exceptions can occur in multiple places in the application. Just because you can create a connection to the database doesn't mean that the application will work. The Unit of Work pattern describes a method of creating applications where each task receives separate handling to ensure you get the anticipated results. However, the example application still doesn't do that. The following procedure will show a weak point and a method for adding handling for that weak point.

Managing entity exceptions

1. Open the *App.CONFIG* file found in Solution Explorer.

2. Locate the *<add>* tag within the *<connectionStrings>* tag.

3. Change the following entry:

```
initial catalog=Rewards2
```

to read:

```
initial catalog=Rewards3
```

4. Click Start or press F5. The application compiles and runs.
5. Click Query. You'll see the EntityException Was Unhandled dialog box shown here:

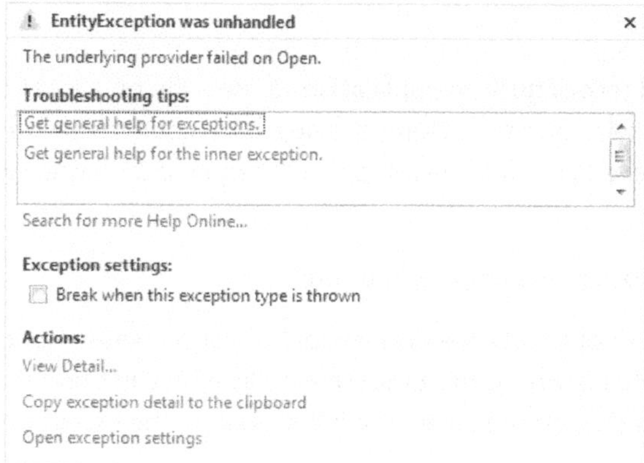

It's important to notice that this exception occurs in an entirely different place in the application. The exception occurs after the connection is made, which means that the connection is fine, but that something else is wrong.

6. Click Stop Debugging. The application stops and the IDE returns to editing mode.
7. Open the *Form1* source code file and locate the *btnQuery_Click()* event handler code.
8. Modify the code so that it now includes exception-handling code, as shown here:

```
try
{
   foreach (var Customer in CustomerList)
   {
      // Create a customer entry for each customer.
      Output.Append("\r\n" + Customer.CustomerName +
          " has made purchases on: ");

      // Process each purchase for that particular customer.
      foreach (var Purchase in Customer.Purchases)
         Output.Append("\r\n\t" + Purchase.PurchaseDate);
   }
}
catch (EntityException EE)
{
   // Show an error message.
   MessageBox.Show("Cannot Open the Database!\r\n" +
```

```
            EE.Message + "\r\n\r\nDetails:\r\n" +
            EE.InnerException.Message + "\r\n" +
            EE.InnerException.GetType().FullName);

        // Exit the event handler.
        return;
    }
    catch (Exception Ex)
    {
        // Show an error message.
        MessageBox.Show("Unexpected Error!\r\n" +
            Ex.GetType().FullName + "\r\n" +
            Ex.Message);

        // Exit the event handler.
        return;
    }
```

In this case, the exception doesn't provide enough information. The message is too generic to be helpful in locating the problem, so you must obtain information from the *InnerException* as well. The code demonstrates how to make the output more useful. As before, the exception handler also includes a generic exception for those situations where the code creates an exception you didn't anticipate.

9. Click Start or press F5. The application compiles and runs.

10. Click Query. This time you'll see the error dialog box shown here:

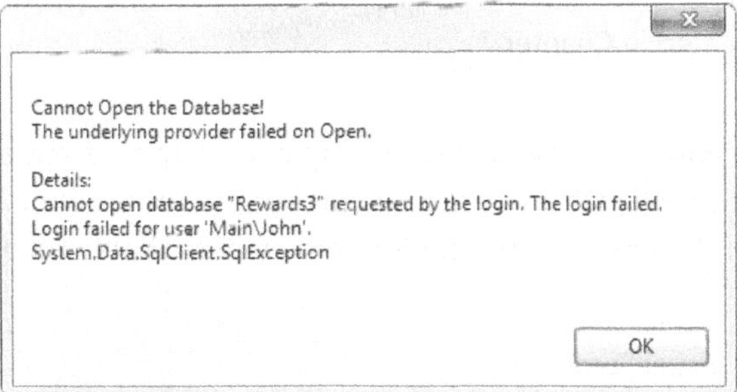

Notice that this output is fairly specific. You know that the provider failed when it attempted to open a resource. The resource is a nonexistent database, *Rewards3*, and the code attempted to open it using a specific set of credentials. The underlying error occurred as part of a *System.Data.SqlClient.SqlException*.

11. Click OK to close the dialog box. Close the application. The application stops and the IDE returns to editing mode.

12. Reverse the edit you made in step 5 and run the application to ensure that the change works as expected. Click Query to ensure you see the desired output from Chapter 6.

Tip There are many locations online that discuss the need to work with inner exceptions when working with the Entity Framework. For example, you can see another developer's interpretation of this issue at *http://www.codeproject.com/Tips/322250/Render-Exceptions-in-an-Entity-Framework-applicati*. The point is that you should consider precisely how to interact with the Entity Framework exceptions so that you get maximum value from them. In many cases, the information you need is buried and doesn't appear as part of the initial exception (which can prove confusing at first).

Dealing with query exceptions

Queries can be annoyingly difficult to create at times. Even simple queries can go awry due to simple typos or a developer thinking one thing when another is required. You can create invalid queries using either LINQ or Entity SQL, but it seems as if Entity SQL is more prone to problems, because it provides less support in the form of IntelliSense and compiler checks. With this in mind, the following procedure shows just two of the many ways in which a query can go wrong.

Observing Bad Queries

1. Copy the Entity SQL query version of the *ModelFirst* example you created in Chapter 7, "Manipulating data using Entity SQL," to a new folder, and use this new copy for this example (rather than the copy you created in Chapter 7).

Note The Entity SQL version of the *ModelFirst* example in Chapter 7 appears in the ModelFirst (Display - Entity SQL) folder of the downloadable source code. If you created your own version of the example, the folder name will probably be different.

2. Open the copied solution in Visual Studio.

3. Locate the *btnQuery3_Click()* method in the Form1.CS source code file and change the *EntitySQLCmd* string so it reads as follows:

```
String EntitySQLCmd =
    "SELECT CustomerList.Id, CustomerList.CustomerName " +
    "FROM Rewards2ModelContainer.Customers " +
    "AS CustomerList " +
    "WHERE CustomerList.Id='Josh Bailey'";
```

In this case, the query is modified so that it uses the wrong field—*Id* instead of *CustomerName*. The query will fail because the *Id* field is an *Int32* type, while the *CustomerName* field is a *String* type.

4. Click Start or press F5. The application compiles and runs.

5. Click Query 3. You'll see the EntitySqlException Was Unhandled dialog box shown here:

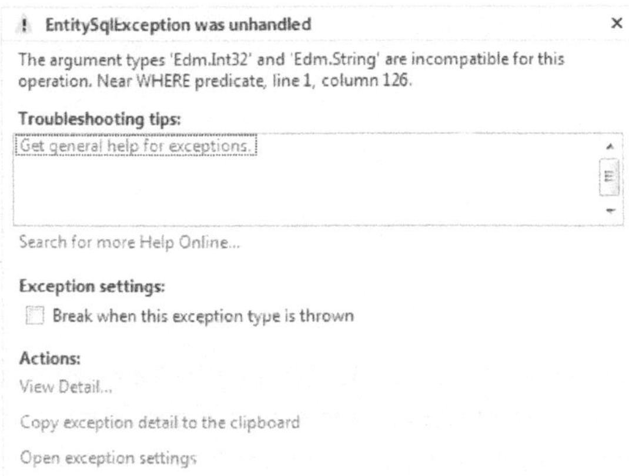

6. Click Stop Debugging. The application stops and the IDE returns to editing mode.

7. Reverse the edit you made in step 3 and run the application to ensure that the change works as expected. Click Query 3 to ensure you see the desired output from Chapter 7.

8. Change the *EntitySQLCmd* string so it reads as follows:

```
String EntitySQLCmd =
    "SELECT CustomerList.Id, CustomerList.CustomerName " +
    "FROM Rewards2ModelContainer.Customers " +
    "AS CustomerList " +
    "WHERE CustomerList.CustomerName>'Josh Bailey'";
```

Notice that the query is performing a greater-than (>) comparison using a *String* type. The comparison is invalid. However, the application will never find the correct error in this case. The Entity Framework doesn't see it, nor does Entity SQL, nor does the database. In fact, the error seemingly has nothing to do with an errant query, as you'll see in the steps that follow.

9. Click Start or press F5. The application compiles and runs.

10. Click Query 3. You'll see the InvalidOperationException Was Unhandled dialog box shown here:

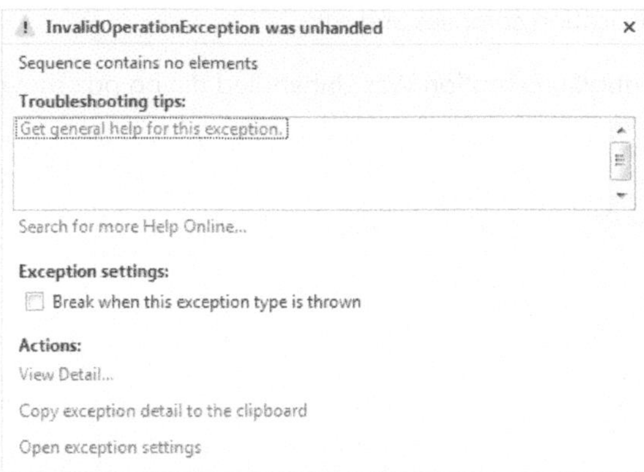

It won't take long for you to discover that some Entity SQL queries look perfectly valid to the application, but don't produce the correct results. This is the reason you must validate the outcome of any queries you make as part of the testing process. Given a specific set of inputs and a test database, you should look for specific outputs. When you don't see those specific outputs, you know there's something wrong with the query.

11. Click Stop Debugging. The application stops and the IDE returns to editing mode.
12. Reverse the edit you made in step 8 and run the application to ensure that the change works as expected. Click Query 3 to ensure you see the desired output from Chapter 7.

Dealing with other data exception types

Entity Framework applications can create a vast number of exception types depending on the precise problem domain you're dealing with at any given time. There isn't space in this book to show you all of the exceptions. However, you'll encounter a number of interesting exception types as you work through your application development. The following procedure demonstrates a few interesting exceptions that fall into the other category of exception types.

Observing Other Exception Types

1. Copy the LINQ query version of the *ModelFirst* example you created in Chapter 6 to a new folder and use this new copy for this example (rather than the copy you created in Chapter 6).

Note The LINQ version of the *ModelFirst* example in Chapter 6 appears in the ModelFirst (LINQ Query) folder of the downloadable source code. If you created your own version of the example, the folder name will probably be different.

2. Open the copied solution in Visual Studio.
3. Open the Rewards2Model.EDMX file found in Solution Explorer. Let's say you decide you need a larger *Id* field for *Purchases* because your customers are buying everything you have (and you even have a backlog).
4. Select the *Id* property in *Purchases*.
5. Change the *Type* property in the Properties window to *Int64*.
6. Click Start or press F5. The application compiles and runs.
7. Click Query. You'll see the MappingException Was Unhandled dialog box shown here:

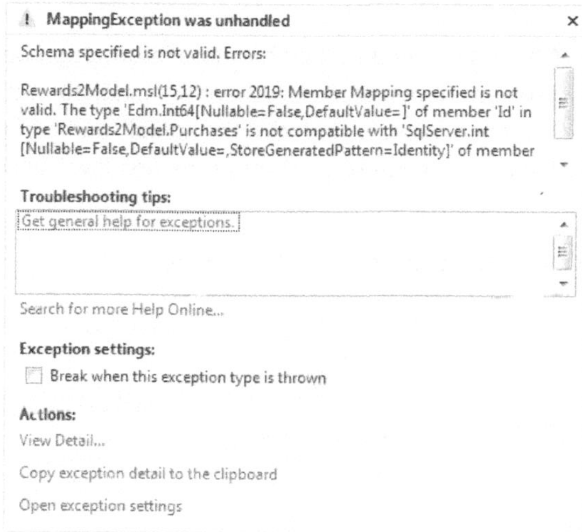

8. Click Stop Debugging. The application stops and the IDE returns to editing mode.
9. Reverse the edit you made in steps 4 and 5 and run the application to ensure that the change works as expected. Click Query to ensure you see the desired output from Chapter 6.
10. Select the *PurchaseDate* property in *Purchases*.
11. Change the Entity Key property in the Properties window to True.
12. Click Start or press F5. The application compiles and runs.
13. Click Query. You'll see the EntityCommandCompilationException Was Unhandled dialog box shown here:

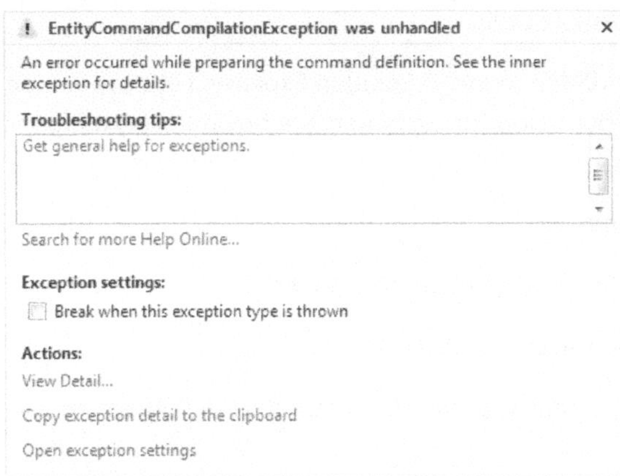

This is one of those situations where you'd need to look for more information before you have any chance at all of fixing problem. When creating exception handling in this case, you'd need to work with the detail information in order to derive the actual source of the problem. Unfortunately, a lot of exception-handling code stops short at the first level, which means you might not ever find the error.

14. Click View Detail. You'll see the View Detail dialog box shown here:

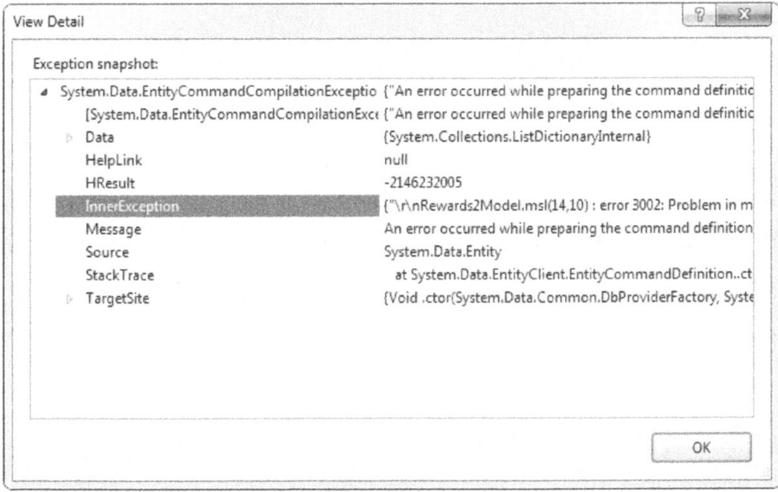

You're getting close to the actual problem. However, just looking at the View Detail dialog box still won't tell you what's wrong.

15. Expand InnerException by clicking the right-pointing arrow. Click the down arrow next to the Message field and you'll see the following information:

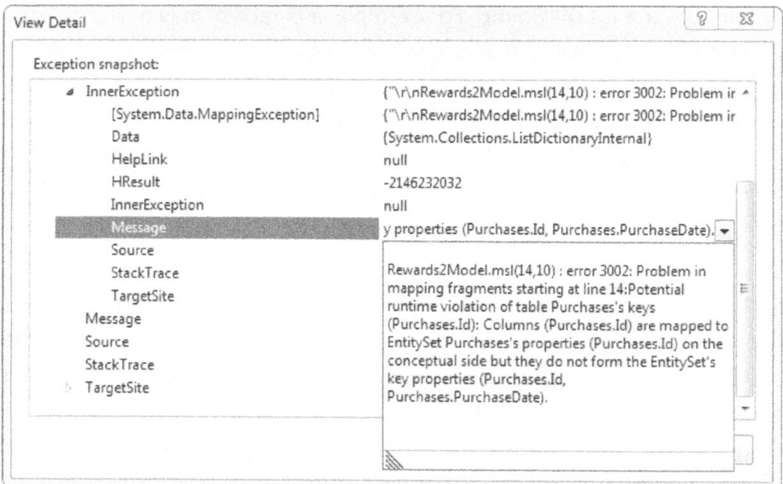

16. Click Stop Debugging. The application stops and the IDE returns to editing mode.

17. Reverse the edit you made in steps 10 and 11, and run the application to ensure that the change works as expected. Click Query to ensure you see the desired output from Chapter 6.

Understanding concurrency exceptions

There's a specific kind of exception—the *System.Data.OptimisticConcurrencyException* exception (see *http://msdn.microsoft.com/library/system.data.optimisticconcurrencyexception.aspx*)—that's thrown whenever there's a conflict updating the database. Conflicts can occur for a number of reasons, such as one user's data overwriting another user's data. Any time two entities are working with the same record at the same time, there's a potential for conflict.

Concurrency refers to the database being used for more than one task at a time. Given that a database may have hundreds of users, trying to keep all of the changes from conflicting with each other is a difficult proposition. In some cases, databases employ *pessimistic concurrency*, where records are locked until an application releases them. This model ensures that there are few, if any, updates for which one user overwrites the changes made by another. However, it also causes problems such as *deadlock*, where two application instances each have a record needed by the other to complete a transaction. Microsoft promotes *optimistic concurrency*, where the records are left unlocked and any issues are resolved when the update is made. You can read more about these two types of concurrency at *http://msdn.microsoft.com/library/aa0416cz.aspx*.

Concurrency rules cover a lot of ground. For example, a database may have a constraint that doesn't appear as part of the Entity Framework model. Because the constraint is unknown to the Entity Framework, it's possible that your application will violate it as part of an update and the database will generate this exception. Because this is a somewhat complex issue that could involve a number of different problems, the book devotes an entire chapter to the topic. Chapter 12, "Overcoming concurrency issues," tells you all about the *System.Data.OptimisticConcurrencyException* and other related exceptions.

Note While the most common concurrency exception that you see is the *System.Data.OptimisticConcurrencyException*, the Entity Framework can present you with other related exceptions, such as the *System.Data.DBConcurrencyException*. In addition, concurrency issues can trigger other exceptions, such as the *System.Data.DeletedRowInaccessibleException*. When working with some exceptions, it's important to keep the source of the exception in mind—the cause may be outside of your application.

Getting started with the Entity Framework

The essential facts to remember about exceptions are that they register an unanticipated condition and that they can come from multiple sources—not just your application code. In handling exceptions, the first line of defense is to keep the exception from occurring in the first place. The second line of defense is to detect the exception as accurately as possible to make it possible to handle the exception without an application crash. Only when you've exhausted every other possibility should you depend on a generic exception. In most cases, it should be possible to recover from an exception and allow the application to continue handling user needs. However, if it becomes impossible to recover, the application should always fail gracefully without any loss of data. Data loss is the ultimate transgression that any application can commit because the value of an application is in the data it protects and manages on the user's behalf.

This chapter contains a number of examples of errant applications and demonstrates how to handle the errors they create. However, the examples don't demonstrate every sort of exception. One useful technique for discovering how a particular exception looks is to simulate it. You might be surprised to discover that some exceptions really don't act the way that you think they might. Knowing how an exception looks can help you diagnose and fix it faster when the boss is breathing down your neck wondering when the application will be running again. Simulations are also a valuable way to ensure that your application adequately handles exceptions that could occur.

Concurrency issues occur when two components try to use the same resource simultaneously. The components can appear in the same application or as part of different applications. In fact, the hardest concurrency issues to diagnose occur when two different applications try to use the same resource at the same time and the developers of those applications don't have much contact with each other. They may not even realize the other application exists. Chapter 12 can't solve every concurrency issue you'll encounter when building applications, but it does provide valuable information on diagnosing and repairing concurrency issues that occur as part of the Entity Framework.

Chapter 11 quick reference

To	Do this
Increase the chances of finding a specific exception cause	Use the most specific exception class as the starting point in a *try...catch* block, and then work your way to toward more generic exception classes.
Increase the chances of locating the specific site of an error in your code	Use multiple *try...catch* blocks around a smaller number of lines of code so that the source of an error is specific to a particular task, rather than a group of tasks within the code.
Determine the cause of exceptions when the message is too generic	Use the *InnerException* and process its contents. In fact, you may have to process several levels of *InnerException* properties to determine the true source of an exception.
Define the actual exception when using a generic exception handler	Obtain the actual exception name using the *GetType().FullName* property of the exception object.
Ensure an exception is actually handled	Rethrow the exception as needed so that a higher level of code in your application can attempt to handle the exception. Never quash or ignore an exception at lower levels.
Reduce the risk of lost data	Include a *finally* clause in your *try...catch* block to ensure that all resources are freed and file handles closed. An exception creates a situation where the .NET application may not properly release resources, resulting in data loss.
Ensure that the application can connect to the server without error	Verify that the *<add>* tag in the *<connectionStrings>* section of the application's .CONFIG file is set up correctly. Although every attribute associated with the *<add>* tag is important, the two most commonly misconfigured attributes are *name* and *connectionString*.

CHAPTER 12

Overcoming concurrency issues

After completing the chapter, you'll be able to

- Describe database concurrency issues and tell how they affect use of the Entity Framework.
- Define optimistic concurrency and describe how its use affects applications.
- Demonstrate how to use optimistic concurrency in an application.
- Define pessimistic concurrency and describe how its use affects applications.

Concurrency is the act of allowing multiple entities to perform multiple tasks on a database at the same time. In order to be useful, a database must provide some level of concurrency to perform Create, Read, Update, and Delete (CRUD) operations in a meaningful way. It turns out that some CRUD operations are more likely to cause problems than others. For example, a read-only database would have few, if any, concurrency problems. The first section of this chapter helps you visualize these issues so you can gain a better understanding of the complexity that concurrency brings.

The issue of concurrency is quite complex. There are different ways to implement it; there are different methods of ensuring that it meets Atomicity, Consistency, Isolation, and Durability (ACID) requirements; and there is a wealth of other topics that would take an entire book to discuss. This chapter discusses concurrency from an Entity Framework perspective in a relatively simple fashion, involving optimistic and pessimistic concurrency (another form of concurrency—semioptimistic—isn't supported in any manner by the Entity Framework or the .NET Framework and is therefore not covered). The combination of the Entity Framework, the .NET Framework, and Microsoft SQL Server reduces the complexity of dealing with concurrency, and this chapter assumes you make use of all the features provided by each technology.

Even with the assistance provided by the tools discussed in this chapter, concurrency can still go wrong at times. For example, when using optimistic concurrency, two users can still fight over the same record in the database, which means you must provide a method for resolving the issue that doesn't involve constant Database Administrator (DBA) intervention. This chapter provides some basics on how to perform this task in order to meet most application development needs.

Warning This chapter takes a very simple view of concurrency. However, it's important to realize that there are many different ways in which to view concurrency, and there are a lot of underlying issues that the automation provided by the tools discussed in this book take care of for you. As the development environment becomes more complex, so do the concurrency issues. The use of multiple platforms complicates the means used to access the database and therefore affects concurrency, as does the use of databases from multiple vendors. This chapter doesn't address these complex issues, but you need to know they exist so you can prepare for them adequately. When in doubt, make sure you research potential concurrency issues before you place an application in production, because once the application is in production, it's actually too late to address the issues without potential data loss.

Visualizing database concurrency issues

The reason that databases are so useful is that they allow any number of people to share the same information. The only limiting factor is how well the database scales (handles the additional burden placed on it by each user who requires access). As the number of users increases, the concurrency issues also increase. The following list describes common concurrency problems:

- User A is trying to read a record that is in use by User B for an update or deletion.
- User A and User B are both changing different fields of the same record.
- User A is trying to update a record that User B deleted.
- User A and User B are both trying to add the same data to the database at the same time.
- User A and User B are both trying to delete the same record at the same time.

These scenarios happen relatively often with just 2 users, so you can imagine what happens when 40 or 50 users are all vying for the same records. In most cases, even with large databases, users are typically vying for control of relatively few records. For example, new customers may require updates, and customers that shop at a particular organization may require more attention than those who don't. On the other hand, some records can sit for years in a database without ever being touched.

There are many situations where you don't need to worry about concurrency. For example, User A and User B can both read the same record at the same time without problem. However, it's helpful to provide yourself with a complete list of potential scenarios and their effects on the database so that you're better prepared to choose policies that work for the greatest number of people as much of the time as possible.

Part of creating a database application is to determine how to handle the concurrency problems before you even create a model. Company policies usually dictate how to handle these issues, but in the absence of clear policies, you need to determine what to do when collisions occur. Here are some examples of ways in which you can handle concurrency issues:

- Provide a user with a read-only copy of a record.
- Create a record that is a composite of the changes that are made in individual fields of a record.
- Accept the changes of one user in favor of changes made by another based on the order of precedence established for various groups in the organization.
- Tell the user that the record has been deleted and that the changes will be discarded.
- Allow the user to re-create the original record and make changes to it.
- Tell a user that there's a duplicate record in the database and discard the duplicate.
- Allow a user to merge differences between duplicate records to create a new composite record.
- Accept the first deletion request and ensure that a second deletion request doesn't cause an exception or other database issues.

> **Note** You should always tell a user how a concurrency problem is handled. Otherwise, the user will think that any changes are accepted and the database may end up containing contaminated, incorrect, or otherwise useless data. Even if the user doesn't have the permissions required to correct record change issues, knowing about the problem will allow the user to ask an administrator to make the required changes.

There's no magic bullet when it comes to concurrency problems. Every policy you put in place will have pros and cons, and more than a few compromises. For example, creating a composite record based on the changes submitted by two users means that neither user fully realizes precisely how the changes are made. In addition, using one or the other user's edits may be correct, but using a composite version may not—the composite record may contain incorrect or incompatible data.

You also need to consider the two forms of concurrency that the Entity Framework supports (pessimistic concurrency is supported only indirectly). The following list provides a quick overview of both types and tells you the pros and cons of using it (you'll read more about both types of concurrency in the sections that follow).

- **Optimistic** Using optimistic concurrency means that when a user requests a record, it's placed in a local cache, and then the user uploads the changed record as a separate task. Using this option means that the database server uses fewer resources to service users because the resources are freed immediately after a request. In addition, multiple users can check out a record at the same time, so there are no deadlocks. Overall, optimistic concurrency focuses on high performance and flexibility with long record modification times. You normally use optimistic concurrency in an environment where users work with a large number of records and there's little contention for records. In addition, this is the only option available for web-based and other disconnected-scenario applications.

- **Pessimistic** Using pessimistic concurrency means that when a user requests a record, the database manager locks the record, and the user gains direct access to that record during the CRUD process. Because the record is locked, there's less chance of a conflict. However, this option also requires a dedicated connection throughout the process, which means it won't work in disconnected scenarios. Overall, pessimistic concurrency focuses on reliability and security with short record modification times. You normally use pessimistic concurrency in an environment where there's a lot of contention for a small number of records.

Note There's a third potential option, called *last in wins*. In this scenario, the user requests a record that is downloaded to a local cache. The user makes any required changes to the record. During the update process, the record is locked by the database manager so that no one else can access the record during that short interval. However, there isn't any attempt made to compare the new record with the old record, so this option could end up overwriting newer changes made by another user. Because of the risky nature of this option, it isn't discussed in this book. You can read about this option at *http://msdn.microsoft.com/library/cs6hb8k4.aspx*.

Considering optimistic concurrency problems

Optimistic concurrency doesn't rely on locks to ensure the integrity of the database. It typically represents the preferred method for working with the database, because most developers view it as more flexible and scalable than working with pessimistic concurrency. The main sticking point with optimistic concurrency is that you must provide some means of resolving conflicts when they occur. Conflicts occur whenever two parties interact with the record at the same time. The most common ways of dealing with this issue are as follows:

- Reject the change completely and ask the user to work with the new data.
- Update only the record columns that haven't changed since the record was read and reject any columns that were already updated.
- Automatically update the record columns that haven't changed since the record was read and then ask the user about any columns that were already updated.
- Ask the user about each updated record column to determine which data to keep.
- Ignore the conflict completely.
- Overwrite any changes with all of the data from the updated record after asking user permission.

- Automatically overwrite any changes with all of the data from the updated record without asking permission.

Each of these solutions to the problem of concurrency conflicts presents problems. There's no perfect solution—there's simply the solution that works best in a particular situation with a specific application. The following sections discuss these options in more detail (in order from more favorable to the server to more favorable to the user).

Considering updates and legal issues

There are a number of settings where you need to consider the legality of allowing mixed updates to a record. For example, allowing multiple updates to a single patient record in a medical database could run afoul of Health Insurance Portability and Accountability Act (HIPAA) regulations (see *http://hipaa.stanford.edu/*). When creating a database for a sensitive application, you need to consider the potential legal ramifications of your update strategy, along with the potential for consistency issues with the record. No one would want to create a situation where consistency issues in a patient record would actually cause injury to the patient. Of course, it's essential to get legal advice from a professional trained in that area before you proceed.

A problem for developers is that most aren't trained to recognize potential legal or other issues outside their professional experience. This is the reason that you must have a development team that includes not only developers, but professionals from all of the areas that will interact with the application. An update strategy that seems perfectly acceptable to a developer may not work for other reasons. As a consequence, you need to get input from people who know about such things and ensure that your design meets these criteria.

Legal or other issues represent the main reason you might need to use pessimistic concurrency. In some cases, you must guarantee that only one person can touch a record at any given time because you must build a chain of authenticated changes. In other words, you must be able to prove that a specific person is responsible for a given change.

Rejecting the change

Detecting that the record has changed since it was last read and sending that updated information to the user instead of performing the update is the best way to ensure the user is performing updates on the most current version of the record. It's also the best way to create truly frustrated users who would rather do anything other than use the application you created. In some cases, you may have to resort to this approach because the integrity of the data—ensuring that the user makes changes to only the most current version of a record—is essential. For example, consider what would happen if someone at your bank showed that you had made a withdrawal from one account, but failed to show that the withdrawal was used as a deposit to another account. Using only the most current records will alleviate this sort of problem.

As an alternative to losing the user's updates completely, you can offer to reapply them after the user reviews the updated record. In this way, the update process is still easier on the user, but it also ensures that the integrity of the data retains first-class status. The Entity Framework doesn't provide any means to perform this sort of update automatically; you must implement the logic within your code as a separate bit of logic.

Note This strategy is also called *store wins* in some texts. Essentially it means that the data store wins every contention issue when it comes to concurrency.

Performing a partial update

Performing a partial update helps ensure that any new information in a record remains there. For example, when User A updates the customer's name and last visit date, and User B updates the customer's birth date and last visit date, the customer name and birth date fields aren't in conflict. Updating them won't cause any problem. A partial update would then either accept the first update to the last visit date and reject the second, or it would give the user the chance to select between the two entries. The advantage to this approach is that it enables the application to accept as many of the changes as possible.

The problem with this approach is that the updates aren't necessarily consistent. The updates could mix in a way that creates an inconsistency and actually makes the data incorrect. Using all of the updates from User A would work, and using all of the updates from User B would work, but the mixture of the two wouldn't. Consistency errors can occur in a number of different settings, so you need to make sure that mixing update information from two users won't cause problems for your particular database.

Obtaining user input

In some cases, you must ensure that there are as few consistency errors as possible. Even when the application performs a partial update, you want to be sure that this update doesn't conflict with existing data or with data that has changed since the application last read the record. To use this strategy, you ask the user to approve every change to the database when there's a concurrency issue. Otherwise, the database accepts all of the changes without problem. The advantages to this approach are that the changes aren't rejected outright and the user's changes aren't overwritten; however, the user is also made aware of how the changes are affecting the information in the record.

Ignoring concurrency issues completely

The Entity Framework ignores concurrency issues by default. However, it assists with them as well, by only updating columns that have changed in the record. In this situation, if two users make nonconflicting changes to a record, then both of those changes will appear, even if you haven't implemented any special logic. For example, User A might update the customer's *name* field, while User B updates the customer's birth date. Both changes will appear when you use the default configuration because the Entity Framework will only update the customer's *name* field in the first case (for User A) and only update the customer's *birth date* field in the second case (for User B). The net result is that both changes appear.

However, you also need to consider the situation where there are conflicting changes. If both User A and User B update the customer's last visit field and User B submits the changes last, then the User B change will be the one that remains, even if the User A change was more accurate. The result of ignoring concurrency issues is that the data could have integrity issues. Some data might be incorrect, and you wouldn't know it without performing a complete audit.

Warning Ignoring concurrency issues only works with small organizations. As the number of people accessing the database increases, so does the number of conflicts. An increased number of conflicts will yield progressively greater integrity issues, eventually making the database unusable. At some point, the data will become so suspect that no one can rely on it for anything other than a guideline as to what the actual data should be.

Performing a forced update

There's a chance that you'll want to force an update even when there are concurrency issues to ensure that just one version of the record appears in the database. Using this approach avoids any potential consistency errors in the record at the expense of changes made by other users. The last application to make a change to the record always wins. When using this strategy, the record is always fully updated, even if the user hasn't changed some of the fields, to ensure that the resulting record appears precisely the same as it did to the end user making the change.

Using this strategy can result in data loss and user arguments. A user could rightfully argue that a change did appear in the database, even though it was later overwritten. A way around this problem is to provide alerts to users who have had changes overwritten. The alert should contain information that was overwritten by the latest record. Implementing this strategy could prove complex because you'd need to track who's making each change, and you'd need some way to ensure they receive the required alerts.

Note This strategy is also called *client wins* in some texts. What it means is that the client application always wins every contention issue when it comes to concurrency.

Implementing optimistic concurrency in an application

There are a number of methods you can use to implement concurrency in an application. For example, you can use the simple approach of verifying that the row version hasn't changed. You can also verify that specific fields haven't changed or check the fields that you want to update for changes before you make the update. Of course, before you can verify anything, you need a test environment in which to do it. The first section that follows shows how to create a test environment. The sections that follow after the first section tell how to implement and test various levels of optimistic concurrency in your application.

Developing the test environment

In order to make it easier to understand how concurrency works, you need a test environment. The following procedure helps you create a test environment for this chapter. The test environment will provide two users, User A and User B. By trying out various changes using User A and User B, you can see how a particular concurrency strategy works. In addition, you can tweak your code to obtain specific effects as part of a concurrency strategy. For example, you need to determine whether to alert the user to changes so that the user can make a decision about which update to accept.

Adding a form to create the test environment

1. Copy the *ModelFirst* example you created in Chapter 3, "Choosing a workflow," to a new folder, and use this new copy for this example (rather than the copy you created in Chapter 3).
2. Open the copied solution in Microsoft Visual Studio.
3. Right-click the TestModelFirst entry in Solution Explorer and choose Add | Windows Form. You'll see the Add New Item dialog box shown here:

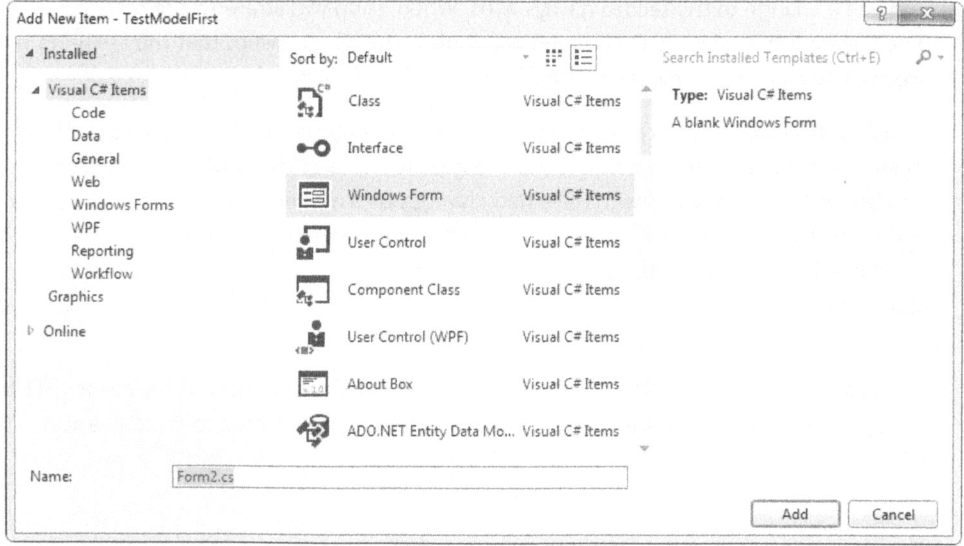

4. Type **UpdateRecord.CS** in the Name field and click Add. Visual Studio adds the new form to the project.
5. Add two buttons (*btnUpdate* and *btnCancel*), three labels (*lblName*, *lblPurchaseDate*, and *lblAmount*), and three text boxes (*txtName*, *txtPurchaseDate*, and *txtAmount*) to the form, as shown here:

6. Double-click *btnClose* to create the *btnClose_Click()* event handler, and add the following code to it:

```
private void btnCancel_Click(object sender, EventArgs e)
{
   // Close the dialog box when finished.
   Close();
}
```

7. Double-click the *UpdateRecord* form to create the *UpdateRecord_Load()* event handler, and add the following code to it:

```
// Provide tracking variables for each field.
String OldName = "";
DateTime OldPurchaseDate = new DateTime();
Decimal OldAmount = new Decimal();

private void UpdateRecord_Load(object sender, EventArgs e)
{
   // Create the context.
   Rewards2ModelContainer context = new Rewards2ModelContainer();

   // Obtain the purchase records.
   var PurchaseData =
      from PD in context.Purchases
      select PD;

   // Add the data from the first record to the form.
   txtName.Text = PurchaseData.First().Customer.CustomerName;
   txtPurchaseDate.Text =
      PurchaseData.First().PurchaseDate.ToShortDateString();
   txtAmount.Text = PurchaseData.First().Amount.ToString();

   // Save the old values.
   OldName = PurchaseData.First().Customer.CustomerName;
   OldPurchaseDate =
      PurchaseData.First().PurchaseDate;
   OldAmount = PurchaseData.First().Amount;
}
```

Notice that the application tracks the original value of each field. You'll see how this comes into play later.

To display the data on screen, the code simply creates a context and retrieves the data from the first record. It also saves the existing values to the global variables for later use.

8. Add the following method to the *UpdateRecord.CS* file:

```
private void DisplayData()
{
   // Create the context.
   Rewards2ModelContainer context = new Rewards2ModelContainer();

   // Obtain the purchase records.
   var PurchaseData =
      from PD in context.Purchases
      select PD;

   // Save the new values.
   OldName = PurchaseData.First().Customer.CustomerName;
   OldPurchaseDate =
      PurchaseData.First().PurchaseDate;
   OldAmount = PurchaseData.First().Amount;

   // Display the content of the first record.
   StringBuilder Output = new StringBuilder();
   Output.Append(PurchaseData.First().Customer.CustomerName +
      "\r\n" + PurchaseData.First().PurchaseDate +
      "\r\n" + PurchaseData.First().Amount);
   MessageBox.Show(Output.ToString());
}
```

When the updating process is complete, you want to display the data on screen. Part of the update process includes saving the new data values, whatever they might be, to the local variables. Otherwise, any additional changes the user makes won't be reflected in the database. Keeping the local variables updated is a requirement if you want to keep your application in sync with the database.

9. Double-click *btnUpdate* to create the *btnUpdate_Click()* event handler, and add the following code to it:

```
private void btnUpdate_Click(object sender, EventArgs e)
{
   // Display the data on screen.
   DisplayData();
}
```

10. Select *Form1* and add a new button, *btnConcurrency*, with a *Text* property value of *&Concurrency*.

11. Double-click *btnConcurrency* to create the *btnConcurrency_Click()* event handler, and add the following code to it:

```
private void btnConcurrency_Click(object sender, EventArgs e)
{
   // Create the User 1 dialog box and display it.
   UpdateRecord User1 = new UpdateRecord();
   User1.Text = "User 1 Update";
   User1.Show(this);

   // Create the User 2 dialog box and display it.
   UpdateRecord User2 = new UpdateRecord();
   User2.Text = "User 2 Update";
   User2.Show(this);
}
```

12. Click Start or press F5. The application compiles and runs.
13. Click Concurrency. You'll see two dialog boxes appear: User 1 Update and User 2 Update. The forms will have the appropriate data entered into the controls.
14. Click Update. You'll see a dialog box containing the current content of the database.
15. Click OK to close the dialog box.
16. Click Cancel on the User 1 Update and User 2 Update dialog boxes. The dialog boxes close.
17. End the application.

Testing the default concurrency

You obviously don't need to implement the default concurrency support; it's already provided as part of the Entity Framework. However, you do need to know how it works. Now that you have a test environment to use, you need to see how default concurrency works. The following procedure helps you understand the default concurrency so that you can determine when it will work best for your particular needs.

Seeing the default concurrency at work

1. Modify the *btnUpdate_Click()* event handler so that it includes the following code to perform updates:

```
private void btnUpdate_Click(object sender, EventArgs e)
{
   // Create the context.
   Rewards2ModelContainer context = new Rewards2ModelContainer();

   // Perform the required updates.
   if (OldName != txtName.Text)
      context.Purchases.First().Customer.CustomerName = txtName.Text;
   if (OldPurchaseDate.ToShortDateString() != txtPurchaseDate.Text)
      context.Purchases.First().PurchaseDate =
         Convert.ToDateTime(txtPurchaseDate.Text);
   if (OldAmount.ToString() != txtAmount.Text)
      context.Purchases.First().Amount =
```

```
        Convert.ToDecimal(txtAmount.Text);
    context.SaveChanges();

    // Display the data on screen.
    DisplayData();
}
```

Notice that the code is designed to update a field only when there's an actual change to make. If you update every field every time, even if there isn't a change, then the Entity Framework will update the entire record. The last user to make changes will win because the changes made by that user will overwrite every other change.

2. Click Start or press F5. The application compiles and runs.

3. Click Concurrency. You'll see User 1 Update and User 2 Update dialog boxes appear. At this point, the content of the two dialog boxes is equal.

4. Select User 1 Update and change the Amount field to read 6.99. Click Update. You'll see a dialog box containing the current content of the database. Notice that the amount is now 6.99, which matches the User 1 Update dialog box. However, the User 2 Update dialog box still shows 5.99.

5. Click OK to close the dialog box.

6. Select User 2 update and change the Purchase Date field to read 2/17/2013. Click Update. You'll see a dialog box containing the current content of the database. The database now reflects the individual changes made by User 1 and User 2, as shown here:

Notice that the dialog box now shows the combined changes of the two users. The changes are melded into a new record that doesn't have any conflicts. However, neither user's form shows the correct information at this point.

7. Click OK to close the dialog box.

8. Select User 1 Update and change the Purchase Date field to 2/18/2013. Click Update. The output now contains 6.99 for the amount and 2/18/2013 for the date. The User 2 change has been overwritten.

9. Click OK to close the dialog box.

10. Click Cancel on the User 1 Update and User 2 Update dialog boxes. The dialog boxes close.

11. End the application.

Coding for field changes

You can add code to your application to mitigate some of the issues with concurrency. This approach doesn't require any special changes to the model or database. The following procedure shows a coded approach you can apply to an application to enforce concurrency by interacting with the user.

Using field-level concurrency enforced by coding

1. Modify the *btnUpdate_Click()* event handler so that it includes the following code to perform updates:

```
private void btnUpdate_Click(object sender, EventArgs e)
{
   // Create the context.
   Rewards2ModelContainer context = new Rewards2ModelContainer();

   // Obtain the purchase records.
   var PurchaseData =
      from PD in context.Purchases
      select PD;

   // Perform the required updates.
   if (OldName != txtName.Text)
   {
      if (PurchaseData.First().Customer.CustomerName != OldName)
      {
         if (MessageBox.Show(
            "Name field value has changed to " +
            PurchaseData.First().Customer.CustomerName +
            " Make the change anyway?", "Updating Newer Data",
            MessageBoxButtons.YesNo) == DialogResult.Yes)
               context.Purchases.First().Customer.CustomerName =
                  txtName.Text;
      }
      else
         context.Purchases.First().Customer.CustomerName = txtName.Text;
   }

   if (OldPurchaseDate.ToShortDateString() != txtPurchaseDate.Text)
   {
      if (!PurchaseData.First().PurchaseDate.Equals(OldPurchaseDate))
      {
         if (MessageBox.Show(
            "Purchase Date field value has changed to " +
            PurchaseData.First().PurchaseDate +
            " Make the change anyway?", "Updating Newer Data",
            MessageBoxButtons.YesNo) == DialogResult.Yes)
            context.Purchases.First().PurchaseDate =
               Convert.ToDateTime(txtPurchaseDate.Text);
      }
      else
         context.Purchases.First().PurchaseDate =
            Convert.ToDateTime(txtPurchaseDate.Text);
   }
```

```
    if (OldAmount.ToString() != txtAmount.Text)
    {
        if (!PurchaseData.First().Amount.Equals(OldAmount))
        {
            if (MessageBox.Show(
                "Amount field value has changed to " +
                PurchaseData.First().Amount +
                " Make the change anyway?", "Updating Newer Data",
                MessageBoxButtons.YesNo) == DialogResult.Yes)
                context.Purchases.First().Amount =
                    Convert.ToDecimal(txtAmount.Text);
        }
        else
            context.Purchases.First().Amount =
                Convert.ToDecimal(txtAmount.Text);
    }

    context.SaveChanges();

    // Display the data on screen.
    DisplayData();
}
```

Notice that the application now checks the old data against the database before making an update. When the database doesn't match the old data, the application asks the user about making the update. Only when the user clicks Yes is the change made.

2. Click Start or press F5. The application compiles and runs.
3. Click Concurrency. You'll see User 1 Update and User 2 Update dialog boxes appear.
4. Select User 1 Update and change the Amount field to read 5.99. Click Update. You'll see a dialog box containing the current content of the database.
5. Click OK to close the dialog box.
6. Select User 2 Update and change the Amount field to read 10.99. Click Update. This time you'll see the Updating Newer Data dialog box shown here:

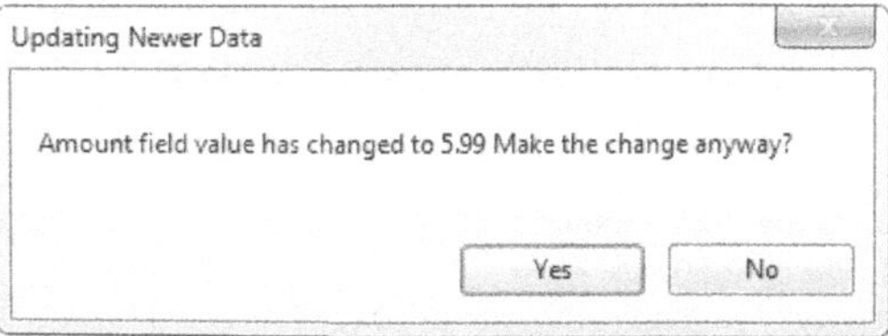

The dialog box shows the new value in the database, which doesn't match the value on the form. You need to tell the application to make the update anyway.

7. Click Yes. You'll see a dialog box containing the current content of the database, which includes the updated Amount field value.

8. Select User 1 Update and change the Amount field to read 6.99. Click Update. You'll see the Updating Newer Data dialog box.
9. Click No. You'll see a dialog box containing the current content of the database. However, this time the Amount field retains the value of 10.99 instead of the new value of 6.99.
10. Click OK to close the dialog box.
11. Click Cancel on the User 1 Update and User 2 Update dialog boxes. The dialog boxes close.
12. End the application.

Using field-specific concurrency

It's possible to tell the Entity Framework to check on concurrency for you. One way to do this is to set the Concurrency Mode property for each of the fields you want to verify. This method works great, even with DBMSs that don't support a row-version strategy. However, it has two shortcomings you need to consider:

- Any field you don't set up correctly won't be checked for concurrency problems.
- Using this approach tends to make your application run slower because the resulting query is larger than if you had used row-version concurrency.

Even so, this approach is relatively straightforward, and you can use it even if your database isn't configured for row-version concurrency. All you need to do is modify the model a little and you're ready to go. The following procedure shows how to use this approach.

Performing field-specific concurrency

1. Open the Rewards2Model.EDMX file found in Solution Explorer.
2. Select the *CustomerName* property in Customers and choose Fixed for the Concurrency Mode property of the Properties window.
3. Select the *PurchaseDate* property in Purchases and choose Fixed for the Concurrency Mode property of the Properties window.
4. Select the *Amount* property in Purchases and choose Fixed for the Concurrency Mode property of the Properties window.
5. Select *Form1* and add a new button, *btnRowVersion*, with a *Text* property value of *&Row Version*.
6. Double-click *btnRowVersion* to create the *btnRowVersion_Click()* event handler and add the following code to it:

```
private void btnRowVersion_Click(object sender, EventArgs e)
{
   // Create contexts for User 1 and User 2.
```

```
    Rewards2ModelContainer context1 = new Rewards2ModelContainer();
    Rewards2ModelContainer context2 = new Rewards2ModelContainer();

    // Get the record for User 1.
    var User1 = context1.Purchases.First();

    // Get the record for User 2.
    var User2 = context2.Purchases.First();

    // Make a change and save it for User 1.
    User1.Amount = Convert.ToDecimal(7.99);
    context1.SaveChanges();

    // Make a change and save it for User 2.
    User2.Amount = Convert.ToDecimal(10.99);
    context2.SaveChanges();

    // Display a success message.
    MessageBox.Show("Update Succeeded!");
}
```

When testing this kind of concurrency, make sure each user has a different context to use. Notice that the users are changing the same field and that the changes from User 1 appear in the database before User 2 begins making a change. The important thing is that the change must be saved to update the concurrency so that User 2 will see a different record.

7. Click Start or press F5. The application compiles and runs.
8. Click Concurrency. Type **4.99** in the Amount field when you see the two user dialog boxes appear. This step ensures that User 1 will actually change the value in the database.
9. Click Update, and then click Cancel twice to close the two user dialog boxes.
10. Click Row Version. You'll see the DbUpdateConcurrencyException Was Unhandled dialog box shown here:

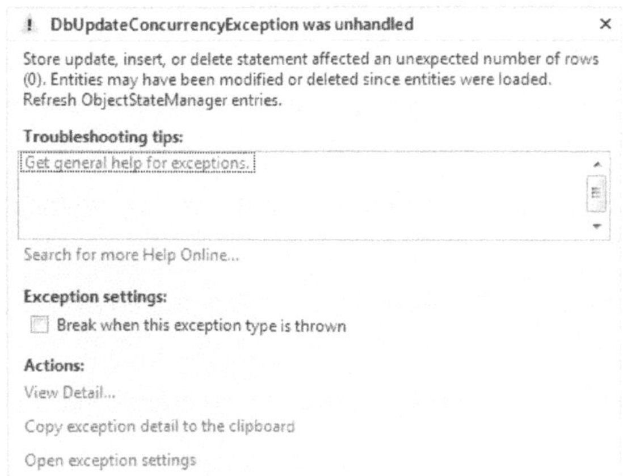
DbUpdateConcurrencyException was unhandled
Store update, insert, or delete statement affected an unexpected number of rows (0). Entities may have been modified or deleted since entities were loaded. Refresh ObjectStateManager entries.
Troubleshooting tips:
Get general help for exceptions.
Search for more Help Online...
Exception settings:
Break when this exception type is thrown
Actions:
View Detail...
Copy exception detail to the clipboard
Open exception settings

11. End the debugging session. Now that you've seen the error, it's time to do something about it in the form of exception handling.

12. Modify the *btnRowVersion_Click()* event handler code so it looks like this:

```
private void btnRowVersion_Click(object sender, EventArgs e)
{
   // Create contexts for User 1 and User 2.
   Rewards2ModelContainer context1 = new Rewards2ModelContainer();
   Rewards2ModelContainer context2 = new Rewards2ModelContainer();

   // Get the record for User 1.
   var User1 = context1.Purchases.First();

   // Get the record for User 2.
   var User2 = context2.Purchases.First();

   // Make a change and save it for User 1.
   User1.Amount = Convert.ToDecimal(7.99);
   context1.SaveChanges();

   try
   {

      // Make a change and save it for User 2.
      User2.Amount = Convert.ToDecimal(10.99);
      context2.SaveChanges();
   }
   catch (DbUpdateConcurrencyException DUCE)
   {
      // Display a message box.
      MessageBox.Show("Initial Attempt Failed!");

      // Obtain the object context.
      var ObjContext = ((IObjectContextAdapter)context2).ObjectContext;

      // Obtain the entry that has failed.
      var Entry = DUCE.Entries.Single();

      // Refresh the object context so that you can perform an update.
      ObjContext.Refresh(RefreshMode.ClientWins, Entry.Entity);

      // Save the changes.
      context2.SaveChanges();
   }

   // Display a success message.
   MessageBox.Show("Update Succeeded!");
}
```

If you've used previous versions of the Entity Framework, the code in this example will look different from what you may have used before. In order to update the record, you must refresh the object context. The *DbUpdateConcurrencyException* provides you with the entity that failed to update. When you call the *Refresh()* method, you must provide a strategy for updating the database. The final step is to call *SaveChanges()*. At this point, the update will succeed with a client-wins approach.

13. Click Start or press F5. The application compiles and runs.
14. Click Concurrency. Type **4.99** in the Amount field when you see the two user dialog boxes appear. This step ensures that User 1 will actually change the value in the database.
15. Click Update, and then click Cancel twice to close the two user dialog boxes.
16. Click Row Version. You'll see an Initial Update Failed message.
17. Click OK. You'll see an Update Succeeded message.

Using row-version concurrency

SQL Server provides a special *rowversion* type, which lets you track the version number of data in each record. By comparing this number to the number that appeared when the data was read, it's possible to determine whether a concurrency problem has occurred. Of course, the example database doesn't include a field that uses the *rowversion* type, so the first order of business is to add such a row to the database (a task you'll probably have to perform on any databases you currently own as well). The following procedure tells how to perform this task. Since you need a copy of the database that doesn't include the *rowversion* row for previous examples in the book, the first step is to create an unmodified copy of the *Rewards2* database.

Performing row-version concurrency

1. Close all connections in Visual Studio (or close Visual Studio for that matter).
2. Create a copy of the *Rewards2* database. You'll need administrator privileges to perform this task.
3. Reopen the *ModelFirst* example in Visual Studio if necessary.
4. Choose View | Server Explorer to open Server Explorer.
5. Open the *Rewards2* database connection and drill down to the *Customers* table.
6. Right-click the *Customers* table and choose Open Table Definition from the context menu. You'll see a designer open, as shown here:

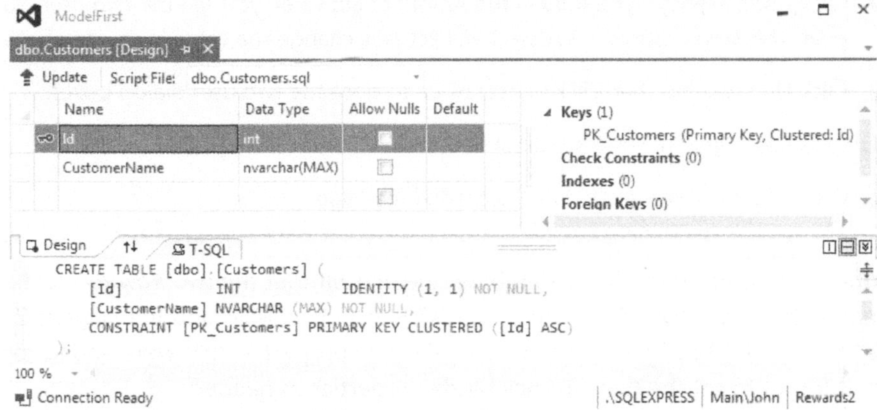

7. Place the cursor in the bottom row of the upper half of the designer. Type **RowVersion** in the Name field. Select rowversion in the Data Type field. Uncheck the Allow Nulls field. You'll see a number of changes made to the SQL script for the table.

8. Place the cursor in the lower half of the designer window (failing to do so will generate an error when you click Update). Click Update. You'll see a Preview Database Updates dialog box that tells what changes the script will make to the database.

9. Click Update Database. After a few moments, the Database Tools Window will show a successful completion.

10. Close the Database Tools Window.

11. Perform steps 5 through 10 for the *Purchases* table. The changes you've made don't appear in the model, so you still can't use them as part of an application.

12. Open the Rewards2Model.EDMX file found in Solution Explorer.

13. Right-click in any clear area of the designer and choose Update Model From Database.

14. Select the Refresh tab, drill down to *Customers*, highlight it, and click Finish. You'll see the *RowVersion* properties added to both the *Customers* and *Purchases* entities.

15. Select the *CustomerName* (*Customers* entity), *PurchaseDate* (*Purchases* entity), and *Amount* (*Purchases* entity) properties in turn, and choose *None* for the Concurrency Mode property in the Properties window. This step ensures that you're seeing the effects of row-version concurrency.

16. Select the *RowVersion* property in *Customers* and choose *Fixed* for the Concurrency Mode property in the Properties window.

17. Select the *RowVersion* property in *Purchases* and choose *Fixed* for the Concurrency Mode property in the Properties window.

18. Click Start or press F5. The application compiles and runs.

19. Click Concurrency. Type **4.99** in the Amount field when you see the two user dialog boxes appear. This step ensures that User 1 will actually change the value in the database.

20. Click Update, and then click Cancel twice to close the two user dialog boxes.

21. Click Row Version. You'll see an Initial Update Failed message.

22. Click OK. You'll see an Update Succeeded message.

Note To return to the original database (the one without the two *RowVersion* fields), simply rename the Rewards2.MDF file to Rewards2 RowVersion.MDF and the Rewards2 (Copy).MDF file to Rewards2.MDF. Delete the two *RowVersion* properties that were added to the model. Don't forget to set the Concurrency Mode properties as needed.

Considering pessimistic concurrency issues

Pessimistic concurrency requires that you lock records in the database before you use them. When you lock a database record for read-only access, other people can also lock that record for read-only access. However, other people are restricted from locking the reader for update access until all of the read-only access locks are cleared. When you lock a database record for update access, no one else can lock it for any purpose. You have exclusive access to the record as long as the lock is in place. The significant advantage of this strategy is that there's no chance of a conflict because access is controlled at the database level. However, pessimistic security presents these problems:

- Using pessimistic security adds to the complexity of an application because you must manage the locks.
- Because of the housekeeping required to manage the locks, the memory used to hold records in a locked state, and the inability to reuse other resources, using pessimistic security slows the application and requires more server resources.
- Application performance suffers as the number of users increases because of the likelihood that two users will require access to a particular record at the same time.
- The developer must create custom code to handle database access because the Entity Framework doesn't support pessimistic security natively.
- There's no direct LINQ to Entities support for pessimistic security. However, when working with Entity Framework 5, you can use the *UPDLOCK* table hint along with the *SqlQuery()* method to obtain satisfactory results.
- Race conditions (where User A has record 1 locked and User B requires access to it, while User B has record 2 locked and User A requires access to it) can occur, resulting in deadlock situations.

The standing theory is that you should never need pessimistic security. The suggestion is that you can create a *TIMESTAMP* column in the table, or use the newer *ROWVERSION* data type. Whenever someone performs a CRUD operation on the record, the timestamp is updated. Before performing an update, the application checks the timestamp and displays an error message if the timestamp on the record is newer than the timestamp of the original record. You must then figure out what has changed and give the user the chance to make a decision about the update (or you must handle the conflict in some other way). In some applications, this technique is simply not useful, which means you must implement pessimistic concurrency using some other custom means.

Even though the Entity Framework doesn't support pessimistic concurrency directly, you still have options for implementing it using custom code. Following are the two most common techniques for accomplishing the task:

- Providing the support using stored procedures. You enclose the action within a transaction and rely on the *ROWLOCK* and *HOLDLOCK* hints to perform the task. The article at *http://www.sqlteam.com/article/row-locking* tells you how to perform this task. Chapter 8, "Interaction with stored procedures," tells you how to work with stored procedures.
- Using specialized LINQ to Entities code with the *SqlQuery()* or *ExecuteStoreQuery()* methods and the *UPDLOCK* table hint to achieve the desired results. However, this technique is extremely complex and well outside the scope of this book. You can read about how this technique works (and why pessimistic concurrency is so hard to achieve with the Entity Framework) at *http://www.ladislavmrnka.com/2012/09/entity-framework-and-pessimistic-concurrency/*.

If you absolutely must have pessimistic security for your application, and the two options mentioned in this section are either undoable or too complex, you can always use a product such as Telerik OpenAccess ORM (*http://www.telerik.com/products/orm.aspx*). You can see the vendor's comparison of OpenAccess ORM to the Entity Framework at *http://www.telerik.com/products/orm/getting-started/openaccess-vs-entity-framework.aspx*. However, there's a more straightforward discussion of the topic at *http://stackoverflow.com/questions/11255583/entity-framework-5-vs-telerik-openaccess-orm-specifically*. The essential trade-off is that you lose some automation and features, like the ability to use enumerations to gain the use of pessimistic concurrency, when using OpenAccess ORM.

Getting started with the Entity Framework

This chapter has provided a good introduction to database concurrency. It's important to remember that concurrency is a complex topic that is still being debated by computer scientists. However, it's also important not to feel overwhelmed by the topic—the tools you have available automate most of the work needed to make concurrency a reality. In fact, if you take one thing away from this chapter, it's that most developers can reduce the entire complex set of choices down to a single decision—the choice between optimistic and pessimistic concurrency. This single choice will make it possible to create the vast majority of applications in a way that ensures the database interactions meet ACID requirements.

This chapter has also demonstrated some of the most common problems with concurrency. Something that even the best tools can't protect you from are environmental factors that conspire to create concurrency errors in your application. Even though SQL Server, the Entity Framework, and the .NET Framework will alert you to these errors, you still need to decide how to deal with them. Trying various strategies with test applications is the best way to start discovering what techniques will work best for your organization. Now that you have some fundamental tools for experimentation (including the sample applications in this chapter), you need to try various scenarios and see how best to deal with them. It's essential that you develop a plan for working through concurrency issues as soon as possible in the development process.

Chapter 13, "Handling performance problems," discusses the final entity error type in this part of the book. Most developers wouldn't view performance issues as an error—strictly speaking. On the other hand, most users view performance issues as one of the most egregious of application errors. Perspective is sometimes everything when it comes to judging the enormity of an error. However, it's no mystery that performance issues often hide deep-seated application problems. If an application has to try multiple times to gain a connection to the server, not only does it affect performance, but it also signifies a problem with the server configuration, network setup, or application design. Chapter 13 discusses matters of application design that you can control and use to create an application with fewer errors that affect overall performance.

Chapter 12 quick reference

To	Do this
Ensure the maximum availability of database resources and the fastest possible response times	Rely on optimistic concurrency, which is the default configuration used by both SQL Server and the Entity Framework.
Ensure maximum reliability and security	Rely on pessimistic concurrency, which requires reconfiguration of your Entity Framework and database setup. In addition, you must create custom code to perform all tasks because the Entity Framework doesn't support pessimistic locking directly.
Reduce the risk of inconsistent changes made as the result of updates to records with a newer version	Reject the changes and provide the user with an updated copy of the new version of the record as it appears in the database.
Allow a cooperative environment where concurrency conflicts are handled	Automatically perform partial updates of fields that have no conflicts, and then optionally ask the user about the application of data in conflicting fields.
Allow a cooperative environment that favors data consistency	Ask the user about each field update when a concurrency issue exists, but automatically accept the updates when there's no conflict.
Allow a cooperative environment where concurrency conflicts aren't handled	Perform partial updates of fields with new data, and ignore any concurrency issues by overwriting fields with the latest information provided by the user (this is the default configuration).
Require that the database accept the latest full record from the client to avoid consistency issues	Perform a forced update of every field in the record without asking the user to confirm the changes. You can optionally inform users whose changes were overwritten about the changes to avoid potential data loss.

CHAPTER 13

Handling performance problems

After completing the chapter, you'll be able to

- Describe the sources of Entity Framework performance issues.
- Show how to obtain information about performance issues.
- Define the elements that define the performance triangle.
- Describe how multithreading speeds performance.

Performance is a measure of how well an application works. It describes how fast, secure, and reliable an application is and defines whether the application meets user productivity requirements. There are many misconceptions about performance, and some developers focus exclusively on just one or two aspects of performance. This chapter focuses on helping you create a well-rounded application that performs well in every respect, rather than focusing on just one or two performance elements. Of course, the question on most readers' minds is why performance is included in a part about entity errors. The fact is that an application that doesn't perform well is subject to a greater range of errors—everything from missed critical timing to frustrated users hitting keys at random to determine why the application is making them wait.

Because the Entity Framework accomplishes so much work automatically (in the background), it's easy to forget that you can tweak it to provide a better-performing application. As part of discovering the Entity Framework and all it can do, you need to know how to determine that there's a performance problem, measure the performance problem to determine its extent, and then tune the application to meet performance requirements. In many cases, you must use multiple techniques to achieve a desired level of performance and still maintain a well-rounded application (one that doesn't focus on one aspect of performance to the detriment of every other area). This chapter provides you with a good overview of the most common techniques for improving performance.

Note This chapter does focus on the Entity Framework. It's important to realize that you have options that you can use to tune performance—other than simply tuning the Entity Framework. The simple act of adding more memory to a server or workstation can often resolve speed issues for an application. Using a better firewall can help with security issues, as can the addition of security-related company policies. Reliability is affected by the use of higher-quality hardware as much as it is by careful coding. User training and policies that help users understand how to interact with applications better can improve application speed, security, and reliability all at the same time. It's essential not to be overcome by a case of tunnel vision when it comes to performance issues. Look at the whole picture and work through performance issues by considering how the application environment can change how the application performs. In many cases, you'll need to combine the information found in this chapter with other kinds of performance tuning to achieve great results, instead of simply obtaining the minimum level of performance that users demand.

Understanding performance issue sources

There are many sources of performance issues on any computer system. For example, not having enough memory or other resources will most definitely cause an application to run slowly. Users who don't understand how to use the application are another source of performance issues. Slow network connections and overloaded servers are other sources. For that matter, even Mother Nature can get into the act—for example, when a thunderstorm affects the processing power of your system. This chapter doesn't discuss any of these sources of performance issues. Instead, it focuses on Entity Framework issues. Even so, you need to consider these other sources as you work through problems with your application, because ignoring them will likely result in less-than-stellar optimizations and a lot of frustration on your part. The following sections describe major sources of performance issues when working with the Entity Framework.

Note This chapter provides a good overview of the most common methods of improving performance using Language Integrated Query (LINQ) to Entities and Entity SQL. You can find a more detailed explanation of these techniques, along with some benchmark figures you can use for comparison purposes, at *http://msdn.microsoft.com/data/hh949853.aspx*. A more generalized listing of benchmarks is available at *http://blogs.msdn.com/b/adonet/archive/2012/02/14/sneak-preview-entity-framework-5-0-performance-improvements.aspx*.

Considering the layers

An essential issue to consider is that layers slow software down. Something developers fail to consider is that the Entity Framework performs a considerable number of tasks for you in the background so that everything just works. The fact is that using the Entity Framework adds three layers to your application as a minimum:

- The query must be translated through either LINQ to Entities or Entity SQL.
- The resulting query is translated through the *EntityClient*.
- The *EntityClient* output is translated through the Entity Framework to ADO.NET.

Note You can find an explanation of how these various layers work in previous chapters of the book. The LINQ to Entities explanation appears in the "Introducing LINQ to Entities" section of Chapter 6, "Manipulating data using LINQ," while the Entity SQL explanation appears in the "Understanding Entity SQL" section of Chapter 7, "Manipulating data using Entity SQL." Knowing how these layers work will make it easier to understand Entity Framework performance.

Each of these layers performs an important task in reducing your workload. However, nothing comes without cost. The price you pay to garner the benefits proffered by the Entity Framework is a reduction in overall application performance. Most organizations consider the trade-off acceptable as long as application performance doesn't suffer too much, but you should keep this in mind. You may find that using ADO.NET directly in critical sections of your code will enhance application performance enough that you can still use the Entity Framework in less critical sections.

Retrieving too many records

A major problem for most developers is trying to create really simple queries that are easy to understand and yet get the job done. The problem is that such simple queries often end up retrieving more records than the application will ever use. The cost of waiting for the server to deliver the records and transporting them over the network connection is high. When every application on the network is attempting to retrieve too many records, the cost is compounded. In fact, asking for too much can quickly bring a server to its knees.

Optimizing your query reduces the load on the server, transfers data quickly over the network, and actually reduces the amount of code you need to write because you perform less filtering when the data arrives at the client. For example, the query

```
var PurchaseData =
   from PD in context.Purchases
   select PD;
```

will actually execute more slowly than

```
var PurchaseData =
   from PD in context.Purchases
   select PD
   where PD.Customer.CustomerName=="Josh Bailey";
```

even though the first query is simpler. The second query will retrieve fewer records and will require less filtering to get the job done. In fact, if you can create a truly specific query—one that results in no excess records—you don't need to perform any filtering at all.

Using the local cache

The Entity Framework provides a local cache that you can use to store queries that you've made in the past. In order to use this feature, you set the *EnablePlanCaching* property to *true*. The advantage of using the local cache is that the client application need only make a request once in order to obtain data from the server. Future requests for the same data are served from the cache so that the application doesn't even tap the server for information. The result is queries that occur almost instantaneously. This feature works exceptionally well for data that doesn't change often. For example, if your application needs a list of states or ZIP codes, using caching is a given since this data will never change.

The negative side of caching is that it can cause problems in situations where data changes relatively often. At the very least, the user could end up seeing outdated information and then make decisions based on that information. In addition, caching makes it more likely that the application will experience concurrency problems (see Chapter 12, "Overcoming concurrency issues," for details). Incurring additional concurrency exceptions means that your application will spend more time handling updates, which could end up costing you more time than if you had simply obtained updated information from the server in the first place.

Note The cached queries are case sensitive. This means that the Entity Framework views *SELECT VALUE CustomerList* as being different than *Select Value CustomerList*. If you find that caching doesn't appear to work, make sure you check the case of the various queries to ensure that they all use the same casing.

Relying on pregenerated views

Normally, you work with the Entity Data Model Wizard to create and manage entities in your application. This wizard creates everything you need in the background, and your application works automatically for you. The Entity Data Model Generator (EDMGen.EXE) tool included with Microsoft Visual Studio makes it possible for you to perform a few tasks that the wizard can't perform automatically. One of the most important additional tasks it can perform is pregenerating the views used with your application so that the runtime doesn't need to generate them when the application runs. This feature works with the *EnablePlanCaching* property to make queries run faster. The following procedure describes how to pregenerate a view into an existing project.

Note As Microsoft continues to improve the performance characteristics of the Entity Framework, some optimizations have less of an effect. Pregenerating views is one of the areas in which the noticeable effect is smaller than with early versions of the Entity Framework unless your application contains a large number of queries or relies on relatively complex queries. Even so, the performance difference might be worth pursuing for an application of any significant complexity.

Pregenerating a view using EDMGen

1. Copy the Entity SQL query version of the *ModelFirst* example you created in Chapter 7 to a new folder, and use this new copy for this example (rather than the copy you created in Chapter 7).

Note The Entity SQL version of the *ModelFirst* example in Chapter 7 appears in the ModelFirst (Display - Entity SQL) folder of the downloadable source code. If you created your own version of the example, the folder name will probably be different.

2. Open the copied solution in Visual Studio.
3. Double-click the Rewards2Model.EDMX file found in Solution Explorer to open it.
4. Click in any open area in the designer. The Properties window shows the properties for the current model.
5. Change the Metadata Artifact Processing property value in the Properties window to Copy To Output Directory, and choose Build | Rebuild Solution. Visual Studio creates the required .CSDL, .MSL, and .SSDL files for you in the output folder for the application.
6. Right-click the Solution 'Model First' entry in Solution Explorer and choose Open Folder in File Explorer from the context menu. You'll see a copy of Microsoft Windows Explorer opened to the folder that contains the solution.
7. Drill down into the TestModelFirst\bin\Debug folder, copy the .CSDL, .MSL, and .SSDL files, and paste them into a new folder such as EDM. Using this approach will allow you to work with the files without having to clutter up the application's output folder.
8. Choose Start | All Programs | Microsoft Visual Studio 2012 | Visual Studio Tools | Developer Command Prompt for VS2012 to open a developer command prompt. This command prompt lets you gain access to the EDMGen utility wherever it might appear on your hard drive from any location on your system.

Note Attempting to use a standard command prompt will result in failure because it doesn't provide access to the EDMGen utility. Make sure you open a Developer Command Prompt for VS2012 to ensure you can access the utility as needed.

9. Type **CD \Microsoft Press\Entity Framework Development Step by Step\Chapter 13\EDM** to change directories to the folder containing the .CSDL, .MSL, and .SSDL files. You're now in the folder that contains the three files you saved earlier.
10. Type **EDMGen /mode:ViewGeneration /inssdl:Rewards2Model.ssdl /incsdl:Rewards2Model.csdl /inmsl:Rewards2Model.msl /p:"..\ModelFirst (Display -**

Entity SQL)\TestModelFirst\TestModelFirst.csproj" /targetversion:4.5. You use these command-line arguments to perform the following tasks:

- **/mode:ViewGeneration** Tells EDMGen that you want to pregenerate the mapping views using the .CSDL, .MSL, and .SSDL files you supply.
- **/inssdl:Rewards2Model.ssdl** Provides the path and name of the .SSDL file to use.
- **/incsdl:Rewards2Model.csdl** Provides the path and name of the .CSDL file to use.
- **/inmsl:Rewards2Model.msl** Provides the path and name of the .MSL file to use.
- **/p:"..\ModelFirst (Display - Entity SQL)\TestModelFirst\TestModelFirst.csproj"** Provides the path and name of the project file for this application. Although the command will work without this switch, the resulting files won't include the appropriate namespaces, which means that you'll spend extra time trying to use the output in your application.
- **/targetversion:4.5** Specifies the target version of the .NET Framework to use. The default version is 4.0. If you try to use the EDMGen utility without this command-line switch, you'll receive a warning message as output. The file will still be generated, but you can't be sure that it will work appropriately with your application. Using the correct version is important.

11. Press Enter. The EDMGen utility will create the required view file for you and add it to the project directory for your application, as shown here:

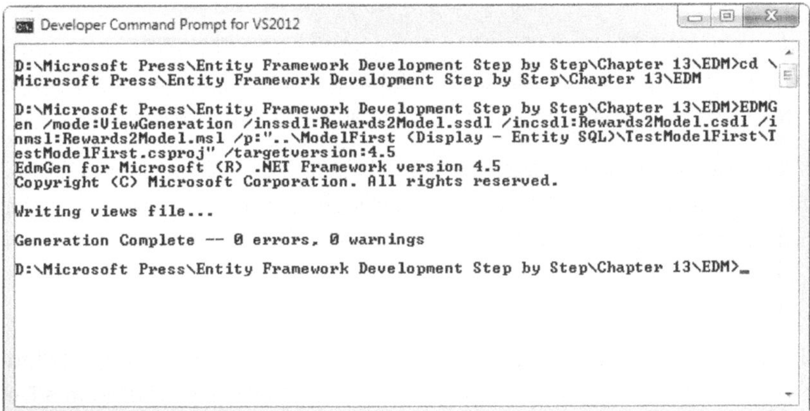

12. Close the command prompt.
13. Change the Metadata Artifact Processing property value in the Properties window to Embed In Output Assembly, and choose Build | Rebuild Solution. Visual Studio removes the .CSDL, .MSL, and .SSDL files for you from the output folder of the application.
14. Right-click the TestModelFirst entry in Solution Explorer and choose Add | Existing Item from the context menu. Drill down into the project folder, and you'll see the list of files shown here:

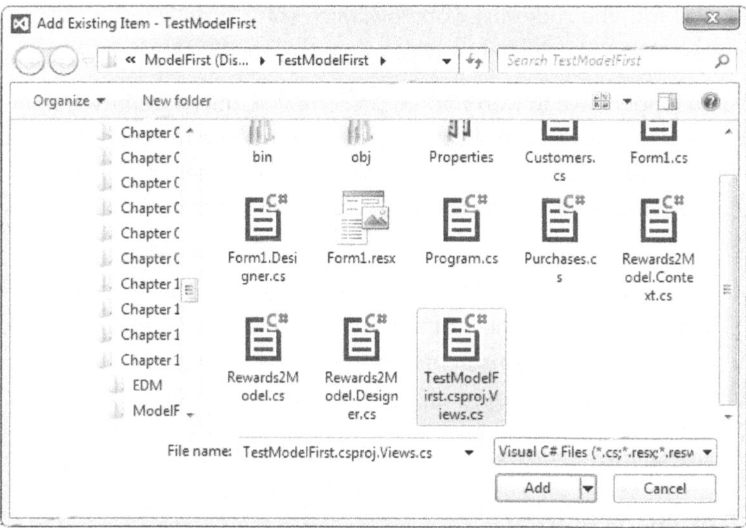

15. Select the TestModelFirst.csproj.Views.cs file from the list and click Add. You'll see the new file added to Solution Explorer. Opening the file hierarchy displays a number of pregenerated views, as shown here:

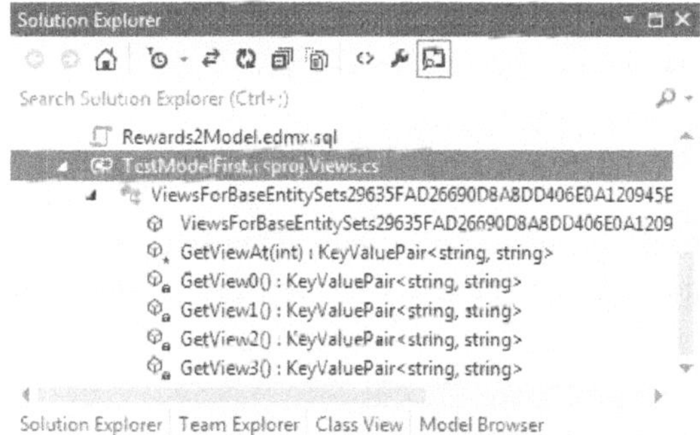

You don't have to do anything special to use this file. The application will automatically use it whenever you run it. The presence of this file means that the application doesn't have to perform as many query compilation tasks when running the application. Because the example is small, you likely won't see any difference when running it with this file in place, but be sure to generate a file of this type when working with larger applications. The more queries your application contains (especially complex queries), the more this process helps improve application performance.

Relying on precompiled queries

If you've worked with previous versions of the Entity Framework, you've likely used precompiled queries to improve performance. Precompiling a query meant that the application didn't have to compile it at run time, resulting in a significant performance boost. However, in order to use the *CompiledQuery* class, you needed to use the *ObjectContext* API for your Entity Framework classes, which doesn't work well with the code-first workflow. Microsoft currently recommends you use the *DbContext* API for all workflows because it provides superior functionality.

Fortunately, you no longer have to worry about precompiling queries. Entity Framework 5 performs this task automatically for you in the background. It compiles each query type you create one time and then caches the query for later use. Each time the query is called, the Entity Framework automatically uses the precompiled query version in the cache, rather than compiling the query again.

Tip If you're working with an older application and really need to know how compiled queries work, you can find an overview of the topic at *http://msdn.microsoft.com/library/bb896297.aspx*. An article at *http://msdn.microsoft.com/magazine/ee336024.aspx* provides more detailed information on the topic, along with some useful example code.

Disabling change tracking

The Entity Framework always makes the entries required to track changes in your data, even when working with a read-only query. If you are only accessing the data to provide it to the user for viewing purposes, you can achieve a significant performance benefit by turning off change tracking. Here's an example of a LINQ to Entities query used earlier in the book with change tracking disabled:

```
// Obtain the customer list without change tracking.
var CustomerList =
    from cust in context.Customers.AsNoTracking()
    select cust;
```

It's also possible to turn off change tracking when working with Entity SQL, but the technique is slightly different. In this case, you turn it off as part of the *ObjectQuery* properties, as shown here:

```
// Create a query object.
ObjectQuery<DbDataRecord> CustomerData =
    context.CreateQuery<DbDataRecord>(EntitySQLCmd);

// Turn off change tracking.
CustomerData.MergeOption = MergeOption.NoTracking;
```

Choosing between lazy loading and eager loading

You can set the model to allow either lazy loading (the default) or eager loading. Lazy loading only loads the entity set when you make a query against it. Consequently, when you want to access the data provided by a navigation property, the application must make another query to obtain that data. The performance benefit is that you access the data only when needed, so the transfers are smaller. When using eager loading, a query obtains not only the target entity, but also any entities accessed through a navigation property. As a result, the data transfer is larger. To configure your application to use eager loading, click any blank area in the entity designer and then set the Lazy Loading Enabled property in the Properties window to False.

Figuring out which form of loading to use can be tricky. The reason that lazy loading is the default is that many queries use only the data provided by the target entity. In addition, the entity set may be quite large, so the user would wait a long time for the query to complete. However, this isn't always the case. In some situations, you always use the navigation properties, and the returned dataset is smaller. As a result, you actually see a performance drop by making multiple requests for data from the server. Here are some guidelines for using eager loading:

- The query will use a limited number of navigation properties.
- You know precisely what data will be returned from the database.
- The data payload is relatively small.
- There's not a large physical distance between the application and the server—long distances can cause network latency problems.

Viewing performance issues

In order to deal with performance issues, you must be able to see them. For example, sometimes a query you create in your application may not translate into a SQL statement that executes quickly. A simple change in your code could translate into tangible performance differences after translation. The following sections describe some methods for viewing the actual queries you send to the database manager and demonstrate how they work. In these sections, you'll also discover methods of measuring the time required to execute the query.

Direct query viewing

Visual Studio provides the means for seeing how your query appears to Microsoft SQL Server. You can directly view the query for either LINQ to Entities or Entity SQL queries. However, simply viewing the query won't tell you too much. What you really need to see is the execution plan associated with that query, which means working with SQL Server Management Studio. The following sections demonstrate both LINQ to Entities and Entity SQL queries, and show you how to generate an execution plan for them.

Working with LINQ to Entities

When working with LINQ to Entities, Entity Framework 5 defaults to using a *DbContext*, rather than an *ObjectContext*. Many of the examples you see online are for older versions of the Entity Framework, which did use an *ObjectContext*. The following procedure shows how to obtain information about the queries you make and then create an execution plan for them, which you can then use to help tune the performance of the query.

Observing the SQL query using LINQ to Entities

1. Copy the LINQ query version of the *ModelFirst* example you created in Chapter 6 to a new folder and use this new copy for this example (rather than the copy you created in Chapter 6).

> **Note** The LINQ version of the *ModelFirst* example in Chapter 6 appears in the ModelFirst (LINQ Query) folder of the downloadable source code. If you created your own version of the example, the folder name will probably be different.

2. Open the copied solution in Visual Studio.

3. Open Form1.CS and place a breakpoint at this line in the *btnQuery_Click()* event handler:

```
StringBuilder Output =
    new StringBuilder("Customer List:");
```

4. Click Start or press F5. The application compiles and runs.

5. Click Query. The application stops at the breakpoint.

6. Choose Debug | Windows | Locals to display the local objects shown here:

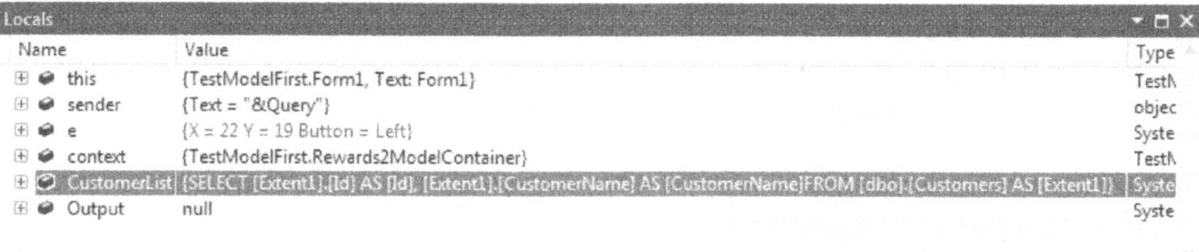

Notice that the *CustomerList* object contains the actual SQL query used to access the information in the database. You can use this information to create a profile of how that query will actually execute, and then decide how best to modify your query to obtain better performance.

7. Right-click the CustomerList entry and choose Edit Value from the context menu. The query text highlights.

8. Select everything but the opening and closing curly brackets and then press Ctrl+C to copy this information to the clipboard.

9. Click Stop Debugging or press Shift+F5. The application stops.

10. Open a copy of SQL Server Management Studio and log in to the database server. This is one case in which you can't use Server Explorer to obtain the information you need.
11. Drill down into the Databases\Rewards2 folder.
12. Right-click Rewards2 and choose New Query from the context menu. SQL Server Management Studio creates the new query for you.
13. Press Ctrl+V to copy the query string into the editor.
14. Click Include Actual Execution Plan or press Ctrl+M to tell SQL Server Management Studio to generate a query execution plan.
15. Click Execute or press F5. Select the Execution Plan tab. You'll see the output from the query, along with the execution plan, as shown here:

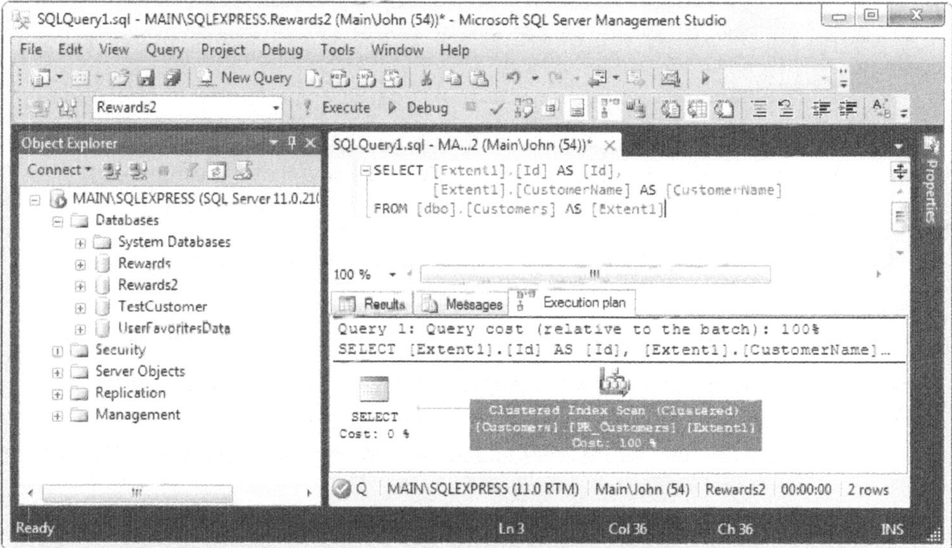

This is a simple query, so all you see are the *SELECT* statement and the background task performed by the server to complete the selection process. Notice that each entry has a *Cost* property that tells you the cost of that item to the query as a whole. When looking for areas of your query to improve, it's the high-cost items that you should consider modifying first.

16. Hover the mouse over the Clustered Index Scan object on the Execution Plan tab. You'll see the cost of this part of the query, as shown here:

Clustered Index Scan (Clustered)
Scanning a clustered index, entirely or only a range.

Physical Operation	Clustered Index Scan
Logical Operation	Clustered Index Scan
Actual Execution Mode	Row
Estimated Execution Mode	Row
Actual Number of Rows	2
Actual Number of Batches	0
Estimated I/O Cost	0.003125
Estimated Operator Cost	0.0032842 (100%)
Estimated CPU Cost	0.0001592
Estimated Subtree Cost	0.0032842
Estimated Number of Executions	1
Number of Executions	1
Estimated Number of Rows	2
Estimated Row Size	4039 B
Actual Rebinds	0
Actual Rewinds	0
Ordered	False
Node ID	0

Object
[Rewards2].[dbo].[Customers].[PK_Customers] [Extent1]
Output List
[Rewards2].[dbo].[Customers].Id, [Rewards2].[dbo].[Customers].CustomerName

This pop-up window breaks down the cost of the item so that you know precisely how much time is used in each activity. For example, you know that the estimated I/O cost is 0.003125 ms (milliseconds).

17. Close SQL Server Management Studio. There's no need to save the query.

Working with Entity SQL

The previous section, "Working with LINQ to Entities," showed the results of viewing a simple query. In this case, there was little you could do to tune the query except limit the number of records returned. The following procedure looks at a more complex query and works with Entity SQL instead.

Observing the SQL query using entity SQL

1. Open the Entity SQL project you worked with in the "Relying on pregenerated views" section of the chapter.

2. Open Form1.CS and add the following code in bold to the *btnQuery7_Click()* event handler in the location shown.

```
// Create a query object.
ObjectQuery<DbDataRecord> CustomerData =
    context.CreateQuery<DbDataRecord>(EntitySQLCmd);

// Discover the query being sent to the server.
String QueryString = CustomerData.ToTraceString();
```

The *ToTraceString()* method returns a string that contains the query being sent to SQL Server. Because *CustomerData* is an *ObjectQuery*, you can use this technique in this situation. This is the same technique used with older versions of the Entity Framework.

3. Place a breakpoint at this line in the *btnQuery7_Click()* event handler:

```
StringBuilder Output =
    new StringBuilder("Purchase Data:");
```

4. Click Start or press F5. The application compiles and runs.

5. Click Query 7. The application stops at the breakpoint.

6. Choose Debug | Windows | Locals to display the local objects shown here:

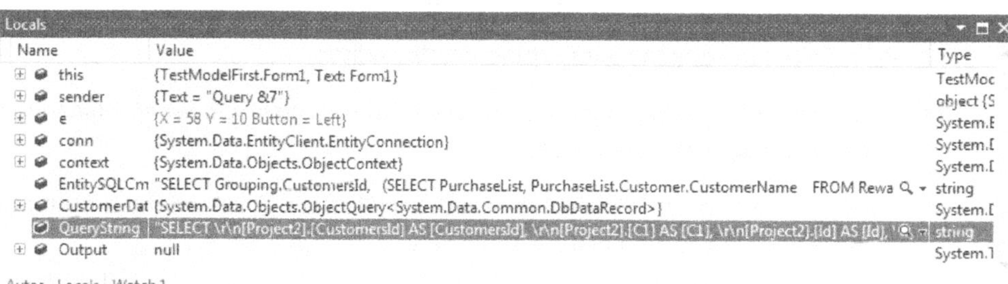

Notice that the *QueryString* contains escape characters that SQL Server won't accept. However, it does contain the complete query.

7. Click the *Text* button in the *QueryString* row. You'll see a usable version of the query, as shown here:

8. Select all of the text in the Text Visualizer dialog box, and then press Ctrl+C to copy this information to the clipboard.

9. Click Stop Debugging or press Shift+F5. The application stops.

10. Open a copy of SQL Server Management Studio and log in to the database server.

11. Drill down into the Databases\Rewards2 folder.

12. Right-click Rewards2 and choose New Query from the context menu. SQL Server Management Studio creates the new query for you.

13. Press Ctrl+V to copy the query string into the editor.

14. Click Include Actual Execution Plan or press Ctrl+M to tell SQL Server Management Studio to generate a query execution plan.

15. Click Execute or press F5. Select the Execution Plan tab. You'll see the output from the query, along with the execution plan, as show here:

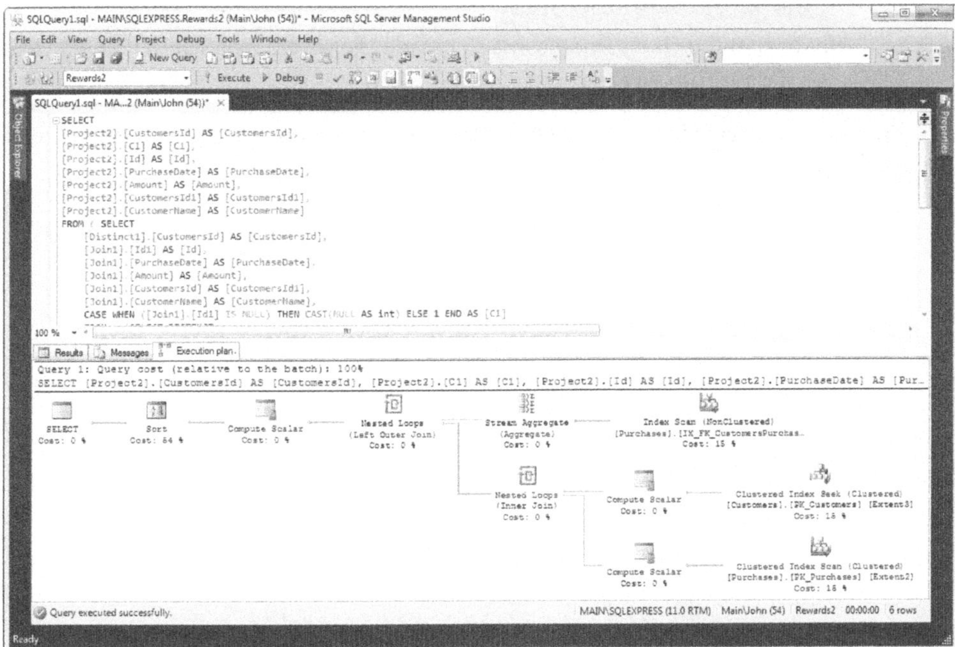

This query is quite complex compared to the query in the "Working with LINQ to Entities" section. Notice that some of the tasks require quite a lot of time, such as the sort operation (54 percent of the total). It might actually be preferable to sort the output at the client to reduce the load on the server and to provide perkier performance.

16. Hover the mouse over the various objects in the plan to see how each affects the overall execution of the query.

17. Close SQL Server Management Studio. There's no need to save the query.

Using third-party products

This chapter shows some quick and easy methods for viewing the queries sent to the server. Of course, you may need a more substantial solution when working with large numbers of queries or want more details about the queries. Fortunately, there are many different options for viewing or profiling your application so that you can see precisely how it sends queries to the server. For example, if you use one of the Visual Studio Ultimate editions, you can use IntelliTrace to profile your application and see how it interacts with the server. The article at *http://msdn.microsoft.com/magazine/ee336126.aspx* describes how to use IntelliTrace to perform this task.

You could also download and rely on the EFTracingProvider (*http://code.msdn.microsoft.com/EFProviderWrappers-c0b88f32*) to provide more substantial profiling of your application. This solution works with all versions of Visual Studio. It's written in C#, and you can obtain the code for it so that you can make any tweaks required for your specific situation. The article at *http://jkowalski.com/tag/efproviderwrappers/* tells you all about the EFTracingProvider and why the author developed it (you may have to rely on the cached version of this article, at *https://webcache.googleusercontent.com/search?q=cache:rrSBLiAIOqgJ:http://jkowalski.com/tag/efproviderwrappers/%2BEFTracingProvider*). Another view of this provider is presented at *http://blog.3d-logic.com/2012/03/31/using-tracing-and-caching-provider-wrappers-with-codefirst/*.

The previous two solutions do the job, but you may want a presentation that's easier to understand and work with. Fortunately, there are two other products you can try. The first is the Entity Framework Profiler from Hibernating Rhinos (*http://www.hibernatingrhinos.com/products/efprof*). This is a real-time visual debugger that you can use to see precisely what is happening with your queries as the application executes, which means that you get a better picture of how the application actually works while it runs. In this case, the output is grouped by object context, so that you can see how each context is doing its work.

The second solution is the Huagati Query Profiler (*http://www.huagati.com/l2sprofiler/*), which provides a log-based approach to working with the queries. The focus is on when queries are executed, so you get a timeline of how your application behaved at any given time during its execution. The advantage of this approach is that you can work back through the data at various points in time while modifying your code to improve performance. Unfortunately, this solution currently works only with SQL Server.

Tip There are a number of other tools that work with profilers or help you create better queries. For example, LLBLGen Pro (*http://www.llblgen.com/*) takes the place of the model designer provided with Visual Studio to help you create models for a number of environments using a single designer. You obtain the files required to work with that specific environment, which can include Entity Framework, NHibernate, LINQ to SQL, and a special LLBLGen Pro Runtime Framework. This product works with a number of databases including SQL Server, Access, Oracle, PostgreSQL, Firebird, DB2, MySQL, Sybase, and Sybase Anywhere. This is a good product to use when you have multiple database managers to work with.

Another good tool to have in your toolbox is LINQPad (*http://www.linqpad.net/*). You use this tool to test your queries before you place them in your application. It's a good way to test out what-if scenarios to determine whether one query or another will produce the best result, without having to go through a long debug cycle. The graphical output of this utility makes it easy to see precisely how your query will work once you add it to your code.

Defining the performance triangle

There are more than a few developers who equate performance with speed. However, an application that performs well offers considerably more than raw speed. In order to perform well, an application must do more than simply run fast. When you think about it, an application can run incredibly fast while providing the wrong answer, or it can run incredibly fast while leaving itself open to attack from outsiders (at which point, it may not run at all). Performance is the combination of a number of elements to define an application that does a task well. The three common elements that make up performance are

- **Speed** The ability of an application to perform a task within a reasonable amount of time to avoid user frustration.
- **Security** The ability of an application to protect the data that it manages so that the purity and consistency of the data are unquestioned.
- **Reliability** The ability of an application to continue performing its task even under adverse conditions without data loss or application crashes.

These three elements form a performance triangle. Increasing one aspect decreases the other two. For example, increased speed often comes at the price of reducing both security features and additional code required to make an application reliable. Likewise, the most secure application in the world is the one that offers no access to the data at all. Adding too much redundancy to make an application more reliable often comes at the price of both speed (in the form of extra code) and security (by being too invasive). In short, high performance is the balanced effect of the speed, security, and reliability. You must have a balance of all three in order to obtain the desired effect.

The following sections discuss speed, security, and reliability from an Entity Framework perspective. However, you can apply these principles to other areas of the application environment, so it's important to get the big-picture view of these elements as you read. For example, you can overclock the hardware to obtain additional speed, but only at the cost of making the hardware less reliable and possibly less secure as well.

Considering the effects of raw speed

Application speed is measured in the number of tasks that the application can perform within a given time frame. Speed doesn't consider the idea that the tasks are performed correctly or that the results are usable—simply that the tasks have been accomplished. It's important to make the distinction between speed and other aspects of performance. Focusing on an application's ability to work fast helps you see redundancies in application code and ways in which you can create code that works more efficiently. Later analysis may show that a particular change is unwarranted, unsafe, or unreliable, but before you can make that determination, you have to experiment with the possibility that the change will improve application speed.

Warning It's never a good idea to tune an application for speed as part of the production environment. Use a test configuration on a test system to perform this task. Otherwise, you risk data errors or even data loss. In addition, the application could crash in a manner that brings down the network or causes other problems. Experimentation is best left to an environment where you can work through issues safely and with less worry as to the consequences of a change.

As part of testing your application, you need to rely on load-testing software that mimics the effects of having multiple users pound away at the application. This chapter doesn't discuss third-party software you use to perform this task, but you need to provide such software as part of your test environment. One of the most commonly used testing frameworks is NUnit (*http://www.nunit.org/*). You can also use the performance-testing tools included as part of the higher-end versions of Visual Studio—the article at *http://blogs.msdn.com/b/visualstudioalm/archive/2012/06/04/getting-started-with-load-testing-in-visual-studio-2012.aspx* describes this process in detail. Load testing is an essential part of any speed tuning because it points out changes that absolutely won't work. For example, it's only with load testing that you can find application concurrency issues or determine that a lock is needed to ensure that a critical section of code that could be accessed by multiple threads works as designed.

Tip If you're really interested in getting everything you can out of Visual Studio and the performance-testing tools created for it, consider downloading the Visual Studio Performance Testing Quick Reference Guide, found at *http://vsptqrg.codeplex.com/releases/view/42484*. This document is based on real-world discussions of issues that developers confront when using performance testing to check application speed. You'll find information in it from a variety of sources (including some from within Microsoft itself). The authors are constantly updating the information, so you won't need to worry about it becoming completely outdated.

You may also want to create your own custom performance counters to monitor application speed. The article "Load Testing with Custom Performance Counters" (*http://visualstudiomagazine.com/articles/2012/10/01/load-testing.aspx*) provides some helpful code and tips that show how to create and use custom counters with your application. An important issue to remember is that the very act of adding custom counters will reduce application speed a little, so you're not seeing the true speed of your application.

Speed takes several forms within an Entity Framework application. In some cases, you can mitigate the need to ensure that the application is both secure and reliable by ensuring the part of the application the user sees is fast. With this in mind, consider these areas of application speed from the user's perspective:

- **User interface** The user interface is the most noticeable part of your application. A user interface that's responsive makes the user feel better about the application and think that it's working faster (even when it isn't). An informative interface is even better. In more than a few tests, users felt that an application that provided information about the task the application was performing was faster than a noninformative application, even when timed tests showed that the noninformative application was faster. Adding a progress bar to your application goes a long way toward giving the user the impression of speed.
- **Partial results display** Displaying the parent records first, and then the details (when possible), gives an impression of speed.
- **Local data sources** Using local data sources whenever possible helps give the application a speed boost because there's no network latency or busy servers to worry about. Optimizing your use of local data sources will produce a significant speed performance the user can see.
- **Optimized queries** The better you can define a query, the less time it takes to obtain the data represented by that query, and the faster the user sees the results.
- **Lazy loading** Even when eager loading is guaranteed to make the application faster, lazy loading often presents the illusion of faster speed because less work is done with each database query. This is one of those situations where you must consider overall application performance against user expectations. In some cases, using other techniques to provide a speedier application will overcome the need to forgo the actual speed advantages of eager loading.

- **Paged results** In some cases, creating a query where only a specified range of records is retrieved will produce the illusion of increased speed. Yes, you'll hit the database every time the user requests more records, but the time required to obtain the subset of records will be less, so the user will see the records faster. When you retrieve all of the records the user needs at one time, the actual speed of the application is improved, but the user sees it as a delay. A way around this issue is to provide the user with an informative interface that indicates the application is performing useful work.

The most important concept to take from this section is that speed is relative to what the user perceives. In order to create an efficient environment that uses client, server, and network resources effectively, you must often provide feedback to the user that gives the illusion of speed, even when the application is working hard in the background and would otherwise present a lag in record presentation. The trade-off in speed is the actual effective use of resources vs. the need to keep the user happy.

Considering the effects of security

The most secure application in the world is the one that no one can access—that has no connectivity with anything. Of course, this truly secure application is completely useless. Even if it could perform useful work, the lack of interactivity would make it pretty much a closed system that no one would ever know about. In order to provide useful functionality, an application must provide some level of access, which means that it must also incur some level of security threat. The irony of this situation appears to escape most developers, who somehow think it's possible to secure an application in a way that makes it truly safe. Of course, there are shades of security. Opening an application to every potential attack ever created isn't a very good idea either. Doing so would also tend to make the application pretty much useless because it could never produce desirable or stable output (despite the hyper-interactivity it would provide). Consequently, application security lies in some level of controlled access.

The Entity Framework presents a few special security issues that you should consider when creating an application. For example, SQL injection attacks (see *http://msdn.microsoft.com/library/ms161953(v=sql.105).aspx* for a description of a SQL injection attack) can severely compromise your system. The way to overcome this problem is to avoid using dynamic SQL queries. This doesn't mean you can't use variables with LINQ to Entities. In this case, the variable is replaced with a value before the query is submitted to the server, so there isn't any chance of a SQL injection attack. The same can't be said for Entity SQL. With enough time and knowledge of the model, an attacker can inject code into an Entity SQL query. However, this second route to a SQL injection attack is significantly harder.

Another serious problem is a connection piggyback, where an attacker uses a connection opened for other purposes to access the database. Whenever you make a query using a direct database connection, the attacker has the level of access provided by that identity. The attacker isn't limited to issuing commands—it's possible to perform every task that the identity has permission to accomplish. The best way to avoid this problem is to limit the rights of the identity you use to make the queries to those required to accomplish the given task.

Neither of these problems is limited to the Entity Framework—the Entity Framework shares them with many other applications. The way you write the application, the interface you provide for it, and the rights you assign to the user all determine the level of exposure that the application provides to the local system, the network, the hosting server, and the target database. The following sections examine several areas of security you need to consider when creating your application.

Considering the connection

It's essential to consider the security of any connection you create. There are a number of ways in which an attacker can gain access to the connection information. The following list provides guidelines on keeping your connection safe:

- Use trusted data source providers The data provider is in the position to do considerable harm to the application and the data it manages. A data provider performs the following tasks, any of which can lead to a security breach:
    - Receives the connection string from the Entity Framework and uses it to create the connection
    - Handles user credentials used to access the server
    - Translates the command tree into something that the data source can understand
    - Assembles and returns datasets to the caller
- Encrypt your data connection The Entity Framework doesn't provide any support for data encryption. Any connection that occurs over a public network should use data encryption to protect data from prying eyes. You can read more about data encryption at *http://technet.microsoft.com/library/ms189067.aspx*.
- Secure the connection string The connection string provides a substantial amount of information about the server and the requirements to access it. If you don't want others to gain access to your server, the first step is ensuring you don't give them the information required to do so. The following methods will help you secure the connection string.
    - Use Windows Authentication to access the server so that you don't need to supply a name and password as part of the connection string.
    - Use protected configuration to encrypt sensitive parts of the connection strings—making them inaccessible to outsiders. Although this technique was originally designed for ASP.NET developers, you can use it with any application. Read more about this technique at *http://msdn.microsoft.com/library/53tyfkaw.aspx*.
    - Store the connection strings in an encrypted configuration file, rather than embedding them within your application. If you embed the connection strings in your application, someone can disassemble the application and read the connection string directly from it. The Entity Data Model Wizard stores the connection string in the application's .CONFIG file by default, so you need to secure this file before releasing the application in a production environment.

- Never use dynamically created connection strings unless absolutely necessary, because they're subject to injection attacks. To reduce the potential for an injection attack, use an *EntityConnectionStringBuilder* (see *http://msdn.microsoft.com/library/system.data.entityclient.entityconnectionstringbuilder.aspx* for details) to create the connection string. The article at *http://msdn.microsoft.com/library/bb738533.aspx* tells how to use an *EntityConnectionStringBuilder* to create a connection string.

Keeping memory secure

The Entity Framework relies heavily on memory to perform tasks. Because attackers can use a number of methods to examine memory, you must be careful to create applications that use memory safely. The following list presents a number of potential issues with memory security that you need to address in your application.

- **Remain within the current security context** Crossing the line between security contexts represents a huge potential security risk. Sometimes this issue can occur in odd ways. For example, in a multithreaded application, one thread may have access to the connection, while another doesn't. If the application stores the connection in a globally accessible area, the untrusted thread could gain access to it. The connection should remain within the confines of the trusted thread to keep it safe.

- **Assume login information and passwords are visible in a memory dump** Whenever you request login information or passwords from the user, the objects holding that information remain available until the garbage collector reclaims their resources. If an attacker can cause an application crash, the memory dump that results from the crash will contain the login information or password. The best way to avoid this problem is to use Windows Authentication whenever possible.

- **Restrict large result sets** A large result set can actually overwhelm the application and cause it to crash. An attacker could force a crash by requesting an abnormally large result set. Make sure that the application automatically filters or otherwise restricts result sets to a size that the client can handle. Otherwise, when the application crashes, the attacker can read sensitive application information from the memory dump.

- **Avoid returning *IQueryable* results to untrusted callers** An untrusted caller could use the *IQueryable* methods to obtain access to sensitive data or increase the size of the result set enough to cause an application crash. In addition, the caller could modify the *IQueryable* result in ways that cause an exception, and the exception could contain sensitive information.

- **Don't share an *ObjectContext* between application domains** It's important to maintain the integrity of the *ObjectContext* by keeping it within the current application domain. If you let other application domains use the *ObjectContext*, it could expose information that the application domain couldn't normally access. For example, if a parent application within a firewall spawns a child application that resides outside a firewall and then shares the *ObjectContext* with that child, the *ObjectContext* is vulnerable to outside parties. You can read more about application domains at *http://msdn.microsoft.com/library/2bh4z9hs.aspx*.

- Prevent type safety violations Any time an application causes a type safety violation, the integrity of the data is at stake. This means that someone could gain unwanted access to underlying data or interact with it in ways you hadn't envisioned. For that matter, the attacker could change the data in a way that will cause the application to crash and expose the contents of memory in the resulting memory dump.

Interacting with users

Users will always present security challenges. There's nothing you can do to change basic human nature, which means that you must interact with users carefully. The following list provides guidelines on creating a safer environment to work with users when employing the Entity Framework in your application:

- Work with trusted users Any time you create an *EntityConnection*, the user can potentially modify the connection parameters or use the underlying connection to access the server. When you must work with untrusted users, make sure the user has no access to the *EntityConnection*.
- Secure the data source Giving users a limited number of permissions in the data source is one of the better ways to enhance overall application security. The data source controls access to the data, so you can use it to control precisely what the user sees and how the user can interact with the data.
- Run the application with minimum permissions Users have a habit of overwhelming local security and then using the ill-gotten permissions to perform tasks that you hadn't expected. In order to ensure that all of the other security features you have in place remain intact, you must limit the user's ability to make changes by running the application with the minimum required permissions.
- Restrict untrusted applications The Entity Framework doesn't check security restrictions. This means it will execute any application code that the user supplies. The best way to keep this from happening is to disallow unauthorized application installations.
- Handle exceptions It's amazing to see the amount and types of information presented by the exception dialog boxes. If an application presents one of these dialog boxes to an untrusted user, the user could rely on the information obtained to thwart other security measures and eventually gain access to the application.

Maintaining configuration integrity

The way in which you configure the application for use makes a big difference in how secure it remains. Maintaining the application configuration as you intend it to be prevents the user from performing acts you hadn't envisioned. The following list describes ways in which you can keep the application configuration secure:

- **Restrict configuration file access** You need to restrict access to all of the configuration files associated with .NET, including *EnterpriseSec.CONFIG*, *Security.CONFIG*, *Machine.CONFIG*, and *<application name>.EXE.CONFIG*.
- **Restrict entity file access** The various Entity Framework files (.EDMX, .CSDL, .SSDL, and .MSL) describe the database model in detail. Your application only requires read access to these files at run time, so you should secure these files to keep them safe from prying eyes.
- **Keep logging for debugging only** When you deploy an application, make sure you turn logging off. Otherwise, the application could expose all sorts of unwanted information in the form of log entries. Make absolutely certain that a release configuration of your application doesn't provide any logs that an attacker can use to surmise the inner workings of your application.
- **Use only trusted *MetadataWorkspace* objects** The *MetadataWorkspace* object (see *http://msdn.microsoft.com/library/system.data.metadata.edm.metadataworkspace.aspx* for details) provides a complete picture of the Entity Framework configuration for an application. Accepting such an object from an untrusted source opens the application to attack. The recommendation is to build such an object internally as needed.

Note You may wonder where these untrusted sources come from. An untrusted source is any data source that you don't personally manage and don't personally know is secure. There are some data sources that are obviously untrusted. For example, when your organization uses a third-party web service as a data source, you must trust that data source as untrusted. Any objects created to manage that data source are therefore untrusted as well. Data that comes from a partner is also untrusted. This sort of data may fall into a political gray area, but from a security perspective the data source is untrusted because you can't vouch for it unless you personally manage it. Likewise, even the data that comes from subsidiaries of your own organization is untrusted. You have no way to verify that the data is properly secured and managed. This viewpoint sounds extremely paranoid, but it's the paranoid developer who produces the most secure code.

Considering how raw speed and security affect reliability

Reliability is one topic that's hard to pin down in some respects because it means something different to each individual. There's also some overlap between reliability and both speed and security. For example, when you make an application faster, the user is less likely to become frustrated. Users who aren't frustrated with the application tend to make fewer mistakes, which improves application reliability indirectly. Likewise, when you handle errors to improve security by keeping the information presented by an exception dialog box out of user hands, you also increase reliability by making it possible to recover from an error. There are, in fact, many areas of overlap. However, from the perspective of this book, reliability is the ability of an application to interact with both user and database in a consistent, efficient, and predictable manner, while protecting the data from harm.

Countering reliability criticisms of the Entity Framework

You'll encounter some negative feedback from others for using the Entity Framework to create applications from a reliability perspective, especially when working with large enterprise applications. The following list describes the most common of these reliability issues and helps you understand why they're important.

- **The Entity Framework is a Black Box** Some developers need to feel completely in control of the application development cycle. However, there aren't any modern programming languages that don't employ black boxes. Classes, methods, events, and properties all represent kinds of black boxes. If you truly want full control, you need to write your application in machine code. The Entity Framework makes the work environment more reliable by making it possible for the developer to focus on what needs to be done, rather than how to accomplish it. Creating a simpler programming environment tends to reduce developer error, which is a prime source of reliability errors in applications.
- **There are too many options to consider** The flexibility provided by the Entity Framework does create an environment where you need to think through the development process and use the options best suited to your needs. However, this flexibility also means that you can fine-tune the application and make it possible to create the specific output you want. The fact that the Entity Framework is flexible makes it possible for developers to get what they want without creating error-laden workarounds.
- **Frameworks tend to produce noisy applications** It's true, custom code can create applications that are more efficient and easier to trace than frameworks can, because you can tune the code specifically for that application. However, frameworks tend to perform tasks consistently, which means that you can be sure a certain call will always result in the same actions in the background. Custom-built code creates inconsistencies that often lead to reliability problems.
- **Custom code is easier to troubleshoot because the developer understands it** Yes, the developer does understand the inner workings of any custom framework written exclusively by that developer. However, large applications are created by teams, not by individuals. The team must understand the framework in order to use it, which means having great documentation for everyone to use. The Entity Framework is already documented well enough that everyone in a team can understand how it works—what namespaces, classes, methods, events, and properties it provides. In addition, using the Entity Framework means that you're using code that has been tested by thousands of developers—not just your in-house staff. In short, the chances are that the Entity Framework will be more easily understood by your team, and therefore the team will make fewer mistakes when using it.

There are a number of reliability issues you can't control directly, but must either handle indirectly or consider a fail-gracefully strategy when you encounter them. For example, if the user's machine fails due to a hardware issue in the middle of a transaction, there isn't much you can do about it except to ensure the transaction is rolled back at the server. The most important thing to remember is that a transaction doesn't actually occur until the application calls *SaveChanges()*. Before that time, any changes the user makes are locally stored, so when the machine fails, all you've really lost is the set of changes that haven't been saved as of yet.

One reliability technique that most developers use when working with databases is to ensure that every set of related queries is wrapped in a transaction so that it's possible to roll back the changes when a particular change fails. For example, if someone transfers money from one account to another, it's a two-step process. First, the money is withdrawn from the first account. Second, the money is deposited into the second account. Allowing the first operation to succeed and then allowing the second operation to fail means that the customer would suffer a monetary loss. Fortunately, you don't have to specifically create transactions when using the Entity Framework. The Entity Framework automatically wraps any changes within a transaction when you call *SaveChanges()*. If any of the changes fail, all of the changes in the transaction are rolled back. For this reason, you want to be sure to call *SaveChanges()* whenever you've completed a unit of work. Using the unit-of-work approach means that the number of changes that will be rolled back after a failed change are fewer, and it's easier to diagnose and potentially recover from the error.

Note The same sorts of issues that apply to the underlying Entity Framework for both speed and security also apply to reliability. For example, you want to be sure that the provider you use is from a known good source and that the provider has been thoroughly tested. You don't want to use a beta provider in a production environment. In addition, you want to consider the sorts of users that will interact with the application—trusted users are less likely to provide input that will cause unreliable application performance.

Reliability also comes from testing the application thoroughly at various levels. Many of the procedures in this book have emphasized the usefulness of testing individual queries and checking the results before using them. You need to extend this process even further and ensure that you check all of the code for potential errors both locally and when interacting with other code. The Entity Framework doesn't provide some magical means of ferretting out bad code. If anything, the automation could potentially hide some errors from view—at least until you find them during the testing process.

The most difficult yet important reliability consideration comes from the user interface. It's essential to design the user interface in a manner that allows the user freedom in making queries, yet reduces the probability that the user will make unusable queries. This is especially important when working with untrusted users who might be more interested in crashing the application than working with it. For example, instead of using text boxes, rely on other controls that provide specific input to the application so that the acceptable entries are quantified at the outset, and you have a better chance of recognizing unusable patterns. When you must rely on text input, validate the input to verify that it doesn't pose potential problems, such as those that occur with a SQL injection attack. Even when working with trusted users, it's essential to check input to ensure the user doesn't become frustrated during the session and purposely make mistakes that could cause errors.

As with every other aspect of development, you must assume that the application will fail at times, and that you'll need to either recover from the failure or fail gracefully, rather than allow the application to crash. The Entity Framework makes it possible for you to create consistent applications quickly, but it doesn't provide anything special in the way of automatic error handling. When there's a chance for failure, assume the worst and handle every situation as if the worst has already occurred. Make sure you add any redundancies required to create a robust application.

Using multithreading as an aid to speed

Multithreading makes it possible to offload a processing task while the main thread continues doing something else. Using multithreading carefully can make the user interface feel significantly faster and definitely be more responsive, which results in less user frustration and fewer reliability issues. The procedure that follows uses the simple LINQ to Entities example you've been working with and turns it into a multithreaded version.

Creating a multithreaded query

1. Open the LINQ to Entities project you worked with in the "Working with LINQ to Entities" section of the chapter.
2. Begin by adding the following *using* statement to the beginning of Form1.CS:

   ```
   using System.Threading;
   ```

3. Add the following delegate after the current *btnQuery_Click()* event handler:

   ```
   // This delegate defines the method used to retrieve data from the thread.
   public delegate void ContextCallback(IQueryable<Customers> CustomerList);
   ```

   This example uses a callback method to return data from the thread you'll create to actually execute the query. The callback accepts an *IQueryable* collection of *Customers* as input.

4. Add a new button to *Form1*. Name the button *btnThreaded* and set its *Text* property to *&Threaded.*
5. Double-click *btnThreaded* to create a new click event handler.
6. Type the following code for the *btnThreaded_Click()* event handler, along with code needed to define a delegate and private list of customers returned by the query:

   ```
   // This delegate defines the method used to retrieve data from the thread.
   public delegate void ContextCallback(IQueryable<Customers> CustomerList);

   private void btnThreaded_Click(object sender, EventArgs e)
   {
      // Create an instance of the thread class.
      MultiThreadedQuery MTQ = new MultiThreadedQuery(
         new ContextCallback(ResultsCallback));
   ```

```
    // Create a thread to perform the task.
    Thread MyThread = new Thread(MTQ.GetCustomers);

    // Start the thread.
    MyThread.Start();
}
```

The example begins by creating an instance of a thread class that you haven't designed yet (but will in a moment). Part of this class defines a callback that's used to return the data from the query to the caller. The next step is to create a thread, *MyThread*, and call *Start()*. At this point, the application can perform some other task while waiting for the query to complete.

7. Create the following event handler to handle the results of the query:

```
public static void ResultsCallback(IQueryable<Customers> CustomerList)
{
    // Process each customer in the list.
    StringBuilder Output =
        new StringBuilder("Customer List:");
    foreach (var Customer in CustomerList)
    {
        // Create a customer entry for each customer.
        Output.Append("\r\n" + Customer.CustomerName +
            " has made purchases on: ");

        // Process each purchase for that particular customer.
        foreach (var Purchase in Customer.Purchases)
            Output.Append("\r\n\t" + Purchase.PurchaseDate);
    }

    // Display the result on screen.
    MessageBox.Show(Output.ToString());
}
```

This event handler is called the moment the query completes. It receives a list of customers from the thread that executes the query. The code should look familiar because you've used it several times already to display results on screen.

8. Create the following worker class to perform the actual query. This class should appear in Form1.CS, but should be outside of the *Form1* class (yet inside the *TestModelFirst* namespace).

```
public class MultiThreadedQuery
{
    // The context used to access the data source.
    private Rewards2ModelContainer context;

    // A list of customers retrieved from the database.
    private IQueryable<Customers> CustomerList;

    // This delegate is used to call the callback method when the task is
    // complete.
    private readonly Form1.ContextCallback _Callback;
```

```
    public MultiThreadedQuery(Form1.ContextCallback CallbackDelegate)
    {
       // Assign a method to the callback delegate.
       _Callback = CallbackDelegate;
    }

    public void GetCustomers()
    {
       // Make sure the context points to the data source.
       if (context == null)
          context = new Rewards2ModelContainer();

       // You must lock this section of code to ensure it's thread safe.
       lock (context)
       {
          // Obtain the customer list.
          CustomerList =
              from cust in context.Customers
              select cust;

          // Return the result to the caller, when there is a caller.
          if (_Callback != null)
             _Callback(CustomerList);
       }
    }
}
```

The code begins by creating some variables, which include a *Rewards2ModelContainer* context, a list of customers to return to the caller, and a variable used to hold a series of event handlers to call after a query completes. The constructor for this class assigns the address of an event handler to *_Callback*, which is later used to fire an event signifying that the query has completed.

The *GetCustomers()* method is the focus of this class. It begins by obtaining a context when the current context object is null. It then places a *lock()* on the context. If you don't perform this act, another thread could call this method and cause a host of problems for the application. The *lock()* makes the application thread safe. The code then performs the query and returns the list of customers to the caller by firing an event.

9. Click Start or press F5. The application compiles and runs.
10. Click Threaded. You'll see the result shown here:

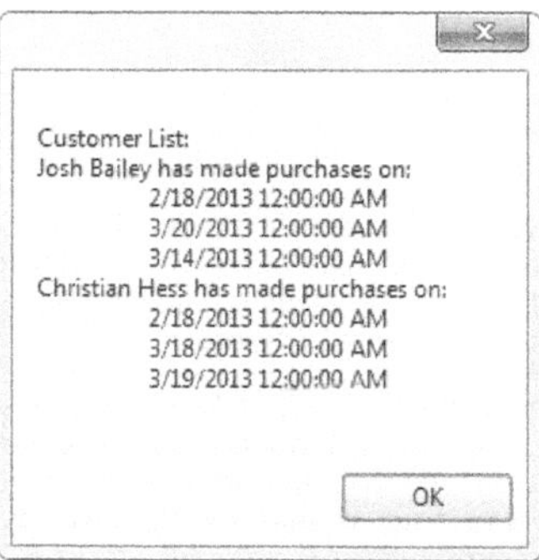
Customer List:
Josh Bailey has made purchases on:
2/18/2013 12:00:00 AM
3/20/2013 12:00:00 AM
3/14/2013 12:00:00 AM
Christian Hess has made purchases on:
2/18/2013 12:00:00 AM
3/18/2013 12:00:00 AM
3/19/2013 12:00:00 AM
OK

11. Click Threaded. You'll see the same results as before. The fact that you can click this button again without first closing the dialog box tells you that the application is indeed multithreaded. Attempting to click Query twice without first closing the dialog box wouldn't work.

Getting started with the Entity Framework

This chapter has helped you understand the subject of performance better. At this point, you should have a better idea of why performance issues can cause application errors of all sorts. Applications that perform well tend to be more efficient and require fewer organization resources. Consequently, a little time spent tuning an application and its environment pays dividends far beyond simple added speed and fewer user complaints. Crafting an application that performs well saves you time, effort, and frustration in the long run as well.

The trick to creating applications that perform well is to look at the big picture to discover elements that may not work up to specification, and then view the details of those elements to determine areas where you can make improvements. This chapter discusses Entity Framework performance. However, simply viewing the Entity Framework isn't enough. As part of your continuing efforts to improve application performance, create a picture of the application and its environment as a whole. Make sure you include things like infrastructure, hardware, and user training in your assessment of application performance.

Chapter 14, "Creating custom entities," begins a new part in the book—one that focuses on advanced management techniques. Managing the Entity Framework means working outside the automation so that you have control over the Entity Framework, rather than allowing it to control you. There's no doubt that the automation works incredibly well and that you should use it as often as possible, but there are times when you need to overrule the automation in order to garner a desired result. Chapter 14 discusses the issue of creating custom entities to meet needs that the Entity Framework automation isn't quite designed to handle. It's true that you won't often need to perform this task (especially given the new features that Microsoft continuously adds), but knowing how to build custom entities will save you considerable time later.

Chapter 13 quick reference

To	Do this
Enhance performance beyond the optimizations available in the Entity Framework	Remove layers by working with a lower-level technology such as ADO.NET. The trade-off is additional development time and increased complexity, which can translate to security and reliability issues.
Reduce the amount of work performed by both server and client in obtaining data	Make your queries as specific as possible using the *where* clause. Anything you do to reduce the number of records retrieved from the server reduces both server and network resource requirements, as well as client-side processing.
Reduce the need to obtain data from the server	Ensure that your queries are configured to use caching by setting the *EnablePlanCaching* property to *true*.
Develop views with better performance profiles	Use pregenerated views as often as possible to ensure the application works with views as efficiently as possible.
Pregenerate application views	Use the EDMGen command-line utility provided with Visual Studio 2012. Make sure you open a Developer Command Prompt for VS2012 command prompt to access this tool.
Eliminate the need to compile queries during run time	Use precompiled queries so that the application doesn't need to parse the query at run time to create a command tree.
Improve the performance of read-only queries	Turn off change tracking so that the application doesn't have to manage the overhead of tracking changes that won't occur because the query is read-only.
Reduce delays that occur when large numbers records referenced by multiple navigation properties	Use lazy loading by setting the Lazy Loading Enabled property of the model to True.
Reduce the effects of network latency on small data payloads	Use eager loading by setting the Lazy Loading Enabled property of the model to False.
Create a balanced application	Ensure that you keep both application and application environment in mind as you work through performance issues. In addition, maintain a balanced view of speed, security, and reliability issues.
Provide a speedier application	Consider the user's perception of speed, as well as the need for actual speed. Use tricks such as an informative interface to make up for lags in obtaining information from the server.
Provide a secure application	Ensure you exercise best practices when writing your application, including limiting user rights to those that the user must absolutely have to accomplish the task. If necessary, provide multiple accounts for various needs so that each task is given only the required level of access.
Provide a reliable application	Use techniques that tend to produce consistent results in a manner that both user and database understand. Making the application efficient tends to produce fewer user-related and time-related errors. Creating a predictable application means that the user can better anticipate how to interact with the application to produce a desired result.
Improve the user experience by returning control to the application faster	Rely on multithreaded queries.

PART V

Advanced management techniques

At some point, you'll have a mostly finished model put together, a database to go with it, and the starting of some amazing code. At this point, you need to start managing the intricacies of your project, or else you'll find that it doesn't quite work as you expected it to work when you're done. This part of the book focuses on the management techniques you most commonly use to create Entity Framework applications.

Chapter 14, "Creating custom entities," begins the process by helping you understand and use custom entities. A custom entity is one for which no standard .NET type exists. You use custom entities with any custom objects that you create to describe specialized data or elements of the real world that aren't modeled well by existing .NET types. Many texts refer to these objects as Plain Old CLR Objects (POCOs). Custom entities aren't necessarily hand coded. The various tools provided with Microsoft Visual Studio can make using POCO entities relatively straightforward and fast, so this chapter helps you use the automation whenever possible.

In Chapter 15, "Mapping data types to properties," you discover techniques for mapping data types to Entity Framework properties. It's an essential part of working with complex data. The chapter begins by looking at some ways in which you can map standard types. You'll also see how to map enumerated, geography, and geometry spatial data types.

The last chapter of the book, Chapter 16, "Performing advanced management tasks," focuses more on administration. For example, you learn how to create multiple diagrams for the same model so that you can see the model in different ways. This chapter also shows how to import multiple stored procedures in batch mode, rather than one at a time. One of the more complex tasks that a developer can perform is mapping a stored procedure that returns multiple result sets—this chapter tells you how. The last part of this chapter takes one more look at Entity Framework performance enhancements from an administrative perspective.

CHAPTER 14

Creating custom entities

After completing the chapter, you'll be able to

- Describe and use classes.
- Describe and use event handlers.
- Describe and use methods.
- Describe and use properties.

So far, this book has relied fully on automatic generation of all entity information. Yes, you've poked and prodded it a bit, but essentially, the examples have used whatever the Entity Framework provided. Unfortunately, despite advances in the way the Entity Framework works, there are still times when you need to create custom entities to address special application needs. The two most common times you'll need to create special entities are

- When updating data classes from an existing application to use the Entity Framework.
- When you need better control over how data classes are generated to ensure you meet organizational requirements (those provided by your own workgroup, department, or enterprise), standards requirements (those created by outside groups or organizations), or legal requirements (those created by the government).

In general, you can use your custom data classes with the Entity Framework without modification as long as the entity types, complex types, and properties in the custom data class match the names you provide for the entity types, complex types, and properties in the conceptual model. This means you can use POCOs, such as domain objects, with the data model. POCO data classes tend to be persistence ignorant. However, once mapped to entities, they can still perform the same Create, Read, Update, and Delete (CRUD) operations as any other Entity Framework entity.

The easiest way to think about a POCO class is as any class that is supported as an entity by the Entity Framework that doesn't inherit from *EntityObject*. POCO support is necessary to support a broad range of programming styles. For example, you must have POCO support in order to support the Domain-Driven Design (DDD) and agile programming styles. The lack of POCO support also makes it hard to transition between technologies, such as moving from an Object-Relational Mapping (ORM) tool such as NHibernate (see *http://nhforge.org/* for details) to the Entity Framework.

In addition, you require POCO classes to support things like unit testing. The problem with using standard entities is that it's hard to break them up into small pieces for testing purposes. In addition, the entities interact directly with the database, so it's hard to create unit tests where such interaction is simulated. With this in mind, this entire chapter takes a step-by-step approach to working with POCO classes in a manner that works best with the Entity Framework and allows you to optimize your use of automation.

Note This chapter doesn't actually discuss DDD or agile programming. These topics require one or possibly more books for a full treatment, and even an entire chapter wouldn't really suffice for much of an introduction. However, it's important to at least know about these programming strategies. You can learn more about DDD at *http://msdn.microsoft.com/magazine/dd419654.aspx* and agile programming at *http://agileprogramming.org/*. Both of these philosophies are important in today's programming environment to help improve developer productivity, so it's good that the Entity Framework can support them. The techniques in this chapter aren't specific to either of these philosophies, but rather are general enough to apply to either (along with a number of other POCO strategies that developers use).

Developing POCO classes

Some developers might confuse using POCO classes with code-first techniques. The fact is that they're entirely different. When working with POCO classes, the classes remain absolutely free of encumbrances from the Entity Framework. In fact, the classes have no idea that the Entity Framework even exists. You can actually start out with a model-first implementation and convert it to a POCO implementation, which is the focus of the example described in the following sections.

Configuring the model

At this point, you've manually added classes to the example that match the model. However, the Entity Framework is still configured to automatically generate code every time you make a change. In order to complete the process of converting to POCO classes, you must configure the model to use the POCO classes and not automatically generate code. The following procedure tells you how to perform this task.

Configuring a model for use with POCO classes

1. Copy the LINQ query version of the *ModelFirst* example you created in Chapter 6, "Manipulating data using LINQ," to a new folder, and use this new copy for this example (rather than the copy you created in Chapter 6).

Note The LINQ version of the *ModelFirst* example in Chapter 6 appears in the ModelFirst (LINQ Query) folder of the downloadable source code. If you created your own version of the example, the folder name will probably be different.

2. Open the Rewards2Model.EDMX file by double-clicking its entry in Solution Explorer.

3. Click in any open area of the designer window. Set the Code Generation Strategy property to None as shown here:

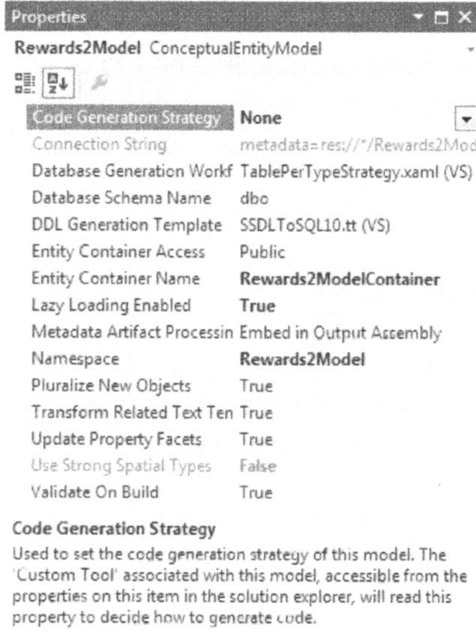

This action doesn't get rid of the template-generated classes—the ones created using the ADO.NET Entity Data Model template. It simply ensures that the model won't generate classes automatically as part of any build process.

4. Right-click the Customers.CS file found under the Rewards2Model.EDMX\Rewards2Model.tt entry in Solution Explorer, and choose Delete from the context menu. You'll see a warning message about the deletion being permanent.

5. Click OK. Microsoft Visual Studio removes the file.

Warning Attempting to delete the files using Microsoft Windows Explorer will cause problems because the .CSPROJ file isn't updated. This file will instruct Visual Studio to continue looking for the files you've deleted.

6. Repeat steps 4 and 5 for the Purchases.CS and Rewards2Model.Context.CS files. At this point, attempting to compile the application will display a number of error messages due to missing references. This is normal, and you shouldn't worry about it.

7. Choose Save All or press Ctrl+Shift+S to save the changes you've made.

Adding the classes

Before you can do anything else, you need to create classes that will support the model. The classes won't derive from *EntityObject*, nor are they even aware of the model, but they'll support it just the same. The way this magic happens is in the technique used to create the classes. The class names and properties must match. All of the classes and properties in the model must also appear in your classes, including the navigational properties. The following procedure describes how to create the classes used as a POCO replacement for the classes that the Entity Framework would normally generate automatically for you. (This procedure assumes you've completed the steps in the "Configuring the model" section of the chapter.)

Creating the *Customers* and *Purchases* classes

1. Open the Rewards2Model.EDMX file by double-clicking its entry in Solution Explorer (if necessary). It's helpful to have the model open as you create the required classes. You'll need to create two classes for this example—one for each entity, as shown here:

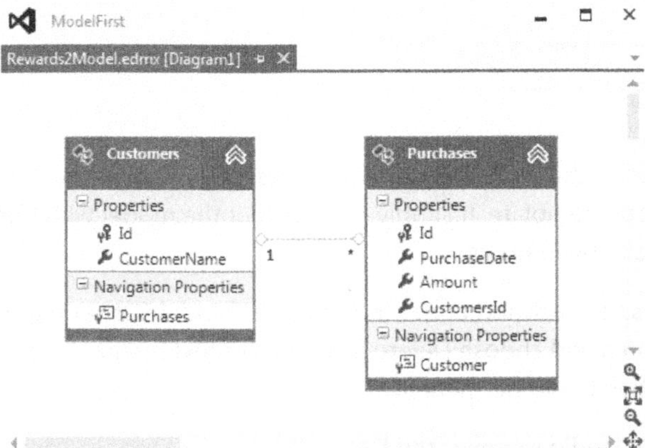

2. Right-click the TestModelFirst entry in Solution Explorer and choose Add | New Item from the context menu. You'll see the Add New Item dialog box shown here:

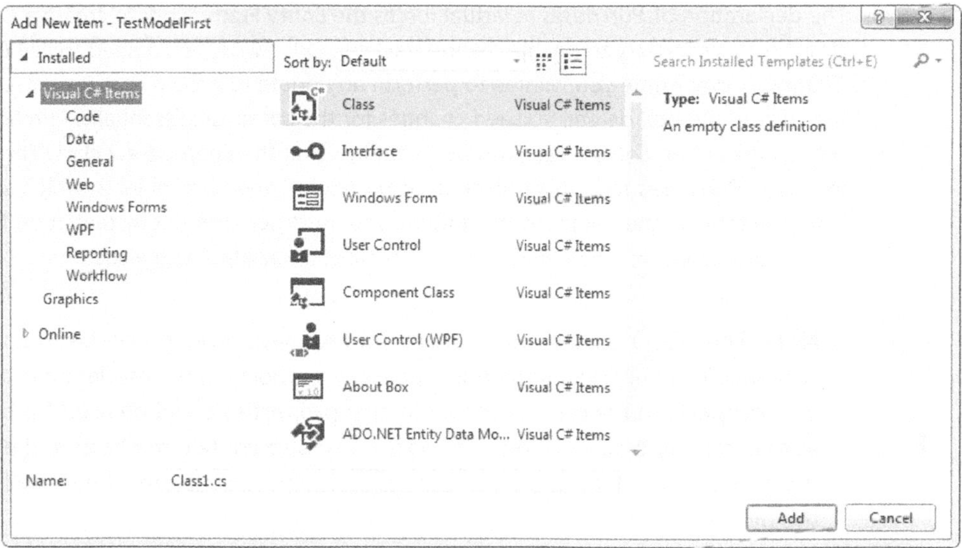

3. Select the Class template as shown, and type **MyCustomers.CS** in the Name field. Click Add. Visual Studio creates a new class file for you.

4. Type the following code into the *Customers* class:

```
namespace TestModelFirst
{
   using System;
   using System.Collections.Generic;

   public class Customers
   {
      public Customers()
      {
         // Automatically obtain a list of purchases from the database.
         this.Purchases = new HashSet<Purchases>();
      }

      // Declare the table properties.
      public int Id { get; set; }
      public string CustomerName { get; set; }

      // Declare the navigational property.
      public virtual ICollection<Purchases> Purchases { get; set; }
   }
}
```

The example code creates a simple set of properties that mimic those used by the model. In order for the code to work at all, you must define properties that match those for both the table and the navigational properties in the model.

Notice that the *Purchases* property is defined as *ICollection<Purchases>*. This declaration ensures you receive a list of purchases to work with from the *Purchases* table.

The declaration of *Purchases* as virtual forces the Entity Framework to create a *DynamicProxy* class for this property to enable change tracking. Otherwise, you'd need to call *Detect Changes()* every time you wanted to perform an update to ensure that *Purchases* contains the current update, delete, and add changes for the database. Essentially, *Purchases* obtains the features of an *EntityObject*, without actually using the *EntityObject* class. The constructor initializes *Purchases* to hold a collection of *HashSet<Purchases>* objects, which are then filled from the table in the database. In addition, you must perform this instantiation to avoid a null-value exception when there are no purchases associated with a customer.

Note The POCO classes you create can always have more properties than the model contains. The only requirement is that every property in the model be represented by a property in the class. These additional properties could be used for tasks such as maintaining business logic. The classes can also contain methods and events—there's no limit on the extra elements you provide, but you must minimally mimic the model.

5. Repeat steps 3 through 5 for the *Purchases* class (using the MyPurchases.CS file). However, you need to type the following code for the *Purchases* class instead of the code shown for the *Customers* class:

```
namespace TestModelFirst
{
   using System;
   using System.Collections.Generic;

   public class Purchases
   {
      // Declare the table properties.
      public int Id { get; set; }
      public System.DateTime PurchaseDate { get; set; }
      public decimal Amount { get; set; }
      public int CustomersId { get; set; }

      // Declare the navigational property.
      public virtual Customers Customer { get; set; }
   }
}
```

Again, this class defines the table and navigational properties. However, because *Customer* is a single object of type *Customers*, you don't need to perform all of the fancy footwork required to make the *Purchases* navigational property work. You can simply declare it as shown.

6. Choose Save All or press Ctrl+Shift+S to save the changes you've made.

Creating an *ObjectContext* class to interact with the POCO classes

At this point, you have a model and a set of classes—neither is aware of the other. While it's desirable for the classes to know nothing about the Entity Framework, the Entity Framework must know about the classes in order to perform any useful work. As a consequence, you need to build an *ObjectContext* class to provide the required connectivity. The following procedure shows how to create the required class to provide the connectivity the Entity Framework requires. (This procedure assumes you've completed the steps in the "Adding the classes" section of the chapter.)

Defining an *ObjectContext* class to manage the POCO

1. Right-click the TestModelFirst entry in Solution Explorer and choose Add | New Item from the context menu. You'll see the Add New Item dialog box.
2. Select the Class template as shown, and type **OCSimplePOCO.CS** in the Name field. Click Add. Visual Studio creates a new class file for you.
3. Type the following code into the *OCSimplePOCO* class:

```
namespace TestModelFirst
{
   using System.Data.Objects;

   class Rewards2ModelContainer : ObjectContext
   {
      // Define internal variables for managing the POCO objects.
      private ObjectSet<Customers> _Customers;
      private ObjectSet<Purchases> _Purchases;

      public Rewards2ModelContainer() :
         base("name=Rewards2ModelContainer", "Rewards2ModelContainer")
      {
         // Instantiate the internal variables.
         _Customers = CreateObjectSet<Customers>();
         _Purchases = CreateObjectSet<Purchases>();
      }

      public ObjectSet<Customers> Customers
      {
         get
         {
            // Return the previously created customer data.
            return _Customers;
         }
      }

      public ObjectSet<Purchases> Purchases
      {
         get
         {
            // Return the previously created purchase data.
```

```
                return _Purchases;
            }
        }
    }
}
```

This is an extremely simplified version of the code you could build to provide full *ObjectContext* support. However, it does serve to demonstrate what is possible. The code begins with a constructor that instantiates two private variables: *_Customers* and *_Purchases*. These two variables provide a context for interacting with the database. The two properties in the example provide read-only access to these private variables. It doesn't look like enough linkage to the do the job, but you'll be surprised when you try it out.

This example provides simplified access to the database in the interest of simplicity. However, you can extend the *Rewards2Container* to provide complete CRUD operation functionality. In the meantime, you do need to comment out the code used to add new records in the example from Chapter 3, "Choosing a workflow."

4. Comment out the following lines in the *btnAdd_Click()* event handler:

```
context.Customers.Add(NewCustomer);
context.Purchases.Add(NewPurchase);
context.SaveChanges();
```

5. Choose Save All or press Ctrl+Shift+S to save the changes you've made.

Testing the POCO application

You've now configured the model, added the necessary POCO classes, and created a class to manage the POCO classes so the Entity Framework can interact with them. The following procedure demonstrates the functionality of the resulting application.

Testing an application that uses POCOs

1. Open Form1.CS and place a breakpoint at this line in the *btnQuery_Click()* event handler:

```
StringBuilder Output =
    new StringBuilder("Customer List:");
```

2. Click Start or press F5. The application compiles and runs.
3. Click Query. The application stops at the breakpoint.
4. Choose Debug | Windows | Locals to display the local objects shown here:

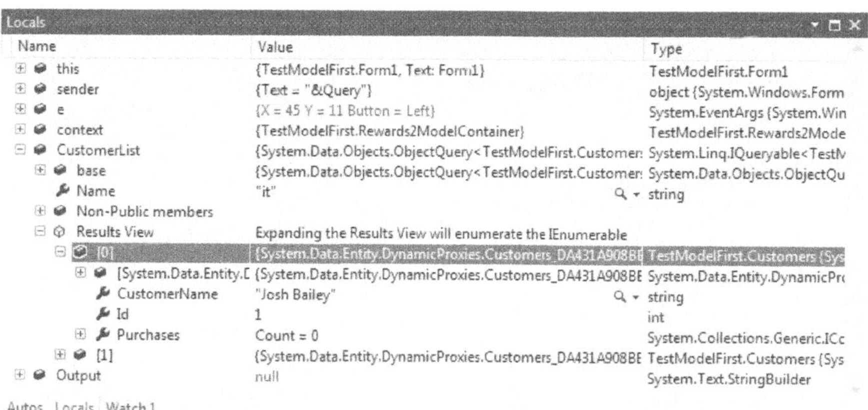

The *CustomerList* object contains a *DynamicProxy* object for each customer, as expected. Each of these entries is assigned a hash value to ensure it retains a unique position within the collection. You can see the *CustomerName* and *Id* values for the first of these entries. In addition, the *Purchases* navigational property is there, and it contains a collection of the correct type. However, the collection says there are zero entries, so let's see what happens next.

5. Click Continue. You'll see the result shown here:

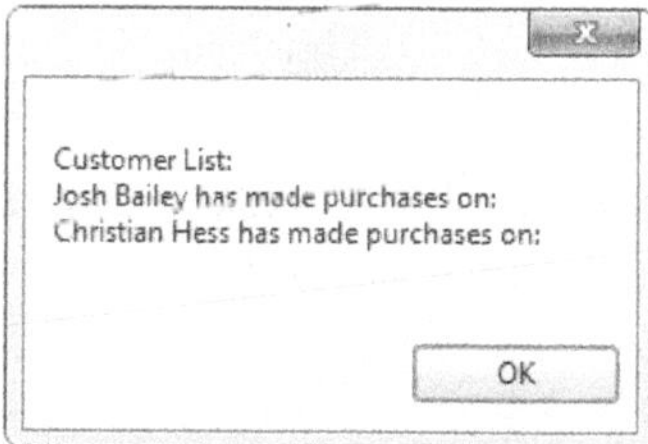
Customer List:
Josh Bailey has made purchases on:
Christian Hess has made purchases on:
OK

The problem is that there's nothing to show for each of the customers. When using POCOs, you must provide some means for retrieving the purchases, because there's no *EntityObject* to provide the required code.

6. Click OK to close the dialog box. Close the application.

7. Modify the query to tell it to obtain the list of purchases, like this:

```
// Obtain the customer list.
var CustomerList =
    from cust in context.Customers.Include("Purchases")
    select cust;
```

8. Click Start or press F5. The application compiles and runs.

9. Click Query. The application stops at the breakpoint.

10. Choose Debug | Windows | Locals to display the local objects. Notice that this time there are purchases in the list.

11. Click Continue. You'll see the result shown here:

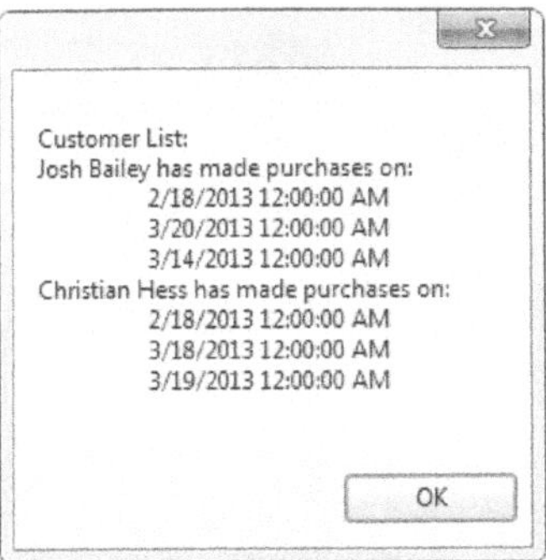
Customer List:
Josh Bailey has made purchases on:
2/18/2013 12:00:00 AM
3/20/2013 12:00:00 AM
3/14/2013 12:00:00 AM
Christian Hess has made purchases on:
2/18/2013 12:00:00 AM
3/18/2013 12:00:00 AM
3/19/2013 12:00:00 AM
OK

12. Click OK to close the dialog box. Close the application.

Creating a *DbContext* class to interact with the POCO classes

Microsoft actually recommends that your connectivity class inherit from *DbContext*, instead of *ObjectContext*. In fact, the setup that the book has used so far automatically generates POCO classes to go with a *DbContext* management class. Unfortunately, if you edit those POCO classes, the automation will overwrite them. This section shows how to manually create POCO classes that you can modify as needed to meet specific needs.

Note The reason this chapter shows both *ObjectContext* and *DbContext* is that many organizations will have existing code that will use *ObjectContext*. It's essential to know how to work with both classes.

A good rule of thumb to follow is to use *DbContext* when creating new projects. Microsoft isn't going to phase *ObjectContext* out any time soon, but *DbContext* offers functionality that *ObjectContext* doesn't provide. In addition, using *DbContext* is much simpler than using *ObjectContext* (see the discussion at *http://blogs.msdn.com/b/efdesign/archive/2010/06/21/productivity-improvements-for-the-entity-framework.aspx* for details). However, even when you contemplate these advantages, you need to also consider whether the third-party products you use rely on *ObjectContext* or *DbContext* to perform their work (some companies have opted to use *ObjectContext* to support people who are using older versions of the Entity Framework). The following procedure shows how to create a class that interacts with POCO classes and inherits from *DbContext*.

Defining a *DbContext* class to manage the POCOs

1. Configure the model to work with POCOs using the steps found in the "Configuring the model" section of the chapter. Don't reuse the *ObjectContext* example.

2. Create POCO classes to use with this example using the steps found in the "Adding the classes" section of the chapter.

3. Right-click the TestModelFirst entry in Solution Explorer and choose Add | New Item from the context menu. You'll see the Add New Item dialog box.

4. Select the Class template as shown, and type **DCSimplePOCO.CS** in the Name field. Click Add. Visual Studio creates a new class file for you.

5. Type the following code into the *DCSimplePOCO* class:

```
namespace TestModelFirst
{
   using System;
   using System.Data.Entity;
   using System.Data.Entity.Infrastructure;

   public partial class Rewards2ModelContainer : DbContext
   {
      public Rewards2ModelContainer()
         : base("name=Rewards2ModelContainer")
      {
      }

      // Create properties to access the POCO classes.
      public DbSet<Customers> Customers { get; set; }
      public DbSet<Purchases> Purchases { get; set; }
   }
}
```

   The first thing you'll notice is that this code is considerably shorter than the *ObjectContext* version. You'll also find out that it's a lot more functional. Using *DbContext* adds a layer to the overall framework, but in doing so you greatly reduce the work you need to perform. All that you really need to do is provide a constructor with the name of the container you want to create and then provide *DbSet* properties for each of the POCO classes.

   When working with *DbContext*, you also don't need to comment out the code for the *btnAdd_Click()* event handler. The proper methods are already in place for adding records using the *Add()* method.

6. Open Form1.CS and place a breakpoint at this line in the *btnQuery_Click()* event handler:

```
StringBuilder Output =
    new StringBuilder("Customer List:");
```

7. Click Start or press F5. The application compiles and runs.

8. Click Query. The application stops at the breakpoint.

9. Choose Debug | Windows | Locals to display the local objects. Notice that all of the data you need is already in place in the *CustomerList* variable.

10. Click Continue. You'll see the output you expected with both the customer and associated purchase data.

11. Click OK to close the dialog box. Close the application.

Creating the classes in a different project

Any large organization is going to have multiple applications that depend on the same Entity Framework model. Trying to keep all of those applications synchronized when each of them creates a separate version of the model would be a nightmare. The best way to perform the task in larger enterprise settings is to use a separate project to hold the model and reference the class from that project. The following sections look at two methods for accomplishing this task.

Using automatic generation

In many cases, you really want to generate POCO classes automatically and have Visual Studio maintain them automatically using the techniques discussed to this point in the book. Fortunately, the automatic method is relatively straightforward. There are a few twists, but nothing you haven't dealt with when creating other application types. The following procedure shows how to create a model in a separate project and access it from an application. The automatically generated model uses POCO classes and a *DbContext* to manage them. However, the POCO classes are automatically generated, which means you can't modify them manually.

Creating an external model automatically

1. Open Visual Studio and choose File | New | Project. You'll see the New Project dialog box.
2. Select the Windows Forms Application template, type **AutoGenerate** in the Name field, provide a path in the Location field, check Create Directory For Solution, and click OK. Visual Studio creates a new Windows Forms project for you.
3. Right-click the Solution entry in Solution Explorer and choose Add | New Project. You'll see the New Project dialog box.
4. Select the Windows folder. Within the Windows folder, select the Class Library template, type **Rewards2Model** in the Name field, and click OK. Visual Studio creates a class library project for you.
5. Close Class1.CS. Right-click its entry in Solution Explorer and choose Delete from the context menu. Click OK when asked whether you'd really like to delete the file.
6. Right-click Rewards2Model in Solution Explorer and choose Add | New Item from the context menu. You'll see the Add New Item dialog box shown here:

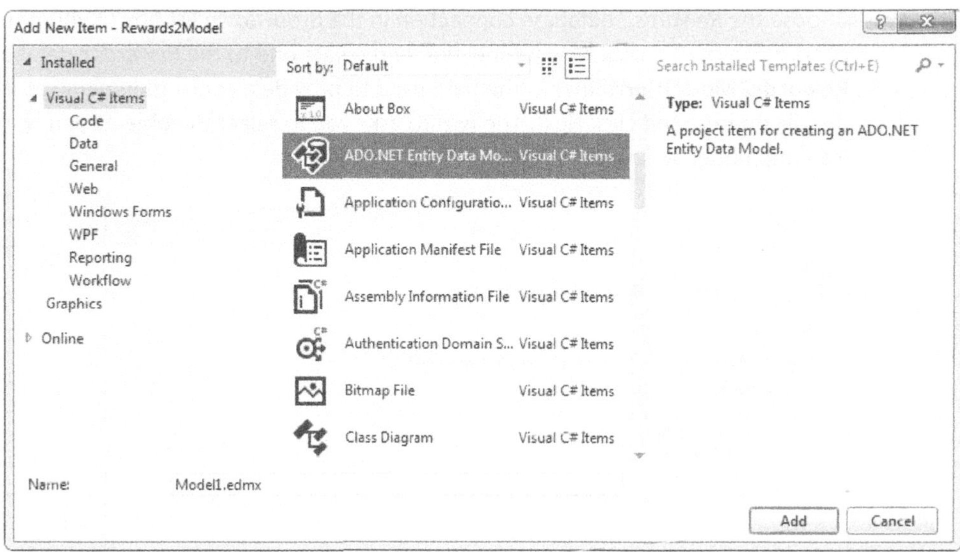

7. Select the ADO.NET Entity Data Model template, type **Rewards2Model** in the Name field, and click Add. Visual Studio starts the Entity Data Model Wizard as shown here:

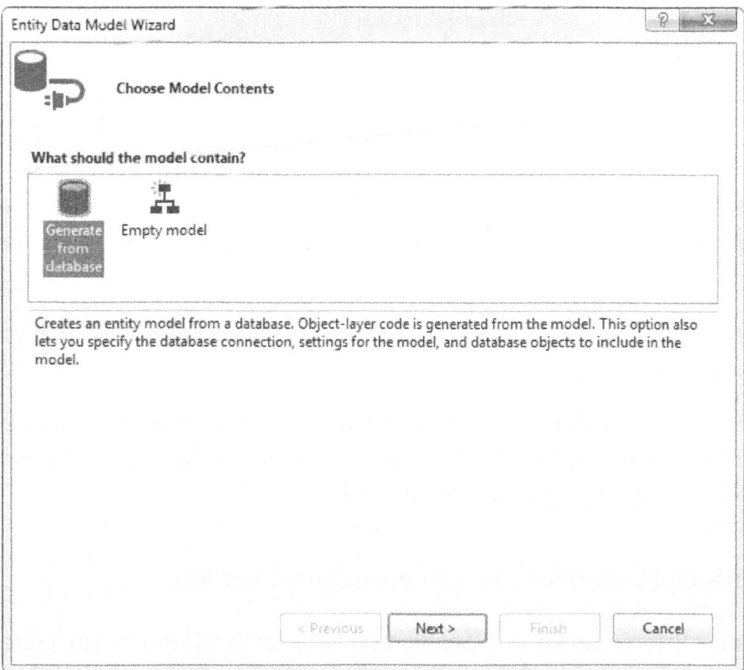

8. Click Next. The wizard asks you to provide details about the connection. This means selecting a database connection (which you should have set up in Visual Studio during earlier examples) and providing a name for referring to that connection.

9. Choose the *Rewards2* database connection in the drop-down list box (if you don't have a connection to use, click New Connection and create one to the *Rewards2* database), type **Rewards2ModelContainer** in the field used to provide a connection name at the bottom of the dialog box, and click Next. The wizard asks you to select the objects you want to import into the model, as shown here:

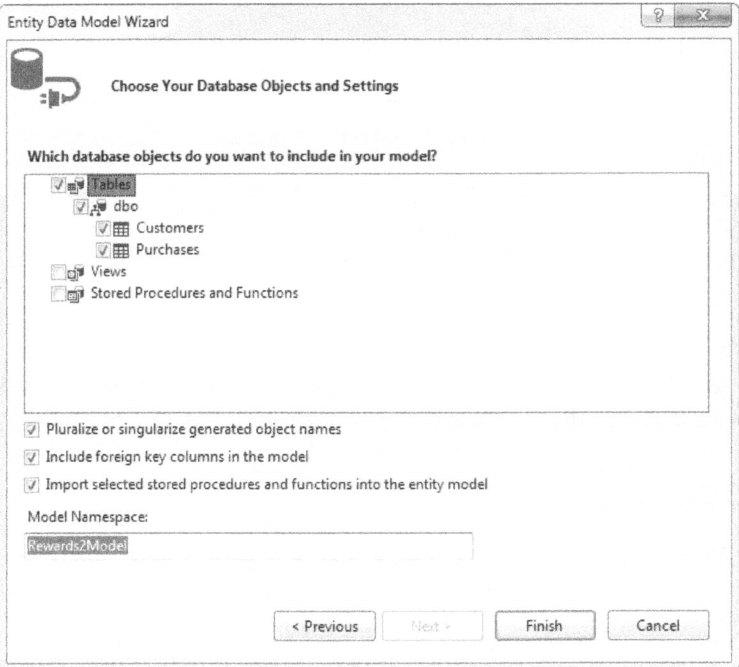

10. Click Tables. The wizard automatically selects both the Customers and *Purchases* tables for you.

11. Click Finish. You'll see an entity diagram appear that contains the entities that you've been working with up until now.

At this point, the model is usable, even though it exists in a separate project. However, you now need to access that model from within the example application. The following steps will help you configure the application for use with the external model.

Configuring the application for use with the external model

1. Right-click the References folder in Solution Explorer for the *AutoGenerate* project and choose Add Reference. You'll see the Reference Manager dialog box.

2. Select the Solution folder and check Rewards2Model, as shown here:

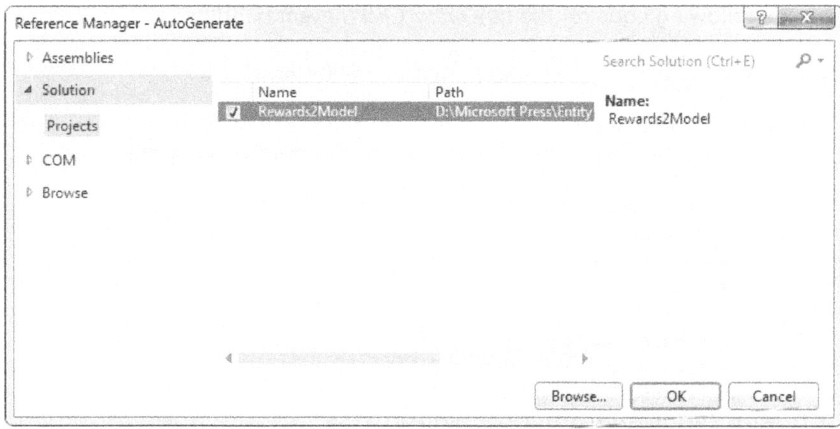

3. Select the Browse folder and use it to locate the SeparateProject\packages\EntityFramework.5.0.0\lib\net45 folder. Within this folder is an EntityFramework.DLL file that you need to select, as shown here:

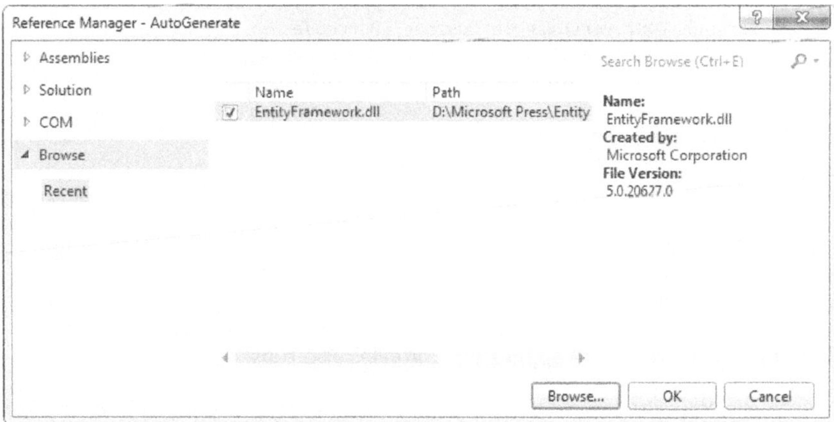

4. Click OK. Visual Studio adds the required references. In addition to these references, you must also use the same connection string as provided by the *Rewards2Model* class. In order to do this, you simply copy the string from one project to the other.

5. Open the App.CONFIG file for the *Rewards2Model* project. Locate the *<connectionStrings>* tag and highlight the entire tag (both the opening and closing tag, plus the *<add>* tag it contains). Press Ctrl+C to copy this information to the clipboard.

6. Open the App.CONFIG file for the *AutoGenerate* project. Place the cursor immediately before the closing *</configuration>* tag and press Ctrl+V to copy the *<connectionStrings>* tag. At this point, you're ready to test the model.

7. Add a new button to *Form1*. Name the button *btnQuery* and set its *Text* property to *&Query*.

8. Double-click *btnQuery* to create a new click event handler.

9. Type the following code for the *btnQuery_Click()* event handler:

```
private void btnQuery_Click(object sender, EventArgs e)
{
    // Create the context.
    Rewards2ModelContainer context = new Rewards2ModelContainer();

    // Obtain the customer list.
    var CustomerList =
        from cust in context.Customers
        select cust;

    // Process each customer in the list.
    StringBuilder Output =
        new StringBuilder("Customer List:");
    foreach (var Customer in CustomerList)
    {
        // Create a customer entry for each customer.
        Output.Append("\r\n" + Customer.CustomerName +
            " has made purchases on: ");

        // Process each purchase for that particular customer.
        foreach (var Purchase in Customer.Purchases)
            Output.Append("\r\n\t" + Purchase.PurchaseDate);
    }

    // Display the result on screen.
    MessageBox.Show(Output.ToString());
}
```

10. Add the following *using* statement to the beginning of the file:

```
using Rewards2Model;
```

11. Click Start or press F5. The application compiles and runs.

12. Click Query. You'll see the expected result in the dialog box (the same result shown for the other examples in this chapter).

Using manual generation

There are many situations in which you won't want to use automatic code generation, but will still want to put your code in a separate project. Of course, the most common time you'll want to take this approach is when the code already exists before you begin using the Entity Framework. As with automatic code generation in a separate project, you'll often see this technique used in the environments of larger organizations, where multiple applications will require access to the same model. The following procedure shows how to create the model code in a separate project.

Creating an external model manually

1. Open Visual Studio and choose File | New | Project. You'll see the New Project dialog box.

2. Select the Windows Forms Application template, type **ManuallyGenerate** in the Name field, provide a path in the Location field, check Create Directory For Solution, and click OK. Visual Studio creates a new Windows Forms project for you.

3. Right-click the Solution entry in Solution Explorer and choose Add | New Project. You'll see the New Project dialog box.

4. Select the Windows folder. Within the Windows folder, select the Class Library template, type **Rewards2Model** in the Name field, and click OK. Visual Studio creates a class library project for you.

5. Right-click the References folder for the *Rewards2Model* project and choose Manage NuGet Packages from the context menu. Select the Online\All folder in the resulting dialog box so that you see the various packages available from online sources. You'll see the Rewards2Model - Manage NuGet Packages dialog box shown here:

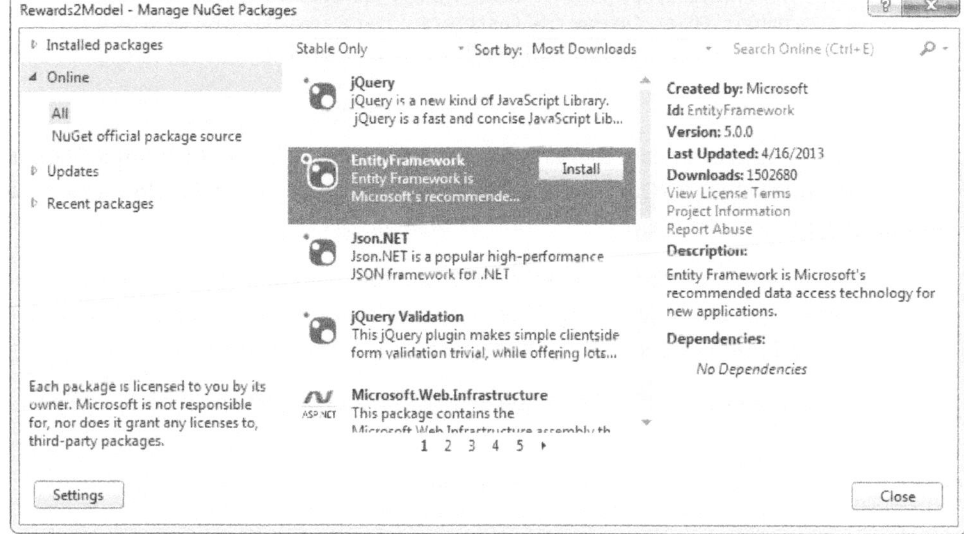

6. Click Install. If you see a licensing agreement dialog box, simply click I Accept to accept the licensing terms and to continue the installation process.

7. Click Close to close the Rewards2Model - Manage NuGet Packages dialog box.

8. Close Class1.CS. Right-click its entry in Solution Explorer and choose Delete from the context menu. Click OK when asked whether you'd really like to delete the file.

9. Create POCO classes to use with this example using the steps found in the "Adding the classes" section of the chapter. However, create these classes within the *Rewards2Model* project, rather than the *ManuallyGenerate* project. In addition, you place the classes within the *Rewards2Model* namespace.

10. Right-click the Rewards2Model entry in Solution Explorer and choose Add | New Item from the context menu. You'll see the Add New Item dialog box.

11. Select the Class template as shown, and type **DCSimplePOCO.CS** in the Name field. Click Add. Visual Studio creates a new class file for you.

12. Type the following code into the *DCSimplePOCO* class:

```
namespace Rewards2Model
{
   using System;
   using System.Data.Entity;
   using System.Data.Entity.Infrastructure;

   public partial class Rewards2ModelContainer : DbContext
   {
      public Rewards2ModelContainer()
         : base("name=Rewards2ConnectionString")
      {
      }

      // Create properties to access the POCO classes.
      public DbSet<Customers> Customers { get; set; }
      public DbSet<Purchases> Purchases { get; set; }
   }
}
```

This code is essentially the same as the code you used in the "Creating a *DbContext* class to interact with the POCO classes" section of the chapter. The main difference is that it appears in a different namespace.

However, notice that the *base()* method accepts a string that provides access to a container name or a connection string. There's no connection string in App.CONFIG. As a consequence, the code won't work. The next several steps will address this issue.

13. Open the App.CONFIG file for the *Rewards2Model* project and type the following code:

```
<connectionStrings>
   <add name="Rewards2ConnectionString"
        providerName="System.Data.SqlClient"
        connectionString="Server=.\SQLEXPRESS;
            Database=Rewards2;
            Trusted_Connection=True"/>
</connectionStrings>
```

Notice that this is a simple connection string and not any sort of entity connection. In this case, you're using a code-first approach to create a connection, which means the application isn't using .SSDL, .CSDL, or .MSL files. The Entity Framework takes care of all of these requirements for you in the background. In this case, you provide a name for the connection string, the name of a provider, and the connection string itself. This connection string points to the *Rewards2* database in the local copy of SQL Server Express.

14. Perform the steps shown in the "Configuring the application for use with the external model" procedure found in the "Using automatic generation" section to configure the application for use with the manually generated model. Of course, you'll use the *ManuallyGenerate* project,

rather than the *AutoGenerate* project. In addition, you must provide the *Include()* method as part of your query, as shown here, or the Entity Framework won't load the purchases information:

```
// Obtain the customer list.
var CustomerList =
    from cust in context.Customers.Include("Purchases")
    select cust;
```

Creating and using event handlers

In some situations, you want to know when a particular event occurs when working with the Entity Framework. For example, you may want to know when the Entity Framework is about to save changes to the database to ensure the changes are correct, or simply to display status information to the user about the changes. Events typically occur in two situations:

- When standard Entity Framework events are fired. These events, *ObjectMaterialized* and *SavingChanges*, are part of the *ObjectContext* object underlying the *DbContext* object.
- When a POCO class includes custom events that are used to handle business logic or to signify task status.

Of course, you can probably make a case for other scenarios in which events could occur, but these are the most typical. The following sections explore these two typical event-handling situations.

Handling *ObjectContext* events

Beneath every *DbContext* object lies an *ObjectContext* object that you can access when needed. The situations in which such access is required are few, but important. One of the most important reasons to access the *ObjectContext* is to gain access to the *ObjectMaterialized* and *SavingChanges* events so that you can provide a handler for them. The following procedure shows how to create an event handler for *ObjectMaterialized* so that you can display a status message to the user. However, working with *SavingChanges* follows the same pattern as this example does.

Handling default Entity Framework events

1. Create a copy of the *ModelFirst (DbContext)* example described in the "Creating a *DbContext* class to interact with the POCO classes" section of this chapter. Use this new copy in place of the original for this example.
2. Open the DCSimplePOCO.CS file. You handle Entity Framework events in the class used to provide the interface between the Entity Framework and the POCO classes.
3. Add the following *using* statements to the others provided with the class:

```
using System.Data.Objects;
```

```
using System.Windows.Forms;
```

4. Add the following code (in bold) to the class constructor:

```
public Rewards2ModelContainer()
   : base("name=Rewards2ModelContainer")
{
   // Add an event handler for the ObjectMaterialized event.
   ((IObjectContextAdapter)this).ObjectContext.ObjectMaterialized +=
       this.ObjectContext_OnObjectMaterialized;
}
```

Notice the technique used to provide access to the *ObjectContext* underlying the *DbContext* object. You work with the current instance of the object and coerce it to an *IObjectContextAdapter* type. This cast allows access to the *ObjectContext*, which provides access to the *ObjectMaterialized* event. Of course, *ObjectContext_OnObjectMaterialized()* is the event handler. In this case, the event handler simply displays a status message.

5. Add the following event handler to the *Rewards2ModelContainer* class:

```
// Define an event handler for the ObjectMaterialized event.
public void ObjectContext_OnObjectMaterialized(
   object sender, ObjectMaterializedEventArgs e)
{
   // Verify the type is correct.
   if (sender.GetType() == typeof(ObjectContext))

      // Display messages only for customers.
      if (e.Entity.GetType().BaseType == typeof(Customers))

         // Display a status message.
         MessageBox.Show(((ObjectContext)sender).DefaultContainerName +
            " has materialized " + e.Entity.ToString() + " for " +
            ((Customers)e.Entity).CustomerName + ".");
}
```

Both *sender* and *e* provide useful information, so the example shows both. The *sender* is an *ObjectContext*, so you can discover information such as the container's name.

The *e* is the actual entity created from the POCO class. Remember that these objects are created as dynamic proxies. In order to determine the actual type of the object, you must access the *BaseType* property as shown.

In order to work with the *Entity*, you must cast the *e.Entity* property as the proper type first, and then access the individual properties as shown. The output is simply a message box telling you that a particular customer entry has been materialized.

6. Click Start or press F5. The application compiles and runs.

7. Click Query. You'll see the materialized object information shown here for each customer. After the individual customers are displayed, you'll see the expected query output.

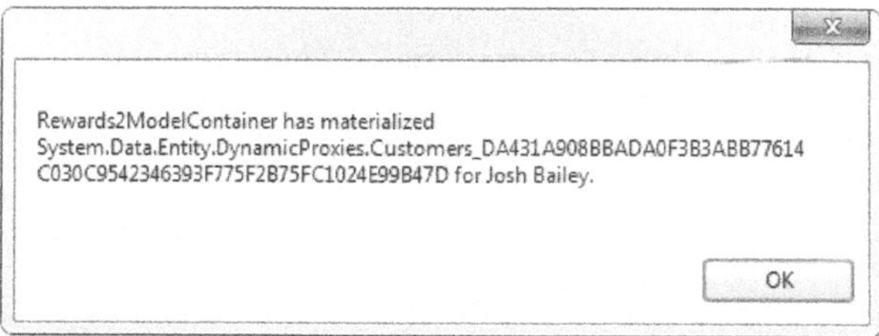
Rewards2ModelContainer has materialized
System.Data.Entity.DynamicProxies.Customers_DA431A908BBADA0F3B3ABB77614
C030C9542346393F775F2B75FC1024E99B47D for Josh Bailey.
OK

Creating and handling custom events

You can use custom events in all sorts of ways with your application. In this example, the purpose is simple: to register the occurrence of a specific event. Whenever the *CustomerName* field is accessed, the *Customers* object will fire an event telling about the kind of access and which customer was accessed. An event like this could be used in all sorts of ways, such as informing an administrator about potentially unauthorized access to sensitive information. The following procedure shows you a generalized technique for adding custom events to your application (with an emphasis on the particular event that occurs in this case).

Developing and using a custom status event

1. Create a copy the *ModelFirst (DbContext)* example described in the "Creating a *DbContext* class to interact with the POCO classes" section of this chapter. Use this new copy in place of the original for this example.

2. Open the MyCustomers.CS file. The custom events you create appear within the POCO class files for the most part. However, you could realistically create them anywhere.

3. Create a delegate and event within the *Customers* class using the following code:

```
// Define a delegate to signify that a customer has been created.
public delegate void NameAccess(object sender, NameArgs e);

// Define an event.
public event NameAccess NameAccessed;
```

   Notice that the delegate relies on a custom event arguments class. You'll create this class later in the procedure. In most cases, you want to create one or more custom event arguments instead of shoehorning an existing event arguments class—except when the existing class is a precise fit (there aren't any precise fits in this case).

4. Redefine the *CustomerName* property as shown here:

```
private String _CustomerName;
public string CustomerName
{
   get
   {
      // Tell everyone there has been name access.
      if (this.NameAccessed != null)
```

```
            this.NameAccessed(this,
               new NameArgs { Name = this._CustomerName, IsGet = true });

         // Return the default value.
         return _CustomerName;
      }

      set
      {
         // Tell everyone there has been name access.
         if (this.NameAccessed != null)
            this.NameAccessed(this,
               new NameArgs { Name = this._CustomerName, IsGet = false });

         // Set the default value.
         _CustomerName = value;
      }
   }
```

This code simply fires the event each time the *CustomerName* property is accessed in some way. The *NameArgs Name* property contains the name of the customer that's affected by the change, and the *IsGet* property is *true* when the change is a *get*, rather than a *set*. The two properties tell you how the property has changed so that you can better gauge what sort of access is being performed. You could extend the *NameArgs* class to include additional information.

5. Add a new class immediately after the *Customers* class, as shown here:

```
// A custom event arguments class used to define access target and type.
public class NameArgs : EventArgs
{
   // Defines the customer's name.
   public string Name { get; set; }

   // Determines whether this is a get or a set.
   public bool IsGet { get; set; }
}
```

6. Open the DCSimplePOCO.CS file. You handle Entity Framework events in the class used to provide the interface between the Entity Framework and the POCO classes.

7. Add the following *using* statement to the others provided with the class:

```
// Added for the event handler.
using System.Windows.Forms;
```

8. Add the following code (in bold) to the class constructor:

```
public Rewards2ModelContainer()
   : base("name=Rewards2ModelContainer")
{
```

```
    // Add an event handler for each customer.
    foreach (var Customer in this.Customers)
        Customer.NameAccessed += Customer_NameAccessed;
}
```

One of the mistakes that would be easy to make is to forget that you're working with a *DbSet* object that contains multiple customers. In order to ensure that every customer change is recorded, you must attach the event handler to each customer separately, as shown in the code. This might seem like a painful way to do things at first, but it's actually quite useful. Using this approach, you can filter the records and attach event handlers only to those that meet certain criteria.

9. Add the following event handler to the Rewards2ModelContainer class.

```
// Provide an event handler for the event.
void Customer_NameAccessed(object sender, NameArgs e)
{
    if (e.IsGet)
        MessageBox.Show(e.Name + " Retreived!");
    else
        MessageBox.Show(e.Name + " Changed!");
}
```

This event handler simply tells you which event has happened and on which record. In this case, *sender* isn't very helpful because it contains the dynamic proxy. The values within the proxy haven't been filled out yet, because the event is fired before the property returns a value. Consequently, you really do need to use *NameArgs* to access the information.

10. Click Start or press F5. The application compiles and runs.

11. Click Query. You'll see the access information shown here for each customer. After the individual customers are displayed, you'll see the expected query output.

Creating custom methods

Your POCO classes could contain custom methods for any number of reasons. One common reason to include a method is to output formatted data. This ensures that the output meets company requirements and also reduces the time each developer spends providing formatted output. The following procedure shows how to create a custom method that outputs the customer data in a formatted manner.

Developing and using a custom method

1. Create a copy of the *ModelFirst (DbContext)* example described in the "Creating a *DbContext* class to interact with the POCO classes" section of this chapter. Use this new copy in place of the original for this example.

2. Open the MyCustomers.CS file.

3. Add the following method to the *Customers* class to allow for formatted output:

```
// Declare a custom method.
public string ToFormattedString()
{
   // Create a StringBuilder to hold the formatted string.
   StringBuilder Output = new StringBuilder();

   // Add the customer's name.
   Output.Append(this.CustomerName +
            " has made purchases on: ");

   // Add each purchase on a separate line.
   foreach (Purchases Purchase in this.Purchases)
      Output.Append("\r\n\t" + Purchase.PurchaseDate);

   // Return the formatted string.
   return Output.ToString();
}
```

   This method essentially draws the formatting code out of the event handler you've been working with up to this point. Placing the formatted output in the POCO class reduces the work needed to create formatted output later.

4. Add a new button to *Form1*. Name the button *btnQuery2* and set its *Text* property to *Query &2*.

5. Double-click btnQuery2 to create a new click event handler.

6. Type the following code for the *btnQuery2_Click()* event handler:

```
private void bntQuery2_Click(object sender, EventArgs e)
{
   // Create the context.
   Rewards2ModelContainer context = new Rewards2ModelContainer();

   // Obtain the customer list.
   var CustomerList =
       from cust in context.Customers
       select cust;

   // Process each customer in the list.
   StringBuilder Output =
       new StringBuilder("Customer List:");

   // Create a customer entry for each customer.
```

```
    foreach (var Customer in CustomerList)
        Output.Append("\r\n" + Customer.ToFormattedString());

    // Display the result on screen.
    MessageBox.Show(Output.ToString());
}
```

Using the new *ToFormattedString()* method does make the event handler code shorter, simpler, and easier to understand. Of course, it also hides implementation details.

7. Click Start or press F5. The application compiles and runs.
8. Click Query 2. You'll see the output you expected with both the customer and associated purchase data.
9. Click OK to close the dialog box. Close the application.

Creating custom properties

Properties take many forms in database applications. The database contains raw data. In the interests of using less space, making the database more reliable, and enhancing application performance, many Database Administrators (DBAs) only include raw data. If you want a calculated value, you need to use the raw data as a starting point and perform the calculation. In the following example, the class performs the calculation for you. All you need to do is access the custom property that contains it. The following procedure shows a technique for creating and using custom properties with your POCO class. This example continues using the example from the "Creating custom methods" section of the chapter.

Developing and using a custom calculated property

1. Add the following property to the *Customers* class to calculate the total purchase amount for each customer:

```
// Declare a custom property.
public Decimal PurchaseTotal
{
    get
    {
        // Create a variable to hold the total.
        Decimal Total = 0;

        // Calculate the purchase total.
        foreach (Purchases Purchase in this.Purchases)
            Total += Purchase.Amount;

        // Return the total to the caller.
        return Total;
    }
}
```

Notice that this property is read-only. Most calculated properties take the same form because you won't save the information to the database. The information is calculated each time the records are loaded to ensure you get the correct result.

2. Add a new button to *Form1*. Name the button *btnQuery3* and set its *Text* property to *Query &3*.

3. Double-click btnQuery3 to create a new click event handler.

4. Type the following code for the *btnQuery3_Click()* event handler:

```
private void btnQuery3_Click(object sender, EventArgs e)
{
   // Create the context.
   Rewards2ModelContainer context = new Rewards2ModelContainer();

   // Obtain the customer list.
   var CustomerList =
       from cust in context.Customers
       select cust;

   // Process each customer in the list.
   StringBuilder Output =
       new StringBuilder("Customer List:");

   foreach (var Customer in CustomerList)
   {
      // Create a customer entry for each customer.
      Output.Append("\r\n" + Customer.CustomerName +
          " has made these purchases: ");

      // Process each purchase for that particular customer.
      foreach (var Purchase in Customer.Purchases)
         Output.Append("\r\n\t" + Purchase.PurchaseDate +
            " for $" + Purchase.Amount.ToString());

      // Add the purchase total.
      Output.Append("\r\nwith a total of: $" + Customer.PurchaseTotal);
   }

   // Display the result on screen.
   MessageBox.Show(Output.ToString());
}
```

This event handler adds some information about the customer to the output. In this case, you see each purchase amount and then the total of the purchases on a separate line.

5. Click Start or press F5. The application compiles and runs.

6. Click Query 3. You'll see the output shown here:

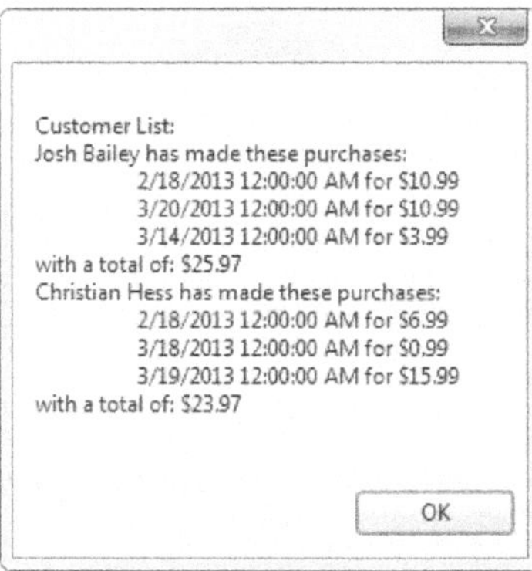
Customer List:
Josh Bailey has made these purchases:
2/18/2013 12:00:00 AM for $10.99
3/20/2013 12:00:00 AM for $10.99
3/14/2013 12:00:00 AM for $3.99
with a total of: $25.97
Christian Hess has made these purchases:
2/18/2013 12:00:00 AM for $6.99
3/18/2013 12:00:00 AM for $0.99
3/19/2013 12:00:00 AM for $15.99
with a total of: $23.97
OK

7. Click OK to close the dialog box. Close the application.

Getting started with the Entity Framework

This chapter has demonstrated techniques for including POCO classes in your Entity Framework application. For the most part, these techniques are generalized so that developers from a wide range of disciplines can use them. The important concept to take away from this chapter is that your entity classes need not actually inherit from *EntityObject* to work with the Entity Framework. Yes, there are significant benefits to inheriting from *EntityObject*, including the use of automation to maintain your application, but it isn't absolutely essential.

This chapter has discussed a relatively complex topic. What you'll want to do is to perform a little more research if you're not familiar with some of the technologies involved, such as DDD and agile. It's also a great idea to work with the examples and spend time viewing how they work with the debugger. Try variations of the examples on your own until you know that you fully understand the concepts presented in the chapter. Most importantly, start thinking about how you can apply what you've learned in the chapter to actual working applications that you maintain. It may be that you'll be able to use the Entity Framework in ways that you hadn't envisioned at the outset because of the POCO support it provides.

Chapter 15, "Mapping data types to properties," moves on to the topic of mapping data types to properties. In this chapter, you discover techniques you can use to make data types that the .NET Framework doesn't support natively work with the Entity Framework. Manually mapping data types to the Entity Framework is another task that you commonly perform when working with POCO classes. However, it's also something you may have to do even when using standard *Entity* objects because some database projects require these custom complex types to describe a particular kind of object fully.

Chapter 14 quick reference

To	Do this
Ensure your application has maximum compatibility with older versions of the Entity Framework	Create a management class that inherits from *ObjectContext*. Using *ObjectContext* also makes it possible to use a number of third-party libraries that don't support *DbContext*. In addition, most online examples rely on *ObjectContext*, rather than *DbContext*, so using *ObjectContext* allows you to receive more sources of information.
Ensure your application reduces complexity and obtains the latest functionality provided by the Entity Framework	Create a management class that inherits from *DbContext*. Using *DbContext* means that your code will be easier to follow and far simpler to create. In addition, *DbContext* performs many tasks automatically for you behind the scenes.
Create POCO classes that offer the maximum performance and are easy to manage	Manually create the classes so that the class names and properties precisely match the model you plan to use. While this option does offer opportunities for performance optimization and better documentation, it's also more error prone.
Save time and create POCO classes that are generally error free the first time	Use an automatic generation tool to create the POCO classes. This chapter shows how to use a template-driven tool that creates acceptable code for most needs.
Create new projects that use the same model in an enterprise environment	Use automatic code generation techniques and place the result in a separate project so that each of the applications can access the model separately.
Use existing code within an enterprise environment	Rely on manual code generation techniques and place the result in a separate project so that each of the applications can access the model separately.
Handle Entity Framework–specific events	Access the *ObjectContext* object underlying the *DbContext* object and use it to define an event handler for either the *ObjectMaterialized* or *SavingChanges* event.
Create and use custom events	Add the delegate and event to your POCO class. Add the event handler code to the class used to provide an *ObjectContext* or *DbContext* for the POCO class.
Create and use custom methods	Simply add the method to the POCO class best suited to meet the requirement. You access the method as you would any other .NET method.
Create and use custom properties	Determine the property type and add it to the POCO class best suited to meet the requirement. Remember that most calculated properties are read-only because the information isn't saved anywhere. You access the property as you would any other .NET property.

CHAPTER 15

Mapping data types to properties

After completing the chapter, you'll be able to

- Define and configure typical automation mapping configuration options.
- Specify and map the standard data types.
- Specify and map enumerated data types.
- Specify and map complex data types.
- Specify and map geography and geometry spatial data types.

Entity Framework automation generally does a great job of mapping types in your database to types that the .NET Framework can understand. In fact, you've seen this automation at work in many of the chapters of this book so far. Most applications will make use of the automatic mappings that the Entity Framework provides.

There are situations where you want to provide custom mapping of standard data types, or you need to provide the Entity Framework with the information required to properly map data types. An example of the first situation is when you want to use a code-first workflow with an existing database that already has a schema defined or when working with Plain Old CLR Object (POCO) classes. Not only will you need to define a custom connection string (as shown in the "Using manual generation" section of Chapter 14, "Creating custom entities"), but you'll very likely need to create a custom data mapping to accommodate both the existing classes and the existing database schema. An example of the second situation is when you use an enumerated type or create a complex custom type (or rely on a complex custom type that already exists). This chapter explores both situations using enumerated data types and the geography and geometry spatial types.

Part of the problem for most developers is determining precisely when to employ custom mapping techniques. There are many situations where you really do want to use the automation simply to make the application-programming environment a little simpler. However, it's equally important not to pound your head against the proverbial wall trying to make the automation do something it can't. This chapter helps you understand when to use custom mapping, as well as how and why to use it.

Defining custom mapping

There are some misconceptions as to what custom mapping is all about. For example, when you use the Entity Data Model Designer to add support for an enumeration, as you did in the "Working with enumerations" section of Chapter 2, "Looking more closely at queries," you aren't really performing custom mapping. Some texts may talk about it as custom mapping, but what you're really doing in this case is configuring the automation, which is an entirely different task. Configuring the automation is the step after relying on the automation alone to discover the data types and map them automatically for you. However, you're still relying on the automation to perform its task.

Custom mapping is the act of coding a mapping solution. In other words, you take control over the mapping process away from the Entity Framework. You draw the Entity Framework a map using code and describe precisely how to represent the data types in the database to the .NET application. Of course, full control over the mapping process comes with additional coding, a higher chance for errors, additional debugging, and potential reliability problems. It's important to create custom mapping solutions carefully and to test them thoroughly before you deploy them to the production environment.

Understanding mapping automation configuration

The book has shown you a number of methods for configuring the Entity Framework automation so that it performs tasks in a reliable manner that specifically meets your needs. For example, you can use enumerations to ensure that a user can't provide inaccurate data to the database when the values for the field in question are known during design time. In the "Making views writable" section of Chapter 9, "Interaction with views," you relied on the automation to make it possible to insert data into a table using a view. The point is that you can use the automation in all sorts of ways to create a customized model. With this in mind, the following sections provide an overview of some of the ways in which you can use the automation to solve specific types of mapping issues.

Note This chapter doesn't discuss the complex topic of inheritance relationships, where one entity inherits from another. In this case, you'd see the base class used for inheritance purposes in the Base Type property for that particular entity. The base class is normally defined as *abstract*. You can learn more about the mechanics of performing this task at *http://msdn.microsoft.com/library/bb738479.aspx*. Another good article on the topic appears at *http://blogs.microsoft.co.il/blogs/gilf/archive/2010/01/22/table-per-type-inheritance-in-entity-framework.aspx*. Chapter 16, "Performing advanced management tasks," will also touch on the topic from a design perspective.

Configuring properties

There are many situations in which you can achieve a desired result by modifying a model property. In some cases, the change immediately affects the application. For example, change the visibility of a getter or setter, and the application will automatically reflect the change. In other cases, you must update the database (by right-clicking the model and choosing Generate Database From Model from the context menu) to see the change you've made. For example, changing the Max Length property won't make the application behave differently until you make that change to the database itself.

Configuring model properties

1. Copy the LINQ query version of the *ModelFirst* example you created in Chapter 6, "Manipulating data using LINQ," to a new folder, and use this new copy for this example (rather than the copy you created in Chapter 6).

> **Note** The LINQ version of the *ModelFirst* example in Chapter 6 appears in the *ModelFirst* (LINQ Query) folder of the downloadable source code. If you created your own version of the example, the folder name will probably be different.

2. Open the Rewards2Model.EDMX file by double-clicking its entry in Solution Explorer.

3. Choose View | Other Windows | Entity Data Model Browser. You'll see the Model Browser window shown here:

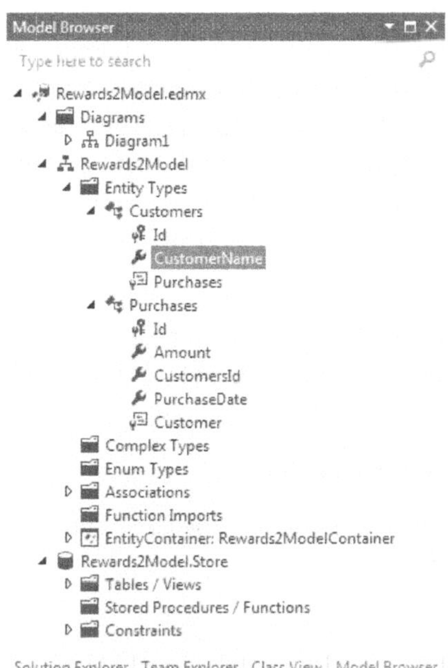

The vast majority of property changes you make will appear as part of the model structure, which is *Rewards2Model* in this case. Each entity type is placed in a different folder to make it easier to find a particular type when working with a complex model. Selecting various folders, entities, and properties, and viewing their properties in the Properties window, will help you get a better idea of what sort of configuration changes are available.

4. Drill down to the *Rewards2Model\Entity Types\Customers\CustomerName* property and highlight it.

5. Choose View | Properties Window. You'll see the Properties window shown here:

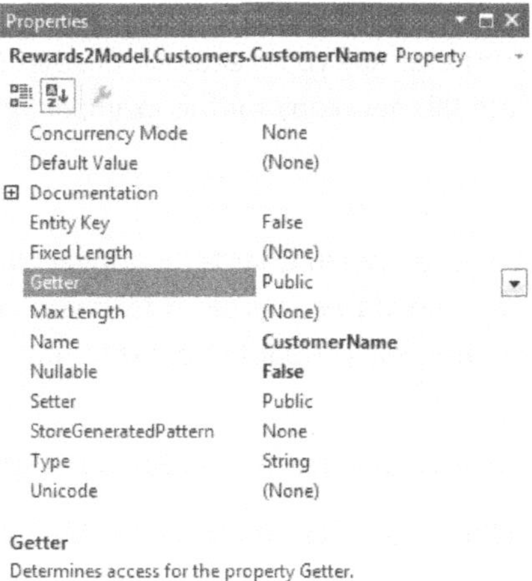

You have already seen the *Concurrency Mode* property used in the "Using field-specific concurrency" section of Chapter 12, "Overcoming concurrency issues." A number of the examples have also explored the *Entity Key* and *StoreGeneratedPattern* properties. The *Default Value* property makes it possible for you to assign a default value to any given field, which reduces the risk of exceptions when a user doesn't supply a value for fields that have the *Nullable* property set to *False*, as shown here. In some cases, setting the *Type* property can help you reduce the risk of errors and make it easier to code a solution. You'll see this type of change used later in the chapter.

6. Set the *Getter* property to *Private*. This will make it impossible to access the value. You could use this setting to hide information from the viewer in a way that works at one of the lowest levels of the application.

7. Choose Build | Build Solution. The application won't build.

8. Choose View | Error List. You'll see a message telling you that the application can't use this property because it's inaccessible, as shown here:

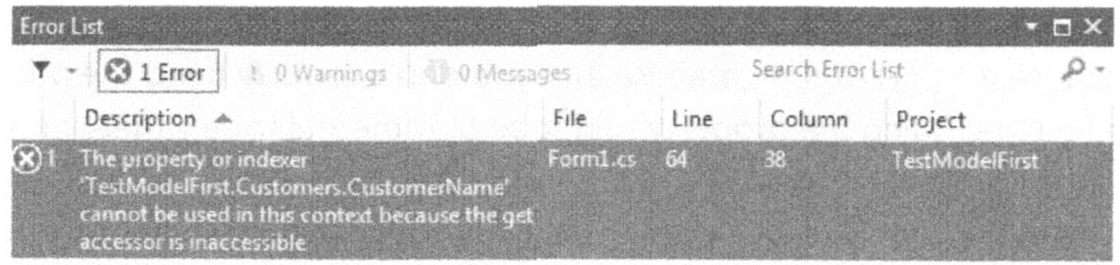

9. Set the *Getter* property to *Public*.

10. Choose Build | Build Solution. The application builds as it did before. The changes you make to the model reflect how and when the user interacts with the database. For example, you could choose to make the *Setter* property of the *Id* field private to keep the user from attempting to change the generated identifier value (not that the database would allow this change anyway, but it would reduce the probability of an exception).

Changing property mapping

You've already seen one case of property mapping in the book—when you worked with an enumerated type in the "Working with enumerations" section of Chapter 2. In that case, you converted an *Int32* property, *FavoriteColor*, to an enumerated type using the automation provided by this latest version of the Entity Framework (before this version, working with enumerated types required more than a little effort on the part of the developer). Chapter 2 didn't show the effect of using an enumerated type on the mapping. Open the *GetUserFavorites* example from Chapter 2 again. Open the *UserFavoritesModel.EDMX* file by double-clicking its entry in Solution Explorer. Select the *FavoriteColor* property and choose View | Other Windows | Entity Data Model Mapping Details. You'll see the Mapping Details window shown here:

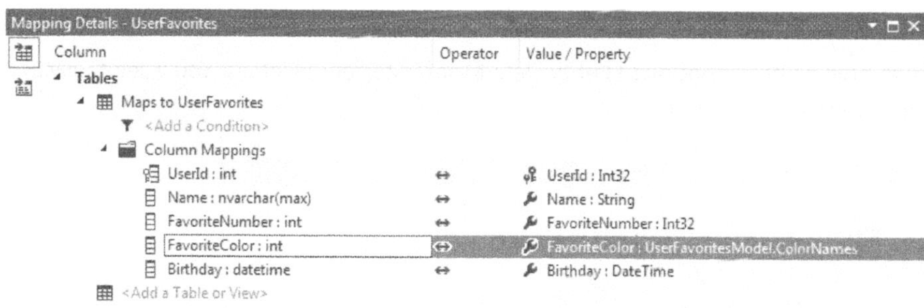

Even though the property mapping is accomplished through the designer, in this case, it shows up as part of the Mapping Details dialog box. The Mapping Details dialog box tells you that the mapping is a particular kind of enumeration that's supplied as part of the XML in the *UserFavoritesModel.EDMX* file. You'll see later that the mapping can start out as part of an application code file.

In some cases, you don't want to map a particular column to a property. The column appears as part of the model because it's part of the database, but you don't actually need the property as part of the application. In fact, including the property might be detrimental for a variety of reasons, such as maintaining application security. In this case, you can click the drop-down list box in the Value / Property column for the particular field you want to remove from the result set and click <Delete>. Microsoft Visual Studio will remove the mapping, and that particular field will be inaccessible.

Filtering the data

It's possible to filter data as part of the model. Using this approach means the application sees less data without using any filtering as part of the query. You use this approach when the application only requires a subset of the information from the database during normal operation. For example, a user may only need to see customer records that have a specific characteristic. Downloading all of the records from the database wastes resources and makes the application slower, so this form of model-based filtering enhances overall application speed. Reducing the availability of records the user doesn't need to see also enhances overall application security. The following procedure describes how to filter data at the model level.

Configuring a model to use filtering

1. Copy the LINQ query version of the *ModelFirst* example you created in Chapter 6 to a new folder, and use this new copy for this example (rather than the copy you created in Chapter 6).
2. Open the *Rewards2Model*.EDMX file by double-clicking its entry in Solution Explorer. You'll see the model appear on screen.
3. Select the *Customers* entity.
4. Choose View | Other Windows | Entity Data Model Mapping Details. You'll see the Mapping Details window shown here:

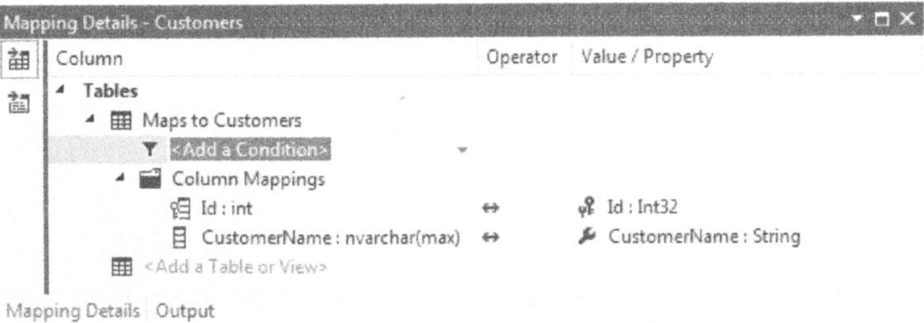

Notice that the <Add A Condition> entry is highlighted. This is the entry you use to add a filter to the model.

Note Filtering works in a peculiar way at this level. You can check for null values or you can check for specific values. For example, you could check for all of the entries for Josh Bailey or you could check for null values in the *CustomerName* field. It isn't possible to filter on key fields. For example, you couldn't filter on *Id*. In addition, filtering is limited to certain data types. Filtering on a *DateTime* field such as *PurchaseDate* or a *Decimal* field such as *Amount* isn't possible. However, you can filter on other field types, such as strings and *Int32* values. In many cases, you simply need to experiment to find the best way to filter the data from the database.

5. Click the down-pointing arrow next to <Add A Condition> and select *CustomerName* from the list. You'll see When CustomerName added to the condition list.
6. Type **Josh Bailey** in the Value / Property column. When you filter on a specific condition, as is the case in this example, you can't use that field as part of the mapped result. The assumption is that you already know the value of the field.
7. Highlight the *CustomerName* entry in the model and press Delete. Not only does this remove the property from the designer, but it also removes the mapping for it from the Mapping Details window (note that the Value / Property column is now blank—indicating that the *CustomerName* field isn't mapped). The Mapping Details window should now look like the one shown here:

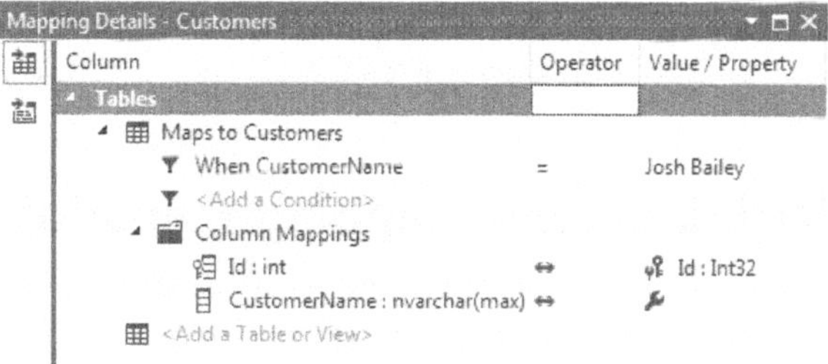

It's important to realize that the *CustomerName* field is no longer mapped. This means you can't use it as part of a query or within the application output. The reason for this change is that *CustomerName* is now a constant: Josh Bailey. Because of this change, you must also modify the example code.

8. Open *Form1.CS* and comment out the code for the *btnAdd_Click()* event handler.
9. Comment out the following lines for the *btnQuery_Click()* event handler:

```
//// Create a customer entry for each customer.
//Output.Append("\r\n" + Customer.CustomerName +
//    " has made purchases on: ");
```

Because there are no customer entries, except for those from Josh Bailey, you could further simplify the code to work exclusively with the *Purchase* table data. For the sake of simplicity, this is the only change you really need to consider.

10. Click Start or press F5. The application compiles and runs.
11. Click Query. You'll see the result shown here:

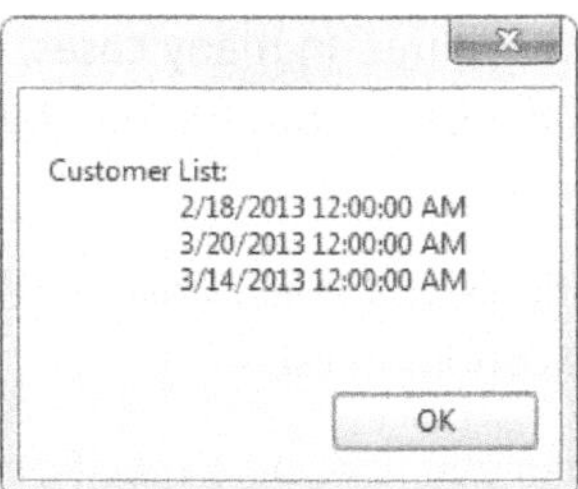

Notice that there are no customer entries this time. The only customer is Josh Bailey. However, the output does show all three of Josh Bailey's purchases.

Working with standard data types

You can perform a variety of manual mapping tasks, especially when working with POCO classes. The Entity Framework does an admirable job of mapping your classes for you. However, in some cases, you must perform some manual mapping to obtain the desired result. The following sections discuss how to manually map standard types between Microsoft SQL Server and the .NET Framework.

Considering the standard data type mapping scenarios

It would be nice if you could start every database application with a new database where naming isn't too important and you don't have to worry about a host of organization conventions. The reality is that the world is filled with legacy databases that often rely on older naming strategies and a wealth of incompatible structures. Organizations do create database-naming and structural policies that might not fit Microsoft's way of viewing things. In addition, you might have to make all of this work with POCO classes that also don't fit well with the database you're working with at any given time.

A typical scenario to consider is the organization that's either absorbed by another organization or is attempting to absorb a new purchase. In either case, both organizations have databases, and both organizations have to merge into a single entity. However, getting the databases to work together can be daunting, and moving the data from one organization to the other might be out of the question. In short, you need some means of performing custom mapping so that the Entity Framework and your POCO classes work as they should, yet the existing data remains intact.

It's also possible that you need to make your application work with databases that aren't even under your control. You might need to interact with databases owned by business partners or even entities that you purchase database information from. In many cases, these sorts of interactions are now addressed through the use of web services, but you may still find situations where you need to address them as part of your application using specialized code you create. Custom mapping is a requirement in such a situation because you can be certain that the host organization is going to be unwilling to make any changes to their database-naming conventions or structure.

Custom mapping goes beyond simple interface needs. You may have noticed that Microsoft makes certain assumptions about the database, especially when you employ a code-first workflow. For security and speed reasons, you may choose not to allow the database to accept an unlimited number of characters in a given field. To ensure database reliability, you might choose to avoid using identity fields and specifically assign identifier information instead. There are many situations where custom mapping of standard data types is an essential part of creating the application because you require more control over how the data is managed by the database.

Creating the *Rewards3* database

This chapter makes some changes to the *Rewards2* database structure. To ensure that your previous applications continue to work, it's important to create a new database you can play around with in this chapter. Of course, you don't necessarily want to re-create the database from scratch either. With this in mind, the following procedure shows how to copy the *Rewards2* database and access it as the *Rewards3* database. The remaining examples in this chapter will use the *Rewards3* database to make any structural changes.

Warning While you can use the existing *Rewards2* database for the examples in this chapter, doing so will make the previous examples in the book unworkable. If you make the changes in this chapter to the *Rewards2* database, it's important to realize that the process is one-way and you won't be able to reverse the changes with ease.

Copying the *Rewards2* database

1. Open the folder containing your databases using Microsoft Windows Explorer.
2. Create copies of *Rewards2*.MDF and *Rewards2_log*.LDF, and rename them *Rewards3*.MDF and *Rewards3_log*.LDF.
3. Open SQL Server Management Studio and log in as normal.
4. Right-click Databases in Object Explorer and choose Attach from the context menu. You'll see the Attach Databases dialog box.
5. Click Add. You'll see the Locate Database Files dialog box shown here:

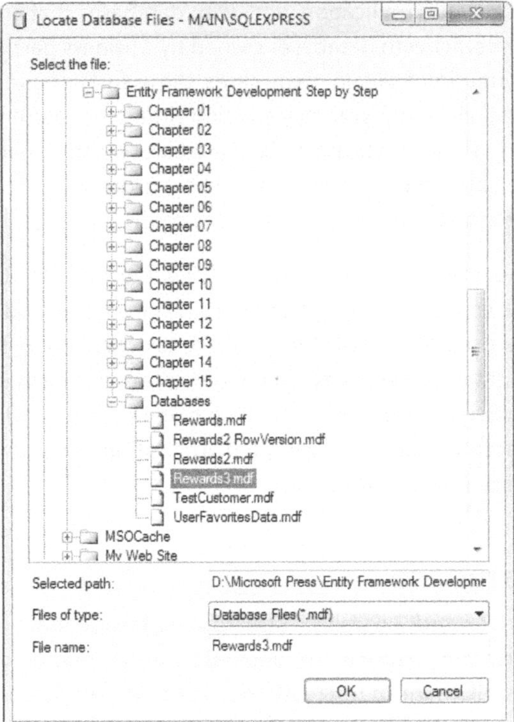

6. Highlight *Rewards3.mdf* and click OK. You'll see the entries listed in the Attach Databases dialog box as *Rewards2*, not *Rewards3*. This is normal.
7. Change the Attach As column entry in the Databases To Attach list to read *Rewards3*.
8. Click the ellipses next to the *Rewards2.mdf* entry in the "Rewards2" Database Details list. You'll see a Locate Database Files dialog box. However, in this case, the dialog box contains both .MDF (database) and .LDF (log) file entries.
9. Highlight the *Rewards3*.mdf file and click OK.
10. Check the log file entry. The *Rewards2_log.ldf* file entry should automatically change to Rewards3_log.ldf. If not, perform steps 8 and 9 again to change the log file entry. Your Attach Databases dialog box should look like the one shown here:

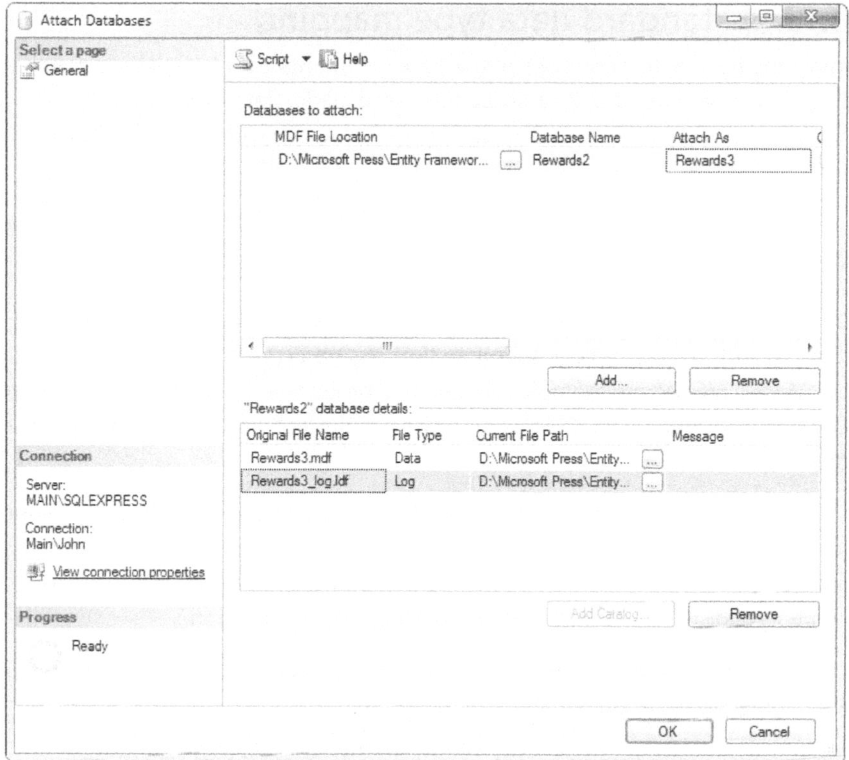

11. Click OK. SQL Server Management Studio will create an attachment to the *Rewards3* database. If you receive an error message, it means that you didn't configure something correctly in the Attach Databases dialog box. Make sure you check the Attach As field, as well as both database file entries.

12. Verify that the task completed successfully by expanding the Databases folder in Object Explorer. You should see the new database, as shown here:

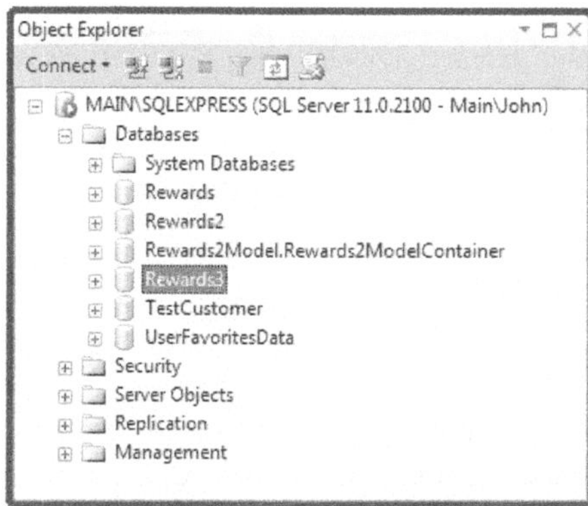

13. Close SQL Server Management Studio.

Performing standard data type mapping

At this point, you have a new database to use for experimenting with data type mapping. This is essentially a copy of the *Rewards2* database that you'll manipulate in various ways. The following procedure helps you better understand how custom mapping can work and benefit you in your development efforts.

Creating a custom data type mapping

1. Copy the *ManuallyGenerate* example you created in Chapter 14 to a new folder and use this new copy for this example (rather than the copy you created in Chapter 14). Remember that the *ManuallyGenerate* example relies on two projects to interact with a database using the Entity Framework and POCO classes, which is a perfect way to see how these mapping strategies can work.

2. Open the example application in Visual Studio and use Server Explorer to create a connection to the *Rewards3* database you created in the "Creating the *Rewards3* database" section of the chapter. (Simply right-click Data Connections and choose Add Connection from the context menu—follow the steps in the wizard to create the connection.)

3. Drill down into the new connection. You'll see entries in the Views, Stored Procedures, and Functions folders, as shown here:

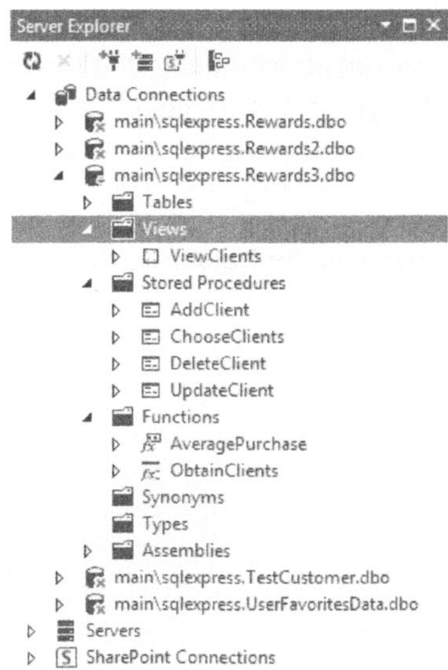

4. Right-click each of the entries, such as ViewClients, in turn and choose Delete from the context menu to remove them. Click Update Database when you see the Preview Database Updates dialog box. Visual Studio will make the required changes to the database each time. The reason you want to remove these entries is to make it easier to change the database structure without having to rewrite every view, stored procedure, and function.

5. Open the *Tables* folder in Server Explorer, right-click the *Customers* entry, and choose Open Table Definition from the context menu. You'll see a Table Definition designer like the one shown here:

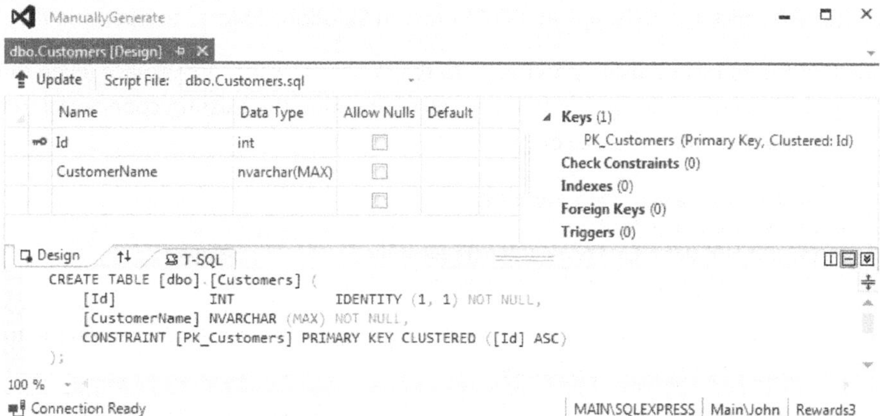

6. Change *CustomerName* to *Cust_Name*. This change will cause the application to malfunction.

7. Click Update in the upper-left corner of the designer window. Visual Studio displays a Preview Database Updates dialog box.

8. Click Update Database in the Preview Database Updates dialog box. Visual Studio will make the requested structural change and then show a Data Tools Operations dialog box that contains the result of running the update script.

9. Close the Data Tools Operations dialog box.

10. Click Start or press F5. The application compiles and runs.

11. Click Query. You'll see the exception dialog box shown here:

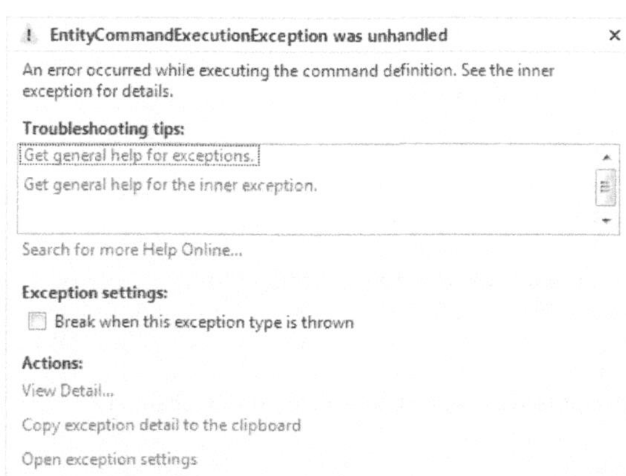

12. Click View Detail. You'll see the View Detail dialog box.

13. Expand the details and look at the *InnerException* property. You'll see that this property correctly identifies the change in the field name as the problem.

14. Click OK to close the View Detail dialog box and stop the program execution.

15. Double-click the *DCSimplePOCO.CS* entry in Solution Explorer to open the file.

16. Add the following *using* statements to the *Rewards2Model* namespace (even though you're using the *Reward3* database, you're updating the existing code, which relies on the *Rewards2Model* namespace):

```
// Added for manual data mapping.
using System.Data.Entity;
using System.Data.Entity.ModelConfiguration;
using System.ComponentModel.DataAnnotations.Schema;
```

    You normally need to add all of these *using* statements to create even simple manual mapping functionality for your application.

17. Add the following method override to the *Rewards2ModelContainer* class:

```
// Perform some manual mapping of the data.
protected override void OnModelCreating(DbModelBuilder MB)
{
   // Load the custom configuration.
   MB.Configurations.Add(new CustomerMap());
}
```

    A custom mapping configuration requires that you create a special class to hold the information. The *OnModelCreating()* event handler is called just once every time the application starts and creates its first query. The configuration you create is loaded and cached for later use.

18. Create the following class within the *Rewards2Model* namespace in the *DCSimplePOCO.CS* file:

```
public class CustomerMap : EntityTypeConfiguration<Customers>
{
   public CustomerMap()
   {
      // Specify the name of the table to use.
      this.ToTable("Customers");

      // Define the key for this table.
      this.HasKey(key => key.Id);

      // Specify the mapping for each of the table properties.
      this.Property(prop => prop.Id)
         .HasColumnName("Id")
         .HasColumnType("int")
         .HasDatabaseGeneratedOption(DatabaseGeneratedOption.Identity)
         .IsRequired();

      this.Property(prop => prop.CustomerName)
         .HasColumnName("Cust_Name")
         .HasColumnType("nvarchar")
```

```
            .IsRequired();
    }
}
```

The configuration you create can contain all sorts of information. This class shows the configuration for the database as you configured it. The class begins by specifying the name of the table you want to use and identifies the primary key for that table. Notice that the key is identified using a lambda expression that identifies the name of the field in the POCO class, not in the database table itself.

The properties come next. Notice how each property is defined by a succession of method calls that further define its functionality. The most important feature here is the lambda expression that identifies the POCO class property and the mapping to a database table field using the *HasColumnName()* method. There are a number of methods not shown here. You can see a full list at *http://msdn.microsoft.com/library/gg696686.aspx*.

19. Click Start or press F5. The application compiles and runs.

20. Click Query. You'll see the expected output. It's possible to reconfigure the tables in any way you want and still have the application work when you create a custom mapping of this sort.

Working with enumerated data types

Enumerated types have all sorts of benefits when working with properties that have a fixed number of responses. The security and reliability of an application both increase when you use enumerations, because enumerations make it much harder for the user to make mistakes, and issues such as injection attacks are nonexistent. The following procedure shows one method for adding an enumerated type to the *Rewards3* database. In this case, the database adds a field that describes the kind of user entry: standard customer, customer with a high discount, employee, or management.

Creating a custom enumeration mapping

1. Open the *Tables* folder in Server Explorer, right-click the *Customers* entry, and choose Open Table Definition from the context menu to open the Table Definition designer (if necessary).
2. Type **Cust_Type** in the first blank row in the upper half of the designer window.
3. Set the *Cust_Type* Data Type field entry to *int*.
4. Type **0** in the Default field. These three entries make it possible to add a new field to the database that will work with the enumerated type.
5. Click Update in the upper-left corner of the designer window. Visual Studio displays a Preview Database Updates dialog box.

6. Click Update Database in the Preview Database Updates dialog box. Visual Studio will make the requested structural change and then show a Data Tools Operations dialog box that contains the result of running the update script.

7. Close the Data Tools Operations dialog box.

8. Double-click the *MyCustomers.CS* entry in Solution Explorer to open the file.

9. Add the following enumeration to the *Rewards2Model* namespace:

```
// Define the kind of customer that has made the purchase.
public enum CustomerTypeEnum
{
   Standard,
   SpecialDiscount,
   Employee,
   Manager
}
```

   As you can see, this enumeration simply defines the four kinds of customers that can make purchases.

10. Add the following property to the *Customers* class:

```
public CustomerTypeEnum CustomerType { get; set; }
```

   This property forces the use of the enumeration within the code and therefore by the user as well. Of course, now you need to map this property to the database table.

11. Double-click the *DCSimplePOCO.CS* entry in Solution Explorer to open the file (if necessary).

12. Add the following property to the other property entries in the *CustomerMap()* constructor:

```
this.Property(prop => prop.CustomerType)
   .HasColumnName("Cust_Type")
   .HasColumnType("int")
   .IsOptional();
```

   Notice that this entry uses *IsOptional()*. That doesn't seem like an appropriate call given that the field can't be null in the database table. When a field has a default value, as this one does, you can map it using *IsOptional()* to allow the caller to rely on the default value, rather than supplying a specific value. Of course, you'll want to see whether the mapping actually works, so it's time to change the query a little.

13. Open the Form1.CS file.

14. Modify the query so that it appears like the query shown below (with the new code in bold):

```
foreach (var Customer in CustomerList)
{
   // Create a customer entry for each customer.
   Output.Append("\r\n" + Customer.CustomerName +
       " (" + Customer.CustomerType +
```

```
            ") has made purchases on: ");

      // Process each purchase for that particular customer.
      foreach (var Purchase in Customer.Purchases)
         Output.Append("\r\n\t" + Purchase.PurchaseDate);
   }
```

15. Click Start or press F5. The application compiles and runs.

16. Click Query. You'll see the output shown here:

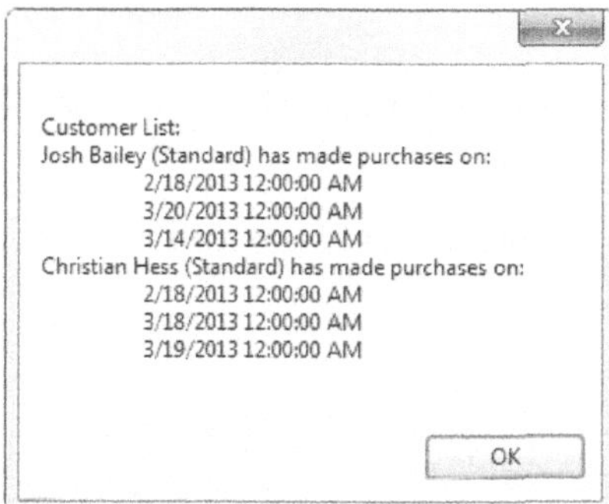

Customer List:
Josh Bailey (Standard) has made purchases on:
2/18/2013 12:00:00 AM
3/20/2013 12:00:00 AM
3/14/2013 12:00:00 AM
Christian Hess (Standard) has made purchases on:
2/18/2013 12:00:00 AM
3/18/2013 12:00:00 AM
3/19/2013 12:00:00 AM
OK

Both customers are standard customers because you haven't set the values for either one of them. As a result, the database assumes a value of 0, which is the Standard entry in the enumeration.

Working with complex data types

Sometimes you need to handle data as a complex type in your application, even if it appears in separate fields in the database. Complex data type mapping is only a little more difficult than other sorts of mapping that you have performed so far. The following procedure describes how to add the complex type fields to the database, create the complex type in code, and then perform the required mapping.

Creating a custom complex data type mapping

1. Open the Tables folder in Server Explorer, right-click the Customers entry, and choose Open Table Definition from the context menu to open the Table Definition designer (if necessary).
2. Type **Cust_ZIP** in the first blank row in the upper half of the designer window.
3. Set the *Cust_ZIP* Data Type field entry to *nvarchar(10)*.
4. Check the Allow Nulls field entry for *Cust_ZIP*.
5. Type **Cust_Telephone** in the first blank row in the upper half of the designer window.
6. Set the *Cust_Telephone* Data Type field entry to *nvarchar(13)*.

7. Check the Allow Nulls field entry for *Cust_Telephone.*

8. Click Update in the upper-left corner of the designer window. Visual Studio displays a Preview Database Updates dialog box.

9. Click Update Database in the Preview Database Updates dialog box. Visual Studio will make the requested structural change and then show a Data Tools Operations dialog box that contains the result of running the update script.

10. Close the Data Tools Operations dialog box. Of course, now there are null values in the database that you'll want to fill with data.

11. Right-click the Customers entry in Server Explorer and choose Show Table Data. You'll see a Data editor containing the data found in the table.

12. Type some appropriate values for the two customer entries. Here are the values used for this example:

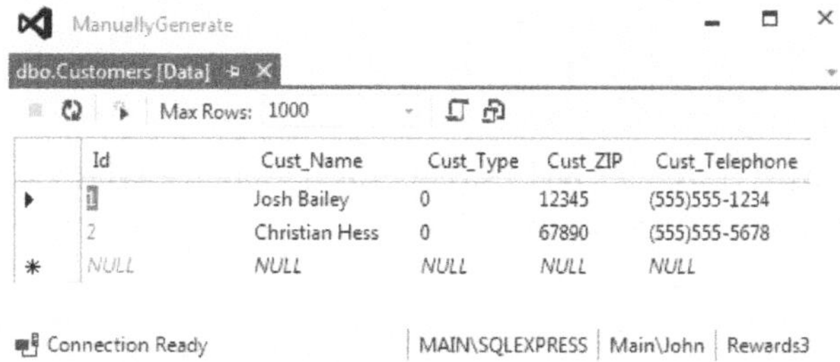

13. Double-click the MyCustomers.CS entry in Solution Explorer to open the file (if necessary).

14. Add the following *using* statement to the *Rewards2Model* namespace:

```
// Added for complex data type support.
using System.ComponentModel.DataAnnotations.Schema;
```

Warning A considerable number of sites online use the wrong namespace for the *using* statement. You must use the one shown or you won't gain access to the required attributes.

15. Add the following class to the *Rewards2Model* namespace:

```
[ComplexType]
public class Location
{
   // Create the two properties of this type.
   public string ZIPCode { get; set; }
   public string Telephone { get; set; }
}
```

To ensure the Entity Framework recognizes your class as a complex type, make sure you add the *[ComplexType]* attribute as shown. This complex type contains just two properties: *ZIPCode* and *Telephone*.

16. Add the following property to the *Customers* class:

```
public Location CustomerLocation { get; set; }
```

17. Double-click the DCSimplePOCO.CS entry in Solution Explorer to open the file (if necessary).

18. Add the following property entries to the other property entries in the *CustomerMap()* constructor:

```
this.Property(prop => prop.CustomerLocation.Telephone)
   .HasColumnName("Cust_Telephone")
   .HasColumnType("nvarchar")
   .HasMaxLength(13)
   .IsOptional();

this.Property(prop => prop.CustomerLocation.ZIPCode)
   .HasColumnName("Cust_ZIP")
   .HasColumnType("nvarchar")
   .HasMaxLength(10)
   .IsOptional();
```

Notice that you must map the two database fields separately. Also, since these two fields have length limits, you must provide them using the *HasMaxLength()* method. In other words, to create *nvarchar(13)* using the mapping features, you must combine the *HasColumnType()* and the *HasMaxLength()* properties. Trying to combine the two criteria into a single method call won't work.

19. Open the Form1.CS file.

20. Modify the query so that it appears like the query shown below (with the new code in bold):

```
foreach (var Customer in CustomerList)
{
   // Create a customer entry for each customer.
   Output.Append("\r\n" + Customer.CustomerName +
        " (" + Customer.CustomerType +
        ")\r\nZIP: " + Customer.CustomerLocation.ZIPCode +
        "\r\nTelephone: " + Customer.CustomerLocation.Telephone +
        "\r\nhas made purchases on: ");

   // Process each purchase for that particular customer.
   foreach (var Purchase in Customer.Purchases)
      Output.Append("\r\n\t" + Purchase.PurchaseDate);
}
```

21. Click Start or press F5. The application compiles and runs.

22. Click Query. You'll see the output shown here:

Customer List:
Josh Bailey (Standard)
ZIP: 12345
Telephone: (555)555-1234
has made purchases on:
2/18/2013 12:00:00 AM
3/20/2013 12:00:00 AM
3/14/2013 12:00:00 AM
Christian Hess (Standard)
ZIP: 67890
Telephone: (555)555-5678
has made purchases on:
2/18/2013 12:00:00 AM
3/18/2013 12:00:00 AM
3/19/2013 12:00:00 AM
OK

Working with geography and geometry spatial data types

Many organizations now require the use of Global Positioning System (GPS) data as part of their database. Fortunately, working with this sort of data (or any other geometric data for that matter) isn't a problem with the Entity Framework. You simply create a mapping for it, as you would any other data type in your application. The "Performing standard data type mapping" section earlier in the chapter shows the technique you'd use to create the mapping in this case.

The differences come with the data itself. SQL Server provides two special data types—*sys.geography* and *sys.geometry*—that you use when working with data of this sort (see *http://msdn.microsoft.com/library/ff848797.aspx* for details). The corresponding .NET types, *DbGeography* and *DbGeometry*, appear in the *System.Data.Spatial* namespace (see *http://msdn.microsoft.com/library/system.data.spatial.aspx* for a description of this namespace and associated classes). The difference between the two classes is that geography types perform tasks using an ellipsoidal (round earth) coordinate system, while geometry types use a Euclidean (flat) coordinate system.

Note Although using geographic and geometric data types doesn't require any special mapping, you do need to provide the coordinates in a form that the .NET Framework understands. The walkthrough at *http://blogs.msdn.com/b/adonet/archive/2011/06/30/walkthrough-spatial-june-ctp.aspx* provides some additional helpful examples that you might find useful in working with these data types.

Getting started with the Entity Framework

The main focus of this chapter has been to demonstrate techniques for mapping various database data types to types that the .NET Framework can understand. What you should take away from this chapter is that the automation normally performs the task admirably and that you can configure the automation to adjust for most schema differences without a problem. The techniques described in this chapter are for those few situations where the automation fails to perform well. Unfortunately, when the automation fails, it usually does so in a manner that will be frustrating to understand at first. When you find yourself working just a little too hard to fix a mapping problem with the automation, that's when you need to look at the techniques in this chapter.

An important part of understanding the complex material in this chapter is going through each of the examples at least once. In fact, it's helpful to go through the examples several times with modifications that you try to see what happens when you perform the tasks in a different way. For many developers, trying to figure out precisely how mapping works involves hands-on activity that includes actual coding and working through the code with the debugger to see how the application reacts to change.

The examples in this chapter are typical demonstrations of situations where you need to perform manual data mapping. Of course, the information isn't all that helpful if you don't apply it to your particular situation. Take time to start looking at your data setup and any custom POCO classes that you're currently using. Performing this survey while you're thinking about the need for custom mapping will likely save you time and frustration later. Document any situations you feel may require custom mapping—there should be few (if any) of them in a typical setting.

Chapter 16, the last chapter of the book, discusses advanced management techniques. What this chapter is really about is managing your model so that it performs better in a number of ways. For example, you can create multiple diagrams for your model so that people viewing the model can understand it better. You can also import stored procedures in batches, rather than one at a time, as you've done throughout the rest of the book. The goal of this chapter is to help you get the most out of the functionality that the Entity Framework provides so that you actually end up performing less work in the long run.

Chapter 15 quick reference

To	Do this
Control access to a particular database field	Change the access level to the Getter or Setter properties of the entity property in question.
Remove a particular field from use within the application	Right-click its entry in the Mapping Details window and choose <Delete> from the context menu.
Limit the number of records returned from the database at the model level	Create a filter in the Mapping Details window. The filter will extract a specific record value or look for records that contain a null value in that field. The field becomes inaccessible when a specific value is used.
Create custom mapping for data elements that don't match the properties in a class	Define a class that describes the required mapping and then override the *OnModelCreating()* event handler to load that class during the first query the application makes. The class you create must inherit from the *EntityTypeConfiguration* class.
Allow for the use of default values even when a field won't allow null values	Rely on the *IsOptional()* method. When the caller doesn't supply a required value, the database automatically uses the default value so the field won't be null.
Define a class as a complex data type for the Entity Framework	Add the *[ComplexType]* attribute to the class declaration. The actual complex type declaration, inclusion in the POCO class, and mapping are no different from a standard type, except that you must provide one property declaration for each field in the database.
Specify an *nvarchar* type with a specific length, such as *nvarchar(10)*	Use a combination of the *HasColumnType("nvarchar")* method and the *HasMaxLength(10)* method when defining the mapping between the application and the database. Never try to declare the type and length as a single entity, because the application won't compile.

CHAPTER 16

Performing advanced management tasks

After completing the chapter, you'll be able to

- Demonstrate how to create and configure a multiple-diagram model.
- Describe and demonstrate techniques for performing batch imports of stored procedures and functions.
- Map a stored procedure that returns multiple result sets.
- Demonstrate techniques for creating and using entities with inheritance.
- Describe context actions for automatically generated classes.

Working with the Entity Framework is a matter of managing data in a specific way. This book has discussed many techniques for managing your database projects, rather than allowing them to manage you. This chapter is the culmination of all of the other concepts you have learned so far. You'll discover the advanced techniques that will set you apart from other developers. For example, this chapter discusses the use of multiple diagrams to create models that are easier to understand and to present to others. Anyone can create a huge model that no one can understand (not even the developer creating it, at times), but it takes finesse to create a series of seemingly simple diagrams that make a complex database project easy to understand.

This chapter is also about saving time. Most developers don't have a lot of time to spare, so performing tasks one at a time when there are techniques for performing multiple tasks at once is just a waste of time. In this case, you discover how to import multiple stored procedures using a batch process, rather than importing them one at a time.

The remainder of the chapter provides you with some advanced methods of working with entities. For example, it's possible to create entities that rely on inheritance. You can create a single base entity and inherit from it to create a number of similar entities; for example, you can start with a people entity and then inherit from it to create customer, employee, and manager entities. This chapter also provides you with additional techniques for interacting with classes, properties, and methods. Developing methods to make the automation work better is always a worthy goal, and this chapter adds several new techniques to your toolbox.

Developing multiple diagrams for a model

Throughout the book, you've worked with relatively simple models. Of course, the real world isn't so easily modeled. The models you work with in the real world are significantly more complex than those found in this book. Of course, that means more entities displayed on screen and a greater potential for confusion. As the model becomes more complex, it becomes more difficult for anyone to figure out what it does—how the various elements interact.

The Entity Framework is supposed to reduce complexity—to make it easier for developers to create robust models that present the database in a way that's both simple and understandable. With this in mind, there are times when you need to display the model for your application using multiple diagrams. Just as an architect relies on multiple pages of blueprints when designing a house, you can use multiple diagrams to make the model easier to understand. Each diagram models a different functional area of the database structure.

The following sections describe how to create, configure, and manage multiple diagrams for applications that rely on the Entity Framework. The basic goal of these sections is to help you understand the mechanics of working with multiple diagrams. Your organization will need to create a plan for defining how elements should appear on each diagram to ensure maximum understandability and flexibility (the "Techniques for organizing model diagrams" sidebar, which follows, can help).

Techniques for organizing model diagrams

There isn't a certain way to create any particular Entity Framework diagram—no right or wrong method. The method that people using the diagram understand the best is the method that you need to use. However, there are some practical methods for organizing diagrams that you might consider when creating your own diagrams. These techniques were derived from various real-world sources.

- **Functional area** Organizing the model by functional area means dividing the database into tasks performed with a particular kind of data. For example, you might have one functional area devoted to user settings, another to employee data, and still another to customer entries. Dividing data by function can be tricky, however, because some data isn't really associated with any specific function—rather, it's used on an organization-wide level. For example, price information may seem associated with the sales department, but it could also be used by the shipping department to help determine shipping costs or with employee data to determine how much to pay in commissions.
- **Department** Specific data is often associated with a particular department. Even though the data might be used by other departments, only one department manages the data. The problem in this situation is that not all data is managed by a particular department, and some static data isn't managed by any department at all. You'd need to consider adding special diagrams for data that doesn't conveniently fit any particular department.

- **Location** A large organization may spread data across regional boundaries. Placing each region on its own diagram would make it easier to find based on where the information is used. In this case, you'd need some method of handling data that's used equally by all locations. It might also be necessary to combine this technique with other techniques for further dividing information that appears in heavily used locations.
- **Unit** Many organizations are divided into units. This is different from the department organization in that each unit might have duplicates of some departments, such as sales or accounting. An organization might have units that deal with appliances, electronics, and apparel. The point is that each unit is a separate entity.
- **Application Element** You may decide to simply give up trying to organize the diagrams based on some physical entity and work with the application design itself. For example, some database elements may only affect the user, while others affect employees as a whole or customers as a whole. You'll likely encounter some database elements that don't fit neatly into a specific application area, however, and will need to create a more generalized diagram to hold these entities.

Creating the new diagram

Before you can do anything, you need to create one or more diagrams to use to organize your model. Working with multiple diagrams is somewhat different from working with a single diagram, but most principles are the same. For example, you can add entities to any diagram you want, and you can create associations between entities on any diagram. The following procedure shows how to add a diagram to one of the existing projects and then move elements around so that you get essentially the same model, but organized in a different way.

Creating multiple diagrams

1. Copy the LINQ query version of the *ModelFirst* example you created in Chapter 6, "Manipulating data using LINQ," to a new folder, and use this new copy for this example (rather than the copy you created in Chapter 6).

Note The LINQ version of the *ModelFirst* example in Chapter 6 appears in the ModelFirst (LINQ Query) folder of the downloadable source code. If you created your own version of the example, the folder name will probably be different.

2. Open the Rewards2Model.EDMX file by double-clicking its entry in Solution Explorer.
3. Choose View | Other Windows | Entity Data Model Browser. You'll see the Model Browser window shown here:

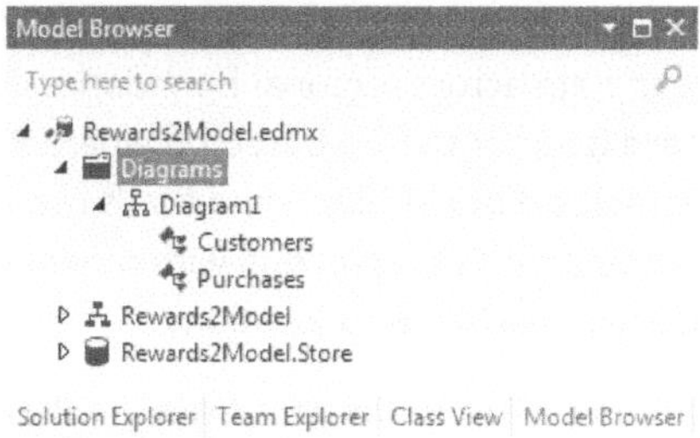

Whenever you start a new Entity Framework project using the model-first workflow, you get a single diagram to start drawing on. This diagram is named Diagram1. Unfortunately, Microsoft Visual Studio doesn't ask you for any other name (and none is really needed until you start creating other diagrams). However, now you need to start thinking about how the model is organized, despite the fact that the model currently contains just two entries.

4. Drill down to the Diagrams\Diagram1 diagram and highlight it.
5. Change the *Name* property value in the Properties window to *People*.
6. Right-click Diagrams and choose Add New Diagram from the context menu. You'll see a new diagram added to the Model Browser window. Notice also that you now have two Rewards2Model.EDMX file entries displayed in Visual Studio—one marked [People] and the other marked [Actions].
7. Highlight the new diagram in the Model Browser and change the *Name* property value in the Properties window to *Actions*.
8. Select the Rewards2Model.edmx [People] tab in Visual Studio. Notice that nothing has changed.
9. Right-click Purchases and choose Cut from the context menu. The entity disappears from the Rewards2Model.edmx [People] tab.
10. Select the *Rewards2Model.edmx [Actions]* tab. Right-click anywhere within the designer and choose Paste from the context menu. You should now have two tabs, each containing an entity, as shown here:

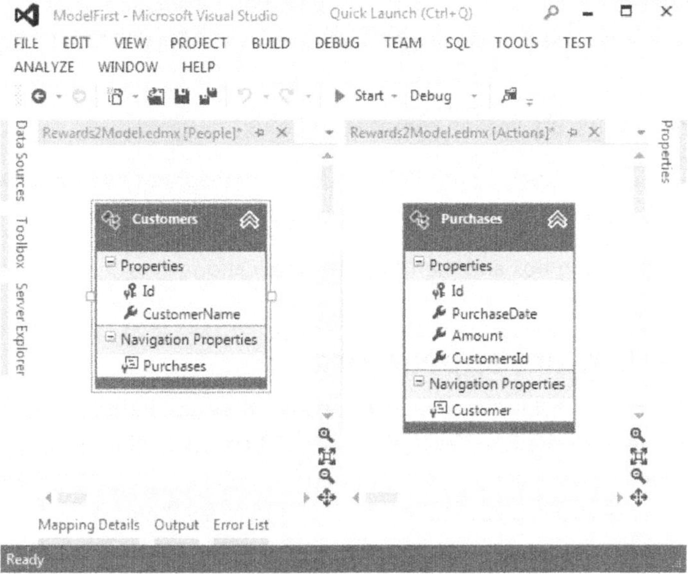

This is a method of separating the entities by functional area. In this case, you have two areas: one for people and another for actions. If you were to add other kinds of people, these people could still perform the same actions. For example, you might have an *Employees* entity that could still make purchases. The Model Browser window also reflects this change.

Notice that there's no longer an association line between the two entities. The association still exists, but now you must modify it by accessing it through the Model Browser window. However, it's a good idea to verify that the association still exists.

11. Choose View | Other Windows | Entity Data Model Browser. Drill down into the Associations folder. You'll see the Model Browser window shown here:

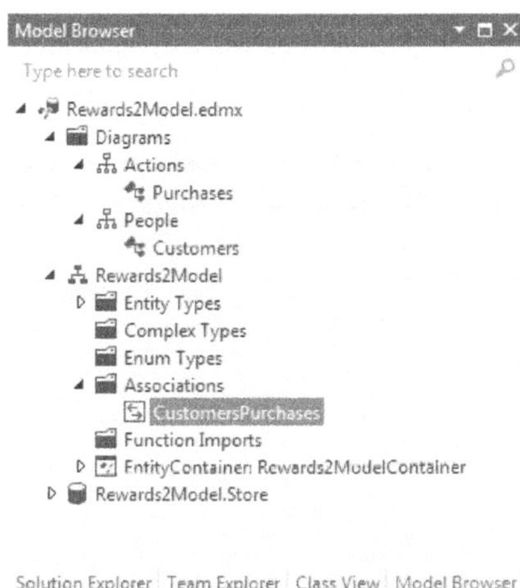

Everything appears to be the same as before, despite that missing line. To satisfy yourself that you have simply reorganized the one diagram into two, it's important to test the application out.

12. Click Start or press F5. The application compiles and runs.
13. Click Query. You'll see the expected result. The number of diagrams used and the presentation of entities on those diagrams don't affect how the model works.
14. Click OK to close the dialog box and then stop the application.

Configuring the diagram appearance

The diagrams you create aren't just there to meet your needs—they also help you explain your database design to other people. Presentation is everything when it comes to discussing complex topics with other people who need to know about them, but don't necessarily have the same knowledge level as you do. You can, for example, place the entities in a grid to lay them out in a manner that's more easily viewed, or you can rely on color to help distinguish entity types. The following sections describe some techniques you can use to modify the presentation of your model and then export it for use in presentation materials.

Using a grid

Grids make it possible to precisely align elements on screen. The precise alignment of display elements will make your model look more professional and prove less distracting to the people viewing it. It may seem like a small thing, but creating a pleasing appearance doesn't take that much time, and it actually makes the model a lot easier to work with later. There are two levels of grid support provided by the designer—both of which you can access by right-clicking anywhere within the white space of the designer window and choosing an option from the Grid menu. The following are the two options:

- **Show Grid** Displays a series of dots on the design area that you can use to align display elements.
- **Snap to Grid** Automatically places any item you add to the model onto one of the grid lines so that it's easier to precisely align the elements. This feature is turned on by default.

Color-coding the entities

As your models become more complex, you'll want to color code the entities by type. You can accomplish this task by selecting an entity and then changing the Fill Color property value in the Properties window. Clicking the down arrow displays a color selector you can use to choose a predefined color. You can choose one of the named colors that appear in the color selector, or you can type three color values in the Fill Color property. The default setting is a custom color of *0, 122, 204*. Note that you must separate the red, green, and blue color values with commas.

Adding type to the display

The default Scalar Property Format value is Display Name, which gives someone an idea of what purpose a particular property serves, but not the type used to represent it. When working with less-skilled viewers, the display name is probably fine, and using it will make it less likely that the viewer will become confused. However, when working with your peers, you need to change the setting to Display Name and Type so that the audience knows which data type is used for a particular property. To change this value, right-click anywhere in the white space of the designer and choose Scalar Property Format | Display Name And Type from the context menu. Here's how the *Customers* entity looks with type information displayed:

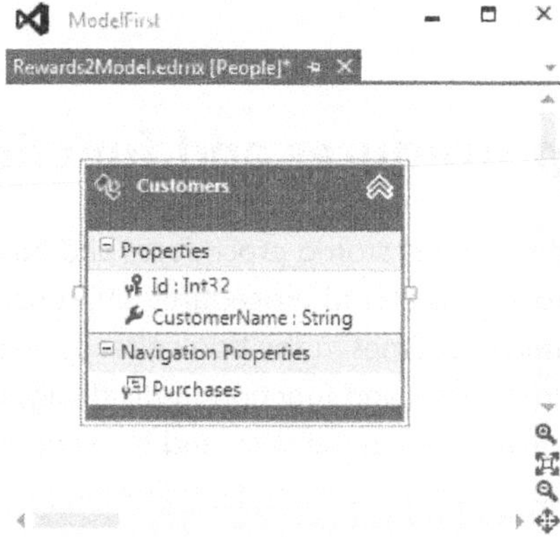

Exporting the diagram as an image

After you have your diagram created precisely as you want to see it in your presentation, you can export it as an image that you can use anywhere it's needed. To perform this task, right-click anywhere within the white space in the designer window and choose Diagram | Export As Image from the context menu. You'll see an Export Diagram As dialog box similar to this one:

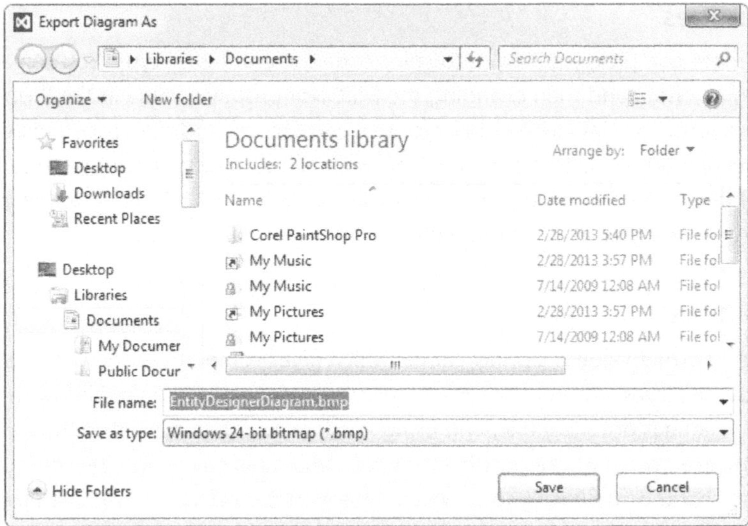

The Save As Type field provides a variety of file formats from which to choose, including .BMP, .JPG, .GIF, .PNG, and .TIF. Select a file type and then type a name in the File Name field. Click Save, and you'll find the diagram on the hard drive in the location you selected. The resulting image will contain just a little white space around the perimeter of the entities.

Performing batch imports of stored procedures and functions

In previous versions of the Entity Framework, you needed to import stored procedures and functions one at a time. It was a painful process. You've been able to import stored procedures and functions in batch mode using techniques that have appeared a number of times in the book already (even though the examples necessitated the import of stored procedures and functions individually, for the most part). However, because this was an issue for many developers in the past, and many developers still have questions about it, this section takes a special look at the process in the following procedure.

Using the Update Wizard to batch import stored procedures and functions

1. Create your Entity Framework application using any of the techniques described in Chapters 1 through 3 (making sure you add the required Entity Framework support).
2. Right-click anywhere in the white space of the Model Designer and choose Update Model From Database from the context menu. You'll see the Update Wizard.
3. Check the Import Selected Stored Procedures And Functions Into The Entity Model option (if necessary). You'll see a list of stored procedures and functions (if the database contains any), as shown here:

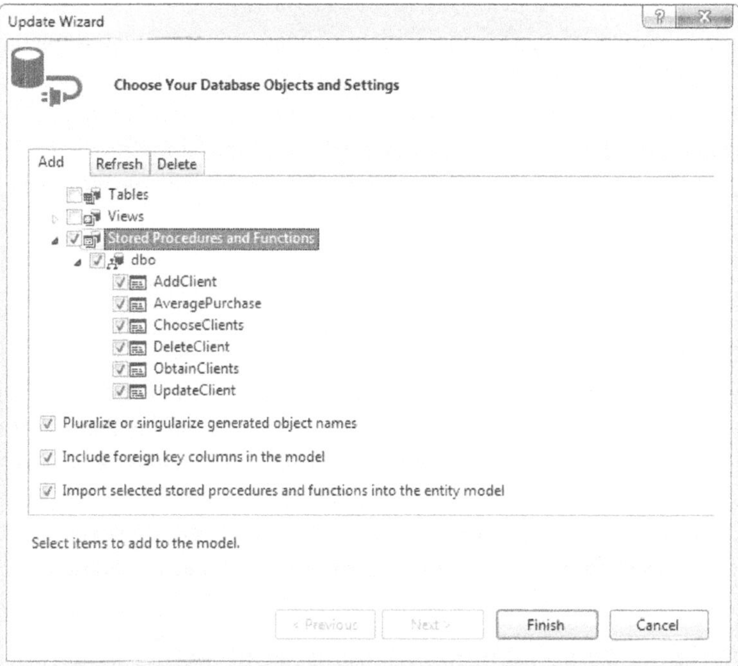

4. Check the Stored Procedures And Functions folder if you want to import all of the stored procedures and functions found in the database. Otherwise, check individual stored procedures and functions as needed by your application.

5. Click Finish. Visual Studio will import the stored procedures and functions you've selected into the model. Chapters 7 through 10 discuss various issues surrounding the use of stored procedures and functions with the Entity Framework. The batch import process doesn't change any of these conditions or results—it simply makes it possible to perform the task in one step.

Mapping a stored procedure that returns multiple result sets

Some stored procedures return multiple result sets. Normally, a developer uses this technique to reduce the number of round trips made between the client and the server. Returning multiple result sets can improve overall application speed and reduce the load on the server by returning just what that application requires, rather than a larger result set that includes both smaller result sets.

A problem with earlier versions of the Entity Framework is that you would see only the first result set. In fact, Entity Framework 5 still has this problem when you use just the automation to interact with the result set. However, with Entity Framework 5, you have two ways to overcome the problem. The following sections describe both techniques.

Note There isn't any way to overcome a multiple-result-set problem when using the database-first workflow. The techniques described in this chapter work only with the model-first and code-first workflows. When using the database-first workflow, you'll need to write code that relies on the code-first approach to work around the problem. This can be a tricky and error-prone approach that isn't recommended (and is therefore not covered in this book).

Creating the stored procedure

Before you can see the problem in working with multiple result sets, you need a stored procedure that performs the task. As part of testing this stored procedure, you can see that the stored procedure does indeed return multiple result sets, but that the automation only interacts with one of them. Sections that follow this one contain the two techniques you can use to overcome this problem. The following procedure helps you create the example application setup and the example stored procedure, and then test the resulting stored procedure to ensure it works as anticipated.

Creating a stored procedure that returns multiple result sets

1. Open your copy of Visual Studio. You don't need to have a project loaded because you're going to be interacting with Server Explorer and Microsoft SQL Server.
2. Choose View | Server Explorer to open the Server Explorer window if it isn't already open. Under Data Connections, you should see closed connections to the databases used in the book.
3. Open the connection to the *Rewards2* database by clicking the right-pointing arrow next to it. You'll see a list of folders associated with the database, including the Stored Procedures folder.
4. Right-click the Stored Procedures folder and choose Add New Stored Procedure from the context menu. You'll see a new window appear that has a template for creating a stored procedure in it.

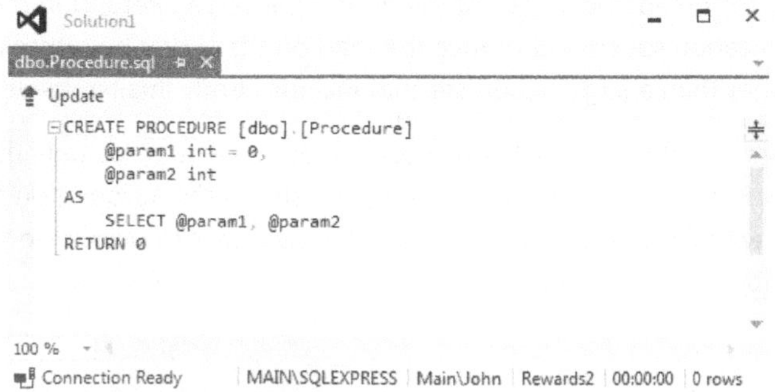

5. Overwrite the template code with the following code:

```
CREATE PROCEDURE MultipleResultSet
AS
   SELECT * FROM Customers AS C
   INNER JOIN Purchases AS P
   ON C.Id = P.CustomersId
   WHERE C.CustomerName = 'Josh Bailey';

   SELECT * FROM Customers AS C
   INNER JOIN Purchases AS P
   ON C.Id = P.CustomersId
   WHERE C.CustomerName = 'Christian Hess';
RETURN 0
```

6. Click the Update button that appears on the left side directly above the editor. Visual Studio prepares the update and displays a Preview Database Updates dialog box showing the changes that it will make.

7. Click Update Database. Visual Studio begins the database update. You can follow the progress of the update in the Data Tools Operations window. When the process is complete, you'll see Data Tools Operations dialog box, containing a success message like the one shown here:

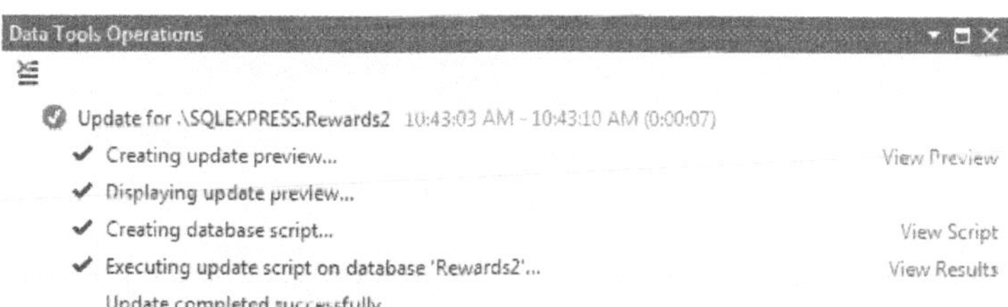

8. Close the Data Tools Operations dialog box by clicking the *X* in the upper-right corner.

9. Right-click the Stored Procedures folder and choose Refresh from the context menu. You should now see the *MultipleResultSet* stored procedure, as shown here:

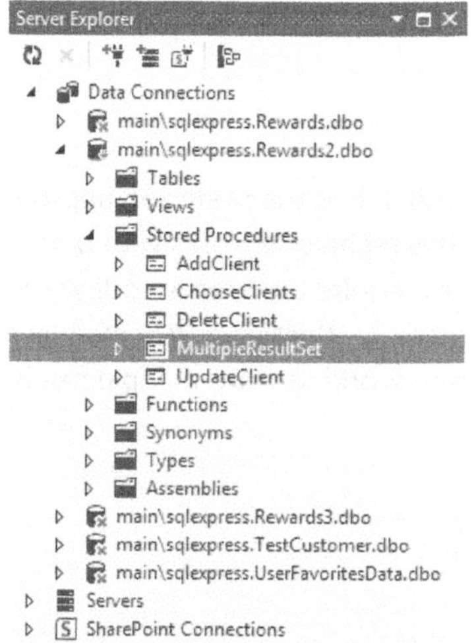

10. Right-click the MultipleResultSet entry and choose Execute from the context menu. Visual Studio creates and executes a new SQL query. You'll see results similar to the ones shown here:

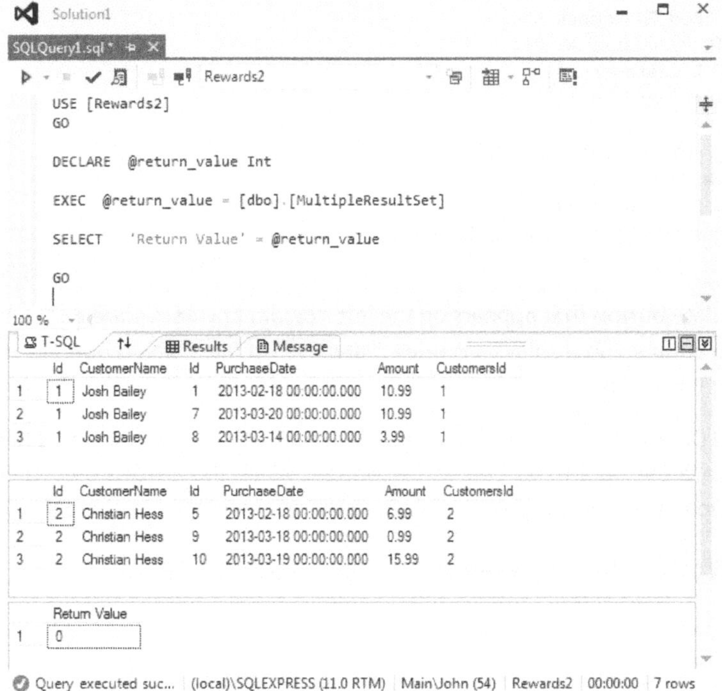

Notice that there are actually three result sets. The first contains all the purchase records for Josh Bailey, the second all the purchase records for Christian Hess, and the third the return value of 0. The example purposely includes this third result set because many stored procedures use a return value to indicate the success or failure of the stored procedure. In other words, the stored procedure might normally return just one result set, but the inclusion of a return value makes it return multiple result sets.

11. Close the stored procedure. You don't need to save the results.

Using the code-access technique

The code-access technique for working with multiple result sets is the preferred approach because it doesn't modify the automation in any way. In addition, this technique works with both the code-first and model-first workflows. Of course, this technique does require a bit more coding on your part, and there isn't any way to add the functionality to the automation—this is a purely manual approach. The following procedure describes how to use this approach to working with multiple result sets.

Creating multiple diagrams

1. Copy the LINQ query version of the *ModelFirst* example you created in Chapter 6 to a new folder and use this new copy for this example (rather than the copy you created in Chapter 6).
2. Add a new button to *Form1*. Name the button *btnCoded* and set its *Text* property to *&Coded*.
3. Double-click *btnCoded* to create a new click event handler.
4. Type the following code for the *btnCoded_Click()* event handler:

```
private void btnCoded_Click(object sender, EventArgs e)
{
   // Create the context.
   Rewards2ModelContainer context = new Rewards2ModelContainer();

   // Create a command to execute.
   var Cmd = context.Database.Connection.CreateCommand();

   // Set the command to execute.
   Cmd.CommandText = "MultipleResultSet";

   try
   {
      // Open a connection to the database.
      context.Database.Connection.Open();

      // Execute the stored procedure and save the results.
      var Reader = Cmd.ExecuteReader();

      // Access the first result set.
      var Results = ((IObjectContextAdapter)context)
         .ObjectContext
         .Translate<MultipleResultData>(Reader);

      // Process the first result set.
      StringBuilder Output = new StringBuilder("Josh Bailey Purchases: ");
      foreach (var Result in Results)
      {
         Output.Append("\r\n\t" + Result.PurchaseDate +
            " for " + Result.Amount);
      }

      // Access the second result set.
      Reader.NextResult();
      Results = ((IObjectContextAdapter)context)
         .ObjectContext
         .Translate<MultipleResultData>(Reader);

      // Process the second result set.
      Output.Append("\r\nChristian Hess Purchases: ");
      foreach (var Result in Results)
      {
         Output.Append("\r\n\t" + Result.PurchaseDate +
            " for " + Result.Amount);
      }
```

```
        // Display the result on screen.
        MessageBox.Show(Output.ToString());
    }
    finally
    {
        // Make certain the database connection is closed.
        context.Database.Connection.Close();
    }
}
```

The code begins by creating a context, as is normal for most of the examples in the book. It then uses the context to create a SQL command, *Cmd*. The command has to describe what to do using the *Cmd.CommandText* property. In this case, it runs the *MultipleResultSet* stored procedure.

The execution process begins by opening a connection to the database—something the Entity Framework normally does for you. It then calls *Cmd.ExecuteReader()* to execute the stored procedure and place the results in a *SqlDataReader* object, *Reader*.

The next step is a little odd looking but a required part of reading the result set. The application accesses the *ObjectContext* object and uses its *Translate()* method to translate the first result set in the Reader object to something that the application can understand. You'll see in a few steps that the *MultipleResultData* object simply places the data in a form that the application can readily use. The application then uses the results to create output that includes the purchases that Josh Bailey has made.

In order to get to the next result set, the code calls *Reader.NextResult()*. It then performs the translation process all over again and uses the translated results to create output. In this case, you see the purchase records for Christian Hess. You can continue to perform this loop of reading the next result set for as many result sets that the *Reader* can access.

Notice that the last step is to close the database connection by calling *context.Database.Connection.Close()*. You must perform this step or the database connection could remain open. At the very least, the application will have a memory leak.

5. Add the following *using* statements to the top of the Form1.CS file:

```
// Using statements added for processing multiple result sets.
using System.Data.Entity.Infrastructure;
using System.Data.Objects;
```

6. Add the following class to the Form1.CS file:

```
public class MultipleResultData
{
    public Int32 Cust_Id { get; set; }
    public String CustomerName { get; set; }
    public Int32 Purchase_Id { get; set; }
    public DateTime PurchaseDate {get; set;}
```

```
    public Decimal Amount { get; set; }
    public Int32 CustomersId { get; set; }
}
```

All this class does is describe the format of the data that comes from the result set; it helps the Entity Framework translate the information into a form that you can use more easily. If you were working with a single table that's already described as part of the model, then you could use an entity class instead. However, it's far more likely that you'll need to create a class such as this one to help with the translation.

7. Click Start or press F5. The application compiles and runs.

8. Click Coded. You'll see the result shown here:

Using the EDMX modification technique

This technique does offer the advantages of automation and reduced coding when working with the result set. Once the model changes are in place, working with the model is considerably easier than with the hand-coded approach discussed in the "Using the code-access technique" section of the chapter. So, from a certain perspective, this approach does provide some usefulness in a large development setting where you need to work with less-skilled developers.

However, this isn't the recommended approach for a number of reasons—the most important of which is that your changes can be wiped out if someone updates the model from the database. This technique also works only with the model-first workflow, so it has limitations in development flexibility. Validation checks won't work anymore either. Every time you validate the model, you'll receive an error message, even though the model will work just fine. (When working with this example, you'll see "Error 10021: Duplicated ResultMapping element encountered." every time you open the model or validate it). With this in mind, the following procedure shows how to implement the EDMX technique for working with multiple result sets.

Creating multiple diagrams

1. Copy the LINQ query version of the *ModelFirst* example you created in Chapter 6 to a new folder and use this new copy for this example (rather than the copy you created in Chapter 6).
2. Open the Rewards2Model.EDMX file by double-clicking its entry in Solution Explorer.
3. Right-click in any white-space area of the designer and choose Update Model From Database. You'll see the Update Wizard dialog box.
4. Check the Import Selected Stored Procedures And Functions Into The Entity Model option (if necessary). You'll see a list of stored procedures and functions (if the database contains any).
5. Check the *MultipleResultSet* stored procedure found in the Stored Procedures and Functions folder and click Finish. Visual Studio imports the *MultipleResultSet* stored procedure. The result set will contain an *Id1* field that will be incompatible with the actual data in the tables, so you must modify it in some way. The easiest way to deal with the situation is to simply remove the offending field.
6. Choose View | Other Windows | Entity Data Model Browser. You'll see the Model Browser window shown here:

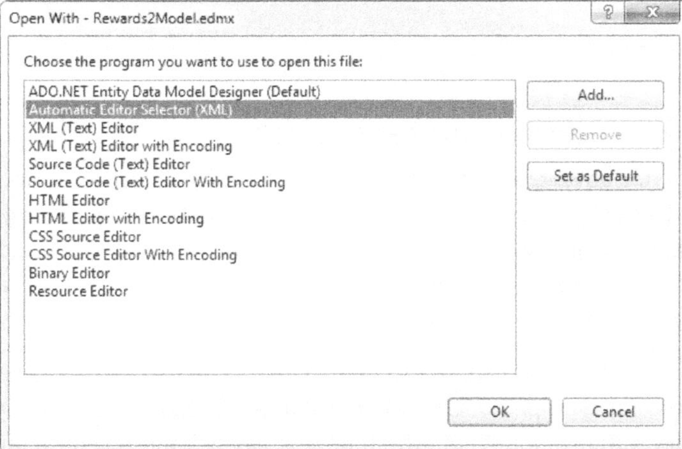

7. Drill down into the Rewards2Model\Complex Types\MultipleResultSet_Result complex type folder, right-click Id1, and choose Delete From Model from the context menu.
8. Click Save All and then close the Rewards2Model.EDMX file. The information currently placed in the model won't work. You need to modify this information so that it will work with a multiple-results set.
9. Right-click the Rewards2Model.EDMX file in Solution Explorer and choose Open With from the context menu. You'll see the Open With - Rewards2Model.edmx dialog box shown here:

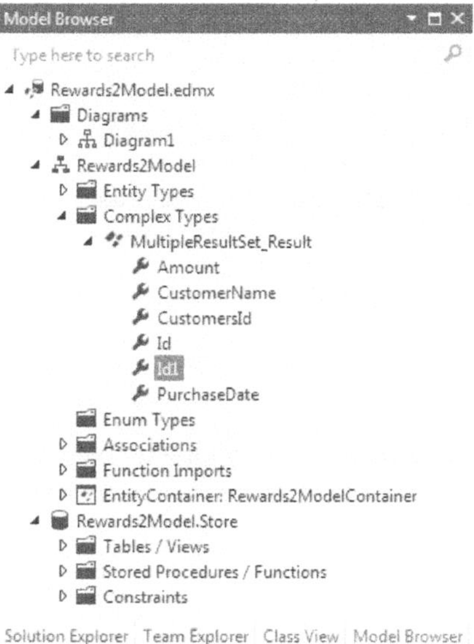

10. Select the Automatic Editor Selector (XML) entry and click OK. You'll see the file opened in the XML editor.

11. Choose Edit | Find and Replace | Quick Find. Type **MultipleResultSet_Result** in the window that appears. You should see the first occurrence of the result set—the one that defines the return value from the *MultipleResultSet* function import. Change this entry so it looks like this:

```
<FunctionImport Name="MultipleResultSet">
   <ReturnType Type="Collection(Rewards2Model.MultipleResultSet_Result)" />
   <ReturnType Type="Collection(Rewards2Model.MultipleResultSet_Result)" />
</FunctionImport>
```

You create one *<ReturnType>* entry for each result set. The two result sets are the same in this case, so the *Type* attribute is the same. If you were working with different result set types, then you would provide each type as needed. The types must appear in the order in which they're returned from the stored procedure. Otherwise, the output data won't make sense (assuming you don't see an exception).

12. Click Find Next (the right-pointing arrow) or press F3. You'll find the function import mapping entry for *MultipleResultSet_Result*. The number of complex type entries in the map must match the number of results sets that the stored procedure will return.

13. Change the mapping so it looks like this (with two copies of the same complex type):

```
<FunctionImportMapping FunctionImportName="MultipleResultSet"
                       FunctionName="Rewards2Model.Store.MultipleResultSet">
  <ResultMapping>
    <ComplexTypeMapping TypeName="Rewards2Model.MultipleResultSet_Result">
      <ScalarProperty Name="Id" ColumnName="Id" />
      <ScalarProperty Name="CustomerName" ColumnName="CustomerName" />
      <ScalarProperty Name="PurchaseDate" ColumnName="PurchaseDate" />
      <ScalarProperty Name="Amount" ColumnName="Amount" />
```

```
      <ScalarProperty Name="CustomersId" ColumnName="CustomersId" />
    </ComplexTypeMapping>
  </ResultMapping>
   <ResultMapping>
      <ComplexTypeMapping TypeName="Rewards2Model.MultipleResultSet_Result">
         <ScalarProperty Name="Id" ColumnName="Id" />
         <ScalarProperty Name="CustomerName" ColumnName="CustomerName" />
         <ScalarProperty Name="PurchaseDate" ColumnName="PurchaseDate" />
         <ScalarProperty Name="Amount" ColumnName="Amount" />
         <ScalarProperty Name="CustomersId" ColumnName="CustomersId" />
      </ComplexTypeMapping>
   </ResultMapping>
</FunctionImportMapping>
```

If you were working with different result set types, then the mapping area would reflect those differences. You must map the data in a way that reflects the actual output of the stored procedure or your code won't work.

14. Save and close the Rewards2Model.EDMX file.
15. Add a new button to *Form1*. Name the button *btnEDMX* and set its *Text* property to *&EDMX*.
16. Double-click *btnEDMX* to create a new click event handler.
17. Type the following code for the *btnEDMX_Click()* event handler:

```
private void btnEDMX_Click(object sender, EventArgs e)
{
   // Create the context.
   Rewards2ModelContainer context = new Rewards2ModelContainer();

   // Call the stored procedure.
   var Results = context.MultipleResultSet();

   // Process the first result set.
   StringBuilder Output = new StringBuilder("Josh Bailey Purchases: ");
   foreach (var Result in Results)
   {
      Output.Append("\r\n\t" + Result.PurchaseDate +
         " for " + Result.Amount);
   }

   // Obtain the second result set.
   var Second = Results.GetNextResult<MultipleResultSet_Result>();

   // Process the second result set.
   Output.Append("\r\nChristian Hess Purchases: ");
   foreach (var Result in Second)
   {
      Output.Append("\r\n\t" + Result.PurchaseDate +
         " for " + Result.Amount);
   }

   // Display the result on screen.
   MessageBox.Show(Output.ToString());
}
```

When you compare this code to the code used in the "Using the code-access technique" section of the chapter, you see that this code is both shorter and simpler. In fact, it looks much like the code you use for a single result set, except for the call to *Results.GetNextResult()*. This call obtains the next result set and places it in *Second*. You must supply the type of result set to return as part of the call.

18. Click Start or press F5. The application compiles and runs.

19. Click EDMX. You'll see the same results shown for the example in the "Using the code-access technique" section of the chapter.

Creating entities with inheritance

Inheritance makes it possible to create complex models that better reflect how developers think and also reduce the work required to interact with those models. Inheritance used with entities serves the same purpose as inheritance used with classes, so developers already know the basics of how this feature works. The following sections describe how to work with inheritance as part of creating or using databases.

Creating the *Rewards4* database

The two inheritance examples in this chapter will significantly modify the database used to interact with them. Only the *Purchases* table will remain the same, and the new database will contain several additional tables with different names than before. With this in mind, it's important to create a new database. The following procedure helps you create the required database.

Warning While you can use the existing *Rewards2* database for the examples in the "Creating entities with inheritance" section, doing so will make the previous examples in the book unworkable. If you make the changes in this chapter to the *Rewards2* database, it's important to realize that the process is one-way and you won't be able to reverse the changes with ease.

Defining a new database connection

1. Choose View | Server Explorer to open Server Explorer.

2. Right-click Data Connections and choose Create New SQL Server Database from the context menu. You'll see the Create New SQL Server Database dialog box shown here:

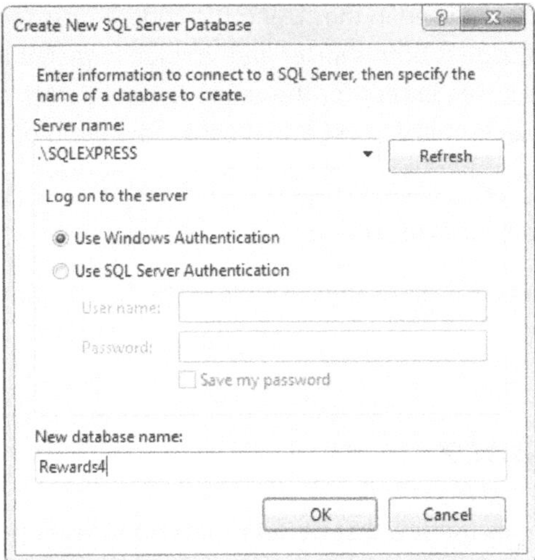

3. Select or type a server name in the Server Name field and type **Rewards4** in the New Database Name field. Click OK. Visual Studio creates the new database.

Using inheritance with the model-first workflow

When working with the model-first workflow, you add inheritance through the model itself. The model provides special functionality that makes it possible to use inheritance and have that inherited functionality show up in the actual model. The following procedure guides you through the process of working with a model-first workflow design that implements inheritance. In this scenario, you want to start tracking purchases made not only by customers, but also by employees and managers.

Using a model-first design that implements inheritance

1. Copy the multiple-diagrams version of the *ModelFirst* example you created in the "Developing multiple diagrams for a model" section of this chapter to a new folder and use this new copy for this example (rather than the copy you created earlier).

Note The multiple-diagrams version of the *ModelFirst* example appears in the ModelFirst (Multiple Diagrams) folder of the downloadable source code. If you created your own version of the example, the folder name will probably be different.

2. Open the App.CONFIG file by double-clicking its entry in Solution Explorer. You need to modify the name of the database used for this example to ensure you can continue to work with previous examples. In this case, modify the *connectionString* attribute of the *<add>* tag so that it reads like this:

```
data source=.\SQLEXPRESS;initial catalog=Rewards4
```

This change simply tells the application to use the *Rewards4* database.

3. Save and close the App.CONFIG file.

4. Open the Rewards2Model.EDMX file by double-clicking its entry in Solution Explorer. If you don't see the People diagram, choose View | Other Windows | Entity Data Model Browser to display the Model Browser window, and double-click the People entry in the Diagrams folder to open it.

5. Create a new entity named *People* by right-clicking the white space in the designer and choosing Add New | Entity from the context menu. You'll see a new entity displayed on screen.

6. Configure the new entity as shown here:

7. Change the *Abstract* property in the Properties window to *True*. This value prevents anyone from creating a *People* object. What you really want is to use the *derives* objects in the application.

8. Right-click People and choose Add New | Association from the context menu. You'll see the Add Association dialog box shown here:

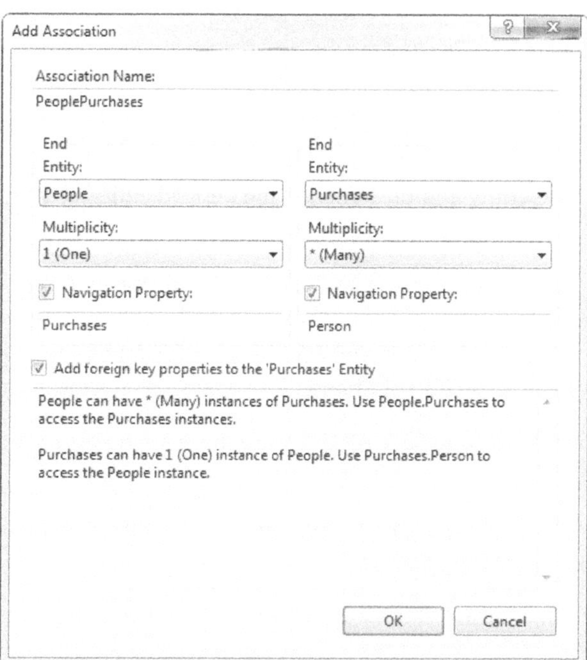

9. Configure the association information in the dialog box so that it matches the association shown in the figure. The purpose is to create an association with *Purchases*. At this point, you have effectively created a copy of *Customers*.

10. Remove the properties from *Customers* by right-clicking each property in turn and choosing Delete From Model.

11. Double-click the *CustomersPurchases* association found in the Associations folder of the Model Browser. The *Purchases* entity will reappear in the People diagram.

12. Click the association line between *Customers* and *Purchases*. Press Delete. You'll see the association removed.

13. Right-click Purchases and choose Remove From Diagram from the context menu. *Purchases* disappears from the People diagram, but not from the Actions diagram (you can open the Actions diagram to verify that the *Purchases* entity is still there).

14. Right-click Customers and choose Add New | Inheritance. You'll see the Add Inheritance dialog box shown here:

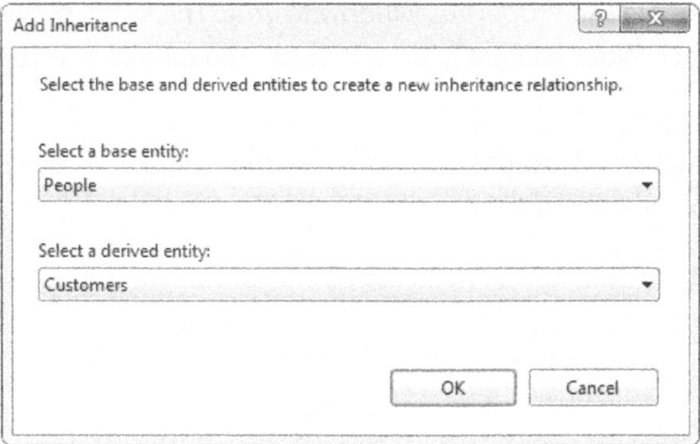

15. Ensure that *People* is the base entity and *Customers* is the derived entity, as shown in the screen shot, and click OK.

16. Add two properties to *Customers*: *CustomerType (type Int32)* and *Discount* (type *Decimal; Nullable: None; Precision: 18; Scale: 2*; and *Default Value: 0*). Make *CustomerType* an enumerated value with values of *Standard*, *Discount*, and *HighDiscount*, using the procedure found in the "Working with enumerations" section of Chapter 2, "Looking more closely at queries."

17. Save the model at this point by clicking Save All to ensure there are no errors in the changes you've made.

18. Create an *Employees* entity that inherits from *People* and has an *EmployeeType* enumerated property that has values of *Hourly* and *Salaried*.

Tip The Add Entity dialog box contains a Base Type field you can use to specify that *Employees* inherits from *People*. Use this Base Type field whenever you want to define inheritance for a new entity, rather than adding the inheritance later, as was done for *Customers*.

19. Create a *Managers* entity that inherits from *People* and has a *Discount* property (type *Decimal*; Nullable: *None*; Precision: *18*; Scale: *2*; Default Value: *.15*). Your model should look like the one shown here:

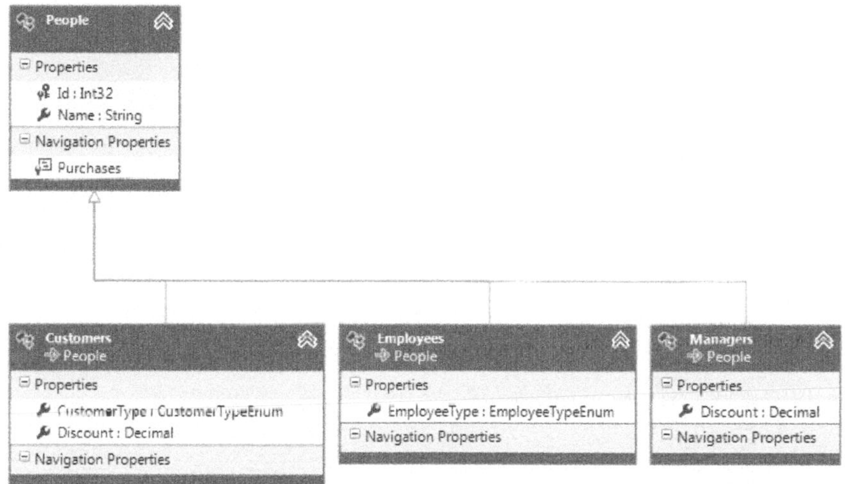

At this point, you have a new model that's created as an extension of the old model. There are now three kinds of people: customers, employees, and managers. Each shares an *Id* and *Name* property in common and each has unique properties that define it. The following procedure generates a new database based on this updated model.

Upgrading the database model

1. Right-click any white space within the model and choose Generate Database From Model from the context menu. You'll see the Generate Database Wizard dialog box. Make absolutely certain that the script shown on the DDL tab says "USE [Rewards4];" as one of the first lines.
2. Click Finish. You'll see a DDL Overwrite Warning dialog box that tells you this process will overwrite the previous DDL file.
3. Click Yes. You'll see an SSDL/MSL Overwrite Warning dialog box that tells you this process will change the .SSDL and .MSL files for this example.
4. Click Yes. Visual Studio creates a new *Rewards2Model.EDMX.SQL* file and opens it for you.

5. Right-click anywhere within the editor for this file and choose Execute from the context menu. You'll see a Connect To Server dialog box.

6. Log in to the server as usual and click Connect. SQL Server executes the script and displays "Command(s) completed successfully."

7. Open Server Explorer. Right-click the *Rewards4* connection shown here:

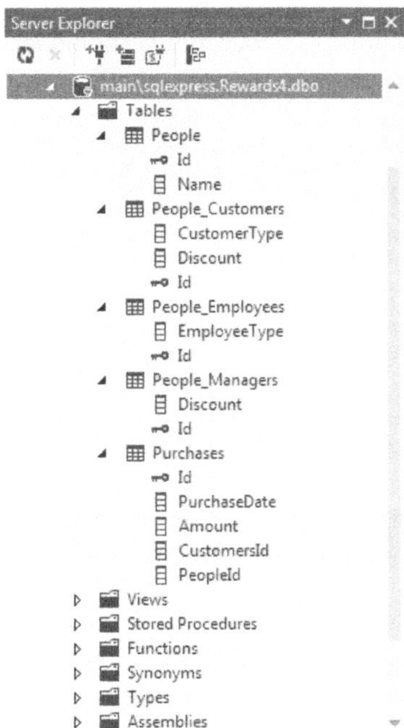

There's one oddity in this example. Notice that even though the *CustomersPurchases* association has been removed, the automation still generated a *CustomersId* column for the table. Manually editing the .EDMX file would have solved this issue. However, it's not a major issue for this example, and it's important to know where the automation could fail when updating a model. Be sure to look for idiosyncrasies such as this one when working on a production system.

At this point, you'll want to interact with the new database. The code used with previous examples will require remarkably few changes. The process of working with the new model is slightly different, but not horribly so. The following procedure shows how to add and query the new model by making small changes to the existing code.

Adding records and querying the model

1. Open the Form1.CS file. Make the following changes (in bold) to the *btnAdd_Click()* event handler:

```
private void btnAdd_Click(object sender, EventArgs e)
{
```

```
    // Create a new purchase.
    Purchases NewPurchase = new Purchases();
    NewPurchase.Amount = new Decimal(5.99);
    NewPurchase.PurchaseDate = DateTime.Now;

    // Create a new customer and add the purchase.
    Customers NewCustomer = new Customers();
    NewCustomer.Name = "Josh Bailey";

    // Create the context.
    Rewards2ModelContainer context = new Rewards2ModelContainer();

    // Add the record and save it.
    context.People.Add(NewCustomer);
    context.Purchases.Add(NewPurchase);
    context.SaveChanges();

    // Display a success message.
    MessageBox.Show("Record Added");
}
```

The first change was probably expected by you. The new model uses *Name*, rather than *CustomerName*, to identify a particular individual.

The second change is to use the *People* object, rather than an individual person type, to access the people in the database. The Entity Framework treats everyone as a member of *People* because that's the name of the base object. You can cast a particular entry as a specific kind of *People* object: *Customers*, *Employees*, or *Managers*.

2. Make the changes shown in bold below to the *btnQuery_Click()* event handler:

```
private void btnQuery_Click(object sender, EventArgs e)
{
    // Create the context.
    Rewards2ModelContainer context = new Rewards2ModelContainer();

    // Obtain the customer list.
    var CustomerList =
        from cust in context.People
        select cust;

    // Process each customer in the list.
    StringBuilder Output =
        new StringBuilder("Customer List:");
    foreach (var Customer in CustomerList)
    {
        // Create a customer entry for each customer.
        Output.Append("\r\n" + Customer.Name +
            " has made purchases on: ");

        // Process each purchase for that particular customer.
        foreach (var Purchase in Customer.Purchases)
            Output.Append("\r\n\t" + Purchase.PurchaseDate);
    }
```

```
    // Display the result on screen.
    MessageBox.Show(Output.ToString());
}
```

As you can see, the example code requires the same changes as before. Everyone is a *People* object now, and customers simply have a *Name* property, rather than a *CustomerName* property.

3. Click Start or press F5. The application compiles and runs.
4. Click Add. The application adds a record and displays the Record Added dialog box.
5. Click OK to close the dialog box.
6. Click Query. You'll see the expected output—a dialog box showing that Josh Bailey has a single purchase made just moments ago.
7. Click OK to close the dialog box and then stop the application.

The dynamics of this application have changed significantly. For example, the query used to access the data is significantly more complex than before because of the effect of inheritance. If you were to look at the individual tables in the database, you'd see that there's a single entry in the *People* table and a single entry in the *People_Customers* table. There aren't any entries in either the *People_Employees* or *People_Managers* table. The Entity Framework makes it extremely easy to interact with a model of this sort without requiring the developer to jump through hoops.

Using inheritance with the code-first workflow

Setting up inheritance in a code-first workflow is about the same as working with inheritance in every other way. The biggest difference is in mapping your classes to the database. The following procedure helps you create a code-first version of the example found in the "Using inheritance with the model-first workflow" section of the chapter.

Creating the code-first inheritance classes

1. Copy the *ManuallyGenerate* example you created in Chapter 14, "Creating custom entities," to a new folder, and use this new copy for this example (rather than the copy you created in Chapter 14).
2. Open the App.CONFIG file in the *Rewards2Model* project by double-clicking its entry in Solution Explorer. You need to modify the name of the database used for this example to ensure you can continue to work with previous examples. Change the *<add>* tag *Database* attribute as shown here:

   ```
   Database=Rewards4;
   ```

   This change simply tells the application to use the *Rewards4* database.
3. Save and close the App.CONFIG file.

4. Perform steps 2 and 3 for the App.CONFIG file in the *ManuallyGenerate* project.

5. Right-click the *Rewards2Model* project and choose Add | Class from the context menu. You'll see the Add New Item dialog box shown here:

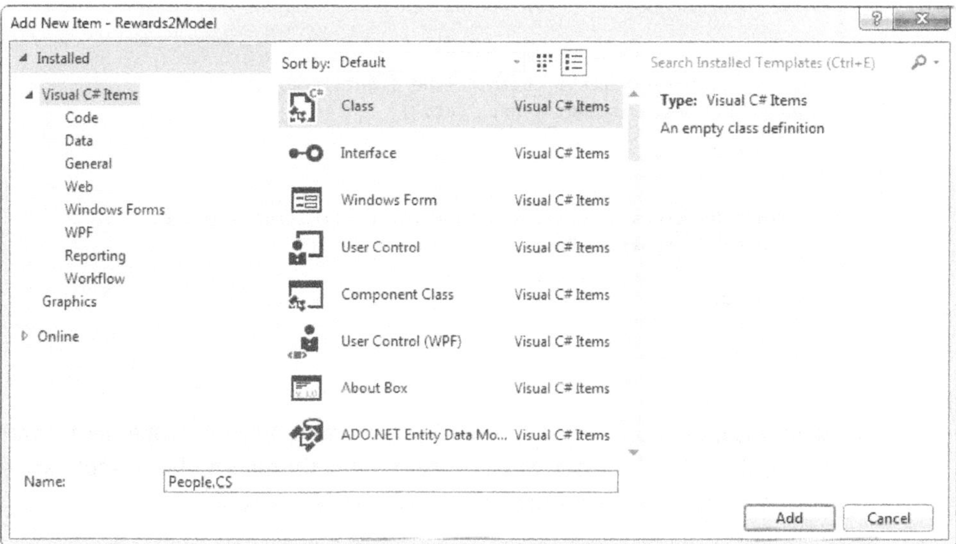

6. Type **People.CS** in the Name field and click Add. Visual Studio adds the new class to the project.

7. Repeat steps 5 and 6 for Employees.CS and Managers.CS. At this point, you have all the files you need. Every code file will require some level of change, so move carefully through the steps that follow.

8. Open the file and add an entry for the *PeopleId* column in the table. Simply add it after the *CustomersId* property, like this:

```
public int PeopleId { get; set; }
```

9. Copy and paste the existing code from MyCustomers.CS to People.CS and modify it so it looks like this (the modifications don't actually change the way this code works):

```
public abstract class People
{
   public People()
   {
      // Automatically obtain a list of purchases from the database.
      this.Purchases = new HashSet<Purchases>();
   }

   // Declare the table properties.
   public int Id { get; set; }
   public string Name { get; set; }

   // Declare the navigational property.
```

```
    public virtual ICollection<Purchases> Purchases { get; set; }
}
```

10. Modify the MyCustomers.CS file so it looks like this:

```
public class Customers : People
{
   // Declare the table properties.
   public CustomerTypeEnum CustomerType { get; set; }
   public Decimal Discount { get; set; }
}


// Define the kinds of customers that the application supports.
public enum CustomerTypeEnum : int
{
   Standard,
   Discount,
   HighDiscount
}
```

It's important to note that MyCustomers.CS contains only the properties that are unique to this object's table. However, when working with a *Customers* object, you'll find that you also have access to all of the properties found in the *People* class.

11. Modify the Employees.CS file so that it looks like this:

```
public class Employees : People
{
   // Declare the table properties.
   public EmployeeTypeEnum EmployeeType { get; set; }
}

// Define the kinds of employees supported by the application.
public enum EmployeeTypeEnum : int
{
   Hourly,
   Salaried
}
```

12. Modify the Managers.CS file so it looks like this:

```
public class Managers : People
{
   // Declare the table properties.
   public Decimal Discount { get; set; }
}
```

At this point, you have the classes done. There are many texts online that will try to tell you that the Entity Framework will automatically find the data it needs and that you don't require mapping when working with inheritance. You'll also note that these examples rely on a single table to hold the data no matter what sort of data is being saved. A production application doesn't work that way. The various data elements will appear in separate tables, much as they do for the example shown in the "Using Inheritance with the model-first workflow" section of the chapter. When your application relies on a number of tables to store the individual data elements, you must use mapping. The following steps describe how to modify the mapping for this example so that it can handle entries of any type.

Updating the DCSimplePOCO.CS file

1. Open the DCSimplePOCO.CS file.
2. Modify the properties used to access the data (as shown in bold) to accommodate the new class structure:

    ```
    // Create properties to access the POCO classes.
    public DbSet<People> People { get; set; }
    public DbSet<Purchases> Purchases { get; set; }
    ```

    As with the model-first example, you access all three kinds of people entries using a *People* object. The Entity Framework will map between the various types after you provide the required mapping information.
3. Create maps for each of the tables that deal with people entries in the example, as shown here:

    ```
    public class PeopleMap : EntityTypeConfiguration<People>
    {
       public PeopleMap()
       {
          // Specify the name of the table to use.
          this.ToTable("People");

          // Define the key for this table.
          this.HasKey(key => key.Id);

          // Specify the mapping for each of the table properties.
          this.Property(prop => prop.Id)
             .HasColumnName("Id")
             .HasColumnType("int")
             .HasDatabaseGeneratedOption(DatabaseGeneratedOption.Identity)
             .IsRequired();

          this.Property(prop => prop.Name)
             .HasColumnName("Name")
             .HasColumnType("nvarchar")
             .IsRequired();
       }
    }

    public class CustomerMap : EntityTypeConfiguration<Customers>
    {
       public CustomerMap()
       {
          // Specify the name of the table to use.
          this.ToTable("People_Customers");

          // Define the key for this table.
    ```

```
            this.HasKey(key => key.Id);

            // Specify the mapping for each of the table properties.
            this.Property(prop => prop.Id)
               .HasColumnName("Id")
               .HasColumnType("int")
               .IsRequired();

            this.Property(prop => prop.CustomerType)
               .HasColumnName("CustomerType")
               .HasColumnType("int")
               .IsRequired();

            this.Property(prop => prop.Discount)
               .HasColumnName("Discount")
               .HasColumnType("decimal")
               .IsOptional();
         }
      }

      public class EmployeeMap : EntityTypeConfiguration<Employees>
      {
         public EmployeeMap()
         {
            // Specify the name of the table to use.
            this.ToTable("People_Employees");

            // Define the key for this table.
            this.HasKey(key => key.Id);

            // Specify the mapping for each of the table properties.
            this.Property(prop => prop.Id)
               .HasColumnName("Id")
               .HasColumnType("int")
               .IsRequired();

            this.Property(prop => prop.EmployeeType)
               .HasColumnName("EmployeeType")
               .HasColumnType("int")
               .IsRequired();
         }
      }

      public class ManagerMap : EntityTypeConfiguration<Managers>
      {
         public ManagerMap()
         {
            // Specify the name of the table to use.
            this.ToTable("People_Managers");

            // Define the key for this table.
            this.HasKey(key => key.Id);

            // Specify the mapping for each of the table properties.
            this.Property(prop => prop.Id)
               .HasColumnName("Id")
               .HasColumnType("int")
```

```
            .IsRequired();

        this.Property(prop => prop.Discount)
            .HasColumnName("Discount")
            .HasColumnType("decimal")
            .IsOptional();
    }
}
```

Each of these maps follows the same pattern described in the "Performing standard data type mapping" section of Chapter 15, "Mapping data types to properties." However, unlike in that example, you absolutely must use mapping in this case because every *People* object subtype—*Customers*, *Employees*, and *Managers*—relies on input from two separate tables. The Entity Framework won't provide the proper mapping for you without these manually generated maps.

4. Create an *OnModelCreating()* override in the *Rewards2ModelContainer* class that looks like this:

```
// Perform some manual mapping of the data.
protected override void OnModelCreating(DbModelBuilder MB)
{
   // Load the custom configuration.
   MB.Configurations.Add(new PeopleMap());
   MB.Configurations.Add(new CustomerMap());
   MB.Configurations.Add(new EmployeeMap());
   MB.Configurations.Add(new ManagerMap());
}
```

As with the maps, these configuration additions follow the same pattern shown in Chapter 15. It's essential to add each map to the configuration separately.

At this point, your application is almost ready to test. However, you need to make two changes to the Form1.CS code.

5. Open the Form1.CS file and make the following changes (shown in bold) to the *btnQuery_Click()* event handler:

```
private void btnQuery_Click(object sender, EventArgs e)
{
   // Create the context.
   Rewards2ModelContainer context = new Rewards2ModelContainer();

   // Obtain the customer list.
   var CustomerList =
       from cust in context.People.Include("Purchases")
       select cust;

   // Process each customer in the list.
   StringBuilder Output =
       new StringBuilder("Customer List:");
   foreach (var Customer in CustomerList)
   {
      // Create a customer entry for each customer.
```

```
         Output.Append("\r\n" + Customer.Name +
            " has made purchases on: ");

         // Process each purchase for that particular customer.
         foreach (var Purchase in Customer.Purchases)
            Output.Append("\r\n\t" + Purchase.PurchaseDate);
      }

      // Display the result on screen.
      MessageBox.Show(Output.ToString());
   }
```

The changes of *Customers* to *People* and *CustomerName* to *Name* are the same changes you made to the model-first example. Interestingly enough, you can process any of the three *People* types using this single query.

Tip If you want to see a specific *People* type, then add the *OfType()* method after the *Include()* method in the query. Specify the kind of *People* object you want to see. For example, if you want to see just *Customers*, then you use *OfType<Customers>()*.

6. Click Start or press F5. The application compiles and runs.
7. Click Query. You'll see the expected output—a dialog box showing that Josh Bailey has a single purchase.
8. Click OK to close the dialog box and then stop the application.

Controlling context actions for automatically generated classes

There are situations where you want better control over how the Entity Framework deals with your data. For example, you may not ever want entries actually deleted. You may want them moved to another table or simply marked as deleted in some way. For that matter, you might not want certain users to have the ability to add records based on their role within the organization. The following procedure demonstrates a technique you can use to control the actions of the automatically generated classes as needed.

Overriding the *SaveChanges()* method

1. Copy the LINQ query version of the *ModelFirst* example you created in Chapter 6 to a new folder and use this new copy for this example (rather than the copy you created in Chapter 6).
2. Right-click the project entry in Solution Explorer and choose Add | Class from the context menu. You'll see the Add New Item dialog box.

3. Type **Override.CS** in the Name field and click Add. Visual Studio adds the new class to the project.

4. Add these *using* statements to the top of the file:

```
// Added to support the override.
using System.Data;
using System.Data.Objects;
```

5. Replace the default class code with the following code:

```
public partial class Rewards2ModelContainer
{
   public override int SaveChanges()
   {
      // Obtain a list of the added entries.
      var AddedEntries = ChangeTracker.Entries()
         .Where(entity => entity.State == EntityState.Added);

      // Change the state of the added entries so they
      // aren't added to the database.
      foreach (var Entry in AddedEntries)
      {
         Entry.State = EntityState.Unchanged;
      }

      // Perform the normal level of processing.
      return base.SaveChanges();
   }
}
```

In this case, you intercept the *SaveChanges()* call and perform some preprocessing with it. The code uses a query to obtain a list of added entries in the change list. It sets the state of these entries to *EntityState.Unchanged* so that the application won't actually add them to the database. Notice that the last step is to call *base.SaveChanges()*. You must make this call or your application will fail to work as anticipated.

6. Open the Form1.CS file.

7. Change the *Amount* value to *22.99* and the *CustomerName* value to *John Kane*. These changes will make it easy to determine whether the application works as anticipated.

8. Click Start or press F5. The application compiles and runs.

9. Click Add. The application adds a record and displays the Record Added dialog box.

10. Click OK to close the dialog box.

11. Click Query. You'll see the records for Josh Bailey and Christian Hess, but no entry for John Kane. The application has prevented the addition.

12. Click OK to close the dialog box and then stop the application.

Note The technique shown in this section works for far more than simply overriding *SaveChanges()*. You can use it with any automatically generated class to override the default behavior, add new methods or properties, or generally change the way in which the application works. Using this technique has the advantage of allowing you to tweak the automatically generated classes without having to rely on manually generating the code. You get the best of both worlds—automation with nearly full control over the low-level processing of the application.

Getting started with the Entity Framework

If you don't take anything else away from this chapter, at least take away the knowledge that you can always create some way to manage your application development process better. The Entity Framework is a powerful and flexible tool that makes it easy to model even complex database configurations. The problem is figuring out how to make your model work with the database. This chapter has shown several new ways to accomplish that feat. You want to make tasks as easy as possible, so it's important to understand how these management techniques can help you.

The examples on inheritance have a lot more to show you than you experienced while working through them in the chapter. Going through these examples step by step with the debugger is a great idea. Make sure you look at all of the things you've worked through in other areas of the book. For example, check out the query used to access the data—you'll be amazed to discover what happens in the background with these inherited models.

One of the more important things you can do now is to apply what you've learned to the real world—to try using the techniques you've encountered in this book with the applications you work with daily. Of course, you don't want to start with the most complex application you work with. Always start employing a new technique with something simple. It's also a good idea to use a test setup. You don't want to trash a production setup by applying techniques incorrectly. This chapter provides the last bit of knowledge that you need to perform those real-world tasks in a meaningful way—but remember that you're still discovering the Entity Framework.

You've reached the end of the book, but you haven't reached the end of your journey. There are many ways in which you can use the Entity Framework to create robust applications. Of course, you'll want to practice the many techniques found in this book and apply them to your own application requirements. It's also a good idea to check the blog for this book, at *http://blog.johnmuellerbooks.com/categories/263/entity-framework-development-step-by-step.aspx*. As people write to me or I find interesting Entity Framework topics to discuss, you'll see posts that will most definitely help you get more out of this book in general and the Entity Framework in particular. Speaking of writing to me, make sure you ask me any book-specific questions you might have at *John@JohnMuellerBooks.com*. I'm always willing to help readers get more out of my books (after all, that's why I've written them).

Chapter 16 quick reference

To	Do this
Reduce the complexity of a database model	Rely on multiple diagrams to represent various database elements. Each diagram can represent a functional unit or application interaction with the database.
Add a new diagram to your project	Right-click Diagrams in the Model Browser window of Visual Studio and choose Add New Diagram from the context menu.
Export your diagram as an image for use in reports and presentations	Right-click anywhere within the white space in the designer window and choose Diagram | Export As Image from the context menu. Type a file name, select a file type, and choose a storage location, and then click Save in the Export Diagram As dialog box to save the image to disk.
Import stored procedures or functions in a batch process	Right-click anywhere in the white space of the Model Designer and choose Update Model From Database from the context menu. Check the Import Selected Stored Procedures And Functions Into The Entity Model option. Check the stored procedure and function entries you want to import in the Update Wizard dialog box and click Finish.
Provide the means for working with a multiple-results set for either the code-first or model-first workflow	Rely on the coding technique for interacting with the multiple-results set.
Enforce the use of automation with a multiple-results set	Rely on the EDMX modification technique for interacting with the multiple-results set.

Index

Symbols

A

B

D

E

F

G

H

I

J

K

L

M

N

O

P

Q

R

S

T

U

V

W

About the Author

JOHN PAUL MUELLER is a freelance author and technical editor. He has writing in his blood, having produced 92 books and over 300 articles to date. The topics range from networking to artificial intelligence and from database management to heads-down programming. Some of his current books include Windows command-line references, books on HTML5 and JavaScript, several books on C#, and an IronPython programmer's guide. His technical-editing skills have helped more than 65 authors refine the content of their manuscripts. John has provided technical-editing services to both *Data Based Advisor* and *Coast Computer* magazines. He's also contributed articles to magazines such as *Software Quality Connection, Mendix.com, DevSource, InformIT, SQL Server Professional, Visual C++ Developer, Hard Core Visual Basic, asp.netPRO, Software Test and Performance,* and *Visual Basic Developer.* Be sure to read John's blog at *http://blog.johnmuellerbooks.com/.*

When John isn't working at the computer, you can find him outside in the garden, cutting wood, or generally enjoying nature. John also likes making wine and knitting. When not occupied with anything else, he makes glycerin soap and candles, which comes in handy for gift baskets. You can reach John on the Internet at *John@JohnMuellerBooks.com.* John is also setting up a site at *http://www.johnmuellerbooks.com/.* Feel free to take a look and make suggestions on how he can improve it.

How To Download Your eBook

Thank you for purchasing this Microsoft Press® title. Your companion PDF eBook is ready to download from O'Reilly Media, official distributor of Microsoft Press titles.

To download your eBook, go to

http://aka.ms/PressEbook

and follow the instructions.

Please note: You will be asked to create a free online account and enter the access code below.

Your access code:

RQDMZXW

Microsoft ADO.NET Entity Framework
Step by Step

Your PDF eBook allows you to:

- Search the full text
- Print
- Copy and paste

Best yet, you will be notified about free updates to your eBook.

If you ever lose your eBook file, you can download it again just by logging in to your account.

Need help? Please contact:
mspbooksupport@oreilly.com
or call 800-889-8969.

Please note: This access code is non-transferable and is void if altered or revised in any way. It may not be sold or redeemed for cash, credit, or refund.

CPSIA information can be obtained at www.ICGtesting.com
Printed in the USA
BVOW10s1259050813

327735BV00005B/8/P